Sixty, Sexy, and Successful

SIXTY, SEXY, AND SUCCESSFUL

A Guide for Aging Male Baby Boomers

Robert Schwalbe, PhD

Sex, Love, and Psychology
Judy Kuriansky, Series Editor

 PRAEGER

Westport, Connecticut
London

Library of Congress Cataloging-in-Publication Data

Schwalbe, Robert.
    Sixty, sexy, and successful : a guide for aging male baby boomers /
Robert Schwalbe.
        p. cm. — (Sex, love, and psychology, ISSN 1554–222X)
    Includes bibliographical references and index.
    ISBN-13: 978–0–275–99928–5 (alk. paper)
    1. Aging—Psychological aspects.   2. Older men—Psychology.   3. Baby boom
generation—Psychology.   I. Title.
    BF724.8.S33   2008
    155.67—dc22   2008000543

British Library Cataloging in Publication Data is available.

Copyright © 2008 by Robert Schwalbe

All rights reserved. No portion of this book may be
reproduced, by any process or technique, without the
express written consent of the publisher.

Library of Congress Catalog Card Number: 2008000543
ISBN-13: 978–0–275–99928–5
ISSN: 1554–222X

First published in 2008

Praeger Publishers, 88 Post Road West, Westport, CT 06881
An imprint of Greenwood Publishing Group, Inc.
www.praeger.com

Printed in the United States of America

The paper used in this book complies with the
Permanent Paper Standard issued by the National
Information Standards Organization (Z39.48–1984).

10 9 8 7 6 5 4 3 2 1

Every reasonable effort has been made to trace the owners of copyright materials in this
book, but in some instances this has proven impossible. The author and publisher will be
glad to receive information leading to a more complete acknowledgments in subsequent
printings of the book and in the meantime extend their apologies for any omissions.

For Janie, with love, always

CONTENTS

FOREWORD

It's the contemporary catch phrase: "60 is the new 40!" Such good news about the youthfulness of this marker age is not just media hype. Thanks to psychoanalyst Robert Schwalbe, there are facts and research to support this good news. In this book, Schwalbe covers every angle you can imagine about what this chronological age means in this new age. The triumvirate of three Ss—sixty, sexy, and successful—is encouraging and exciting.

I knew this story had to be told from the moment I met Dr. Schwalbe when he participated in the group I was leading at a workshop for aspiring authors sponsored by Harvard Medical School Department of continuing education. As he described his idea for this book, I knew it had to be published and be read by all men. Those under 60 need to know what's ahead and those at 60 need to know what they're facing. As impressed as I was then, I am even more pleased now to see this completed work, which exceeded coverage of the subject. Robert leaves no stone unturned, as he explains in detail and with authority, the facts about maturing interspersed with compelling stories of real men. Every aspect of life at 60 and over is covered, from emotional and physical fitness, family and finances, to grandparenting, losing love, and finding it again, making attitude adjustments, and maintaining meaning in life. Essentially this book is 20 books in one—a detailed guide and insight into everything you would ever want and need to know about men at this stage in their lives.

While addressing men's fears and anxieties, and the stark realities of aging imposed not only from within but by society, Schwalbe shows us there is much to be optimistic about. While many men at this age contemplate retirement—often forced by companies and laws—in truth they are reaching their prime, emotionally and professionally, and also sexually. Like his title promises, Schwalbe addresses sex. Yes, there are changes that men go through physically—with hormonal shifts and physical challenges—but I'm glad he hails that 60 can be the sexiest time of life. I've long held that positive view, even from the earliest days of the beginning of sex therapy when I was the protégé of a prominent group of psychiatrists at the Psychiatric Institute at Columbia Medical Center who were asked to evaluate Masters and Johnson's groundbreaking therapeutic techniques. The good news then, as now, is that once men stop focusing on sexual performance, they can enjoy sensuality—and be the type of partner women always say they want. Cheers to Schwalbe's plug for the art of cuddling. The optimism reminds me of groundbreaking films made decades ago hailing the sensuality of the "mature male," showing older men delighting their partners, reaching new confidence, and enjoying themselves freed from pressures of having to perform. Research even decades ago, some of which I also did, has found that people are enjoying intimate relations well into their eighties.

I'm sure every reader also knows men over 60 who are exceptionally vital in their life, who start new career paths and find new interests and meaning in life. Of all the research and clinical work I have done over the years, I've found that the key to the fountain of youth is what Schwalbe hails: having purpose in life and finding new meaning.

The importance of understanding men at different stages of life—commensurate with the intense study of women at stages of life—has become so prominent that the American Psychological Association even has a whole division devoted to the study of men. Geriatrics has become a hot topic in the health field, and those in the second half of life are increasingly focused on living healthy and spryly. Many colleges have women's studies programs, but Schwalbe's book makes a good case that equal attention should be paid to men's studies—and Schwalbe's book should be a required text.

Though filled with academic knowledge, Schwalbe also makes the intense exploration engaging, readable, and hard to put down. There's much to learn for everyone, about trusts, changes in living arrangements, and caregiving. And there's much advice about the importance of "feeding your brain," keeping up social contacts, and going through a "life review."

With changes in today's society, men in their sixties are facing new roles. Schwalbe points out some of these new trends, like late-life divorce, which used to be a rarity. I recall doing a television story a long time ago about the shocking news about famous "baby doc" Benjamin Spock and his wife getting a divorce after 48 years of marriage. Another new trend is step-grandparenting—when your children remarry and you inherit new sets of grandchildren. With new constellations of families and changes in parenting, grandparenting has taken on yet another new role: custodial grandparenting, as Schwalbe points out has happened for 10 percent of grandparents in the United States who assume primary responsibility for raising their grandchildren. This role recently came to light when the sister of troubled star Britney Spears, Jamie Lynn Spears, became pregnant at age 16 and her mother agreed to raise the child (reportedly so her daughter could lead a "normal" teenage life).

Readers will be interested in other new information Schwalbe presents, like Syndrome X (a cluster of symptoms that predispose a person to diabetes and heart disease) and the "hereafter" phenomenon (signaling increasing interest in Alzheimer's and maintaining a healthy brain and cognitive functioning).

Fortunately, the definition of *old* and words used to describe an age has changed. Men in their sixties are now being considered at the upper range of midlife, which has extended downwards to age 35 and upwards to 65. The "New Man" as Schwalbe accurately points out, is working out, coloring his hair, using face cream, and even getting plastic surgery. Schwalbe himself admits to having had Botox, a treatment to eliminate wrinkles. Like their female partners over 60, men may have senior moments but they are still on the tennis court and even taking dancing lessons.

While Schwalbe gears his message to men, every relative, friend, and professional associate, and particularly intimate partner, also needs to read this book to understand the new 60 male. Famed psychoanalyst Freud pondered "what do women want?" Psychoanalyst Schwalbe makes us confront what men want, and need, specifically at this transitional and what-can-be-magical age of 60.

Dr. Judy Kuriansky
Series Editor

ACKNOWLEDGMENTS

I wish to express my gratitude to those who are part of my practice currently, or have been in the past, for permitting me to use their experiences in my chapters. Suffice it to say that all identifying characteristics have been changed in order to protect their confidentiality. Thank you to Dr. Jim Twaite, for his valuable research and involvement in the writing of this book. In addition, I thank Saul Agus, MD, Ron Livesey, MD, and Jonathan Waitman, MD for their acknowledgment of the medical contents. My ongoing gratitude to Doug Ingram who helps me find my balance and my depth. And significantly to the many people who have encouraged the writing of this book. In particular, to the baby boomers who have come of age or who are at its threshold. This book leads the way to flourish in the best of life's periods.

And most of all to my wife Janie. All that I am today I owe to your understanding and encouragement, your vibrant personality and your compassionate love. I am happiest when with you.

Chapter One

THE MYTHS AND REALITIES OF LIFE AFTER 60

John's Sixtieth Birthday

John came into my office for the first time on the morning of his sixtieth birthday. He didn't tell me that it was his birthday. I noticed it on the contact form that he had filled out. John got right down to describing his problems. He complained that over the past few months he had been feeling anxious, depressed, disorganized, and ineffective. His successful marketing business had begun to fall off, and he couldn't seem to muster up enough energy to turn it around. He was plagued by increasingly annoying physical aches and pains, to the point that he had cut back on the golf game that he had always loved so much. He couldn't get a good night's sleep. His sex drive was non-existent. He felt as if he was losing control. He said his life was "falling apart" in front of him, and there was nothing he could do about it. He was afraid of where it all might end up, but at the same time he wondered if it was even worth the effort to try to turn things around.

I commented that this was a pretty substantial laundry list, and I commented that trying to deal with such a broad range of issues must indeed be an overwhelming task. John readily concurred that he was overwhelmed. That's why he came to me for help. I suggested that it might be helpful if we could prioritize the various problem areas that he listed, and then work on one problem at a time. To help in developing our strategy, I asked John to give me some additional details regarding each of the problems that he had mentioned. As he considered the various problem areas in turn, two things became clear. First, the problems that he mentioned were quite complex and even more serious than one might have expected on the basis of John's capsule summary. Second, all the problems he mentioned were related in one way or another to growing older and/or to his ideas about growing older.

John discussed his business problems first. He said that he had lost business to competitors who were offering customers better prices on items that were reordered on a regular basis. They were using new inventory control technologies that allowed the suppliers to anticipate and meet the customer's needs automatically, with little effort on the part of either the seller or the buyer. This allowed the suppliers to reduce their prices substantially, and John was losing substantial amounts of business, even with clients of long-standing. John complained that it wasn't enough to know an industry anymore: You had to be a computer engineer to succeed. John said that he was techno-phobic and could not keep up with younger competitors who were all so comfortable around computers. He also said that he had considered hiring someone to handle this aspect of the business, but he feared that he would not be able to supervise such an individual, and he feared losing control. Furthermore, technical people were expensive, and since business had begun to fall off, John was not sure that he could even afford to hire such a person. When I asked John if there was more business out there that he might get if he brought his technology up to date, he said that there probably was, but he no longer had the drive or the physical stamina to run around courting new accounts.

When I asked John to tell me about his physical complaints, he said, "I'm just getting old I guess. I used to play golf two or three times a week, and I never had any problems. I loved being out there. I enjoyed the walking. I was a good player, and I got a lot of satisfaction out of playing well. Now there are always problems. My back is stiff and I have arthritis in my hands and elbows. I can't get loose, and my swing has gone to pot. My handicap is going up steadily, and I am very frustrated that I cannot play as well as I used to. Some days I plan to go, but I'm either too stiff or too tired to bother. What's the point of going when you know it's going to be a painful, frustrating struggle? I'd rather just stay at home and watch the professionals on the TV."

John said that he had always slept very well, but not anymore. He said that he had trouble falling asleep at night because he couldn't stop himself from thinking about his problems, and he couldn't help worrying about just how bad things might get. Sometimes he took a glass of brandy to help him fall asleep. Sometimes the brandy worked, and sometimes it did not. If John did fall asleep, he rarely slept through the night. Sometimes he would get up in the middle of the night to go to the bathroom, and then he could not go back to sleep. Sometimes he would wake up because he was having a troubling dream, and then he could not go back to sleep either. He felt sleep-deprived during the day. Sometimes he would doze off at his desk. John said that most days he felt as if he were walking around in a cloud.

John said that he and his wife had a good sex life for most of their marriage, but lately it had pretty much faded into oblivion. He said that after his wife went through menopause, she seemed to lose interest in sex, and she often made excuses if he expressed any romantic interest. He said that for a while he had used alcohol to get her "in the mood." This worked off and on for a time, but in the long run using alcohol seems to have been counterproductive. John drank along with his wife while he was attempting to seduce her, and eventually the alcohol became a regular and even indispensable prerequisite to sexual activity. Unfortunately, John found that alcohol did not enhance his sexual prowess, and he developed intermittent erectile dysfunction. He found this terribly embarrassing, especially when his wife criticized him for "working so hard to get me in the mood and then losing interest yourself." During the extended period over which their sex life languished, John occasionally turned to the services of prostitutes. At first he found this exciting and liberating, but he recognized that having sex with prostitutes did not help his ability to perform with his wife. In addition, the need for alcohol carried over to sex with the prostitutes as well as sex with his wife. Eventually, John began experiencing erectile dysfunction with the prostitutes as well, leaving him totally frustrated.

Now, it doesn't require a psychotherapist to see the common thread of advancing age that runs through all of John's presenting issues. Rapid changes in business technology made it difficult for him to compete in business; and his self-concept as an aging technological dinosaur prevented him from addressing this fixable issue in a timely and appropriate manner. He felt incapable of learning the "new tricks" of marketing technology, and he felt threatened by anyone who had such expertise.

Normal aspects of the aging process also impacted John's golf game, but he allowed the appearance of stiff muscles and arthritis pains to have a much greater effect than they might otherwise have had because he did not take the steps that are necessary to minimize these issues, such as stretching out and loosening up before beginning the golf game, undertaking other forms of exercise to enhance one's golf game, and taking an appropriate inflammatory medication to ease the aches and pains when they occur. John also made matters worse by refusing to accept the fact that one will naturally lose a stroke as the years go by. Even worse, he allowed his physical complaints and his mental frustration to reduce his level of participation in the game he loved. Of course, playing less frequently makes it even more difficult to maintain one's performance, as well as reducing the amount of time spent each week engaging in pleasurable activities.

Aging most likely contributed to John's problems with insomnia as well. As we grow older we tend to sleep less. It is normal for older individuals to spend an extra hour or so reading before they fall asleep, and it is also normal for older individuals to get up rather early in the morning. It is better to accept such changes than to struggle against them. However, John made matters worse by obsessively worrying about other age-related problems while trying to force himself to fall asleep, and by self-medicating with alcohol. A drink can indeed help to induce sleep, but those who take a drink to go to sleep often wake up in the middle of the night when the alcohol has been metabolized. John would have been far better off getting some additional exercise during the day to help to make him tired at night. If he did require some medication to sleep, he would have been much better off to obtain an effective sleep aid from his physician.

John's sexual dissatisfaction also appears to have been in part the result of normal aging processes, but to a much greater degree the result of John's ineffective attempts to understand and cope with these changes. First of all, John's wife may have experienced a decline in sexual interest due to age-related physical changes, such as reduced vaginal lubrication, which may make sex uncomfortable for post-menopausal women. If such issues are recognized and discussed, they can be remedied easily. If they are not discussed, they can be misinterpreted, and they can become serious problems. Similarly, as men age their testosterone levels fall. This lessens the sex drive and impacts their sexual performance. Older men may take longer to achieve an erection, and erections may not be as hard as they were when they were young. But these issues do not preclude sex. They simply mean that we must take more time for sex. This is a good thing, not a bad thing. However, John's insecurities surrounding aging led him to do all the wrong things to demonstrate that he was still sexually capable. He relied on alcohol, which only makes the problem worse. And he went to prostitutes, which clearly indicates that he was not communicating his sexual needs to his wife.

John is a good example of what can happen to men over 60 if they are not knowledgeable regarding the actual changes that occur as we grow older, and they fail to take the simple steps that are required to maintain optimum health and wellness. In this book I will tell you what men need to know about the normal effects of aging and how to maintain a high level of satisfaction with life in the face of these changes. Notice that I am addressing this book to men. Why do men more than women need help as they enter and pass their sixtieth year?

MEN AND WOMEN PASSING 60

Have you noticed that men seem to have more problems than women with turning 60? They do. In my practice I frequently see men like John, whose lives have gotten increasingly out of control as they approach their seventh decade of life. Many men passing 60 find themselves feeling restless and depressed as they contemplate the rest of their lives. They experience *aging anxiety*, and they often respond to their discomfort in irrational ways. Some have affairs. Some turn to alcohol or other drugs. Some start to gamble, or they start to gamble more than they ever have before.

Women at 60 tend not to experience these problems to the same extent as men. Women at 60 have already undergone the significant and undeniable passage of menopause. They have already been told by their bodies that they are beyond the reproductive stage of their lives, and they have had to come to terms with the implications of this reality. They know that they are growing older. In addition, when women are experiencing menopause, they tend to seek out the support of their friends who have shared or are sharing the same experience. Women know what to expect after menopause, because they talk about it.

Men tend to avoid talking about their problems in general. If they can avoid dealing with an issue by denial, they will. For this reason, the lack of a discrete and unmistakable physical marker of the aging process such as menopause leaves men free to indulge their tendency to deny their concerns and avoid talking about them. Men do experience age-related physical and mental changes and concerns, but these changes are more gradual in nature, easier to deny, and therefore more apt to sneak up on us and suddenly leave us in a state of overall agitation and depression like John. Therefore, men need a book like this one far more than women, because they are in far greater danger of denying their fear of aging until it has become so strong that it will paralyze them.

THE FEAR: IT'S ALL OVER NOW

Why Do We Fear Aging So?

We men really fear growing old. We fear it because we believe that growing old is synonymous with becoming sick, incapable, dependent, unattractive, and miserable. Men in particular dread the thought of becoming physically frail. Many of us have personal identities founded upon physical prowess and competence, and the idea of losing this aspect of one's identify is disturbing, even terrifying. In addition, we want to think of ourselves as sexually attractive and as commanding respect through our strength. Therefore the idea that advancing age will reduce our sexual attractiveness and our physical strength is especially threatening to men.

Perhaps even more powerful than the fear of losing our attractiveness and our physical strength is the fear that as we grow older we will become dependent upon others. Men are socialized to take care of themselves. This is why we refuse to ask for directions while driving. We cannot admit that we are lost, because being lost requires that someone find us. For the same reason, we may choose to undertake certain home repairs ourselves when it would make far greater practical sense to hire a professional. We do it ourselves, simply because we need to demonstrate that we *can* do it *ourselves*. We don't *need* anyone to do it for us. Given our masculine need for independence and self-sufficiency, the idea that growing old may make it necessary for us to depend on others for certain forms of help is extremely threatening. We men do not want to be dependent in any way, not emotionally, not physically, not socially, and not financially.

Why Do We Avoid Confronting the Issue of Aging?

In addition, we men tend to avoid displaying our emotions, because we have been taught to view emotional breakdowns as a sign of weakness. We have all been offended at some point in our lives by something that a friend or colleague said about us. Maybe it was a remark about putting on a few pounds. It might have been a comment on how we let a fish get off our line or how we missed a foul shot in a big game. Or perhaps someone criticized us because the team we picked to win the world series never made the play-offs. Regardless of the nature of the offense, one thing is clear. *No matter how offended we may actually feel, we men will not admit that we have been hurt or humiliated.* We will not tell the offender that his remarks are insensitive, be-cause then he will know that he has gotten to us. And under no circumstances will we complain to a third male friend about how insensitive to our feelings the offender was.

So here's how it is: If Mary inadvertently offends Sue by criticizing her choice of floral arrangements, Sue will not only make it clear to Mary that she is offended, but she will also tell all their other friends how insensitive Mary was to her. But if Sam tells Jim that the new SUV he bought was given a poor rating by *Car and Driver* magazine, Jim will first tell Sam that he's full of shit, and then Jim will find as many of their friends as he can and tell all of them that Sam is full of shit as well. Deep inside, Jim may feel like an asshole for not doing better research on the car he bought. He may very well call himself a jerk every time he gets in the car. But he's not going to let Sam or anybody else see that he has been offended.

And so it is with the fear of growing old. We all have it, yet none of us want to acknowledge that we have it. To the greatest extent that we can manage, we deny the fear. For a good long while, we deny getting older at all.

Why Do We Regard Aging as a Problem?

•But eventually, the little signs of growing old rise to a level of awareness that does not allow us to deny the fact of aging any longer. Then, because we fear aging so much, we tend to consider the reality of growing older as a problem that we must somehow overcome. For this reason, many men engage in pro-digious efforts to hang on to their youth for as long as they possibly can, in a futile attempt to avoid growing older (or at least to deny the reality that we are growing older).

Sometimes these efforts become quite silly. We spend large sums of money on restoring and/or coloring our thinning and graying hair. We go to tanning salons to get a rugged outdoor look, but at the same time we use skin creams to keep our skin looking young. Some of us have even resorted to plastic surgery to remove age-related wrinkles.

There are many other ways in which we can attempt to hang on to our youth. Many of us ingest unproven dietary supplements and drugs that are reputed to have anti-aging effects. Some men even engage in extreme and possibly dangerous physical activities in an effort to prove that they have not "lost their edge." We may suddenly feel compelled to take up bungee jumping, mountain climbing, or white-water rafting, or big game hunting. Even if we do not carry our efforts to maintain our youth to quite such extreme lengths, we may take other steps to preserve our youthful image. We may simply buy a little red sports car or have an affair with a woman who is half our age.

THE TRUTH: LIFE AFTER 60 CAN BE VERY GOOD INDEED

What Are the Misconceptions That We Hold Regarding Aging?

It is ironic that these questionable efforts to hang on to our youth are based on the idea that growing old means becoming weak, frail, unattractive, and dependent, because the truth is that growing old does not mean this at all. In fact, the great majority of men over the age of 60 are healthy and independent.

Nevertheless, most people subscribe to the widely held stereotypical belief that life after 60 is generally characterized by significant decreases in both physical health and mental acumen. Most people also believe, consciously or unconsciously, that these decrements in physical and mental functioning will eventually lead to diminished participation in occupational, social, and leisure time activities.

Many people believe that men over 60 are neither interested in nor capable of engaging in sexual relations. Moreover, there is a general perception that diminished engagement in occupational, social, recreational, and sexual activities will inevitably lead to a sense of purposelessness, boredom, and depression.

However, these commonly held negative stereotypes are much more myths than realities. In this chapter, I will consider these erroneous beliefs in turn and try to differentiate between the frightening myths and not so frightening reality. I will also consider a number of other inaccurate stereotypes regarding aging that you really need to recognize as you approach and enter the seventh decade of your life. The more you know about the reality of aging, the better prepared you will be to make the years after 60 successful and satisfying.

Physical Health after 60

We generally assume that most people over the age of 60 are in poor health. Even those who should know better tend to hold on to this misconception. These inaccurate views even extend to people in the medical professions. For example, gerontologist Cary Kart surveyed third year medical students, and he reported that among this group "the consensus was that more than half of the older population are in ill health, and perhaps half of that population (25 percent of the total) are in institutions."[1] But the views expressed by these medical students are completely inaccurate. Kart noted that in fact the majority of older individuals do *not* have health problems that are significant enough to limit their ability to work or to manage their households. Kart also reported that "fewer than 5 percent of those sixty-five and over can be found in an old-age institution on a given day."[2]

Research studies indicate that most men over 60 are in good health and that they can expect to live for a long time and to remain healthy for much of their lives. The MacArthur Foundation Study of Successful Aging resulted in the conclusion that most men over the age of 65 are quite healthy. Rowe and Khan, the principal investigators of this study, reported that in 1990 the average 65-year-old American male had a life expectancy of more than 15 years, and that on the average 12 of these 15 years "are likely to be spent fully independent."[3] They noted that over the period from 1960 through 1990 there had been a dramatic reduction among seniors in the prevalence of three important conditions that are associated with chronic disease, that is, high blood pressure, elevated cholesterol levels, and smoking. They also reported that over the period from 1982 to 1989, there were significant reductions in the prevalence of arthritis, hardening of the arteries, hypertension, stroke, and emphysema.

These reductions in the incidence of various risk factors and chronic conditions among older Americans have resulted in an unprecedented level of freedom from disability. Kart noted in 1990 that fewer than one-fifth of all individuals over the age of 60 reported any health problem that limited their ability to work or to perform regular household chores.[4] Rowe and Kahn reported in 1998 that 89 percent of all adults between the ages of 65 and 74 "report no disability whatsoever."[5] In addition, Rowe and Khan reported that 73 percent of those between the ages of 75 and 84 had no physical disability, and that even among those over 85, nearly half reported no disability whatsoever.

Furthermore, these descriptions of the population in general must be evaluated against the reality that there is considerable variability in the health status of individual men. As I will discuss in detail in chapters 2 and 3 below, there is a great deal that a given man can do to maintain good physical health as he grows older. The appropriate use of preventive medicine, along with proper exercise and nutrition, can greatly increase the chance of remaining healthy literally for decades beyond the age of 60. Please keep in mind that I am not saying that any man can avoid growing older but rather that growing older should not be automatically equated with poor health and loss of independence.

Mental Functioning after 60

Another inaccurate stereotype of aging is that once we get past 60 or so we inevitably experience decrements in intelligence, memory, and the capacity to learn. In its extreme form, this belief is manifested in a fear of becoming senile. We dread the possibility that Alzheimer's disease may leave us unable to care for ourselves, find our way home, or even recognize our loved ones. Less extreme forms of this stereotype depict older individuals as unable to learn new skills or to keep up with technological innovations.

This latter belief may be less terrifying than the fear of senility, but it is potentially a serious misconception nevertheless, because it may lead us to restrict the scope of our professional endeavors, to avoid entering into competition with younger individuals, or to fail to participate in new and potentially rewarding leisure time or recreational activities. In the event that the fear of declining mental alacrity leads us to avoid situations involving new learning, we are engaging in and perpetuating a self-fulfilling prophecy. The failure to undertake new intellectual challenges may indeed lead to boredom and mental stagnation.

In reality, few men over 60 suffer from Alzheimer's disease or any other form of dementia, and age-related changes in learning ability tend to be very small. The MacArthur Foundation Study reported that no more than 10 percent of the population aged 65 or over are Alzheimer's patients, and that "among those aged seventy-four to eighty-one, a full half show no mental decline whatsoever over the following seven years."[6] It is true that as we age, our brains lose some neurons and there is a decrease in the production of the neurotransmitters that carry impulses to and from brain cells.[7] It is also true that these changes can result in minor sleep disturbances and disruptions in short-term memory.[8] However, it is also true that the brain retains its plasticity as we age, allowing the possibility for new growth.[9] Assuming continued mental stimulation and experience, neuronal loss may be lessened and neuronal connections may be regenerated. In addition, as some neurons are lost, other neurons may be used more frequently to maintain necessary cognitive function. The result is that knowledge, the capacity to reason, judgment, and long-term memory may remain relatively unaffected by aging.[10]

The key to maintaining our cognitive functioning is to continue to engage in mentally stimulating activities, including new learning. Thus to some extent keeping sharp mentally is a use it or lose it phenomenon. In addition, as I will consider in some detail in chapter 4 of this book, physical activity, proper diet, and mental exercise may contribute to continued high levels of cognitive functioning.

Occupational and Leisure Roles after 60

At least until rather recently, it would have been fair to say that society expects that after the age of 60 men will naturally reduce their participation in a broad range of occupational roles and recreational activities. This expectation is supported by the inaccurate stereotypes of aging with regard to declining physical health and mental acumen that I discussed in the two previous sections of this chapter. To the extent that we believe that aging is synonymous with weakness and frailty, we will likely also assume that it is appropriate for older men to withdraw from participation in strenuous physical activities.

This assumption seems to be based on the idea that for an older man to continue with such activities is inconsiderate of others, since he is risking an injury that might disrupt the activity for those participants who are younger and more fit, and perhaps even require a rescue or medical evacuation. Similarly, to the extent that we believe that aging is synonymous with decrements in mental alacrity and the capacity to learn, we will likely assume as well that older men should withdraw from occupational roles that are intellectually demanding in order to make room for younger, better educated, and more energetic workers.

Any social expectation that men over 60 should dramatically reduce their participation in cherished leisure and work roles is not only potentially very damaging but also wholly irrational. It is damaging because reducing activities can have an extremely wide ranging negative impact on a man's psychosocial well-being; and it is irrational because such reductions are generally largely unnecessary. Consider a man whose primary recreational activities throughout his lifetime have involved strenuous physical activities like hiking, bicycle racing, mountain climbing, or big game hunting. To the extent that he conforms to social expectation and gives up this favored activity when he passes the age of 60, he will not only suffer the loss of the enjoyable activity itself but he will likely also suffer the loss of the companionship of the peers with whom he participated in the activity. Similarly, consider a man who has engaged in a rewarding professional activity over the course of a lifetime. If he retires from this work simply because he feels that it is time to make room for younger workers, he will not only lose the enjoyment of engaging in the work but also the enjoyment of his daily interaction with his colleagues and clients.

These are major losses, and there is probably no good reason why they should occur. We have seen that older men generally retain their physical health and their mental capability well beyond the age of 60, so the need to discontinue participation in strenuous physical activities and intellectually demanding occupational roles is largely a myth. Even in the event that some cutting back is in order, changes in role participation can be measured and calculated so as to minimize the disruption of the rewarding aspects of the role. A man who has run marathons may elect to do so somewhat less frequently, or he may cut back his training schedule somewhat without discontinuing the sport entirely. A man who has climbed major peaks may reduce the difficulty level of the climbs that he undertakes. He may also become involved in working with younger climbers and derive satisfaction from passing on some of the lessons that he has learned over the course of his climbing career.

The same is true of professional activity. Any disadvantage that the older worker may experience based on decrements in cognitive processing speed, memory, or the ability to learn is most likely small, and most likely more than adequately compensated for by his extensive knowledge and experience. In addition, adjustments can be made in one's workload to accommodate a desire to work fewer hours or to focus one's efforts on areas of special expertise. The empirical research indicates clearly that "older workers produce a quality of work equal or superior to that of younger workers."[11]

Therefore it should not be surprising that more and more men past the age of 60 are continuing their old activities or taking up new ones, and more and more men are opting to continue working at their careers or to begin entirely new careers. Many older men are even going back to school in order to prepare for a second (or third) career that may well begin after the traditional retirement age. The reality is that very few men over 60 are compelled to discontinue enjoyable and productive activities simply because of their age. It is therefore important to remember that there is no rule that says men over 60 cannot continue to climb mountains or run businesses. You are the only one who knows what you are capable of doing and what makes you happy.

Family Roles after 60

There is a widespread belief that men over 60 tend to be isolated and lonely. We tend to believe that the extended family is a defunct institution in the United States. Not only do we not expect that our children will be available to care for us in our old age, but we are likely to expect that they will move off to the opposite coast and have very little to do with us. This belief is also inaccurate. The reality is that men over 60 tend to continue to have meaningful contact with their children and grandchildren and that they continue to perform valued roles within the family. The truth is that we tend to continue to take care of them and that they in turn provide us with both emotional and tangible support.

Sex after 60

The same applies to sex. The stereotypical view of aging men is that they are typically completely or at least substantially incapable of sexual activity, but that this doesn't matter much, since they are pretty much uninterested in sex anyway. However, neither of these beliefs is accurate. There are some age-related changes in the male genital system that may develop after the age of 60 and have an impact on the male sexual response. These changes include a decrease in the production of testosterone, the thickening of the tubules in the testes, and the enlargement of the prostate. Such changes may have the effect of lengthening the amount of time that a man requires in order to achieve and erection and orgasm following erection.[12] They may also result in a less firm erection and less forceful ejaculation. After 60, the man's erection tends to subside more rapidly following orgasm than it did earlier in his lifespan, and a longer time is typically required to have a second orgasm.

However, these changes do not preclude sex, and they do not necessarily diminish a man's interest in having sex. An early empirical study of 254 men and women between the ages of 60 and 94 indicated that there is no age-related decline in sexual interest.[13] Rowe and Kahn reported the results of a study that indicated that at the age of 68, approximately 70 percent of all men were sexually active on a regular basis.[14] Studies also show a strong correlation between sexual activity in the later years of life and sexual activity in the younger years: If an individual has an interest in sex and satisfying sexual activity during his early years, then he is also likely to have an interest in sex and to engage in satisfying sexual activity after 60 as well.[15]

There is great variability in the sexual activity of men beyond the age of 60. Some men implicitly accept the stereotypical view that they should lose interest in sex as they get older. This may make them feel embarrassment in connection with their sexual interests and lead them to avoid sex.[16] Some may feel embarrassed by diminished sexual potency due to poor health or age-related changes and may avoid sexual behavior because they fear embarrassment. Married men over the age of 60 are far more likely to be sexually active than unmarried men because of the availability of a partner.[17]

There is also great variability in the nature of sexual behavior among men beyond the age of 60. When we consider sexual intercourse per se, we must keep in mind that age-related physical changes in both men and their female partners may require adjustments. More time must be allowed for sex, and more foreplay may be required to achieve arousal. Greater emphasis may be placed on oral and manual forms of sexual stimulation. Lubricants become important, and their use may be incorporated into the lovemaking. Furthermore, sexual intimacy may take the form of touching and embracing one another in various ways other than or in addition to vaginal penetration.

The key here again is that the prevailing stereotype is inaccurate, and one should use his own sexual interests and desires to determine his sexual behavior, rather than conforming to a socially prescribed formula for how a man over the age of 60 is supposed to feel and behave. In chapter 7 of this book, I will consider the topic of sexuality after the age of 60 in some detail, providing specific suggestions for increasing your satisfaction with your sex life.

FEAR OF AGING REVISITED

Having seen that most of the negative stereotypical beliefs regarding life after 60 are inaccurate, I hope that at this point I have succeeded in greatly diminishing your fear of growing older. I also hope that the clarity of thought that accompanies this reduction of fear will enable you to distinguish between: (1) senseless and futile efforts to avoid growing old; and (2) perfectly sensible efforts to insure that the many years of your life that come after your sixtieth birthday are as rewarding and satisfying as they possibly can be. These efforts are aimed at maintaining your physical health, your mental fitness, and your active involvement with life after the age of 60. Most of these steps involved are straightforward, and most do not require prodigious efforts on your part. I invite you to proceed through this book with the idea that each new chapter contains recommendations for actions that represent a very good investment in your long and happy future life.

Chapter Two

FITNESS

WHY ISN'T EVERYBODY FIT?

Whether you are young or old, physical fitness is an important predictor of your satisfaction with your life. The more fit you are, the better you feel. Being fit makes you feel better about yourself. Being fit lets you participate in more activities that are fun. Being fit fights depression. I'm not telling you anything that you don't know. If you were to ask 100 people whether they would rather be physically fit or not so fit, they would all certainly choose to be fit.

Yet few people are fit. In fact, the *majority* of Americans are either substantially overweight or obese. The majority of Americans are so out of shape that they couldn't walk a mile on flat ground. Many men past the age of 60 are so out of shape that they couldn't walk a quarter of a mile on flat ground.

How can this be? How can it be that so many people are so unfit? Of course, the answer is obvious. We do not exercise, and we eat too much of the wrong foods. This chapter is about *exercise* and *nutrition*.

EXERCISE

Let's start with exercise. I am going to convince you that exercise is not just good for your health but also fun. I am going to start with the fun part, because most of us already know that exercise is good for us. We know that we should exercise, but most of us do not. It is not enough that we know it is good for us. Those of us who exercise regularly also enjoy exercising.

Why Do We Not Exercise When We Know We Should?

There are two major reasons why we do not exercise regularly: Either we think that exercise is unpleasant; or we think that we don't have the time to exercise. Some of us think that exercise is unpleasant because it is downright painful. And indeed, for those who are really overweight and out of shape, the wrong kind of exercise can be uncomfortable. It can even be painful or dangerous. But even if you are not physically fit, the right kind of exercise is not painful or dangerous. The right kind of exercise will still be fun.

Among those of us who are not quite so out of shape, there is still a tendency to view exercise as unpleasant and therefore to fail to engage in regular physical activity. This is due to the perception that exercise is boring. Many people think that going to the gym to walk on a treadmill or use an elliptical machine is just too tedious. Simply, they would rather be somewhere else doing something interesting or somewhere else doing nothing at all. Many of these folks say that they would exercise a lot if the exercise were hiking through Yellowstone Park on a gorgeous fall day or participating in some exciting sporting activity, but obviously they can't be in Yellowstone on a regular basis, and they have never been good enough athletes to feel comfortable being a member of a competitive athletic team. These folks are the so-called weekend warriors, who will engage in physical activities from time to time when opportunities present themselves. However, their exercise is so irregular that they do not ever really become physically fit, and they may even risk injury by plunging into rigorous activity for which they are not physically prepared. But once again, I am here to tell you that there are many ways to get exercise regularly that are not boring at all. I would also argue strongly that even working out in a gym on a regular basis does not need to be boring. I work out in a gym almost every day, and I look forward to it.

The second major reason why we fail to exercise regularly is that we think that we do not have time. We are too concerned with making a living to stick to a regular exercise schedule. There are appointments to keep and deadlines to meet, and the easiest part of the schedule to change is the time that we have allotted for exercise. Perhaps our work involves travel, which can also make regular exercise difficult. However, those of us who have made a commitment to a regular exercise routine do not allow the demands of work or other time pressures to interfere with our workouts. We know that our exercise time is at least as important as our work time. In fact, the exercise routine is probably the most important part of our daily schedule. I enjoy the act of exercising, and I enjoy how good I feel after I have exercised; therefore, I exercise regularly. Since I have been exercising regularly, I have become so motivated that I actually feel just a little uncomfortable on the rare days when I *do not* exercise. Exercise is indeed a positive addiction.

The Joy of Exercise: Where the Motivation Comes From

Now I'm going to tell you about three men, all over 60, all of whom exercise regularly. These three men are quite different, and their motivations for exercising are quite different as well. However, they all have one thing in common. None of them exercises regularly just because he feels that he *should exercise*. They all receive major positive reinforcement from the exercising itself, and it is this reinforcement that motivates them to return to the gym each day.

Sam

Sam is an old gentleman who works out each day at my gym. I was quite impressed by this man when I first noticed him, because I could tell that he was quite a bit older than I, yet he was clearly in excellent shape. Sam is about six feet tall and he cannot weigh more than 145 pounds. He always smiles and says hello, and he has a twinkle in his eye that suggests real joy. He works out a lot each day.

His workouts are not that intense, although he does build up a sweat by the time he's finished. He starts with a lot of stretching. He is very flexible and seems to have very good balance and body control. Then he does a large number of resistance exercises, using very light weights and many repetitions. He takes his time between sets of resistance exercises. He varies the resistance exercises that he does each day. He uses every weight machine in the gym, and he uses free weights as well. He concludes his workout by using either an elliptical machine or an exercise bicycle for about 15 minutes. He reads the newspaper during this part of the workout.

One day I mentioned to him that he was really inspiring to me, and would he think that I was hopelessly rude if I asked him how old he was. He smiled and said that he was 92, and that he had been working out for years, since he was just a "young man" like me (I am 63). I was blown away. I probably would have guessed his age as being in the mid-70s.

I told him that I only wished I was in half as good shape as he is when I am his age, and I asked him what his secret was. He didn't hesitate for a second in responding. He had obviously given the matter some thought. He said that he exercised almost entirely because he loved the way that exercising made him feel. He said that he had always known that exercise is good for you, but he had never had enough self-discipline to make himself work out, just because he knew that it was good for his health or because it would likely make him live longer. Rather, his motivation came from remembering *before* the start of each workout just how good he would be feeling a few minutes later.

Without using the jargon, my old friend had stated and had put into practice two fundamental principles of motivational psychology: (1) the principle that positive reinforcement is more powerful than negative reinforcement; and (2) the idea that an immediate reward (like the euphoric feeling we get when we exercise) is a much more powerful determinant of behavior than a delayed reward (like the knowledge that exercising may help us to live longer). The first principal is illustrated by the fact that the good feelings that Sam gets from the actual exercising (positive reinforcements) are much stronger motivators for him than the fear of any potential illness that he might get if he did not exercise (negative reinforcements). And the second principle is illustrated by the fact that the euphoric feelings he gets from exercising (immediate rewards) are more powerful motivators than the knowledge that exercising may help him to live longer (delayed rewards). At any rate, my friend Sam is still enjoying his workouts, and he is still inspiring me.

Me

I also work out regularly, and I also do so primarily because I enjoy the work out. I am very much aware that my exercising will help me to look better, feel better about myself, and make me healthier and happier. Like Sam, I really enjoy my workout each day. I look forward to it, and I have no need to rely on the knowledge that it is good for me to force myself to go. I have been engaging in regular workouts for the better part of 25 years, and I have always thought of myself as being in reasonably good shape, although by no means an athlete. Much of this time I have used the services of a personal trainer to maintain my motivation and to insure that my workouts are sufficiently strenuous as to have a positive impact. My trainers use their knowledge of physical assessment and motivational strategies to help me to work very hard indeed to achieve a level of fitness that is substantially higher than the reasonably good shape that I was in when I began working out with him.

There is no age at which we should assume that we are no longer capable of becoming increasingly physically fit, which is defined in terms of increasing endurance, adding muscle mass, and enhancing flexibility. Based on the belief that we can always raise our level of physical fitness, my trainer is constantly challenging me to increase the weights I use in resistance training and to do more strenuous cardiovascular training. He correctly recognized that I had the type of personality that would respond to a challenge, so he introduced a subtle element of competition with him into our workouts. He has even introduced boxing into our workouts. Boxing is an extremely strenuous form of physical activity, and of course it involves physical contact and intense competition. I love it.

All of these strategies have worked very well with me, and I cannot stress enough the value that a really competent personal trainer can be to an individual seeking to become physically fit. Moreover, this advice applies not only to individuals who are already in pretty good shape. A trainer can also be highly beneficial to an out of shape individual who needs to have a more modest exercise program designed for him, a program that will make him enjoy the exercise immediately and begin to feel more fit fairly quickly. My trainer tells me that some people respond best to challenge, while others respond best to support and encouragement. Most folks need a little bit of each at different points in their journey toward fitness. A good trainer will understand when to use the carrot and when to use the stick, thus achieving the maximum gains while always keeping the experience an enjoyable one.

The key aspect of my training experience for our discussion here, however, is the idea that my trainer motivated me by making it a pleasure for me to come to work out each day. He recognized that I would derive great pleasure not only from the endorphins released during my exercise sessions but also by successfully meeting or exceeding the goals he set for me, by showing him that I could push myself and succeed, and by recognizing how much more fit I was becoming. He was right.

William

I have a 60-year-old friend who also works out almost every day. He goes to a gym religiously, but he does not use a trainer, and he does not push himself quite the way that I push myself. I asked William if he could describe to me his motivation in working out. What I got from William was quite a different motivational set from my own, much lower key and not as competitive in nature. However, William's motivations for working out were similar in one important way to the motivations expressed by Sam and to my own motivations. William made it clear that he was definitely driven much more by the positive rewards associated with the workout itself than the knowledge of the possible long-term gains in health and longevity associated with the exercise. He loves both the natural high that he gets from working out and the social environment in the gym. He views his buddies in the gym as part of his extended family.

He explained that

> My attitude toward working out goes through the same sequence each day. Without fail, as the time for my workout approaches, I need to convince myself to go ahead and do it. I think about the time and energy involved in getting to the gym, and I think about how I could use that time to do other work that needs to be done. I think about how I had a good workout yesterday, and I rationalize that I could certainly get away with skipping a day with no ill effects.
>
> In spite of this predictable daily resistance, however, I almost always do get myself together to go to the gym and do my work out. As I'm driving to the gym and getting dressed to work out, I think about how good it will feel to stretch out and relax. Then I think about who I might see at the gym and what we might talk about. Then I think of how good I'll be feeling mid-way through the workout.

William said that he works out nearly every day for about an hour and a quarter. He went through his typical routine for me to describe his motivations at each point. He said that first he takes about 20 to 25 minutes to stretch out

completely and to loosen up his muscles. During this period he assumes different positions that he has learned in yoga classes. He varies the positions from
day to day, using a different list for each day of the week. However, each list will
contain stretching exercises aimed at the lower body, the torso, and the upper
body, and each list will contain several deep breathing exercises aimed at relaxing. William said that he works at a computer most of the day, and the stretching exercises are particularly pleasurable and particularly helpful in working
out the "kinks and stiffness that come from sitting at a desk." He said that he
does the stretching first not only because it makes good sense physically but
also because he looks forward to this part of the exercise routine a lot, and the
anticipation of the stretching helps him to motivate himself to go to the gym.

After stretching thoroughly, William does about 20 minutes of resistance
training. He described weight training part of the workout as "hard work and
a little boring." He said, "I can't honestly tell you that this part of my workout
is fun, though it is a rewarding when I can increase the resistance for a particular exercise, or when I perceive that I was able to complete a set of exercises
more easily this time than last time. Still I have to force my self through the
weight training." However, William said that by this point in the workout he
knows that he has already gone through the effort of getting to the gym and
getting changed to workout clothes. Also by this point, he has already gotten
all stretched out, and he is ready to work. Therefore, "by the time the weight
training part comes around, there is no chance that I will skip this part of the
workout."

In addition, William said that he had written down several different se-
quences of weight training exercises, and he works through a different set
each day. He remarked that even though the weight training is hard work, it is
quite manageable, because no one set of weight training exercises is too long,
because he can stretch out between sets of weight exercises, and because during the weight work he can talk with some of the other folks who are working
out at the same time. He particularly likes the encouragement that he receives
from friends at the gym. Finally, William said that he like the way his muscles
feel immediately following the weight training.

In the final part of his daily workout, William spends one half-hour on an
elliptical exercise machine or treadmill. During this last half hour of aerobic
exercise, he said, "I get my heart rate up to about 125 beats per minute, and
I burn approximately 550 calories (or so my elliptical machine tells me). The
numbers are not really too important. I can tell that my level of intensity is
about right, because I sweat quite a lot and I breathe a bit heavier than usual,
although I do not ever feel out of breath." In this regard, William's motivational level is quite different from my own. I need to feel that I have pushed
myself, and I don't really feel completely satisfied unless I have gotten quite
out of breath.

William said that the beginning of the aerobic training is tedious. He said that he wears headphones and listens to some good rock music to overcome the initial boredom and get him "up" for the effort. He said that he needs the music initially to help the time go by and to energize him. However, after about 10 or 12 minutes on the elliptical machine, "I begin to feel really good. The endorphins kick in, and I settle into a very comfortable frame of mind. By the time I get off the elliptical machine, I am feeling really good. What's more, I am acutely aware of this good feeling for several hours after the workout. During these hours immediately following my workout, there is no doubt whatsoever in my mind that my exercise hour is the most important part of my day."

Notice that even though William did express some resistance to exercising at several points in his workout, his description of his state of mind during the workout contained no "should" references to the long-term benefits of exercise with respect to health and longevity. Rather, he talked almost entirely about the feelings that he had before and during the workout. He acknowledged that feelings of laziness and inertia tend to inhibit exercise, as do concerns with other responsibilities that need to be taken care of. In opposition to these resistances, William described feelings of comfort and relaxation that come from stretching out; and he described feelings of well-being that result from prolonged aerobic exercise. For William, the positive feelings associated with exercising clearly greatly outnumber and overshadow the negative feelings. He recognizes this, and it keeps him coming back to the gym each day.

Summary: The Motivation to Exercise

In the remainder of this chapter I will discuss the many positive effects of exercise on one's health and longevity, and I hope that this discussion will encourage you to begin an exercise program. However, in the final analysis, the daily decision to go to the gym and "get it done" will not depend on your knowledge of the long-term benefits of exercise. It will depend on your immediate awareness of how good exercising makes you feel—and you'll feel it *today,* right smack in the middle of exercising. So the bottom line with regard to exercise is that you should do it, because you will enjoy doing it, and because it will make you feel a great deal better, *right now.* Start easy with two or three days a week and gradually build up the amount and intensity of your exercise. The more you keep at it, the more you will like it. If you think you could use a push now and then, a trainer might be a good idea. But a trainer is certainly not required for you to enjoy the exercising. Keep it in the back of your mind that you are probably making yourself healthier and that you may very well be extending your life span. But don't use that knowledge as your primary motivation to exercise. Those benefits are just too far off in the future to provide you with much incentive when the time comes to go to the gym. Concentrate on how good exercising makes you feel.

Now, having made that crucial point, I will give you some specific information regarding the nature and importance of physical fitness, the specific benefits of exercise, and the prevalence and negative consequences of inactivity. I believe that having this information will help to motivate some readers to begin a regular exercise program. However, if you have already made the decision to begin working out, you can skip the next section. If you are ready to start exercising, get a check up from your physician and get ready to start your workouts. To begin planning, read the section of this chapter on what exercises you must do to experience the benefits of fitness.

THE IMPORTANCE OF PHYSICAL FITNESS AMONG MEN OVER 60

Whether you are young or old, being physically fit is the most important single factor in reducing your risk of dying. Experts have defined physical fitness as comprising a broad range of components, including agility, balance, body composition (fat vs. muscle), coordination, flexibility, muscular strength, cardiovascular and muscular endurance, and speed.[1] The relative importance of these components may vary somewhat depending upon the particular individual whose fitness we are discussing. For example, the components of muscular strength and speed might be somewhat more important for a 30-year-old professional athlete than for a 60-year-old investment banker. However, each of these elements has a role in determining the ability of each individual to meet the demands of daily living.

As individuals grow older, they tend to experience reductions in both the capacity of the cardiovascular system to deliver oxygen to the muscles and the capacity of the muscle tissue to use the oxygen to do work. These reductions are associated with a tendency for individuals to become less physically fit as they grow older.[2]

Some older individuals, particularly those who lead inactive lives, will ultimately experience a condition known as sarcopenia. This condition is characterized by reductions in the strength and size of the muscles, problems with one's sense of balance, and a tendency to walk in a slow and hesitating manner. Changes such as these would clearly have a negative impact on a man's ability to get around easily and take care of himself properly.

Thus physical fitness is certainly as relevant to the average individual as it is to the athlete. Rowe and Kahn observed that "To most people, the physical decline that accompanies aging is not so important on the basketball court as it is in regular daily life. Walking upstairs, reaching for a can on the top shelf of the kitchen, getting out of bed in the morning, dressing oneself—if we become unfit, all of these mundane tasks become more like chores as we age."[3]

Fortunately, however, the frail health and loss of function that we associate with aging is due only in relatively small measure to unavoidable age-related decreases in the capacity to deliver and use oxygen. Much more important is the amount of physical exercise one gets. When our bodies give us indications that physical exertion is more difficult than it was when we were younger, we have a choice to make. We can give in and become sedentary, or we can make up our minds to follow a program of physical activity and exercise.

If we choose the former course of action, if we give in and stop exercising, the likely outcome is what Rowe and Kahn have described as "a terrible downward spiral" in which "the experience of feeling weak leads us to become more sedentary, and this inactivity in turn leads to further frailty."[4] On the other hand, if we choose to remain (or become) physically active, we can remain physically fit and avoid the loss of function associated with declining physical capacities, at least for the great majority of our remaining years.

The Agency for Healthcare Research and Quality of the Centers for Disease Control has observed that "investing a small amount of time in becoming more active can produce big dividends in better health."[5] They suggested that nature has been very kind to us in terms of the amount of physical activity that is required to promote health. There is no need to spend hours a day in vigorous activity to obtain health benefits. On the contrary, "Significant health benefits can be obtained by including a moderate amount of physical activity on most, if not all, days of the week. Spending at least 30 minutes in moderate activity, such as a brisk walk or raking leaves, on all or most days of the week has remarkable health benefits for older adults."[6]

The Centers for Disease Control has also stressed that it is never too late to become physically active:

> No one is too old to enjoy the benefits of regular physical activity. In fact, older Americans have more to gain than younger people by becoming more active. Older people are at higher risk for the health problems that being active can prevent. In addition, physical activity can be an important part of managing problems that can already be present, such as diabetes, high blood pressure, or elevated cholesterol. Finally, physical activity can improve the ability to function well and remain independent in spite of health problems. Few factors contribute as much to successful aging as having a physically active lifestyle.[7]

People who are physically fit, even if they are smokers or have high blood pressure, are at lower risk of death than nonsmokers with normal blood pressure who are so-called couch potatoes. Because physical fitness often trumps other risk factors, getting fit and staying fit are probably the most important things a man over 60 can do to have a long and healthy life.

THE SPECIFIC BENEFITS OF EXERCISE

I hope that by this point I have convinced you that exercise really is important for your physical health and psychological well-being. I would hope that an appreciation of these benefits of exercise should be enough to inspire you to begin an exercise program. Nevertheless, being a bit of an obsessive type myself, I understand that some readers will want to know a bit more about exactly what happens when we exercise that makes it so good for us. This section of the chapter is for those readers, and I provide it in the hope that it may further motivate those of you who need to have a bit more detail regarding the specific benefits of exercise.

Exercise impacts your health positively because it: (1) improves oxygen delivery to the muscles and increases the efficiency of metabolic processes; (2) increases your strength and endurance; (3) reduces body fat; (4) improves flexibility in the joints and muscles; and (5) promotes a general sense of well-being. Most of the research on the effects of exercise has focused on its positive effect on cardiovascular health. However, recent research indicates that general fitness reduces mortality rates in men from non-cardiac causes nearly as much as it does from heart-related causes.[8]

Exercise Helps to Prevent Disease

In terms of the specific benefits of exercise on the risk of various diseases, Rowe and Kahn have pointed out that physical activity is related directly to heart health. The more you exercise, the less likely you are to suffer from coronary heart disease. Individuals who are inactive are 80 percent more likely to develop heart disease than those who exercise vigorously.[9] Physical activity reduces your risk of developing high blood pressure. If you already have high blood pressure, increasing your physical activity will help to reduce it. Physical activity is related negatively to your chance of developing colon cancer.

Exercise is also related negatively to the incidence of type 2 diabetes and the symptoms of Syndrome X, described in chapter 3 of this volume. Physical exercise reduces the likelihood of all the symptoms that comprise Syndrome X, including high blood sugar, high blood pressure, high cholesterol levels, and the development of belly fat. Physical activity is frequently helpful in reducing the symptoms of arthritis and reducing the progress of osteoporosis. Since physical activity develops strength and balance, it is also related negatively to the incidence of falls and related injuries.

Exercise Promotes Psychological Well-Being

Exercise has particularly positive effects on one's emotional state. Several studies have indicated that 30 minutes of brisk exercise three times a week may be as effective in reducing depression as antidepressant medication. Exercise is especially effective in reducing mild depression among the elderly. Aerobic exercise can increase the production of endorphins, adrenaline, serotonin, and dopamine, which are responsible for the phenomenon known as the *runner's high*. Subjective well-being and self-esteem also tend to go up when we lose weight and develop improved muscle tone.

Thus it is quite clear that men who have reached their 60th birthday benefit from physical activity not only in the sense of general well-being but also in terms of reducing the likelihood of developing life threatening diseases. Unfortunately, most men past 60 do not get sufficient physical exercise to maintain an acceptable level of fitness.

THE PREVALENCE AND CONSEQUENCES OF INACTIVITY IN OLDER ADULTS

Most Men Get Too Little Exercise

Very few men over the age of 60 actually get 30 minutes or more of moderate physical activity five times per week. According to the Centers for Disease Control and Prevention, approximately 30 percent of men between the ages of 65 and 74 and approximately 35 percent of men over the age of 75 are completely inactive, meaning that they engage in no leisure-time physical activity at all.[10] The figures are even worse when we consider the proportion of the older population who engage in moderate or vigorous forms of physical activity.[11]

The Agency for Healthcare Research and Quality of the Centers for Disease Control and Prevention of the U.S. Department of Health and Human Services has reported that through 2030, the growing number of older adults in the population will place increasing demands on the public health system and on medical and social services. The agency also reported that "lack of physical activity and poor diet are the major causes of an epidemic of obesity that is affecting elderly as well as middle-aged and younger populations."[12] The National Heart, Lung, and Blood Institute estimated that 18 percent of adult males over the age of 65 in the United States are obese, and another 40 percent are overweight, putting them at substantially increased risk for diabetes, high blood pressure, heart disease, and other chronic diseases.[13]

The impact of lack of physical activity on the medical care costs of older Americans is increasing. Colditz estimated that the direct medical costs attributable to inactivity and obesity accounts for nearly 10 percent of all health care expenditures in the United States.[14] Being inactive results in the loss of muscle strength and balance and increases the risk of falls.

These data make it clear that we have much to gain as a nation and as individuals by getting physically fit and staying physically fit. It is imperative that we recognize that we can stay fit only by remaining active. The job of maintaining fitness is a continuing one. For this reason, it is very helpful if we can build physical activity into our daily routines. For example, if we can make it a habit to walk to the store instead of riding, we will be that much ahead. Similarly, we can climb the stairs instead of taking the elevator. We can exercise with friends, join a gym, or take an exercise class. Personal trainers are great if you can afford one. They will maximize the efficiency of the time you spend exercising, and they can be terrific motivators. In addition, it is important for you to cultivate activities that are interesting and rewarding and at the same time require physical activity, so that we continue to do them for their own sake, and not simply because it is something that we feel we must do. Such activities include hiking, golfing, cycling, cross-country skiing, and tennis.

WHAT DO I HAVE TO DO TO BE PHYSICALLY FIT?

Guidelines for the amount and nature of the exercise one needs to become and remain physically fit range from very general to quite specific. I noted above that the Agency for Healthcare Research and Quality simply stated that 30 minutes of moderate activity three to five days per week has substantial health benefits, particularly for older individuals.

Aerobic Exercise

Aerobic exercise is really good for you. People who are aerobically fit also tend to be healthy. The American College of Sports Medicine recommends that healthy adults in general should engage in aerobic exercise three to five days a week, with an intensity of 50 to 80 percent of maximal oxygen uptake or maximum heart rate, for a period of 20 to 60 minutes each day.[15] Similarly, Harvey Simon of Harvard Medical School and Massachusetts General Hospital has suggested that older adults specifically should aim for 60 to 73 percent of maximum heart rate when they exercise.[16] This intensity level is not difficult to determine. You can obtain a good estimate of your maximum heart rate by subtracting your age from 220. A 60-year-old man would have a maximum heart rate of approximately 160. Therefore, using Dr. Simon's recommendation, the 60-year-old man would strive to get his heart beating in the range between 96 (0.60 × 160) and 117 (0.73 × 160) beats per minute. You can estimate your heart rate while exercising by taking your pulse for 10 seconds and multiplying by 6. You can take your pulse either from an artery on the inside of either wrist or on a carotid artery, located under the jaw on either side of the neck. You can also purchase an inexpensive and easy to use heart rate monitor at a sporting goods store or a runner's shop.

Moderate Exercise

Although aerobic exercise is required to achieve high levels of aerobic fitness, more moderate exercise is good for you as well. Recent studies have suggested that "it is possible to get nearly all the health benefits of exercise without reaching high levels of aerobic fitness."[17] According to the Harvard Men's Health Watch, the intensity of your exercise is less important than the net amount of exercise, and intermittent activity is as effective as continuous activity. Walking, golf, yard chores, dancing, yoga, and cross-country skiing are all activities that most consider moderate rather than strenuous, yet these activities have significant health benefits when you engage in them regularly.

I believe that the more activity you have, the healthier you will be. If you do not feel up to strenuous aerobic exercise now, begin with moderate exercise like walking. The chances are that you will enjoy it. It will certainly be good for you. And it may open the door that leads to more strenuous aerobic exercise.

Variations in Physical Fitness

I must stress that there are large variations in fitness levels, particularly among men over 60. For this reason the American College of Sports medicine has recommended that individuals who participate in supervised exercise programs complete a brief medical history and risk factor questionnaire.[18] Special diagnostic tolerance tests are recommended for individuals with diabetes mellitus or coronary heart disease and for individuals who are known to be at risk for these diseases. For those planning rigorous exercise programs, the college recommends that trainers make sure that program participants have had a physical examination by a physician within two years of the start of the program. This is particularly important if you start to exercise past the age of 60.

Berg and Cassells pointed out that exercise programs for older adults vary substantially. For those 75 and over, "emphasis may be placed on maintaining flexibility, strength, coordination, and balance, rather than on aerobic training."[19] However, for men between 60 and 75, moderate aerobic training is typically recommended.[20] Pollock recommends that exercise programs for the older men typically include exercises of lower intensity and impact than programs for younger individuals.[21] In addition, exercise programs for men over 60 are typically paced so as to approach the most strenuous portions of the workout quite gradually. Due to the relatively lower levels of intensity of exercise programs for those over 60, greater frequency is often recommended. The American College of Sports Medicine has suggested that older individuals might want to adapt their exercise routine to workout 5 to 7 days each week for periods of 20 to 40 minutes.[22] However, given the great differences among fitness levels among those over 60, it is best to individualize your exercise program in consultation with a physician and/or fitness training professional. Start slowly and build the frequency, intensity, and duration of your workouts gradually.

METHODS OF EXERCISE

There are three major categories of exercise: (1) aerobic exercise; (2) strength building exercise; and (3) stretching exercises. All three types of exercise are typically included in a balanced exercise program, although the relative balance of the three types will vary according to the age and fitness level of the individual man.

Aerobic Exercise

Aerobic exercises include fast walking, jogging, running, hiking, swimming, dancing, and calisthenics. These exercises build cardiovascular fitness and endurance. They do not necessarily increase one's muscular strength. In addition to strengthening the heart and increasing endurance, aerobic exercises boost HDL cholesterol (the good, or high density blood lipids), help to control blood pressure, strengthen the spine and the skeleton, help maintain normal weight, and improve one's sense of psychological and physical well-being.

Although even one hour of aerobic exercise per week is beneficial, three to fours hours per week are optimal. It has been suggested that simply walking quickly for three of more hours per week reduces one's risk for coronary heart disease by 65 percent.[23] Older individuals, particularly those who might be out of shape to start, should begin aerobic training gradually with 5 to 10 minutes of low-impact exercises (e.g., walking, swimming, cross-country skiing) every other day and build toward a goal of 30 minutes per day, three to seven days a week. He also indicated that swimming is an ideal exercise for older individuals.

A good method for moderating the intensity of one's aerobic exercise is to aim for a "talking pace," which means to work out hard enough to sweat, but still be able to converse with a friend without gasping for breath. As your fitness level increases, the pace that fits this definition will gradually increase. For burning calories and elevating one's heart rate and oxygen consumption, treadmills and elliptical trainers are excellent low impact devices.

Strength Training

Strength training involves moving various parts of the body against resistance. This form of exercise is often referred to as weight training. Strength training builds muscle strength and burns fat. It helps to maintain bone density. It improves digestion, and it appears to lower LDL cholesterol (the bad, or low density lipids). Weight training is beneficial to everyone, even individuals in their 90s. It is the only form of exercise that can slow and even reverse the loss of muscle mass, bone density, and strength that tends to occur with aging.

Strength training involves three different types of muscular contractions: (1) isometric contractions; (2) concentric contractions; and (3) eccentric contractions. In isometric contractions, the length of the muscle does not change. An example of an isometric contraction is pushing against an immovable wall. Concentric contractions involve the shortening of muscles, for example, the part of a biceps curl in which the weight is lifted up, shortening the bicep. Eccentric contractions involve the lengthening of muscles, for example, the part of the biceps curl in which the weight is lowered and the arm extended.

Each training session should begin with exercises focused on large muscles and multiple joints. It should end with exercises for small muscles and single joints. Strength training involves repetitions of weight bearing movements. Generally one begins with 8 to 12 repetitions of each movement with low weights. Typically the initial weight used for a given movement would be about one-half the weight that one could move with maximum effort. During the movements, you should try to breathe slowly and rhythmically, exhaling as the movement begins, and inhaling when you return to the starting point. The first half of each movement should take two to three seconds; and the return to the original position should take four seconds. Strength training sessions should allow 48 hours between exercises of the same muscle group, in order to allow the muscles to recover fully. Some people just do weight training every other day. Others divide their movements into two groups using different muscles, and alternate between the two sets of exercises. Strength training requires equipment in the form of weights that may be lifted or exercise machines that can supply resistance against which you can move your muscles.

Stretching

Stretching helps to prevent cramping, stiffness, and injuries. It improves one's range of motion. In addition, certain flexibility training techniques, such as yoga classes, also involve meditation and breathing techniques that function to reduce stress. Some stretching exercises are especially helpful in reducing back pain. In addition, stretching feels good. Yoga is a particularly enjoyable and safe method of stretching that you may engage in alone or with an instructor. Stretching exercises should be performed for at least 10 to 12 minutes at least three times per week.

CAUTIONS WITH RESPECT TO EXERCISE

As beneficial as exercise is, one must exercise some caution when beginning an exercise program. Simon noted that in the United States there are approximately 1.5 million heart attacks each year. Of these, about five percent occur following heavy exertion. Therefore it is good to be careful. Make certain that you are not at high risk for heart attack before beginning a strenuous exercise program. Regardless of the shape you're in, start slow and work up.

High impact aerobic exercise can be problematic, in that such exercise can result in injury to bones, joints, and muscles. Low impact aerobic exercise is an option, and high impact aerobic exercises should be done in moderation. Good footwear can be helpful in reducing impact. Be careful to warm up slowly and cool down following exercise. Take a day off now and then.

Be careful not to become dehydrated during exercise. Drink lots of water during intense exercise. Don't go by thirst, as this is often an inaccurate indicator of the need for hydration, particularly among older individuals. Working out in a warm setting, you can lose two liters of fluid in an hour by sweating alone. Therefore, if you do exercise intensively you should drink six to eight ounces of water about 15 minutes before you begin your workout, and you should take time during the workout to drink more. Drink water. Sports drinks are no better than water for quenching your thirst or improving your endurance. Avoid caffeinated beverages. They can raise blood pressure and reduce fluid.

If you're working out where it's hot, guard against hyperthermia. Rest, and drink lots of water. If your skin temperature rises to 103 degrees F, or if you feel lightheaded, nauseous, clammy, or chilled, rest in a cool place and cool your skin with ice packs or cold wet towels pressed against the skin.

NUTRITION AND SUCCESSFUL AGING

A good diet is one of the most important determinants of successful aging.[24] Of the ten leading causes of death in the United States, five have dietary behaviors as significant risk factors. These are heart disease, cancer, stroke, diabetes, and Alzheimer's disease.[25] Many older people eat poorly, for a variety of reasons. These include life-long bad habits, poverty, dental problems, and often lack of knowledge regarding the nutritional requirements of those over 60. In this section I consider the nutritional needs of men over 60, including the need for energy, water, fat, carbohydrates, protein, and various vitamins and minerals.

Energy (Calories)

As we age, we tend to lose muscle mass; and our metabolism tends to drop. Each of these trends results in a reduction in the number of calories that we require to live. On top of these age-related changes, it is clear that Americans in general are eating more, although they are less and less active. For all these reasons, men over 60 typically take in more calories than they need. This leads to excessive body weight, which becomes a risk factor for the development of chronic disease. Therefore a most basic recommendation for men over 60 is to monitor their caloric intake and their activity level so as to avoid excessive weight gain.

A related issue has to do with nutrient density. Since we need to reduce our caloric intake as we grow older, it may become more difficult to obtain all the nutrients that we need within the necessary caloric limits. This means that it may be necessary to cut down on foods that have many calories but relatively few vitamins and minerals (for example, sugars, starches, fats and oils), and increase the relative proportion of foods in our diets that have few calories but are rich in nutrients (e.g., fruits and vegetables).

Water

Unlike calories, which we tend to get too many of, older individuals tend to be at risk for getting too little water. As we grow older we suffer a diminished capacity to conserve water through the kidneys, and we also tend to experience a reduction in the sensation of thirst. Dehydration in turn increases the risks associated with infections such as flu, sinus infections, and pneumonia. Men over 60 should make a special effort to drink about six glasses of water each day, and they should drink more if they lose water through sweat when they work out.

Fat

Older men, like younger men, should aim to consume no more than 30 percent of their daily caloric intake in the form of fat. This should include 10 percent saturated fat, 10 percent polyunsaturated fat, and 10 percent monounsaturated fat.

Carbohydrates

Carbohydrates should comprise about 55 to 60 percent of our caloric intake. In most people the actual proportion is lower, generally around 45 to 50 percent. This is largely because we are eating too much fat. When choosing carbohydrate foods, it is very important to minimize the number of highly processed carbohydrates, foods such as white bread, sugar, pasta, and pastries. Complex carbohydrates are far better for us. These include foods like peas, beans, lentils, and some fruits. These foods contain soluble fiber, which is helpful in reducing blood fat and blood sugar levels. This may help to prevent heart attacks. Fiber is also helpful in preventing constipation. I really like apples. Apples are a great source of fiber and have the ability to satisfy cravings for unhealthy foods.

Protein

In general, it is recommended that 12 percent of our caloric intake should be in the form of protein, which is necessary to maintain and repair bodily tissue. Today, most Americans actually consume more protein than they need. However, older individuals may find it difficult to provide enough protein to meet tissue maintenance needs. Older individuals are somewhat more likely than younger adults to have surgery, to suffer from infections, or to experience metabolic stresses. Each of these conditions can increase the need for protein.

Therefore it is very important for men over the age of 60 to be sure that they are consuming adequate amounts of protein. Failure to do so over time can reduce the body's capacity to heal wounds and fight disease. It may also interfere with the body's effort to maintain muscle mass.

Vitamins B6, B12, and Folate

These vitamins are involved in the metabolism of amino acids. Deficiencies of one of more of these vitamins can lead to the accumulation of homocysteine in the blood, which elevates one's risk for cardiovascular disease.[26] Elevated blood levels of homocysteine may also constitute a risk factor for dementia and Alzheimer's disease.[27] Vitamin B6 is found in chicken, fish, liver, pork, and eggs. Folate, or folic acid, is found in leafy vegetables, liver, yeast, and some fruits. Vitamin B12 is found in red meat and organ meats.

By age 80, approximately 35 percent of men and women develop atrophic gastritis, an infection that adversely impacts the ability of the stomach lining to secrete the acids required to digest foods. This condition leads to reduced absorption of folic acid and vitamin B12. It has been recommended that all older people should take supplements of at least 400 mg of folic acid per day.[28]

Antioxidants

The antioxidants include vitamins C and E, beta carotene, and the mineral selenium. Antioxidants are important because they act within cells to prevent oxidative activity that is associated with damage to important cell components, including DNA. Research evidence has shown that the presence of so-called free radicals and related oxidative molecules is associated with several age-related diseases, including cardiovascular disease, Parkinson's disease, Alzheimer's disease, and some cancers.[29] As we age, our natural defenses against free radicals tend to weaken, leaving us vulnerable to these diseases. At this point the antioxidants appear to be helpful in neutralizing the effect of these free radicals.

The best food sources of antioxidants in general are "fruits and vegetables with a variety of colors; for instance, red, yellow, green, and orange."[30] Specifically, the best food sources of vitamin C are citrus fruits, berries, peppers, and tomatoes. The best sources of vitamin E are vegetable oils, wheat germ, nuts, and green leafy vegetables. The best sources of beta carotene include carrots, sweet potatoes, and squashes. Selenium is found in tuna fish, asparagus, brazil nuts, as well as in meat and poultry.

Studies have indicated that lifelong consumption of fruits and vegetables provides the best protection from oxidative damage.[31] Several studies have reported that a high dietary intake of vitamins C and E reduces the risk of developing Alzheimer's disease.[32]

With respect to supplementation of the antioxidants, Rowe and Kahn noted that vitamin E deficiency is not common among seniors. However, they also pointed out that vitamin E enhances the immune function of older individuals, and they recommended supplementing the dietary intake of vitamin E with an additional 200 mg per day, but not larger doses. Deficiency of vitamin C is also not very common. However, vitamin C is very important in reducing the risk of cancer, coronary artery disease, and cataracts, and in promoting rapid wound healing. Here again, therefore a modest supplement of 200 mg per day may be in order for those who do not consume many citrus fruits and tomatoes. A note of caution must be added with respect to large daily doses of vitamin C (1000 mg or more), which had been recommended to prevent colds and other viral infections. The evidence that vitamin C prevents colds is weak, and very large does of vitamin C can cause diarrhea and kidney stones. Beta carotene is readily available in foods and generally does not require supplementation. Daily supplementation of selenium (200 mcg per day) has been shown to be related to significant reductions in the incidence of lung, colorectal, and prostate cancer. The side effects of selenium supplementation appear to be minimal.

Vitamin D and Calcium

Vitamin D facilitates the absorption of calcium from foods. Vitamin D is found in milk, butter, eggs, and seafood. Vitamin D is also obtained through exposure to sunlight. Calcium is found in dairy products, broccoli, and green leafy vegetables like kale and collard greens. Men over the age of 60 should get around 1200 mg per day of calcium. Most do not get that much from food. In addition, many men and women over the age of 60 do not get sufficient vitamin D from natural sources, in part because they are not outside enough to get the vitamin from sunlight. For these reasons, men over 60 should probably supplement their calcium intake with 500 mg of calcium per day, and they should also take 700 international units of vitamin D each day to insure that their overall intake of these nutrients is adequate. This will slow down age-related bone loss and help to prevent fractures.

Iron

Iron is necessary to prevent anemia. Iron deficiency among men over 60 is not unusual, due in part to decreased dietary intake and in part to decreased efficiency of the absorption of iron through the stomach and intestine. Iron is found primarily in meat but also to some extent in eggs and various fortified cereals. Efforts to alleviate iron deficiency through food fortification have been very successful in the United States.

There has been considerable discussion of the possible negative effects of iron accumulation among the elderly. Connor and Beard suggested that too much iron in our diet may be associated with certain diseases including cardiovascular disease, cancer, diabetes, and neurological diseases.[33] In addition, the supplementation of iron at high doses (200 mg per day or more) often has some serious immediate side effects, including gastrointestinal distress and constipation. For this reason there is substantial disagreement regarding the advisability of taking iron supplements to augment dietary iron intake. Connor and Beard did not recommend the use of dietary iron supplements but rather concluded that "consumption of the major food groups, with special emphasis on five servings of fruit and vegetables, plenty of grains and legumes, and decreased fat consumption, can go a long way toward the provision of good nutrition."[34]

Chapter Three

REMAINING FREE FROM DISEASE

FITNESS IS NOT QUITE ENOUGH

In the previous chapter I was trying to convince you how important physical fitness is in determining your satisfaction with life, particularly as you pass the age of 60. I focused on exercise and diet because those are the two most important determinants of fitness over which we have considerable control. However, there is one more important determinant of health and life satisfaction that we need to consider, freedom from disease. In addition to promoting general fitness and a sense of well-being, regular exercise and a thoughtful diet also help to reduce the likelihood that we will be afflicted by life altering or life threatening diseases. However, even the most physically fit among us may contract a disease that could destroy the quality of our lives or kill us outright. Therefore, it is very important that we take some additional prudent steps to increase our chances of remaining free from disease.

These steps include taking advantage of available medical knowledge and technology to prevent, detect, and/or treat diseases that could threaten our health and well-being. In this chapter, I hope to encourage you to cultivate your awareness of what it feels like to be healthy, so that you will be aware of any painful or uncomfortable feelings that could indicate the presence of a disease process requiring treatment. I also hope to encourage you to be proactive in defending your health through knowledge of and attention to the warning signs of the diseases that most commonly threaten men over 60. Finally, I hope to encourage you to make appropriate use of available medical technology to detect the presence of possible problems that have no current discernible symptoms.

BELIEVE THAT YOU SHOULD FEEL GOOD

The most important single factor in combating possible threats your good health after 60 is the firm belief that you *should* continue to feel good. You must always expect to feel good, and you must interpret any pain or discomfort that you experience as an indication that something is not as it should be. Unfortunately, many older individuals labor under the misconception that aging necessarily involves "pain and discomfort, debilitation, or decline in intellectual functioning."[1] Kart points out that this belief can lead an older individual to attribute to aging itself a symptom that might actually be a sign of an identifiable disease process.

INTERPRET PAINS AND DISCOMFORT AS INDICATIONS OF A POSSIBLE PROBLEM

This misattribution of pain or discomfort to so-called normal aging could result in your failing to take appropriate action to identify and treat a real problem. For example, if you experience pain in your arm, which could indicate a fracture or possibly bone cancer, you might attribute the pain to age-related rheumatism. You might just say, "That's how it is. I'll just have to live with it and cut back a bit on some of the activities that hurt." But such acceptance of the pain as simply a "fact of life for an older guy" could lead you to fail to have it checked out by your physician. The failure to have it checked could be disastrous. Of course, you could be right. The pain might very well be "just" rheumatism. But even if it is, initiating medical attention could result in getting a prescription for pain medication that would eliminate the pain and get you back to your normal activities. And if it turns out to be something more threatening, early detection could save your life.

Similarly, a change in bowel habits is a well-known danger signal for cancer, but as we get older we might assume that such a change is simply a function of advancing age. Further, if we experience chest pain, which is a possible warning sign of heart disease, we may simply assume that this symptom represents just another attack of heartburn.

Therefore you should *never* assume that it is simply a part of the normal aging process if you feel pain or discomfort, or if you experience insomnia, anxiety, weakness, loss of energy, depression, or any other somatic complaint. You should always assume that such symptoms are possible indications of the presence of a disease process that can be identified and treated. In this way, you can be sure that you do not inadvertently fail to obtain proper treatment for a condition that is quite possibly easily remediable. Obviously, such a failure could have tragic consequences, as in the case of an individual who fails to have appropriate diagnostic tests so as to identify a cancer during the early stages, while it is still highly treatable.

TAKE PROACTIVE STEPS TO DETECT POSSIBLE HEALTH PROBLEMS

Furthermore, you should not wait until you experience a pain or other symptom to take proactive measures aimed at detecting the possible presence of a disease process. We cannot afford to wait until we experience a problem to act because some of the most important early warning signs of disease are silent. There are indications of disease processes that are not within our awareness unless we make a conscious effort to look for them or we employ a medical technology that can reveal the problem. Thus Rowe and Kahn point out that "you don't 'feel' high blood pressure until it makes you sick [and] you don't 'feel' bone loss until you sustain a fracture."[2] For this reason, it is important that we have regular physical examinations, which provide data that may indicate disease processes that have not yet resulted in observable symptoms. In addition, men over 60 should routinely be vaccinated against the possible contraction of certain diseases, including influenza, pneumonia, and tetanus.

In this chapter I discuss: (1) how frequently a well man of 60 or more years should have routine physical examinations and what procedures those examinations should include, including the diagnostic tests that should be included; and (2) the specific diseases for which men over 60 have an elevated risk, along with the risk factors, the screening procedures used to detect these diseases, and the treatment options.

Regular Physical Examinations

Because many health problems do not produce noticeable symptoms until they have reached a relatively advanced stage, most health professionals recommend routine health checks, including a physical examination and screenings for a broad range of conditions that can present a danger but go unnoticed. There also appears to be a consensus among health professionals that men are more likely than women to fail to have regular physical examinations. Scott Hansen, a physician at the Intermountain Health and Fitness Institute at LDS Hospital in Salt Lake City, observed that, "Men, more than women, are either too busy or reluctant to take the time for health screenings when they may be feeling relatively well."[3] Karen Barrow, a medical writer, had a slightly different perspective on the reluctance men have toward visiting the doctor. She wrote that "even the most macho of men can turn into big babies when it comes to going to the doctor [even though] most visits to the doctor are simply uncomfortable, not painful, and routine physical exams and screening can help men prevent many serious diseases."[4]

The consensus among medical professional appears to be that individuals who are 60 and over should have yearly physical examinations.[5] At a minimum, routine examinations should include the following components.

History

If you come with a particular presenting problem, your physician will ask you questions about the history of that problem. Whether you have come for a specific problem or for a routine examination, the physician will ask you questions about your medical history, including surgeries, medications, smoking and alcohol use, sexual activities, family history, and work and leisure time activities. Some of these questions may be of a sensitive nature, but it is important for you to be as forthright as possible, since this information will help your physician detect possible problems and recommend health promoting behaviors.

Body Measurement

Just having measurements of your weight and height will tell your physician a great deal about your physical condition. Your physician can use these data to calculate your body mass index (BMI), which will indicate whether you are overweight. Being overweight increases the likelihood that you will develop a number of significant health problems, including high blood pressure and type 2 diabetes.

Vital Signs Measurement

Your physician or an assistant will measure your vital signs, including temperature, respiratory rate, pulse, and blood pressure. These measures will help the physician to identify any acute medical problem and rapidly determine the severity of any current illness, and how well the body is coping with the stress of such illness. The more disrupted your vital signs, the sicker you are. If you are not sick but simply having a regular physical examination, the measurement of vital signs may indicate the presence of a chronic condition. For example, the measurement of blood pressure may indicate hypertension, a potentially dangerous condition discussed in detail below.

Blood pressure is the force exerted on the walls of the blood vessels by the blood flowing through them. During contraction (a period called systole), the right ventricle pumps blood into the lungs, and the left ventricle pumps blood to the rest of the body. After each contraction, the heart muscle relaxes and the heart is again filled with blood (a period called diastole). There are two types of blood pressure: systolic and diastolic blood pressures. Systolic blood pressure (the first and larger number in a blood pressure reading) is the pressure in the arteries during contraction. Diastolic blood pressure (the second and usually smaller number in the blood pressure reading) is the pressure during relaxation. Blood pressures are determined by the height of the mercury column in a gauge and are expressed in terms of millimeters of mercury or mm Hg.

The inflatable cuff that is placed around your upper arm during a routine physical measures both systolic pressure and diastolic pressure. The American

Heart Association has established the range of 90/60 to 140/90 as representing the normal limits for blood pressure. It is important to know your blood pressure, because high blood pressure is becoming increasingly common among men; and it puts you at risk for heart attack, stroke, kidney damage, and other problems.

Eye Examination

Your physician will check your visual acuity. He or she will examine the sclera (whites) of your eyes. The presence of yellowing of the sclera may indicate liver or blood disorders. The physician will also check for conjunctivitis, an infection of the membrane covering the sclera. The physician will ask you to focus on an object and then move that object in various directions. This allows the physician to determine the functioning of the extra-ocular muscles that control eye movement. Both the visual acuity assessment and the assessment of extra-ocular muscular movement also provide a test for the functioning of the optic nerve.

Your physician will shine a bright light into your eyes to assess the function of the pupils. Failure to respond appropriately to light can indicate the presence of elevated intracranial pressure, which may be a sign of a brain tumor or intracranial bleeding. The physician will use an opthalmoscope to examine the structures within your eye, including the retina.

Head and Neck Exam

During your physical examination your physician will feel and look at various parts of your head and neck to look for possible indications of disease. In this section of the chapter I will provide some indication as to why these different pokings and proddings are done, but you should of course feel free to ask at any point what he or she is doing. A good clinician will routinely explain why each procedure is being performed.

Your physician will feel (palpate) the lymph nodes in your neck to look for swelling that could indicate an infection or possible malignancy. Your physician will also check for possible blockages in the carotid arteries (carotid artery stenosis, discussed in detail later in this chapter) by listening to the sound of the blood flowing through the carotid arteries with a stethoscope. Your physician will use an otoscope to look into your ears. This enables the physician to check for possible damage to the eardrum as well as signs of inner ear infection. The physician may palpate and percuss the sinus areas of the face to detect any possible infection. He or she will also examine inside your mouth and throat to look for signs of infection or growths. The physician will ask you to stick out your tongue and move it from side to side. This is a way of detecting possible nerve damage. Your physician will palpate your thyroid gland to check for possible enlargement, which could indicate a tumor.

Lung Examination

Your physician will probably begin by simply observing you breathe. The physician can learn a great deal from this inspection. He or she can detect signs of pulmonary distress, emphysema, chest and spine deformities. Your physician will percuss your chest and back to provide an auditory indication of possible fluid in your lungs. He or she will listen to you breath with a stethoscope, listening for a variety of sounds that can indicate possible difficulties.

Heart Examination

Your physician will palpate your chest and listen carefully to your heart through a stethoscope to detect a variety of conditions, including heart murmurs that could indicate blockages of the aortic artery or mitral valve regurgitation.

Abdominal Examination

Your physician will palpate, percuss, and listen to your abdomen with a stethoscope in order to gather data regarding the functioning of the digestive system, the liver, the kidneys, and the spleen.

Testicular Examination

Testicular cancer is the most common malignant cancer among American men of all ages. According to the American Cancer Society, during the routine physical the physician should manually check your testicles to detect any change in the size or shape of the testicles that could indicate testicular cancer.

Digital Rectal Examination

During the routine physical examination the physician will perform a digital rectal examination to check for enlargement of the prostate gland, which could indicate benign prostatic hyperplasia (BPH, or simply enlarged prostate) or possibly prostate cancer. The examination involves the insertion of a gloved and lubricated finger into the rectum so that the physician can feel for hard or lumpy areas. This examination is very important for men past the age of 60 because more than 50 percent of men over the age of 60 have BPH. The benign enlargement of the prostate can make urination painful and difficult. Men with BPH can have difficulty starting the urinary stream, or they may experience an intermittent stream. Approximately one-fourth of men with BPH experience symptoms that are sufficiently troublesome as to require treatment.[6]

When symptoms of BPH are sufficiently severe, surgery may be performed to remove excess tissue inside the prostate. Using a special tool called a cystoscope, the physician can view the prostate and remove the tissue without having to make an incision.

Examination of the Extremities and Skin

A thorough physical examination will include a thorough examination of the extremities and the skin. Your physician will examine your hands and feet, checking for joint abnormalities associated with arthritis, and for swelling (edema), which may indicate circulatory problems. The physician should also check the skin for signs of skin cancer (discussed in detail below) and your joints for signs of inflammatory arthritis and structural damage.

Blood Testing

During your routine physical examination blood should be drawn and sent to a laboratory for testing. This testing provides much valuable information and is very important. The Life Extension Foundation notes that "Too often, people fall victim to a disease that could have been prevented if their blood had been tested once a year."[7] For example, prescription drugs can cause liver and kidney problems, as can alcohol consumption, over-the-counter drugs, excess niacin, and hepatitis C. These liver and kidney problems can smolder for years until a life-threatening medical crisis occurs. However, a simple blood chemistry test can detect an underlying problem in time to take corrective actions. The American Medical Association has noted that the average person older than 60 takes several prescription medications each day to treat or prevent chronic medical conditions. Adverse reactions to prescription drugs constitute a leading cause of death in the United States. The physicians who prescribe drugs are responsible for monitoring their patients to prevent such drug-induced deaths. However, cost-conscious health maintenance organizations and overworked physicians are not always mandating the blood tests that would detect damage in time to prevent disability and death. Thus it is very important for you to be sure that your routine physical include all the blood tests that you should have.

The Life Extension Foundation recommends that a basic battery of tests be included with your annual physical examination. For all men, regardless of age, this battery should include a complete blood count (CBC)/chemistry test, homocysteine, testosterone, estradiol, prostate-specific antigen (PSA), and DHEA. In addition, for men over 40, tests should include fasting insulin, thyroid stimulating hormone (TSH), and free triodothyroxine (T3). The Life Extension Foundation also suggests that if a serious abnormality is detected during routine annual blood testing, the testing should be repeated more frequently to determine the benefits of any therapy that you are using to correct to potentially life-shortening abnormality.

The CBC provides your physician with red blood cell count, white blood cell count, hemoglobin, and hematocrit. Red blood cells (erythrocytes) carry oxygen in the blood. Their color is from hemoglobin. The hematocrit is a measure of the percentage of the blood volume that is made up of red blood cells. These tests are used to detect diseases such as anemia. White blood cells (leucocytes) are produced in the bone marrow and defend the body against infection. White blood cell counts can indicate the strength of the immune system, as well as the presence of infection.

Homocysteine is a test used to screen for patients who may be at risk for heart disease and stroke. Homocysteine is a risk factor for the development of coronary artery disease and thrombosis.

Testosterone is tested to evaluate gonadal and adrenal functioning. Low testosterone levels are associated with loss of libido, erectile dysfunction, fatigue, difficulty concentrating, irritability, and depression. This complex is referred to as andropause in men who are middle-aged and older (see section on andropause below).

Estradiol is tested to assess hypothalamic and pituitary functions. In men, it is used in particular to diagnose gynecomastia (breast enlargement) and other feminization syndromes.

The test for PSAs is used to detect possible prostate cancer (see below). A natural steroid hormone, DHEA, is produced from cholesterol in the adrenal glands, the gonads, adipose tissue, and the brain. Testing for DHEA is used to detect excess adrenal activity, as might be found with adrenal cancer. Low levels of DHEA have been shown to be associated with insulin resistance (see section on diabetes below), and depression. Blood insulin levels are also tested to indicate possible diabetes or pre-diabetic conditions.

The level of TSH and T3 in the blood are tested to detect thyroid disease such as hypothyroidism.

Therefore you should realize that the small amount of discomfort associated with obtaining a blood sample during your physical produces a great deal of important data that is relevant to many diseases that can afflict men over 60.

Urine Testing

The urine sample that you provide at your physical examination is also subjected to a number of tests that detect abnormalities in the urine, including the presence of glucose, protein, bilirubin, red and white blood cells, and bacteria. These may be present in the urine because they are at elevated levels in the blood and the body is attempting to decrease the blood levels by excreting them in the urine. These tests may provide indications of possible diabetes, kidney disease, urinary tract infection, and liver disease.

Cholesterol and Triglycerides

Routine blood tests check for levels of cholesterol and triglycerides. Cholesterol is one of the most important blood components because high cholesterol, specifically low density lipoprotein (LDL) cholesterol, is a direct cause of heart attack, the number one killer of American men. Cholesterol testing will measure both LDL and HDL (high density lipoprotein), as well as triglycerides, and total cholesterol. The American Heart Association has determined that a total cholesterol count above 200 constitutes a risk marker for heart disease. A total cholesterol count above 240 is considered to represent a high risk for heart disease.

Triglycerides are a form of stored energy derived from foods that are not used immediately. Normal triglyceride levels range from 45 to 150. Elevated levels of triglycerides can cause pancreatitis, which is an inflammation of the pancreas.

Diseases for which Men over 60 Have Increased Risk

Men who are 60 or older are at increased risk for a number of diseases. It is very important that we screen for disease processes on a periodic basis. These screenings may take place during regular physical examinations, but in some cases special screening tests should be performed in addition to the examination.

Heart Disease

Heart disease is the primary cause of death among both men and women who are over the age of 60. Among the primary risk factors for heart disease are heredity, smoking, lack of exercise, having high blood pressure, and being overweight.

Hypertension (High Blood Pressure)

High blood pressure damages the arteries that supply tissues and organs with blood, leading to disease in these organs. Hypertension causes hardening of the arterial walls, clot formation, and obstruction of the blood vessels, including the aorta and the arteries supplying blood to the heart, brain, kidneys, and legs. Obstruction of the blood flow in these arteries can cause heart attacks, transient ischemic attacks (mini-strokes) in parts of the brain, and pain in the leg muscles due to poor blood supply. High blood pressure is a risk factor for atrial fibrillation (irregular heart beat) in the upper chambers of the heart. The latter condition is associated with an increase in the risk of strokes.

The left ventricle of the heart, which is responsible for pumping blood to the body, becomes enlarged due to the increased workload associated with the greater resistance to blood flow associated with hypertension. The enlargement of the left ventricle means that the heart requires greater blood supply, but the coronary arteries may fail to provide this supply because they too have been narrowed by hypertension. This condition has been associated with increased likelihood of heart attack and congestive heart failure.

Because high blood pressure weakens the walls of the blood vessels, it increases the risk of developing an aneurysm, which is a sack-like bulging in the wall of an artery. Aneurysms are particularly likely to develop in the aorta and in the arteries supplying the brain with blood. Aneurysms may burst, leading to dangerous bleeding.

Hypertension also damages the kidneys by narrowing the main arteries supplying the kidneys with blood and by damaging the smaller arteries within the kidneys. This damage can lead to the progressive loss of kidney function and eventually to renal failure.

Mild hypertension is defined as 140 to 159 mm Hg systolic and 90 to 99 mm Hg diastolic. Moderate hypertension is defined as 160 to 169 mm Hg and 100 to 109 mm Hg diastolic. Even mild hypertension can lead to serious complications. However, hypertension may have no early warning symptoms, and it may go undetected for some time. Most hypertension is discovered during routine physical examinations.

Hypertension may be treated through the use of drugs, including diuretics, beta blockers, calcium channel blockers, and angiotensin-converting enzyme (ACE) inhibitors. Nutritional changes such as reduction of salt intake and increased physical exercise have also been shown to reduce hypertension. Among the drug therapies that are used to reduce hypertension, diuretics function to reduce blood volume by increasing the excretion of sodium through the kidneys. Beta blockers (e.g., propranolol, nadolol, timolol) decrease blood pressure by reducing cardiac output. Calcium channel blockers inhibit the influx of calcium into arterial smooth muscle cells and cause the dilation of peripheral arteries, leading to a reduction of blood pressure. By decreasing peripheral vascular resistance, ACE inhibitors (e.g., Captopril, Enalapril) lower blood pressure. Each of these categories of drugs may have significant side effects, and care should be taken in prescribing the drugs and monitoring their effects.

Colorectal Cancer

Colorectal cancer refers to cancer that starts in the colon or rectum. In most cases, colon and rectum cancers develop slowly over a period of several years. Most of these cancers begin as a polyp, a growth of tissue that protrudes into the center of the colon or rectum. The type of polyp referred to as an adenoma can become cancerous. Removing such polyps early prevents them from becoming cancer. Over 95 percent of colon and rectal cancers are adenocarcinomas, cancers of the cells that line the inside of the colon and rectum.

According to the American Cancer Society, colorectal cancer is the third most common form of cancer among American men and women. The Society estimates that there will be approximately 112,000 new cases of colon cancer and 41,000 new cases of rectal cancer in 2007, and that together these cases will cause over 52,000 deaths.[8] The death rate from colorectal cancer has been decreasing over the past 15 years, due largely to colorectal cancer screening, which enables physicians to locate and remove polyps before they turn into cancer.

Although the exact cause of colorectal cancer is not known, there are a number of known risk factors. Age is a risk factor. Your chance of having colorectal cancer goes up after you reach the age of 50. More than 90 percent of people diagnosed with colorectal cancer are over the age of 50. Having had colorectal cancer before is a risk factor, as is a history of polyps. A history of bowel disease such as ulcerative colitis and Crohn's disease is a risk factor. With these diseases the colon is inflamed for long periods of time, and ulcers may develop. Individuals who have had colitis or Crohn's disease should begin screening for colorectal cancer at a young age, and they should be screened frequently.

A family history of colorectal cancer increases your risk of colorectal cancer, particularly if the other family member was diagnosed with colorectal cancer before the age of 60. Ethnic background appears to be a risk factor. Jews of Eastern European descent (Ashkenazi Jews) have a higher than average chance of getting colorectal cancer. African Americans are also at higher risk of getting this cancer and dying from it.

A diet that is high in fat, particularly animal fat, appears to increase the risk of colorectal cancer. Lack of exercise, being overweight, and smoking are all risk factors. Smokers are 30 to 40 percent more likely than nonsmokers to die of colorectal cancer. Also, people with diabetes have are 30 to 40 percent more likely than others to get colorectal cancer.

For men with average risk, screening for colorectal cancer should begin at age 50. The tests that are typically performed to screen for polyps in your colon or rectum include:

1. the fecal occult blood test (FOBT);
2. the flexible sigmoidoscopy;
3. the colon X-ray; and
4. the colonoscopy.

The FOBT (stool blood test) chemically checks your stool for blood that may not be visible to the naked eye or even under a microscope. A fecal sample is smeared onto a card and sent to a laboratory to be evaluated for the presence of blood. This test should be performed annually.

The sigmoidoscope is a slender, lighted tube about the thickness of a finger. This is inserted into the lower part of the colon through the rectum. This allows the physician to look inside of the rectum and part of the colon for cancer or polyps. Because the tube is only about two feet long, the physician is only able to see about half of the colon. This test is uncomfortable but not painful.

Before the sigmoidoscopy, you will need to take an enema to clean out the lower colon. This procedure takes about 15 minutes and should be repeated every five years.

The colon X-ray involves the introduction of liquid barium into the colon. This is a chalky substance that appears white in an X-ray. This outlines the inside of your colon, allowing the physician to see anything unusual. In addition, air is pumped into the colon, causing it to expand. This allows good X-ray pictures top be taken. You will need to take a laxative the night before the colon X-ray and have an enema the morning of the exam. A colon X-ray take about 20 minutes to complete; and one should be performed every five years.

A colonoscope is a longer version of the sigmoidoscope that allows the physician to see the entire colon. In addition, the colonoscope enables to physician to remove any polyps that may be found. Tissue removed from the colon by means of the colonoscope can then be sent to a lab for a biopsy. A colonoscopy requires about 30 minutes. It is usually performed under mild sedation. Colonoscopies should be repeated every 10 years.

Prostate Cancer

The prostate is one of the male sex glands. It is located just below the bladder and in front of the rectum. The prostate is normally about the size of a walnut. The prostate surrounds part of the urethra, the tube that carries urine from the bladder to the outside of the body. The prostate makes fluid that becomes part of the semen. In the United States, prostate cancer is the most common cancer and the second leading cause of cancer deaths among men. Statistics indicate that the incidence of prostate cancer is increasing. From 1990 to the present, the number of men diagnosed with prostate cancer has tripled.[9] Eighty percent of prostate cancer cases are diagnosed in men who are 65 or older, and 40,000 men die from prostate cancer each year.[10]

In addition to the digital rectal examination performed during your routine physical examination, physicians can screen for prostate cancer using a blood test, called the prostate-specific antigen (PSA) test. Prostate-specific antigen is a protein secreted by the prostate. In men who have an enlarged or infected prostate or prostate cancer, this protein tends to leak into the circulatory system, causing an elevation in the level of PSA found in the blood. In order to obtain an accurate PSA measurement through a blood test, you need to (1) have your blood drawn before the digital rectal examination; (2) avoid ejaculating on the day before the blood test; and (3) inform your physician if you are taking Proscar to treat BPH. If a blood test comes back positive for elevated levels of PSA in the blood, the test should be repeated after approximately three months. For a man over 60, the PSA level considered elevated sufficiently to warrant a biopsy of the prostate is 4.0 nanograms per milliliter. Before ordering a biopsy, some physicians will request that a transrectal ultrasonography

(TRUS) be performed. This procedure uses sound waves generated by a probe that is inserted into the rectum. These waves bounce off the prostate, and a computer uses the echoes to generate a picture of the prostate called a sonogram. The sonogram indicates areas of uneven firmness in the prostate, and this data informs the decisions whether to perform a biopsy.

If prostate cancer is suspected, one of two forms of biopsies will likely be performed. The fine needle aspiration (FNA) involves the insertion of a fine needle through the rectum or through the space between the scrotum and the anus to withdraw cells from the suspicious area. In the sextant biopsy a needle is used to remove six cores of tissue from various portions of the prostate. Once prostate cancer is diagnosed, other tests are issued to determine if the tumors have spread beyond the prostate. These tests include computerized tomography, lymph node biopsies, and bone scans.

It should be noted that the accuracy of the PSA test is not entirely clear and that some organizations do not recommend this test as part of routine screenings. The American Cancer Society does recommend annual PSA screenings, beginning at age 50 for most, but earlier for African American men and others who have an elevated risk for prostate cancer.[11] The National Cancer Institute does not currently recommend screening for prostate cancer but has the question under study. Dollemore and Raymond pointed out that screening for prostate cancer is somewhat controversial, because the disease typically develops so slowly. They noted that most men who have prostate cancer never experience any symptoms, and only one of every 380 men diagnosed with prostate cancer dies of the disease.[12]

The question of whether to screen is complicated by the fact that some biopsied tumors that appear dangerous under the microscope turn out to be very slow-growing, while others that appear to be slow growing can change quite suddenly to become rapid growing. Furthermore, the treatments for prostate cancer, which include radical prostectomy, radiation therapy, and hormone therapy, may have some rather serious side effects, including urinary dysfunction, bowel dysfunction, erectile dysfunction, and infertility.

These considerations complicate both the decision as to whether to screen for prostate cancer, and the decision regarding how to treat the disease when it has been detected. Gerald Chodak, the director of the Prostate and Urology Center at the University of Chicago Hospitals, has recommended that because prostate cancer is most often very slow to develop, only those men who are reasonably sure that they will live another 10 to 15 years should even bother being screened.[13] However, unless you have another disease that is likely to be terminal or a chronic health condition with a very poor prognosis, you really can't be sure that you won't live another 15 years. Therefore this guideline is useful for only a relatively small number of men who are 60 or older.

Assuming that you do screen for prostate cancer and that prostate cancer is diagnosed, the type of treatment that is most appropriate is typically determined on the basis of a judgment regarding the stage (phase or progression) of the cancer. The staging system generally used is as follows:

1. Stage A: Here the prostate cancer cannot be felt and causes no symptoms. The cancer is located only in the prostate. It is typically discovered accidentally when other prostatic surgery is performed, for example, surgery for BPH.
2. Stage B: At this stage prostate cancer can be felt by the physician during a digital rectal examination. It is also indicated by an elevated PSA level. It is confirmed by a biopsy. The cancer is still located in the prostate only.
3. Stage C: Here the cancer cells have spread outside the prostate to tissues surrounding the prostate.
4. Stage D: Here the cancer cells have spread to lymph nodes or organs and tissues far away from the prostate.[14]

Treatment for prostate cancer depends on the progression of the disease, the aggressiveness of the tumor, and the age of the patient. Stage A cancers that are considered slow growing may call for a conservative approach involving "watchful waiting." This approach is quite likely if the patient is older. In younger patients the physician may recommend surgery or external radiation therapy. Surgery and/or external radiation therapy are typically recommended for stage B and stage C prostate cancers. They may also recommend hormone therapy. Men with stage D prostate cancer are typically treated by hormone therapy first, followed by surgery and/or external radiation. Decisions regarding appropriate treatments for prostate cancers at various stages should be made in consultation with prostate cancer specialists of three types: a urologist, a radiation oncologist, and a medical oncologist.

Osteoporosis

Although women are four times more likely than men to develop osteoporosis, about five million American men do have osteoporosis.[15] Osteoporosis is a disorder in which bones become weakened. Specifically, osteoporosis occurs when an individual experiences bone loss that (1) exceeds the loss associated with normal aging; and (2) is sufficiently severe as to place the individual at significant risk of bone fracture. Osteoporosis is sometimes referred to as the silent disease, because it has no symptoms. It typically manifests itself only when the patient experiences a fracture of the hip, wrist, ankle, spine, or other bone.

Although the exact reason for osteoporosis is unknown, it has been established that calcium deficiency is a factor. Leo Lutwak, a medical officer in the FDA's Center for Drug Evaluation and Research, has noted that "calcium intake over a person's lifetime is crucial to preventing bone loss."[16] He pointed out that a diet adequate in calcium starting in childhood will maximize peak bone mass, helping to insure the development of strong bones and reducing the likelihood of osteoporosis later in life.

Osteoporosis occurs less frequently in men than in women for several reasons. First, men generally have larger skeletons and greater bone mass than women. Also in men, bone loss tends to begin later and proceed more slowly than in women, since men do not experience the rapid bone loss that affects women when their estrogen production drops as a result of menopause. However, men do tend to experience a reduction in testosterone levels as they grow older, and this reduction in testosterone can result in an acceleration of bone loss. The National Osteoporosis Foundation has estimated that men over 60 have a 25 percent chance of sustaining an osteoporotic fracture at some point during the remainder of their lives.[17]

In addition to dietary calcium deficiency over the course of the lifespan and lowered testosterone levels, risk factors for osteoporosis in men over 60 include smoking, lack of exercise (particularly weight-bearing activities), and excessive consumption of alcohol. In addition, hyperthyroidism, intestinal disorders, malignancies, and steroid therapy have been shown to be related to osteoporosis.[18]

Screening for osteoporosis is accomplished through a bone density scan, using dual energy X-ray absorptiometry (DXA). This test requires 5 to 15 minutes. The DXA involves low exposure to radiation (between one-hundredth and one-tenth the amount of radiation of a standard chest X-ray). Furthermore, the DXA test is far superior to a standard X-ray for detecting osteoporosis, because standard X-rays are not sensitive enough to detect mild or even moderate bone loss, whereas the DXA can detect such loss. Moreover, the DXA allows the measurement of bone density at multiple sites, including those areas which are the most common sites for bone fractures (wrist, hip, spine).

The treatment of osteoporosis in men involves identifying and treating any specific causes of bone loss, as well as adhering to a balanced diet that includes an adequate intake of calcium and vitamin D. For younger men, 1000 mg of calcium per day is adequate, but men over 60 should have 1200 to 1500 mg per day. The minimum recommended daily intake of vitamin D is 400–800 IU per day. In addition, exercise or physical therapy may be prescribed. Weight-bearing exercise and resistance training are especially helpful. If a testosterone deficiency is found, testosterone replacement therapy may be advised. Pharmacological treatments that have been recommended for men with osteoporosis include calcitonin, biphosphonates (e.g., alendronate), and human parathyroid hormone. However, the National Osteoporosis Foundation notes that there has not really been sufficient research conducted on men to be certain that these pharmacological treatments are effective.

Skin Cancer

Skin cancer is a disease in which cancer cells are found in the outer layers of your skin. Your skin functions to protect your body against heat, light, infection, and injury. The skin also stores water, fat, and vitamin D. The skin has two main layers and several different types of cells. The top layer of the skin is called the epidermis. The epidermis contains three different types of cells: (1) flat, scaly cells on the surface of the skin called squamous cells; (2) round cells called basal cells; and (3) the cells that give your skin its color, called melanocytes.

Skin cancer begins in cells. Normally, skin cells grow and divide to form new cells. Every day skin cells grow old and die, and new cells take their place. This process is normally orderly, serving to maintain the skin. However, sometimes the process gets out of control, so that new cells form when the skin does not need them, and the old cells do not die when they should. In this case, the extra cells that result can form a mass of tissue called a growth or a tumor. Tumors may be benign or malignant. Benign growths are not cancerous. Benign growths are rarely life threatening. They can usually be removed; and they do not grow back. The cells from benign growths do not invade the tissues around them. Benign growths do not spread to other parts of the body. Malignant growths are cancerous. Malignant growths are generally more serious than benign growths, and they may be life threatening. However, the two most common types of skin cancer together cause only about one out of every thousand deaths due to cancer. Malignant growths can often be removed; but they sometimes grow back. The cells from malignant growths can invade and damage nearby tissues and organs. The cells from some malignant growths can spread to other parts of the body (metastasize).

Skin cancers are named for the type of cells that become cancerous. The two most common forms of skin cancer are basal cell skin cancer and squamous cell skin cancer. Basal cell skin cancer usually occurs on areas of the skin that have been exposed to the sun. It is most common on the face. Basal cell cancer rarely spreads to other parts of the body. Squamous cell skin cancer also occurs on parts of the body that have been exposed to the sun; but it may occur in places that are not exposed to the sun. Squamous cell cancer sometimes spreads to lymph nodes and to organs inside the body.[19]

Melanoma is a disease of the skin in which cancer cells are found in the cells that color the skin, the melanocytes. Melanoma is a more serious type of cancer than basal cell skin cancer or squamous cell skin cancer. Melanoma can metastasize quickly to other parts of the body through the lymph system or through the blood. You should see your doctor immediately if you have any of the following signs of melanoma: change in the size, shape, or color of a mole; oozing or bleeding from a mole; or a mole that feels itchy, hard, lumpy, swollen, or tender to the touch. Melanoma can also appear on the body as a new mole. Men most often get melanoma on the trunk (the area of the body between the shoulders and the hips) or on the head or neck. Women most often get melanoma on the arms and legs.[20]

The American Cancer Society estimated that there would be over 60,000 new cases of melanoma in the United States in 2006.[21] In some parts of the world, especially among Western countries, melanoma is becoming more common every year. In the United States, the number of people who develop melanoma has more than doubled in the past 30 years.[22] This has been attributed to the increase in ultraviolet (UV) light associated with the reduction of ozone in the earth's atmosphere over the last 50 years.

Sunburn and UV light can damage the skin, and this damage has been linked to skin cancer. Blistering sunburns in early childhood increase the risk of developing melanoma, but cumulative exposure to sunlight is also a factor. People who live in locations that receive a great deal of sunlight, like Florida, Hawaii, and Australia, get more skin cancer. In addition to the risk posed by exposure to UV radiation, there appears to be a heritability factor in skin cancer. If there is a history of skin cancer in your family, you will have an increased risk of contracting skin cancer. Also, people with fair skin such as those of Northern European heritage appear to be most susceptible. Age is also a risk factor for skin cancer. As we grow older, the amount of skin pigment declines. This increases the penetration of sunlight and UV-related damage.

The American Academy of Dermatology and the Skin Cancer Foundation recommend the following steps to reduce the risk of skin cancer:

1. Minimize your exposure to the sun between the hours of 10:00 AM and 3:00 PM;
2. Apply sunscreen with at least SPF-15 or higher to all areas of the body which are exposed to sun;
3. Reapply sunscreen every two hours, even on cloudy days. Reapply after swimming or perspiring;
4. Wear clothing that covers your body and shades your face (hats should provide shade for both the face and the back of the neck); and
5. Avoid exposure to UV radiation from sunlamps and tanning parlors.[23]

In addition to the skin examination that is part of your annual physical examination, I recommend frequent self examination to detect changes in the skin. Many men who are approaching 60 see a dermatologist who can perform a thorough skin examination, recording the presence of moles, and other skin pigmentations to provide a baseline against which future examinations may be compared.

If a suspicious growth is detected, a biopsy will be performed. There are several different types of biopsies. In a punch biopsy the physician will use a sharp, hollow tool to remove a circle of tissue from the abnormal area. In some instances the growth will be completely excised. In either case, the tissue will be examined microscopically by a pathologist to determine if the tissue is malignant. If skin cancer is detected, the most common form of treatment is surgery. Skin cancer may also be treated by topical chemotherapy, photodynamic therapy, or radiation therapy. Obviously the choice of treatment(s) is made in consultation with a skin cancer specialist based on the specific nature of the cancer.[24]

Regardless of the treatment(s) employed, follow-up care is very important in cases of skin cancer. Individuals who have had a skin cancer are more likely to develop a new skin cancer than those who have never had a skin cancer. If you have had skin cancer, you should see a dermatologist regularly to check for possible new skin cancer. In addition, if you have had skin cancer you should be particularly careful with exposure to the sun, and you should check your skin regularly and carefully to detect any skin changes.

Carotid Artery Stenosis

The carotid arteries are the two large arteries on either side of the neck. Stenosis is a narrowing or blockage of a passageway. Carotid artery stenosis occurs when the carotid arteries become narrow or blocked by carotid artery disease. The most common form of blockage in these arteries is atherosclerosis, generally referred to as hardening of the arteries. Hardening of the arteries occurs when fatty materials collect under the lining of the arterial wall.[25] As the amount of fatty material increases, it forms a thickened area, called plaque, in the artery's inner lining. This plaque can rupture and cause blood clots, which can break away and travel to the brain, causing a stroke. A stroke occurs when the lack of blood flow and oxygen to the brain results in a sudden loss of brain function.

Cerebrovascular disease is the third leading cause of death in the United States, accounting for approximately 150,000 deaths each year.[26] Most stroke-related morbidity and mortality occur in older adults: 87 percent of all deaths and 74 percent of all hospitalizations occur in persons aged 65 years or older.[27] The risk of developing carotid artery stenosis increases with advanced age. Other risk factors are high blood pressure, high levels of cholesterol, high levels of stress, diabetes mellitus, diabetes, cigarette smoking, obesity, and lack of exercise.[28]

Most people with carotid artery stenosis have no symptoms. Some patients do notice a "swishing" sound in either ear with each heartbeat. This is the sound of blood flows past a partial blockage in one of the carotid arteries. If you experience feelings of numbness, partial paralysis, or transient blindness, there is a great risk of a major stroke, and you should see your physician immediately. Symptoms of stroke include paralysis of an arm or leg, speech

and vision problems, and personality changes. These symptoms can be permanent. Cartotid artery stenosis can also cause transient ischemic attacks (TIAs),
also referred to as *mini-strokes*. When a TIA occurs, a small piece of the fatty
material in the arteries breaks away and lodges in the smaller blood vessels
supplying the brain. This temporarily blocks the blood supply to a part of
brain, which may result in numbness or tingling of the skin, weakness of an
arm or a leg, or blindness in one eye. The duration of TIAs generally range
from 2 to 30 minutes. The symptoms are generally temporary and reversible;
however, if you experience one or more TIAs, you are more likely to have a
stroke.

Carotid artery stenosis may be diagnosed during your routine physical examination through neck auscultation. This is listening with a stethoscope to
the sound of blood flowing through the arteries in the neck. A trained physician
can hear the sound of blood flowing past a blockage in the carotid artery.
However, neck auscultation is an imperfect screening test for carotid artery. Favrat, Pecoud, and Jaussi have observed that among physicians "the general
proficiency in physical diagnostic skills seems to be declining in relation to
the development of new technologies."[29] Chambers and Norris observed that
"there is considerable interobserver variation among clinicians in the inter-
pretation of key auditory characteristics—intensity, pitch, and duration—of
importance in predicting stenosis."[30] Arteries that produce sound that are
noticeable to the physician (bruits) often have no significant compromise in
blood flow, and arteries with no audible bruits may nevertheless have significant stenotic lesions.[31]

Due to the uncertainties associated with the results of the neck auscultations
that are performed in the course of regular physical examinations, individuals
with high risk for carotid artery stenosis should consider having additional
screening for the condition. There are several different tests that may be used
to discover narrowing in the carotid arteries, including Doppler ultrasound,
magnetic resonance imaging (MRI), and cerebral angiogram.[32] The Doppler
ultrasound uses sound waves reflected from the structures in the neck to show
if the artery is narrowed. This test is noninvasive, uses no radiation, and is a
reliable test to assess blockages. Magnetic and radio waves are used in MRIs
to generate images of the arteries and the brain. The MRI can detect even
small strokes in the brain. A related magnetic resonance angiography (MRA)
technique developed at the Mayo Clinic allows detailed pictures of the carotid
arteries to be obtained. This technique is also noninvasive and has no related
risk. Techniques of MRI have largely eliminated the need to perform invasive
cerebral angiograms.

Should significant carotid artery stenosis be detected, various surgical options may be recommended, including carotid endarterectomy or a less invasive procedure, carotid angioplasty and stenting.

Diabetes

Diabetes is a disorder of the metabolism. Most of the food we eat is broken down into glucose, the form of sugar in the blood. Glucose is the body's primary source of energy. In order for glucose to get into the cells, insulin must be present. Insulin is a hormone produced by the pancreas, a large gland located just behind the stomach. When we eat, the pancreas automatically produces the right amount of insulin to move glucose from the blood into our cells. In people with diabetes, the insulin produces either too little insulin or none at all, or the cells do not respond properly to the insulin that is produced. Then glucose builds up in the blood until it passes out of the body in urine. Thus the body loses its primary source of fuel, even though there is adequate glucose in the blood.[33]

There are two main types of diabetes that affect men. Type 1 diabetes is an autoimmune disease. In type 1 diabetes the body's immune system attacks and destroys the insulin-producing beta cells in the pancreas. Type 1 diabetes develops most often in children and young adults, but it can develop at any age. Symptoms of type 1 diabetes are increased thirst and urination, constant hunger, weight loss, blurred vision, and fatigue. A person with type 1 diabetes must take insulin daily in order to live. If type 1 diabetes is not diagnosed and treated with insulin, the patient can lapse into a life-threatening diabetic coma.

Type 2 diabetes is the most common form of diabetes. This form of diabetes is associated with older age, and with obesity, family history of diabetes, and physical inactivity. Type 2 diabetes is more prevalent among African Americans, American Indians, Native Hawaiians and other Pacific Islanders, and Hispanics than it is among Caucasians. Non-Hispanic African-Americans are 1.8 times as likely to have diabetes as non-Hispanic whites of the same age.

The prevalence of Type 2 diabetes in the United States is increasing. There are several reasons for this. A large segment of the U.S. population is aging. Hispanics/Latinos and other minority groups who are at increased risk of type 2 diabetes comprise the fastest growing segment of the U.S. population. In addition, Americans are becoming increasingly sedentary and increasingly overweight. The Centers for Disease Control and Prevention (CDC) has estimated that diabetes will affect one person in three born in 2000 in the United States. The CDC has projected that the prevalence of diabetes will increase by 165 percent by the year 2050.

In addition to type 1 and type 2 diabetes, you can be prediabetic. Pre-diabetes is characterized by blood glucose levels that are higher than normal but not high enough to be characterized as diabetes. Many people with pre-diabetes develop type 2 diabetes within 10 years. Pre-diabetes also increases the risk of heart disease and stroke. With modest weight loss and moderate physical activity, people with pre-diabetes can delay or prevent the onset of type 2 diabetes.

Diabetes is diagnosed by means of a fasting plasma glucose test or an oral glucose tolerance test. A fasting plasma glucose (FPG) test measures blood glucose after you have gone at least eight hours without eating. An oral glucose tolerance test (OGTT) measures your blood glucose after you have gone at least eight hours without eating and two hours after you drink a beverage containing glucose. Either of these tests can be used to detect either diabetes or pre-diabetes.

The FPG is the preferred test for diagnosing diabetes due to its convenience. It is most reliable when performed in the morning. A fasting glucose level of 99 mg/dl or less is considered normal. A level between 100 and 125 mg/dl is indicative of pre-diabetes. A level of 126 mg/dl indicates diabetes. The OGTT is more sensitive but less convenient than the FPG for diagnosing pre-diabetes. The OGTT requires that you fast for eight hours before the test. Your plasma glucose level is measured immediately before and two hours after you drink a liquid containing 75 grams of glucose dissolved in water. A blood glucose level under 139 mg/dl two hours after drinking the liquid is considered normal. A blood glucose level between 140 and 199 mg/dl after two hours indicates a pre-diabetic condition referred to as impaired glucose tolerance. A blood glucose level of 200 mg/dl or higher after two hours indicates diabetes.[34]

The National Diabetes Information Clearing House lists the following as risk factors for diabetes among men:

1. being 45 years old or older;
2. being overweight or obese, as indicated by a body mass index of 25 or greater. (This is a stringent cut-off. A man who is 5'10" tall weighing more than 174 pounds would be considered overweight);
3. having a parent, brother, or sister with diabetes;
4. having a family background that is African-American, American Indian, Asian American, Pacific Islander, or Hispanic American/Latino;
5. having high blood pressure (140/90 or higher);
6. having risky cholesterol levels, that is, HDL (good) cholesterol is 35 or lower, and/or triglycerides level is 250 or higher;
7. being inactive (specifically, exercising fewer than three times per week).

Anyone over 45 years old should get tested for diabetes, particularly if your BMI indicates that you are overweight. You should ask your doctor for an FPG or an OGTT. The Diabetes Prevention Program research study demonstrated conclusively that people who follow a low-fat, low-calorie diet, lose a moderate amount of weight, and engage in regular physical activity (e.g., walking briskly for 30 minutes, five times a week) sharply reduce their chances of developing diabetes. These strategies work well for both men and women, and they are particularly effective among participants who are 60 years old or older.

If you are diagnosed with type 2 diabetes, you can manage the condition with sensible meal planning, physical activity, and, if necessary, medications.

Syndrome X (Metabolic Syndrome)

The term *Syndrome X* has recently been used to refer to a cluster of conditions that predispose an individual to diabetes and heart disease.[35] These symptoms include high blood pressure, high levels of blood triglycerides, decreased levels of HDL cholesterol, and obesity. Other symptoms include fatigue, depression, sleep apnea, and heart palpitations.[36] Syndrome X is also linked to insulin resistance. Ten to 20 percent of the population are resistant to insulin. Individuals who have been diagnosed with insulin resistance need to lose 10 to 15 percent of their body weight. They should exercise vigorously for 30 minutes at least 5 times per week. They can help to reduce triglycerides by following diets that are low in alcohol and refined carbohydrates.

Andropause

Between the ages of 40 and 55, men can experience a drop in testosterone levels that occurs gradually and is accompanied by changes in attitudes and moods, fatigue, loss of energy, reduction of sex drive, and decreased physical agility.[37] In addition, low testosterone is also associated with increased risk of heart disease and osteoporosis. It has been estimated that 30 percent of all men in their 50s will have testosterone levels that are low enough to cause symptoms or put them at risk.

Testosterone functions to build protein, and it is essential for normal sexual behavior and producing erections. The hormone also affects many metabolic activities, including the production of blood cells in the bone marrow, bone formation, lipid metabolism, carbohydrate metabolism, liver function, and prostate gland growth.

Low testosterone levels are detected through blood tests, and they may be treated through hormone replacement therapy. Hormone replacement may be accomplished through oral capsules, injections, and skin patches. Testosterone replacement therapy is contraindicated for men who have a prostate tumor and for men who have been diagnosed with breast cancer.

Chapter Four

COGNITIVE FITNESS

THE HEREAFTER PHENOMENON

The "hereafter phenomenon" occurs when you walk into a room and then you can't remember what you walked into the room for. Roger Seip said that this is "walking into the hereafter," because you walk in and you think, "Now what was it that I was here after?"[1] Come on now. Admit it. You have certainly had this experience. We have all had this experience. But does it seem to you that these hereafter events are happening more often now than they used to? Most of us would answer this last question in the affirmative. In fact, most of us assume that as we grow older we will inevitably experience failing memories and decreases in our mental sharpness. For many of us, this belief is a source of considerable dread.

EXAGGERATED FEAR OF COGNITIVE DECLINE ASSOCIATED WITH AGING

In fact, moments of forgetfulness like those described above actually occur throughout our entire lives. However, we become more aware of such moments as we grow older, simply because we fear the loss of mental sharpness and memory that we assume will occur inevitably as a result of aging. Some blame physicians for this mindset. They argue that our doctors tell us to be aware of short-term memory loss because if it starts happening more frequently, it may be a sign of Alzheimer's disease. Such warnings may make us hyper-aware of every hereafter moment. The fearful mindset regarding the possible onset of

Alzheimer's disease makes us notice these moments even more every time they occur. However, the fact is that we do not have hereafter moments any more often at 50 or 60 than we did at 17 or 27. We simply notice them more.

The Fear of Alzheimer's Disease

Most experts on aging agree that fear makes us greatly exaggerate the major cognitive declines associated with aging. For example, Rowe and Kahn observed that, "The greatest dread for many older people is Alzheimer's disease, the debilitating form of dementia which receives tremendous publicity these days."[2] They observed that misplacing one's eyeglasses or struggling to find the right word "might just irritate a younger person. But for the elderly such errors bring to mind the looming threat of Alzheimer's disease or other permanent mental disability."[3] Rowe and Kahn argued that older people worry far too much about losing their mental ability. They pointed out that really serious disruptions in mental (or physical) function will typically lead to living in a nursing home where one can receive professional care. However, only five percent of the population over the age of 65 actually live in nursing homes, and this proportion has been falling rather than rising. Thus the overwhelming majority of older individuals do not experience declines in cognitive function that are serious enough to require such care.

Fears of Alzheimer's disease and other forms of cognitive loss are understandable, because Alzheimer's really is a devastating condition for both the patients and for those who care for them. Alzheimer's disease is caused by brain cell loss or impairment.[4] The most significant symptom of Alzheimer's disease is memory loss. The disease progresses from occasional absentmindedness to a point where the patient loses memory for important facts, names, and even the learned routines associated with daily living. In advanced Alzheimer's, patients may forget the names of their spouse and children. They may not even recognize loved ones. They may forget their own name. They may forget how to put on their clothes, brush their teeth, and prepare meals. Patients may forget social conventions, with the result that they commit social indiscretions.

In addition to these symptoms of memory loss, Alzheimer's patients may exhibit mood swings and physical symptoms including a shuffling gait and a sagging posture. They may experience visual or auditory hallucinations and disorientation. They may wander about aimlessly, and they may become unable to communicate. As the disease progresses, Alzheimer's patients become increasingly difficult to understand, relate to, and care for. Ultimately the disease is fatal. Advanced Alzheimer's patients typically fall into a coma resulting from secondary infections such as pneumonia.

During the early stages of Alzheimer's disease, patients often remain sufficiently intact that they recognize the deterioration in their cognitive functioning.

At this point, many patients become depressed.[5] Sometimes patients who recognize their deteriorating condition make great efforts to conceal their problem. If they lose their way coming home, they may make excuses to conceal the fact they were lost.

Family members may reinforce this denial, preferring to view the problem as a simple manifestation of growing older, rather than the disease that it is.[6] Eventually the symptoms will worsen to the point that the condition is undeniable. However, the insidious aspect of the disease is that patients may live for up to 20 years after they have been diagnosed, placing an incredible strain on those who provide care.[7]

Although Alzheimer's disease is a devastating condition, most experts agree that we worry about it more than we need to. It has been estimated that only 4 to 6 percent of the population over the age of 65 is affected by the disease.[8] About 20 percent of those over the age of 85 show signs of Alzheimer's disease.[9] Thus, *the chance that you will be affected by Alzheimer's disease is small, and the chance that you will have to live with the condition for a considerable period of time is very small indeed.*

Rowe and Khan summarized the probabilities of experiencing serious decreases in cognitive functioning as we grow older as follows: "Even though the proportion of older people in the population has been increasing, and despite the fact that the relative increases have been greatest among the 'oldest-old,' the usual pattern is that older people maintain a good portion of their independence and mental sharpness."[10]

NORMAL AGING AND FUNCTION

On the other hand, we must acknowledge that some changes in cognitive functioning do tend to occur normally as we grow older. We tend to process information a bit more slowly than when we are younger, and we tend to experience small decreases in specific types of memory.

Average Declines Are Small

Research indicates that after the age of 50 we tend to humans become *a bit* slower in processing new information, and they have *a bit* more difficulty remembering names.[11] These decreases in mental functioning are very small in relation to the overall cognitive functioning. For this reason, most individuals who do experience some slowing down of information processing speed or some loss in explicit memory have little difficulty in compensating for these changes through the use of adaptations such as reminder notes. Furthermore, the forms of memory that typically do not decline with age are functionally much more important than speed of information processing and explicit memory. In particular, working memory, which contains the learned routines that we perform each day, shows little or no reduction with age.

Not Everyone Experiences Even These Small Cognitive Declines

Furthermore, even these limited changes *do not affect everyone.* There is a great deal of variability among older individuals in terms of the decreases in mental functioning that we experience; and there is a great deal that one can do to prevent or minimize any such decrements. In the next section of this chapter, I consider the things that men over 60 can do to maximize their cognitive functioning beyond the age of 60.

HOW TO PREVENT COGNITIVE DECLINES

There are many steps that we can take to minimize the impact of aging on our cognitive functioning. These steps involve three different areas: (1) insuring that one's physical condition supports optimum mental functioning; (2) remaining actively involved in life and participating in rewarding and challenging mental activities each day; and (3) maintaining an optimistic outlook and a sense of self-confidence.

Step One: Keep Your Brain in Good Physical Condition

There are a number of specific steps that we can take to insure that our physical condition supports cognitive functioning as we grow older. These include: (1) avoiding the use of substances known to damage the brain; (2) making sure that we have adequate nutrition, including the vitamins that are necessary to promote cognitive fitness; (3) avoiding unnecessary stress; and (4) making sure that we have sufficient cardiovascular fitness to insure that the brain is adequately supplied with oxygen and necessary nutrients.

Avoid Substances That Can Damage Your Brain

There is no question that significant use of alcohol, tobacco, and other powerful drugs will harm the brain over time. However, there is some question regarding the definition of *significant,* particularly with respect to the use of alcohol. Although most experts and the great majority of the public acknowledge that any use of tobacco or illegal drugs is harmful, this is not the case with alcohol. With respect to alcohol, some experts do believe that any use of alcohol will eventually prove harmful to one's cognitive functioning, but others distinguish between acceptable amounts of alcohol use and excessive heavy use.

On the conservative end of the spectrum, the Fitness Habit Web site presents readers with the following "bottom line message": "Don't use alcohol, tobacco, and other powerful illicit drugs—over time they harm the brain."[12]

This message indicates that *alcohol is bad for your brain, period.* It suggests that any use of alcohol, or tobacco, or an illegal street drug, should be avoided.

The Case for Avoiding Alcohol

A careful examination of how alcohol impacts the brain and the nervous system tends to support the view that even moderate alcohol consumption is bad for you. Alcohol is a depressant.[13] The presence of alcohol in the blood stream decreases the activity of the nervous system. It does this by inhibiting the action of a specific set of neurotransmitter receptors in the brain cells. According to the Alcohol Abuse Prevention Program at Virginia Tech University, the consumption of even small amounts of alcohol "affects many parts of the brain, but the most vulnerable cells are those associated with memory, attention, sleep, coordination, and judgment."[14] Alcohol impairs memory by inhibiting the transfer and consolidation of information in long-term memory. Even in small doses, alcohol interferes with REM sleep. When REM sleep is disturbed, we feel tired when we get up. Even in small doses, the consumption of alcohol may interfere with judgment, with the result that we may engage in behaviors that may have negative long-term consequences.

The Case for Moderate Use of Alcohol

Of course, many adults do use alcohol occasionally or regularly, and many who do use alcohol seem to be able to enjoy it without experiencing any obvious problems. Therefore, not many authorities are as unambiguous as those representing the Fitness Habit Web site in recommending that we avoid the use of alcohol entirely. Instead, most authorities stick to a message that is more acceptable to the drinking public and to themselves personally, that is, the message that one should not drink alcohol to excess.

How Much Is Too Much?

Of course, this position immediately raises the question of how to define *to excess.* Unfortunately, there is no consensus on this definition. In fact, when the question of the effects of alcohol consumption on the brain are discussed, the question of how much one can drink without experiencing any harmful effects is often avoided altogether by transitioning quickly to the manifestly negative effects of *really* heavy drinking.

For example, in 2004 the U.S. Department of Health and Human Services published an article in the publication *Alcohol Alert* entitled, "Alcohol's Damaging Effects on the Brain." The first paragraph of this article read as follows:

> Difficulty walking, blurred vision, slurred speech, slowed reaction times, impaired memory: Clearly, alcohol affects the brain. Some of these impairments are detectable after only one or two drinks and quickly resolve when drinking stops. On the other hand, a person who drinks heavily over a long period of time may have brain deficits that persist well after he or she achieves sobriety. Exactly how alcohol affects

the brain and the likelihood of reversing the impact of heavy drinking on the brain remain hot topics in alcohol research today.[15]

This paragraph begins with a description of some rather severe neurological symptoms that are detectable after only one or two drinks. We would probably consider these symptoms to be quite alarming if they occurred when we were not consuming alcohol. The paragraph acknowledges that the symptoms indicate clearly that the consumption of even small amounts of alcohol has significant negative effects on the brain, *but* then the paragraph immediately goes on to say that these impairments quickly resolve when drinking stops. The paragraph does not say whether any underlying long-term brain damage may result from the consumption of small amounts of alcohol. Instead, it jumps to a description of what happens when a person drinks *heavily* over a *long period of time.*

But the article does not define "drinks heavily" or "a long period of time." Instead, the article leaves it up to the reader to judge whether his personal alcohol consumption is too heavy, and whether it has been occurring for a long period of time. I guess in this way the author avoided challenging or offending anyone, either members of the general public or colleagues involved in health-related fields. The paragraph ends with an incontrovertible statement, that is, that exactly how alcohol affects the brain and the likelihood of reversing the impact of heavy drinking on the brain are hot topics in alcohol research.

Nevertheless, in the midst of this complex array of confusing motivational sets and the effects of diverse confounding variables, several publications have actually made specific recommendations regarding the levels of alcohol consumption that may be considered safe. For example, a 1995 publication of the National Institute on Alcohol Abuse and Alcoholism entitled, *A Physician's Guide to Helping Patients with Alcohol Problems,* stated that a male patient may be at risk for alcohol-related problems if alcohol consumption is greater than 14 drinks per week, or greater than four drinks on any one occasion.[16] This *Guide* also provided patients with a series of recommendations for "low risk drinking." Men under the age of 65 were instructed to have no more than two drinks per day.

The Bottom Line on Drinking

I don't know whether you drink or, if you do drink, how much. Given the ambiguity that exists within the literature, I cannot state with certainty that you would be better off if you did not drink alcohol, although I suspect that this may be the case. It does seem clear, however, that if you do drink alcohol, you should really drink *very* little. If you are over 60, you should probably not have more than one drink on any given day. I typically have a glass of wine with dinner, and my cardiologist tells me that this is good for me. I will also enjoy a martini or a scotch or two when out with friends, but I am careful not to overindulge.

In addition, you should not smoke or use tobacco in any other way, and you should stay away from illegal drugs of any kind.

Feed Your Brain Well

In the last chapter I indicated the importance of nutrition in general and specific vitamins for our physical health as we grow older. But nutrition and vitamins are important for maintaining cognitive fitness as well. Research indicates that men over 60 should reduce total fat intake, use plant oils, eat less red meat, and eat more fish, poultry, fruits and vegetables.[17]

Vitamins. Recent research has identified a number of specific vitamins that are important in maintaining cognitive performance as we grow older, including vitamins C, E, B12, B6, and folate.[18] Diamond wrote that vitamin "B6 is vital for the creation of neurotransmitters...A vitamin B6 deficiency can cause memory impairment which diminishes the ability to register, retain and retrieve things from the memory bank."[19] The previous chapter of this book contains recommendations regarding the use of supplements to insure the adequacy of vitamin B6 and these other vitamins in our diets.

Herbal Supplements. In addition to these specific vitamins, a number of herbal products and supplements have been recommended as helpful in maintaining cognitive function as we grow older. Weil mentioned three such products as "promising," while cautioning that the evidence for their efficacy is still somewhat scant.[20] These products are ginkgo biloba, ALC, and PS. Ginkgo is an extract of the leaves of the leaves of the ginkgo biloba tree. This herbal extract increases the flow of blood to the head, and it has been shown to slow the progression of dementia and early-onset Alzheimer's disease. Weil noted that ginkgo is widely believed to enhance short-term memory and that some students even take it before examinations. However, he believes that in reality ginkgo is helpful only for individuals who have impaired or inadequate circulation to the brain. In addition, he pointed out that the effects of ginkgo appear only after six to eight weeks of continuous ingestion. Thus, the efficacy of the supplement as an aid to short-term memory immediately before an examination are questionable. On the other hand, ginkgo has low toxicity and is readily available in health food stores. It won't harm you, and it may help you keep your mental sharpness.

The Bottom Line on Nutrition of the Brain

However, Weil did not say that he was using any of these supplements. Rather, he said that he would not rely on supplements to preserve your memory or other aspects of mental function as you grow older. I would suggest that a healthy diet with reasonable vitamin supplements are more important, and certainly more cost effective. Weil also stressed the importance of lifestyle, including both physical and mental exercise. To these I would add the importance of avoiding excessive stress, a topic to which I now turn.

Avoid Unnecessary Stress

Excessive emotional stress has numerous adverse consequences for health for men and women of all ages, but stress is particularly problematic with respect to cognitive functioning as we grow older. Excessive stress can contribute to high blood pressure, which in turn can lead to the rupture of blood vessels in the brain. These ruptures can result in damage to brain cells and loss of function. Some strokes are very severe, with obvious severe neurological symptoms. However, it is also possible to have smaller strokes that are not immediately detected. These may occur over time, resulting in almost imperceptible decrements in cognitive functioning.

For these reasons, it is helpful for all of us to minimize the amount of stress that we confront in our lives, and it is helpful for us to learn to deal with the stresses that we do encounter. We can minimize stress by avoiding high risk situations. Some individuals cope with stressful situations better than others, and some people appear to thrive on stressful situations. However, every individual has his limits. If you find yourself worrying excessively about the possible outcomes of a business deal or a chosen activity, it is possible that you may have placed yourself in an overly stressful situation, and you may want to rethink your decisions. Regardless of the levels of stress that we may face on a daily basis, we can all benefit from stress reducing techniques, such as yoga, meditation, physical exercise, and relaxation training.

Maintain Your Cardiovascular Fitness

Cardiovascular fitness is important to insure adequate blood supply to the brain. I discussed the benefits of exercise in the previous chapter. The point I would like to make here is that when you exercise you are not only making an investment in your physical health but in your cognitive health as well. The more fit you are, the less the chance that you will suffer from high blood pressure, and the less the chance that you will succumb to dementia resulting from the cumulative effects of small strokes.

Step 2: Remain Active and Exercise Your Mind

The experts all agree that our minds need exercise just as our bodies need exercise. This exercise can come in the form of work, as well as in the form of social and leisure activities. Rowe and Kahn suggested that for most adults, the job is probably the single most important source of both cognitive demands and mental stimulation. They argued that "People whose jobs promote self-direction, use of initiative, and independent judgment tend to boost their intellectual flexibility—that is their ability to use a variety of approaches in order to solve mental problems. On the other hand, workers in routine and monotonous jobs working under close direction from a foreman or supervisor tend to lose intellectual flexibility."[21]

The quest for continuing mental challenge may take many different forms. Some individuals are fortunate enough to have careers that afford them the opportunity to continue to grow and learn. Other individuals retire from one occupation, but take steps to remain engaged in life and active. They may to return to school or take up a new vocation or avocation that is challenging and rewarding. The decision regarding whether to retire is not the crucial element of this challenge. Continuing to work at a boring and repetitive job may be no better than retiring to a boring and repetitive daily routine. Retiring from work to engage in challenging activities that are not income producing is likely to do more to maintain our cognitive capabilities. Changing from one career to another may be the most rewarding path of all, particularly if the new career involves the development and utilization or previously underdeveloped areas of talent.

Active engagement in life is also promoted by maintaining an active social life. Maintaining close ties with friends and family members is not only intrinsically rewarding and stress reducing but also tends to encourage us to broaden the scope of our normal activities. I like fishing, but my friends encourage me to go to the theater. This is something that I might not do on my own. But it turns out that I really enjoy it. It stimulates my thinking, and it encourages me to engage in interesting discussions with my friends.

Beyond structuring our lives so that we are challenged to remain intellectually active, it is possible to engage in specific activities that exercise the brain. Weil recommends card games and word puzzles to individuals who seek to maintain their cognitive functioning.[22] I am learning to play bridge, and I am taking cello lessons. There is simply no need to allow our minds to become lazy. The key is to provide ourselves with a continuous diet of new mental challenges.

Step 3: Remain Optimistic and Self-Confident

The third major way in which we can promote high levels of cognitive functioning as we grow older is to remain optimistic and self-confident in our ability to meet life's demands. Self-confidence builds on success. When we have success meeting specific challenges, we come to believe that we are capable of handling new challenges. This leads us to take on new responsibilities and try out new activities, which provide us with additional opportunities for success. It is important to remember the admonition, "nothing ventured, nothing gained." You may need to convince yourself to take a slight risk, if you are to pick up a new skill or engage in a new activity. When contemplating a new challenge, it is extremely helpful if you can structure the situation to maximize the amount of support and encouragement that you can expect to receive in your efforts. This is another good reason for developing and maintaining close social ties. Often the friends who suggest that you try a new challenge will do the most to encourage your efforts and reward your progress.

Chapter Five

PSYCHOLOGICAL ADJUSTMENT AFTER 60: DEPRESSION, ANXIETY, AND LIFE SATISFACTION

THE RISKS OF DEPRESSION, ANXIETY, AND DIMINISHED LIFE SATISFACTION FOR MEN OVER 60

Depression, anxiety, and a diminished sense of subjective well-being are all potential problems for men passing into the sixties. In the United States, depressive illnesses affect more than seven percent of all men each year, or more than six million men.[1] Depression is particularly problematic among older men. It has been estimated that as many as 15 percent of men over 60 may be clinically depressed at any point in time.[2] Men must cope with several different kinds of stress as they age. If we have been the primary wage earners and we have identified heavily with our jobs, retirement or even cutting back on work can generate stress associated with the loss of important roles. We may experience decreased self-esteem as we see our contributions becoming less relevant, and lowered self-esteem can lead to depression. In addition, the loss of co-workers and professional colleagues that accompanies retirement can be a blow. We may also begin to experience more health-related problems than we did when we were younger, and this can be a source of stress. And of course, when friends and family members begin to die, these losses can be very difficult.

Although it is commonly believed that anxiety is less common than depression among older men, research studies suggest that the opposite is true.[3] The rate of detection of generalized anxiety disorders among older men in clinical settings is low, because most older adults with anxiety are seen in primary care settings rather than specialized mental health settings. Another misconception regarding anxiety disorders in men over 60 is the belief that most anxiety among older men mostly occurs along with depression. In fact, the prevalence of mixed depression and anxiety is lower than the prevalence of either depression or anxiety alone.[4]

Also incorrect is the belief that the onset of generalized anxiety disorder late in life is relatively rare.[5] In fact, more than one-third of older men who are diagnosed with generalized anxiety disorder report that they only became depressed later in life. Anxiety appears to arise when we become more concerned with the state of our health. In addition, some men report that they have become depressed because they have begun to anticipate the situation where they may have to assume a caregiving role for their spouse.[6]

Although anxiety may affect both men and women as they grow older, research indicates that the presence of a generalized anxiety disorder in men may have more serious health consequences than in women. Among men, there is a significant relationship between diagnosed anxiety disorder and mortality. To put it bluntly, anxiety can kill us. No such relationship has been identified for women.[7]

Life satisfaction is particularly at risk as we grow older. The concept of successful aging has been traditionally defined in terms of the goal of maintaining a sense of well-being and continuing to derive satisfaction from our lives as we grow older, given that the process of aging is "a situation implying many biological, social, and psychological crises and risks."[8] The man who can cope successfully with the many age-related stresses noted above is the man who will maintain a positive outlook. He will have the best chance of avoiding depression and anxiety, and he will continue to derive satisfaction from life. In this chapter, I will first describe some of the many threats to life satisfaction that men face as they grow older. These include biological stresses, such as declining hearing and eyesight, as well as sociological stresses, such as the loss of important work, family, and community roles. Chapters 6 and 7 focus specifically on two very important areas in which age-related changes can adversely affect our sense of well-being. These are the areas of social connections after 60 and sexual relations after 60. After considering all of these potential sources of stress for men over 60, I will move on in chapter 8 to focus on some of the strategies that we can use to minimize the impact of these threats to our well-being.

BIOLOGICAL STRESSES AFTER 60

In a youth oriented culture, aging itself tends to be stressful. Gray hair, wrinkles, and a few extra pounds can be viewed as unattractive characteristics that render us undesirable. Increasingly frequent physical complaints are stressful not only because they remind us of our mortality but because they require us to interact more frequently with the health care system, which can be time consuming, frustrating, and expensive. Decreases in libido and changes in the sexual response may be experienced as frustrating.

In addition to acute or chronic conditions that require urgent medical attention, aging also brings with it a number of biological changes which are more subtle. We considered age-related changes in cognitive functioning in the last chapter. In addition, these changes affect vision, hearing, reflexes, and the speed with which we can respond to stimuli.

Vision

Although many individuals maintain normal or nearly normal sight well into old age, many others will experience age-related visual impairment. Statistics indicate that approximately 40 percent of men who are 60 have 20/20 vision. This proportion declines to about 25 percent among men who are 70, and to about 10 percent of men who are 80.[9] Both degenerative changes and disease processes can contribute to visual impairment.

Presbyopia

As we age, most of us become far-sighted. We tend to experience presbyopia, which is a degenerative change in which the lens of the eye loses its ability to focus on near objects. This change explains why the great majority of individuals over the age of 55 require reading glasses. Unfortunately, many people who really need reading glasses do not use them, perhaps due to vanity or perhaps due to the tendency to deny the reality of aging. These are the folks that we see in restaurants holding the menu at arms length in order to read it. While this behavior is typically seen as humorous rather than a serious problem, inadequately corrected farsightedness can be a real problem. We may give up on reading an interesting and informative article in the newspaper, simply because it is too much work to make out the fine print. We may have difficulty reading the directions on a prescription medication. In addition to nearsightedness, presbyopia makes it more difficult for individuals to discern color intensities, especially in the cool colors like blue, green, and violet. This change may diminish our aesthetic enjoyment.

Cataracts

Cataracts constitute the most common disabling visual condition associated with aging. The lens of the eye becomes opaque rather than transparent, and the opaqueness of the lens interferes with the transmission of light to the retina. As a result, the individual experiences blurred and/or dimmed vision. Individuals with cataracts may need very bright light to read, and they may need to hold objects very close in order to be able to see them. As the cataract develops, useful sight is eventually lost. Surgery is required to remove the opaque lens and replace it with a plastic implant. This implant is known as an intraocular lens. The surgery is relatively simple. I know from experience, having had cataract surgery in both eyes.

Glaucoma

Glaucoma is a condition that results from increased pressure within the eyeball. This pressure is the result of excessive production of aqueous humor, the nutrient fluid that fills the anterior chamber of the eye. This fluid is formed more quickly than it is eliminated, producing increased pressure. This pressure can damage the optic nerve and can lead to total blindness. One of the early indications of glaucoma is the loss of peripheral vision. In time so much of the normal range of vision is eliminated that the patient experiences tunnel vision. Other indications of glaucoma are headaches, blurred vision, tearing, and the appearance of halos around sources of light such as streetlights. Untreated glaucoma can lead to blindness. In fact glaucoma is the second leading cause of blindness in the United States. A test for glaucoma is performed at regular eye examinations.

Senile Macular Degeneration

Senile macular degeneration (SMD) is the leading cause of blindness among adults in the United States. The condition involves the degeneration of the macular area of the retina, which normally functions to enable individuals to discriminate fine detail. There are two forms of this disease, referred to as dry (non-neovascular) SMD and wet (neovascular) SMD. Dry SMD is the early stage of the disease, and it appears to result from the aging and thinning of the macular tissues, the depositing of pigment in the macula, or a combination of these two processes. Dry macular degeneration results in gradual loss of central vision, but the symptoms are less severe than those of wet SMD. In about 10 percent of the cases, dry SMD progresses to the more damaging form of the eye disease known as wet SMD. In this condition, new blood vessels grow beneath the retina, a phenomenon known as neovascularization. These vessels leak blood and fluid into the eye, which causes permanent damage to the light-sensitive retinal cells. These cells then die off and create blind spots in central vision.

The leading cause of blindness in the United States is SMD. The *Archives of Ophthalmology* estimated that in 2004 approximately 1.75 million U.S. residents had significant symptoms associated with age-related macular degeneration; and this number is expected to grow to almost 3 million by 2020.[10]

These age-related visual problems can be extremely stressful. Vision links us to the outside world. It is critical to carrying out our daily activities. Of course, people who are blind from birth or have been blind for a long period of time learn to make adjustments that enable them to function with their visual impairments. However, individuals who suffer visual impairments late in life, having relied on their sight for many years, typically experience significant stress. Since the onset of these conditions is gradual, we may be unaware of the changes that are occurring yet nevertheless restrict our activities based on barely perceptible declines in vision. We may read less. We may avoid going out to dimly lit restaurants because we fear the embarrassment of not being able to read the menu. We may stop driving at night, thus restricting our social and recreational activities. Each of these incremental changes may contribute to decreased enjoyment and decreased satisfaction with living. These losses can contribute to depression.

Fortunately, most of the common age-related visual impairments are treatable or correctable. Nearsightedness associated with presbyopia can be treated with glasses, contact lenses, or LASIK eye surgery. Cataract surgery is the most frequently performed type of surgery in the United States, and 95.5 percent of those who have cataract surgery achieve uncorrected vision of 20/40 or better.[11] Glaucoma can be treated with various prescription drugs that promote the flow of fluids within the eye, including prostaglandin drops and beta-blockers. You need to discuss these possible medications with your doctor for possible adverse interactions. For example, the beta blockers are not appropriate for individuals with heart conditions. In addition to pharmaceutical interventions for glaucoma, there are surgical options. In a surgery called a trabeculoplasty, the surgeon employs a laser to make a series of minute holes where the cornea and the iris meet. These holes promote the drainage of ocular fluid. Some have noted that the use of marijuana may be associated with a decrease in intraocular pressure. However, there is no research suggesting that marijuana is better in reducing this pressure than the available legal prescription medications.

The treatment of SMD is somewhat more difficult than the treatment of the other age-related visual impairments. There is as yet no outright cure for macular degeneration. However, there are treatments available that effectively delay the progression of the disease or even reverse tissue degeneration with resulting improvement in vision. Many researchers believe that certain nutrients, including zinc, lutein, zeaxanthin, and vitamins A, C, and E help lower the risk of developing SMD and slow down the progression of dry SMD. For SMD that has already advanced to the neovascular form of the disease, the FDA has approved the drugs Lucentis, Macugen, and Visudyne. These drugs stop the abnormal blood vessel growth that causes damage to the retina. For individuals who have already experienced significant vision loss resulting from wet SMD, complete recovery of lost vision is not common. However, many new low vision devices are available that can facilitate reading and other visual tasks.

Please keep in mind that in order to receive appropriate treatment for these conditions, it is necessary to (1) be aware that there is a problem, and

(2) obtain an exact diagnosis. *Since age-related visual impairments tend to be very gradual in onset, it is quite possible that we may not to notice these gradual changes in vision, even though they can eventually become quite severe.* Furthermore, since timely treatment is important to the success of treatment for some of these conditions, *early detection is very important.* Therefore it is important for men over 60 to have regular eye examinations to check visual acuity and screen for degenerative conditions. These examinations are quite likely to detect problems before they reach the point at which we would become aware that there is a problem. In the case of SMD disease, early detection and pharmacological treatment can prevent potential losses in vision that might be irretrievable.

Hearing

Difficulty hearing is another potential source of stress as we grow older. Men over 60 are much more likely than younger men to experience impaired hearing. Among men in the age range from 18 to 44, approximately five percent have a clinically significant hearing loss. Among men over 65, this proportion increases to 31.5 percent.[12] Between 40 and 50 percent of men over the age of 75 have a significant hearing loss.[13]

The name that is given to the gradual loss of hearing that occurs as we grow older is presbycusis. There are many causes for presbycusis. The most common cause is changes in important structures in the inner ear, which is responsible for transforming sound vibrations into nerve impulses that can be transmitted to the brain and interpreted as sound.[14] Aging itself, as well as exposure to loud noise, certain drugs, or disease, can result in the loss of the delicate hair cells in the organ of Corti that detect sound vibrations. The hearing loss associated with presbycusis is generally more serious for high-pitched sounds than for low-pitched sounds. Thus we may have difficulty hearing a bird singing or a telephone ringing but still be perfectly able to hear a truck rolling down the street. Generally presbycusis affects both ears equally.

Because the process of hearing loss is gradual, we may not be aware that our hearing is diminishing. According to the National Institute on Deafness and Other Communication Disorders, individuals with presbycusis may experience any or all of the following:

1. The speech of others seems mumbled or slurred.
2. High-pitched sounds such as *s* and *th* are difficult to hear and tell apart.
3. Conversations are difficult to understand, especially when there is a background noise.
4. A man's voice is easier to hear than the higher pitches of a woman's voice.
5. Certain specific sounds may seem annoying or overly loud.
6. One experiences ringing, roaring, or hissing sounds in one or both ears (the condition referred to as tinnitus).[15]

Obviously, if you are aware of one or more of these symptoms, you should have your hearing checked by an audiologist. However, because of the gradual onset of presbycusis and the likelihood of being unaware of hearing impairment, you should have your hearing checked periodically whether or not you experience these symptoms. This is particularly important for men over 60.

It is very important to detect and remediate age-related hearing loss because research has shown that hearing loss can have a negative effect on psychological adjustment and subjective well-being.[16] In addition to reduced ability to enjoy music and other sounds that we appreciate, hearing loss can produce social isolation, distorted communication, and stigmatization. Based on a review of the literature on the psychosocial effects of various degrees of hearing impairment, Jakes concluded that "Most of the evidence presented appears to suggest that emotional disturbance of more than a transitory nature does occur with hearing loss, and that it is reduced when that hearing loss is cured."[17] Numerous studies have shown a relationship between hearing loss and depression.[18]

Hearing aids can help to compensate for presbycusis. Hearing aids do not represent a complete solution to the problem, because they do not restore hearing loss across the full frequency range. However, hearing aids can help most individuals suffering from hearing loss to a very substantial degree. An audiologist can conduct tests to determine the type of hearing aid that will maximize an individual's hearing.

Reaction Time

Katz described "psychomotor response" as a process in which the organism takes in information, gives meaning to this information through perceptual and integrative processes, determines whether the information calls for any action, and if necessary activates the appropriate response.[19] This process occurs more or less efficiently in different individuals, and within a particular individual the process tends to become less efficient with increasing age. The process may be limited by weaknesses at any point in the sequence of events. It may be inhibited by increases in sensory thresholds, increases in the time required for the neurological processing leading to the decision to respond, and decreases in the speed and strength of the response. Any of these changes can slow reaction time, and slowed reaction time may have an adverse impact on our ability to exert control over our environment. It may become more difficult to drive a car or operate machinery. It has been pointed out that decreases in psychomotor performance can be more problematic than typical decrements in vision or hearing because decrements in psychomotor performance are not easy to offset mechanically in the way that glasses can compensate for decrements in vision and hearing aids can compensate for decreases in hearing.[20]

SOCIOLOGICAL STRESSES AFTER 60

We have already noted some of the sociological stresses that affect men as they pass the age of 60, including the loss or reduction of the professional role and associated sources of self esteem, including the sense of fulfillment derived from providing for the needs of one's family and the sense of mastery and accomplishment associated with making a contribution to society through the pursuit of one's profession. Reduction of professional involvement will also result in the reduction of social gratifications derived from interactions with one's professional colleagues. In addition to possible reduction in professional activity, aging may make it more difficult for some people to pursue sports and hobbies that they have pursued for a lifetime. These reductions in non-professional roles may also lead to the loss of both the gratifications associated with the activities themselves and the rewards derived from social interactions with others who share these hobbies and pastimes. As our children mature, they may become less dependent upon us, further reducing the perception that we are needed. In the modern world, adult children are more mobile than was once the case. They may be transferred to distant locations by their employers or otherwise required by their own professional responsibilities to live at great distances from us. And where the children go, the grandchildren go as well.

In addition to these age-related changes in social roles and responsibilities, other sociological factors can constitute sources of stress for older men. Socio-economic indicators are obvious correlates of adjustment after 60. Research shows that the subjective well-being of older men is related to their level of income, home ownership, level of education, ethnic/cultural group identification, and religious affiliation.[21] In general, men with higher incomes score higher on measures of psychological adjustment and life satisfaction than men with lower incomes. This stands to reason, of course, because money can provide diverse sources of gratification and can help to buffer the adverse effects of such negative life events as illnesses.

The relationship between income level and life satisfaction applies first of all when income is defined in absolute terms, by the actual dollar value of one's annual income. Interestingly, however, the relationship is even stronger when income is defined in terms of self-perceived adequacy of income. In other words, it is important how much money we *actually* have to spend, but it is even more important that we *believe* the amount of money that we have to spend is sufficient. Men who own homes are more satisfied with life than those who do not. Of course, home ownership is related to income and wealth, so a part of the relationship between home ownership and life satisfaction might be explained by differences in income levels between home owners and non home owners. However, the effect of home ownership on the subjective well-being of men over 60 goes beyond wealth. Men who own very modest homes tend to manifest greater satisfaction than men with similar incomes who do not own homes.

The same is true of level of education. Although individuals with higher levels of education tends to be more affluent than those with less education, there is nevertheless a tendency for better educated men of very modest incomes to score higher on measures of life satisfaction than men of similar incomes with lesser educational achievement levels. It would appear that education gives us an additional repertoire of available areas of interest that entertain us and bring joy to our lives.

Of course, there is a relationship between ethnic/cultural group membership and income level in American society. For example, numerous studies have shown that older black males in America are less affluent than older white males.[22] This would suggest that older black men might well have lower subjective well-being than older white men. However, this is not necessarily true. Research shows that individuals tend to judge the adequacy of their income by comparing themselves to their friends, neighbors, and close relatives, rather than to the population of the nation as a whole.[23] Thus a man of modest income may well feel quite satisfied with life if he compares his position favorably to that of his neighbors. Alternatively, a man who has achieved quite a lot by objective indicators may be dissatisfied, if those around him are clearly more successful.

I have had the opportunity to treat several such individuals. One such patient was Tony, a Ph.D. psychologist who was the director of special education in an affluent New Jersey suburb. He earned close to $100,000 a year, had responsibility for a staff of eight, and was frequently called upon to deliver expert opinion and/or testimony in relation to special education placements. Despite these objective indicators of success, however, he approached retirement age with a sense that he had failed in life.

He felt this way for several different reasons. First, his first generation Italian-American parents had very little idea of what a psychologist does and did not accord very much respect to the fact that he had earned a doctoral degree. Second, his two older brothers ran an extremely successful garbage carting company, and they each earned at least five times his salary. He said that they each had fabulous homes, spent freely, and talked incessantly about their frequent luxurious vacations. They frequently asked Tony and his wife to join them on trips that Tony could not possibly afford. They had fancy cars, and their kids had fancy cars. The brothers made fun of Tony's necessarily more modest lifestyle and questioned the value of his education. His nieces and nephews seemed to go out of their way to let Tony's kids know how much more they had. In addition to the family comparison, Tony also compared himself to the families who lived in his school district. They were also generally much more affluent than he, and the students with whom he worked in school had greater advantages than his own children. At one point Tony complained that his children had to attend colleges where they received financial aid, whereas other kids could go wherever they wanted.

Tony represents an important lesson for men approaching and moving past their sixtieth birthday. The lesson is this: Please avoid the trap of basing your sense of accomplishment and self-worth on comparisons with others. This is a sure way to make you think poorly of yourself, and a pretty sure way to guarantee that you will become dissatisfied and depressed. No matter how objectively successful you may be, you can always find someone out there who is more successful. You can also find someone better looking, someone in better shape, someone with a prettier wife, and someone with smarter kids. Once you've gotten as far in life as you have, you really need to give up competitive comparisons and focus on the good things you have.

Chapter Six

SOCIAL CONNECTIONS AFTER 60

Two Men

Ben

Ben was the director of employee benefits at a Fortune 500 corporation before he reached the mandatory retirement age of 65. He loved his work and spent most of his time at the office. His wife had died of breast cancer when he was 52, and he had never remarried. He was not particularly close to his one child, who was an investment banker living 3,000 miles away. Ben did not have any hobbies that he enjoyed, and the only organizations he belonged to were organizations of employee assistance personnel. Ben derived a great deal of pleasure from helping company employees with their retirement planning and making sure that they all took full advantage of their medical and other benefits. He liked to meet with employees personally and in small groups on a periodic basis to make sure that they were aware of their benefits and to counsel them on how to make sure that they would be prepared financially for comfortable retirements. He always made sure that these meetings were enjoyable for the employees by holding the meetings in nice places and having food provided by the best caterers. He also worked up a bunch of jokes to use during presentations to keep the interest of the employees. Ben developed quite a reputation in the company as an entertaining manager who did a great job preparing his workers for retirement.

Ironically, Ben's own retirement did not work out very well. He was completely comfortable financially, but almost every other aspect of his life after retirement was a disaster. He didn't know what to do with himself. He missed his coworkers, who had become his primary source of social contact and support since his wife had died. He no longer felt that he was performing a valuable service. In fact, he came to perceive of himself as a useless "has been" who no longer served any significant purpose. He had no one to tell his jokes to.

Ben was bored, and depression followed after boredom. He stopped eating, and he began to lose weight. Within six months of retiring, Ben came to me for help with his depression. He said that he was so miserable that he had actually given some thought to suicide. It took the better part of a year to get him out of his funk and involved with life again.

Mark

Mark was 74 when his wife Bella died. She had been disabled to the point of being nearly completely housebound for 10 years. Over that entire time period Mark had been a loving and devoted caretaker. They had an adequate income from savings and from Mark's benefits as a retired airline employee, but Bella's illness made travel impossible. They rarely left their home. They each had grown children who spoke with them regularly on the telephone, but all their children (and grandchildren) lived far away. They could visit only once or twice a year. Mark and Bella had many friends when they were younger, but by the time Bella had become incapacitated, many of their friends had died, and those who were still alive were similarly restricted in terms of their ability to travel. So they spoke to friends occasionally on the telephone, but they did not get many visits.

While Bella was alive, Mark only went out for short periods to do the shopping. He did not travel the long distances that would be required to attend family weddings and Bar Mitzvahs, because he was afraid to leave Bella alone. They loved and comforted each other, but their lives were not exciting. Around the time that Bella died, Mark had been diagnosed with diabetes. He was also on medication for depression. When Bella died, all of their children assumed that Mark would follow her in fairly short order.

Surprisingly, however, after a period of mourning Mark responded to his new situation by renewing social contacts with friends and family. Although it was not all that easy for him, he began to do some traveling to visit old friends, and he visited his children and grandchildren. He spent a good deal of time going through the many possessions that he and Bella had accumulated over the years. He gave many of these items to family members and neighbors, and he also held numerous yard sales, which he greatly enjoyed. He also became quite active in an organization of families who had once lived together in China, eventually assuming the position of editor of the organization's monthly newsletter.

Within six or eight months of Bella's death, Mark had reduced his need for insulin and had eliminated his antidepressant medication. Although he is still an older man with medical issues that require attention, no one is expecting him to die imminently. He has been thinking of moving closer to his children to make it easier for them to spend time together. Mark has also begun to engage in online dating activities.

THE IMPORTANCE OF SOCIAL CONTACT FOR MEN OVER 60

These two stories clearly indicate the importance of social contact for men who have passed the age of 60. Ben, the younger and healthier of the two men, became seriously depressed after he was forced to retire. With the loss of his job he lost not only a way to occupy his time and the sense that he was performing an important role in life but also the most important part of his social network. He lost the gratification of telling his jokes and having them appreciated by others. Without a spouse or close relatives nearby, he was left in a void. He did not respond to this situation by developing new social ties but rather by withdrawing from life and allowing himself to become inactive. His health as well as his mood suffered, and it required professional intervention to get him reengaged with people. In sharp contrast, Mark, considerably older and more challenged with respect to mobility, responded to the loss of his wife by making a conscious effort to renew old social contacts and spend more time with family members. He recreated his social network and reengaged. As a result, his mood and his health both improved, and his outlook for the future became positive.

MEN OVER 60 ARE PARTICULARLY AT RISK FOR THE LOSS OF SOCIAL CONTACTS

Of course, social contact and social support are important for everyone, but aspects of the American social structure combine to make the issue of social contact more difficult for older men than for any other segment of society. In our culture, there seems to be an expectation that older men will withdraw from important roles. Thus Ben was expected, indeed forced, to retire from work. But for Ben this meant more than just the loss of employment. It involved the loss of the important social contact that came with his employment. Although many women in our society have careers, it is still fair to say that work and work-related social contact is relatively more important for men than for women. This is partly because more men work, but it is also partly because men and women tend to form and nourish quite different social constellations. Women tend to have stronger bonds to family and friends than do men, and women tend to be emotionally more open with their friends than men. Whereas women often have these relationships to fall back on when they retire from work, men who retire tend to experience a greater loss. Crowley and Lorge have described this loss as "being cut off from the pack."[1] This term signifies the loss of the important mammalian bond that wolves experience when they cooperate to achieve success in the hunt. Men who retire lose this bond with their coworkers. For many men, work is simply, "who we are."

Another reason why men experience greater loss of social contact than women as they age is that over the course of their lifetimes men are more likely than women to participate in both work and leisure activities that are physically demanding. With respect to work, one can certainly argue that the policy that forced Ben to retire from his executive position at the age of 65 makes very little sense; but there are many men whose work involves strenuous physical labor. These men may really reach a point where they can no longer perform the same job. These men must reduce, modify, or discontinue their work roles;

and with this change they may well lose the camaraderie of their fellow workers. Furthermore, men tend to engage in strenuous recreational activities, such as sports. If a man is forced to give up softball because his arthritis is making participation painful, that man may not only lose the activity but also the teammates. Of course, he can still hang out and watch his friends play, and he can still go for a beer with them after the game; but many men find it frustrating to view such activities from they outside, after having been an active participant for many years.

Both men and women lose social contacts as they age because of aging itself. Friends die. Children become independent and move away. Even grandchildren grow up and become less available. Spouses die. Although these events impact men and women alike, it seems that these losses are tougher on men. This is simply because we men tend to be more independent over the course of our lives, and we find it more difficult to establish and cultivate other social relationships to take the place of those that are lost. It is often painfully difficult for men to initiate social contacts. This is especially true of older men, who may feel that at this point in their lives they have relatively little to offer. Men over 60 must make a conscious effort to develop and cultivate social contact and social support. This is especially important in view of the ample evidence that social isolation is a powerful risk factor for the development of physical illnesses as well as psychosocial adjustment problems, which can destroy our quality of life.

SOCIAL ISOLATION IS A RISK FACTOR FOR POOR HEALTH AND PSYCHOSOCIAL ADJUSTMENT

Social isolation for men over 60 is associated with poor health. This relationship is complex. In the most direct sense, social contact is a fundamental human need. We require interaction with others in the form of conversation, physical contact, and shared interests. In addition to this basic need for contact, the existence of social connections has indirect health benefits. For example, friends may encourage us to engage in activities that are good for us, like exercising and making sure that we see the doctor. Friends may also encourage us to try new activities that turn out to be enjoyable and to make us feel better. For example, they may get us to go to a play or a concert that we would not have considered on out own, or they may encourage us to take a trip to some interesting place, instead of just staying at home. Having friends also provides us with a sense of being there for someone else, which can bolster our sense of personal efficacy and self-fulfillment. Conversely, having friends gives us someone to talk to when things are not going well for us. This form of social support can go a long way toward buffering the impact of life's disappointments and travails.

The scientific literature is very clear on the benefits of social contact for older persons in general and for older men in particular. A number of large scale studies have indicated that older individuals who lack social ties are more likely to die prematurely than individuals who are socially engaged.[2] Several of these studies are noteworthy for specific reasons. For example, a nine-year study of nearly 7,000 adults in Alameda County, California, showed that people who lacked social ties were more likely to die during the follow-up period than those with extensive ties. The study also showed that this effect was independent of initial self-reported health status, socioeconomic status, risky health behaviors such as smoking and alcoholic beverage consumption, and physical activity and obesity, and independent of utilization of preventive health services over the period of the study.[3] In other words, the positive effect of social contact on longevity appears to be due to the social contact itself, rather than to any potential confounding factors. In this study, social ties were defined as including presence of a spouse, contact with friends, membership in a religious group, and membership in one or more community organizations.

In another large sample longitudinal study, a significant relationship between social support and longevity was found for older males but not for older females.[4] In this study social support was defined as consisting of intimate social relationships, formal organizational involvement outside of work, and active involvement in leisure activities having a social component.

Other studies have reported significant relationships among older persons between social ties and specific diseases, including high blood pressure[5] and coronary heart disease.[6] Studies have also demonstrated that among elderly men social ties are related to overall satisfaction with life.[7] Thus there is more than adequate reason to believe that it is extremely important for us to cultivate our social contacts, social relationships, and social roles as we move into and beyond the seventh decade of life. In the sections of this chapter that follow, I want to consider the specific areas in which we can develop and cultivate social connectedness. These include work, family roles and responsibilities, relationships with friends and neighbors, participation in religious, fraternal, and community organizations, and participation in leisure activities. I will also consider the issue of social connectedness among several specific groups of men, those who have lost a spouse or partner, and gay men.

WORK

Many people are like Ben, in that a major portion of their social connectedness occurs in conjunction with work. Even among workers who have families, friends, and interests outside of their work, it is often the case that coworkers provide a very unique form of social interaction that is sorely missed following retirement. For example, a man who has worked in a profession requiring unique knowledge and skills may be able to share this aspect of his interests and personality only with others who have the same knowledge base. These contacts may be lost upon retirement, creating a significant void. Similarly, a man who has worked with a team in a highly competitive work environment such as law or advertising may find that he misses the challenge of the competition and the synergistic creative interactions with his coworkers.

There are various approaches that a man can take to fill the void. One approach available to some is simply to refuse to retire. If you are the owner of your business or a self-employed professional, no one can make you quit. You can continue on at full speed until such time as you are ready to cut back, if indeed you are ever ready to cut back. My friend Dave sold his family electronics firm at age 68, and then went back to school to earn a Master's degree in American history. Now he is teaching at a junior college and is enjoying his new work immensely.

If you are in a position where you are required to retire from one job, you can take another. Many men retire from military or law enforcement careers, then begin another career in a related field. I know a number of academicians who have retired from teaching at one university but have taken another position at another school. There is also the possibility of retiring from a full-time position to take a part-time consulting position in the same field. Some workers even retire from a full-time position at a firm, then assume a part-time consulting position with the same firm. A business proprietor may sell his business, then sign on as a paid advisor to the company.

All of these courses of action represent ways in which an older man can maintain the professional social interactions that he finds so rewarding. There are as many possible solutions to this problem as there are individuals. The key point is that you don't need to think of retirement from work as unavoidable. In fact, retirement is not really a yes or no choice. If you derive a great deal of satisfaction from your job and your interactions with coworkers, you should plan your life after 60 in such a way as to maximize the chance that you will continue to have these interactions. Chapter 11 further examines this question of whether to retire and how to handle retirement if you do retire.

FAMILY ROLES

We men really need to be needed. Having a family is rewarding for many reasons. Supporting our families is a badge of honor and a reason for getting up each day and working hard. Watching our children grow and mature gives us a place in the stream of life. Helping them to master the tasks of growing up gives us a purpose. Seeing them succeed is a source of pride.

When our children go off to college and move out on their own, we feel a void. The nest is empty. We wonder whether we are really needed any longer.

If we are lucky, the children will stay close to home and give us grandchildren. Then we can once again be useful. We can baby-sit. We can give our children respite from their childcare responsibilities, and we can give our grandchildren presents. We can share our knowledge of parenting with our children, and we can teach our grandchildren how to play baseball and how to catch fish. We can take them to the museum and travel with them.

All these roles are personally validating and gratifying. Even helping out financially can be a source of satisfaction. When we are called upon to provide some financial assistance to our grown children, we may complain about it, but it still makes us feel important. Even disagreements have a positive aspect. If we disagree with our children on how our grandchildren should be raised, we may experience some degree of frustration, yet we are nevertheless fully engaged in our roles as the experienced elder. And those of us who are grandparents have all enjoyed watching our grandchildren recreate for their fathers all the annoyances and frustrations that their fathers had previously created for us.

Therefore it is very important for us to do everything in our power to insure that we remain involved in the lives of our children and grandchildren to the greatest extent possible. It is also important to nurture relationships with other family members. When circumstances arise that diminish our involvement with family members, we must do what we can to keep in touch and involved. During Bella's illness Mark was unable to do much visiting, but he kept in touch with family and friends as much as he could, and when Bella passed away he was in a position where it seemed natural that he would resume visiting.

If your own circumstances are such that you do not have a spouse or family members with whom you are close, you need to recognize that there may be a significant void in your life that needs to be addressed. You can get a great deal of gratification and satisfaction out of relationships with individuals who are not family members. These may be friends, neighbors, individuals with whom you share common interests, or even strangers who could use your help.

FRIENDS AND NEIGHBORS

If you have friends, cultivate them. If you have neighbors, get to know them. Men are not naturally prone to form close relationships with other guys the way that women do with other women. Men are socialized to be independent and self-sufficient, and when we have friends our interactions with them tend to focus on an activity rather than how we are feeling. Men can go bowling together once a week for years and never learn very much about each others' lives outside the bowling alley. They can sit for hours watching a football game and never say a word to each other that is not related to the game. But it doesn't have to be that way.

I have had the experience of discussing personal concerns with close male friends. I have discussed my marriage, my frustrations with work, my aspirations, my problems, my anxieties, and my pet peeves. I have found that men are actually very interested in sharing their experiences and helping each other to clarify issues. The difficulty men face in developing close friendships is overcoming their initial reluctance to acknowledge their vulnerabilities and actually disclose their personal concerns and feelings. For men who have particular difficulty in opening up, a group experience may be helpful. Men may join formal therapy groups run by professionals, or they may form informal self-help groups surrounding a particular shared interest of need. For example, men who have recently retired or men who have recently lost a spouse or partner may participate in a self-help support group in which they can share their experiences and exchange strategies.

Neighbors constitute a natural support group, since they will have similar concerns regarding issues confronting the neighborhood. A call to a neighbor regarding the garbage pick-up schedule can be used to break the ice and initiate a more personal relationship. Older men who lack meaningful social connections must come to regard the development of social relationships as an important goal requiring conscious effort and cultivation. It is a good idea to keep a list of acquaintances that you call periodically, just to say hello and see if everything's going well. These contacts will likely generate other activities, such as going out to a movie or a ball game, visiting, or working together on some project of mutual interest. These activities will not only be rewarding in their own right but will provide the basis for deepening friendships. The Internet also opens up opportunities for new relationships.

PARTICIPATION IN RELIGIOUS, FRATERNAL, AND COMMUNITY ORGANIZATIONS

Being a member of a religious group is not simply spiritual. It is also social. Members of the same church or synagogue share religious beliefs; but they also share the most important transitions in life. We share our children's Christenings and Bar Mitzvahs with the members of our religious group. We get married in the church or synagogue. We plan and carry out benefits and community service activities in our houses of worship. We have our funerals there.

Depending on the particular denomination, religious services themselves may constitute a significant social interaction and entertainment. In many religions, participation is not confined to formal religious services that take place a single day a week. There may be evening bible study, choir, youth fellowship, and family pot luck suppers. Our ministers and rabbis are likely to visit us during times of illness, and our fellow parishioners may well provide respite care to the spouse of a sick or dying member of the congregation by shopping, bringing food to the family, or helping to provide transportation to the doctor's office. Members of a religious group can both give and receive these social supports. Whether they are giving or receiving, they are likely to feel better as a result.

Studies of older men have shown that both membership in a religious group and the frequency of involvement in the activities of that group are related to psychosocial well-being.[8] I believe that both the spiritual and the social aspects of religious group affiliation and participation are important to many members. Certainly there are many men for whom religious beliefs provide a sense of comfort and purpose that can help to give meaning to life as they contemplate their lives and their mortality. However, I also note that not everyone who is a member of a religious congregation is particularly devout or observant. Many individuals are affiliated with a church or synagogue primarily because their membership represents a tie to the community and provides them with a place where they can meet and socialize with community members with whom they have various relationships. I have a friend whose grandfather was a church elder for many years, although he cared not a lick for any of the religious rituals, and in fact he was not at all certain that he even believed in God. He didn't object to the religious services. They were simply irrelevant. This man was perfectly clear that he was a member of the church because that is where he met all of the clients for the contracting business that he ran. He felt that being a member of the church was simply a part of being a full member of his community, like being a member of the rotary club.

Therefore, I would suggest that if you are one of the many men who identifies as a member of a religious group but has not been involved for many years, it may be a good idea to consider renewing your involvement by becoming affiliated with a nearby house of worship. Of course, if you are an atheist or have some other philosophical or moral reservation regarding organized religion, then you should be aware that there are secular organizations that can provide a very similar sense of social connectedness and purpose without the accompanying religious beliefs and observances.

A myriad of organizations are available for the purpose of developing social connectedness. Depending on your background and interests, you may join a political party or a political interest group. You may join the Chamber of Commerce or a community organization such as Rotary or Kiwanis. You may join a fraternal organization such as the Elks, a Masonic Lodge, the Veterans of Foreign Wars, or the American Legion. You may become involved in the support of a charitable activity. All of these organizations undertake community service projects that you may find rewarding, and all of them provide opportunities for social contact and connectedness. In most cases, these organizations are anxious to have new members to contribute time and energy to their work. Therefore you may expect to be welcomed when you indicate your interest in joining.

PARTICIPATION IN LEISURE ACTIVITIES

Leisure activities are also rewarding for both the intrinsic enjoyment of the activity itself and the social connections that can be developed and fostered in connection with the activities. I had a friend who was a lifetime member of the Southern New York Fish and Game Association, a large group of sportsmen whose purpose is to promote the sports of fishing and hunting and lobby in the interest of those who engage in these activities. This friend was not really terribly interested in either of those sports. He went fishing only occasionally when his friends organized a group trip, and he had never been hunting. He simply enjoyed spending time with other members. They had a weekly meeting of the local chapter of the organization and monthly meetings of the entire membership where conservation experts typically gave talks on wildlife. He also participated actively in the organization's annual youth fishing tournament, which he found particularly gratifying.

Most leisure activities have organizations comprised of the individuals who participate in these activities. Whether you are an active type who likes hiking and canoeing or a cosmopolitan type who likes theater and opera, there will be a group that you can join to share your activity with similar souls. These groups have the dual advantage of facilitating your enjoyment of your hobby by organizing trips and events while at the same time connecting you with individuals with who you can enjoy the activity and develop personal relationships. Organizations of participants in various activities can be located easily. You can find them advertised in magazines directed toward fans of the activities, and of course you can locate them on the internet. In many cases there is a national or even international umbrella organization that has local chapters. For the purpose of developing social connections, it is the local chapter that you should be most interested in. Generally the umbrella organization will have information on local chapter meetings.

FOR MEN WHO HAVE LOST A SPOUSE

Older men who have lost a spouse or partner are particularly at risk for social isolation and concomitant adverse psychosocial consequences. This is because men tend to rely on their spouses to schedule the couple's social activities. Therefore, when his partner dies, an older man loses not only the companionship of the spouse, but frequently the other social activities that came with the relationship. The widower may eventually complete his mourning and be ready to resume social relationships, only to find that it is not so easy to make the necessary arrangements.

In addition, if the couple had engaged primarily in social activities with other couples, the widower will likely find himself in a kind of limbo because he no longer fits in as a member of a couple. Therefore the widower may need to develop a new network of acquaintances that includes other single individuals.

This possibility gives emphasis to my suggestion to become involved in community organizations and organizations based on common interest in specific hobbies and leisure activities. Membership in such organizations will transcend the death of a spouse and provide a familiar forum and continuing opportunities for social contact following the death of a spouse.

Even assuming that you have places to go to socialize, your new status as a widower will still place you in a different status when you go back. Like it or not, you will be perceived as and treated as a single person. This can be very difficult, particularly for a man who had been with the same partner for a long time. He is simply out of practice when it comes to initiating and developing social relationships. The widower may avoid social situations because he is uncomfortable. It may have been many years since he confronted a challenge of this nature. He has been used to feeling competent and in control, and he has likely settled into a comfort zone that does not involve any particular efforts to be charming or impeccably dressed. The average man may simply prefer being lonely to confronting the challenge of recapturing his social desirability.

If you are in this position, you should be very careful to avoid falling into the trap of accepting a solitary life. You may feel anxious about meeting new people, but you need to work through this. I often see men in my practice who are confronting loneliness and feel paralyzed in their efforts to resocialize. In this context, a peer support group for widowers may be very helpful. Membership in such a group can not only help you with the grieving process but also help you to acknowledge your need for social contact and your fears regarding the initiation of new relationships. Widowers can also derive a great deal of social support from the other members of such groups, based on their shared experiences.

A word of caution is also in order. While widowers frequently experience great difficulty in reestablishing social contacts following the death of a spouse, some widowers find themselves in the position of being pursued by women. Because women tend to outlive men, in most neighborhoods there will be more single women over the age of 60 than there are men. I have heard stories of men in retirement communities who have lost a spouse and in short order have been actively courted by one or more widows.

If this should happen to you, you obviously need to be careful not to jump into a new relationship before you are sure that you really care for the new person and before you are certain that you are compatible with her. After all, you probably had a long period of comfort living with your deceased wife. You may or may not have had a perfect marriage, but if you stayed together for life you almost certainly had achieved a degree of comfort in your daily routine of living. A relationship with someone new will likely bring changes in some established routines, and you need to get a sense of what these changes might be and whether they are going to be acceptable before you jump in. In this situation the support and counsel of other widowers may also prove helpful. No matter what stage of life we have reached, we can always benefit from the counsel of others who have already navigated the transitions that we are facing.

SOCIAL CONNECTIONS AMONG GAY MEN OVER 60

Kooden and Flowers have suggested that gay men face social unique challenges as they age, because "the majority of negatives around aging involve the body...Gay men are deeply invested in their bodies, and many feel that their body is their best asset, not only for sex, but for feelings of attractiveness, power, and success."[9] For this reason, experts on psychosocial development among gay men have argued that as gay men enter their seventh decade, they may experience a loss of social valuation that is proportionately greater than the corresponding loss among straight men.[10] This may make it difficult for gay men to pursue the goal of maintaining social connections as they grow older.

Weizalis has argued that older gay men who hold the idea that physical changes in their bodies lessen physical attractiveness and desirability will be distressed by the aging experience.[11] He and his associates have suggested that clinicians working with such men should encourage such men to seek out social connections "by learning about the community resources, becoming advocates for older gay men, and embracing their own aging with excitement and vigor."[12] I would add that gay men as well as straight men must strive for self acceptance as they grow older. They need to recognize that the potential for rewarding social connections exists everywhere, for older adults as well as younger ones. Lack of self-acceptance always exacerbates the problems of social connectedness and the development of close personal relationships and intimacy.

So much of gay socialization is based on physical attraction, and for men entering their 60s the challenge of maintaining youthfulness can be daunting. I urge men to embrace their age. Of course you want to look your best, but don't feel that you must compete with much younger men. Maintain your personal identity and your integrity. Be who you are.

Chapter Seven

SEX AFTER 60

John's Lost Libido

At the age of 60, John came in to my office complaining that his libido was shot. He said that he never even thought about sex unless his wife let him know that she was in the mood. When that happened, he was happy to please her, but he felt that his performance was marginal at best. He said that when they were younger he was constantly initiating sex. He also said that he remembered when just a touch or a kiss from his wife would excite him and produce an instantaneous erection. Now, however, when he and his wife engaged in foreplay, it seemed to take forever for his penis to get hard, and there were times when he felt that he was barely hard enough to actually enter his wife's vagina. He said that there were times when they would have sex and he would not have an orgasm, and on the occasions when he did have an orgasm, it was "more of a fizzle than an explosion…barely worth the effort."

John's wife sometimes apologized for "bothering him" when he seemed tired, and he had to reassure her that even though his sex drive had diminished, he still loved being close to her and giving her pleasure. He had always enjoyed performing oral sex on his wife, and more and more these days that was how she achieved orgasm. She felt a degree of guilt for apparently getting more pleasure from sex than he did, and even though he reassured her that he genuinely enjoyed the sex they had, it was clear to John that there were times when she would have liked to initiate sexual activity but did not, because she felt that she was being selfish. As a result, they made love less often than they had in the past, and less often than John's wife would have liked. On the other hand, John said that if his wife didn't remind him about sex from time to time, it might very well slip his mind entirely.

AGE-RELATED CHANGES IN THE MALE SEXUAL RESPONSE

John's sex life at 60 is typical of many men his age. There are a number of age-related physiological changes in the male reproductive system that may affect sexual interest and sexual activity. Sometime after the age of 40 or so, the production of the male sex hormone testosterone begins to diminish gradually. This is due to age-related fibrosis in the testes. Fibrosis is an increase in the amount of fibrous connective tissue within the testes. This tissue tends to constrict the blood supply to the testes and reduces the production of testosterone within the interstitial cells of the testes.[1]

Reduced testosterone production and concomitant reductions in testosterone levels in the bloodstream may result in the reduced sexual desire. There is a great deal of variability from one man to another in terms of the age at which this decrease in the production of testosterone begins, as well as in the rate of reduction in the production of the hormone. Some men will experience reductions in blood testosterone levels in their forties, and others will not experience such reductions until well into their sixties. But almost all men will experience a reduction of testosterone production at some point in their lifetime, and this reduction is related to a decrease in the sex drive. This results in a tendency toward decreased sexual activity as we grow older. Researchers at Duke University found that about half of men in their early sixties reported that they were sexually active, compared to only about 10 percent of men in their eighties.[2]

Fibrosis also affects the penis as we get older, reducing the capacity of the organ to become engorged with blood. This vascular change tends to increase the amount of time required to achieve an erection following sexual excitation. This change also tends to make erections less firm in older men than in younger men.

In addition to these vascular changes, there is a tendency for the prostate gland to enlarge as we get older. This also has effects on the sexual response among older men. The ejaculatory duct traverses the prostate. Therefore the enlargement of the prostate has the effect of making ejaculatory contractions experienced during orgasm less forceful than they are in younger men.

Masters and Johnson summarized the changes in sexual functioning that tend to occur among older men.[3] They concluded that because of the physiological changes described above, the following changes are typical: (1) It takes an older man longer to achieve a full erection, and his erection may not be as full or as firm as when he was younger; (2) It typically takes an older man a longer period of time to achieve orgasm; (3) The force and the volume of the ejaculation are reduced, and fewer genital spasms are experienced; (4) The erection of an older man subsides more rapidly following orgasm than does that of a younger man; and (5) It takes an older man longer than a younger man to have a second erection and orgasm.

So it is quite clear that as we enter our seventh decade of life, we may expect to experience some changes in the sexual response. The question for us then becomes, how do we deal with these changes?

HOW DO WE DEAL WITH CHANGES
IN THE SEXUAL RESPONSE?

Experts on male aging have tended to take two different approaches in counseling men on how to cope with these changes. I refer to these two approaches
as the *listen to your own body* approach, and the *keep the testosterone levels up*
approach. I consider these below.

Listen to Your Own Body

The traditional approach to sex after 60 has been to suggest that you listen
to your body, accept what it is saying about sex, and act accordingly. If you feel
the urge to have sex, do so. If not, don't worry about not doing what you don't
want to do.

This approach begins by emphasizing that there is a great deal of variability
among men in the nature and timing of the age-related changes in the male
reproductive system. Therefore, just because you have turned 60, don't assume
that your sexual drive will decrease. It may very well not decrease, at least for
a long time. This approach also points out that even after these changes do
occur, they do not preclude sexual activity and intimacy, although they may
result in changes in the frequency of sex and the nature of sexual behavior. The
basic message in this approach is that our own bodies will tell us what our own
unique sexual needs are at various points over the course of the lifetime. All
that we need to do is to accept the messages we receive and act accordingly.[4]

According to this listen to your own body perspective, we should first of all
recognize that the urge to have sex will probably appear less frequently than
it has in the past, and we should accept this change as OK. Thus Crowley and
Lorge argued that:

> Finally there comes a time when we have all had enough. And we do not want any
> more. Not now, anyway. And we want to go to bed and go to *sleep*. That time will
> come to you, too, and you will just want to go to bed and the hell with it. And you
> will not be howling with regret or resentment for your fading libido. You will not
> see it that way at all. You will just want what you want. And you'll get it. How bad
> can that be?[5]

Crowley and Lorge even stated explicitly that one can have a perfectly good
life, even if one never has sex. They argued that having a good sex life after 60
can be a tremendous help in achieving the good life, but they also pointed out
that "sex is not mandatory for the good life."[6]

Rowe and Kahn have expressed a similar view, arguing that "Certainly there
are older people who have lost interest in sex and are glad to be done with it."[7]
These authors go so far as to quote Sophocles on the subject of waning sex
drive. When he was in his 80s, the poet was asked whether he "had yet any

acquaintance with Venus," to which he responded, "Heavens forbid…I thank the gods that I am finally rid of that tyranny."[8]

Of course, this perspective also recognizes that most men over 60 do continue to have sexual desires and that many men continue to have highly gratifying sexual relations into their eighties and beyond. I have a friend whose grandmother took him aside when she was in her 80s to tell him with a twinkle in her eye that his grandfather, then 86, "still doesn't leave me alone." Grandma was not specific about exactly what grandpa did when he wasn't "leaving her alone," but whatever it was, she clearly enjoyed the attention.

Speaking of attention, another aspect of this take it as it comes approach to sexuality as we grow older involves the promotion of other forms of intimacy when the urge for actual sexual intercourse does not manifest itself. Thus Crowley and Lodge included in their book "a small plug…for the ancient art of cuddling."[9] They suggested that man is basically a pack animal, and pack animals naturally require touching. Therefore we should make it a point to have close physical contact with another person, even if this contact is not sexual intercourse. They urged us to "take off [our] clothes and roll about," and they suggested that we should "make love if you feel like it, but touch regardless."[10] This is certainly good advice when the urge to have sex does not present itself. The moral is to let yourself go. Follow your instincts. Do what feels right to you and your partner.

A closely related proposition of those who emphasize the importance of listening to our own bodies is the idea that our sexual behavior should be determined by our personal needs and capacities, and not by prevailing social expectations regarding appropriate sexual behavior for men over 60. We have all heard the jokes that are made about men and women over the age of 60 who continue to engage in passionate lovemaking. There is still a presumption that as we age it is appropriate for us to give up sexual activity. It is considered unbecoming for seniors. Younger people will tell you that when they imagine older persons (like their parents or grandparents) making love, they experience a negative visceral reaction. They may burst into laughter, or they may feel disgusted by the image. But that is their problem, not yours. I am over 60 and I assure you that I do not find sex disgusting. My wife doesn't look the same as she did when we were 30, but she still looks good to me. In fact, she looks even better to me now than she did then. I don't look the same either, but I feel good about myself and my wife feels good about me as well. If we want to have sex, we will. If you need to imagine what that looks like, that's your issue. Either enjoy the fantasy, or just get over it.

Of course, it takes two to tango, and all this talk about listening to your body must be considered in the context of your partner, and what her body is telling her. Communication of your respective needs and desires is crucial to your relationship and to your mutual happiness. If one partner has a continuing need for sexual relations and the other doesn't, the chances are it can be worked out. When two people live with each other, they are generally happy to accommodate each other. But accommodation requires knowing our partner's needs, and knowing each other's needs requires good communication. Whether you still have a strong need for sex or whether the need has faded away, you need to let your partner know, and you need to encourage your partner to communicate her needs to you as well.

I am an advocate of keeping the romance alive in a relationship. Sex may come and go and return once more, but romance has a profound constancy that creates a unique intimacy for the partners in a relationship. Romantic love can last much longer than the afterglow of sex, and romantic love has an enduring grace that goes far beyond sex.

Up to this point I've been considering sex in the context of a marriage or a long-term committed relationship. However, single men must adapt to changes in their sexual response as well. It is difficult enough to openly discuss changes in our sexual response with a trusted lover whom we know cares about our happiness, but it may be even more difficult to discuss these issues with a new partner with whom we have no such foundation of trust. However, I can only say that if you are close enough with someone that it appears sex is likely, then you are close enough to let them know how you are likely to respond, what your needs are, and what you can do to please your partner. For men with a desire for sexual contact who feel inadequate or inhibited due to limited sexual capacity, another course of action would be to employ a prostitute who will be satisfied with being paid and who will regard your gratification as a matter of professional pride.

Sex can be especially problematic for widowers, for whom changes in their sexual response may combine with the loss of a familiar partner to make the prospect of sex especially anxiety-producing. I had a client who came to me four years after the death of his wife of 35 years. Dave complained that he was lonely and miserable, because he just could not get beyond the grief that he felt for the loss of his long-term partner. Although he felt sexual desires and he thought he would like to develop a new relationship, Dave found himself unable to approach women, because he could not stop remembering and reliving what it had been like to make love to his wife.

Over time Dave revealed to me that toward the end of his marriage he had begun to experience occasional erectile dysfunction. This had not been much of a problem when his wife was alive, because she was a caring and sensitive lover, and together they had developed extensive forms of foreplay to help him achieve erections and enable them to have mutually satisfying sexual relations. However, now that his wife was gone, performance anxiety and the fear of impotence became overwhelming for Dave. In response to this anxiety, Dave had been using his prolonged grieving and his inability to get his wife out of his mind to prevent him from becoming close to another woman, thereby effectively eliminating the possibility of having sex and therefore the possibility of embarrassing himself by failing to perform.

Dave needed to be reassured that some loss of sexual prowess was not uncommon among men over 60 and that this issue could be dealt with in a number of different ways, including the use of drugs like Viagra. He also needed to be reassured that the women with whom he would socialize at this point in his life would probably not expect him to perform like a 20-year-old, and would be likely to be understanding and ready to take things slowly.

Another patient of mine who had lost his wife of many years had a different issue. Steve came into my office complaining that "I miss sex." Steve did not have a problem with meeting women or with impotence. In fact, after his wife died he had taken up gambling, and he met quite a few women at the casinos and clubs where he gambled. Steve's problem was that he considered himself to be a great lover and a master of seduction, and during his marriage his wife had always allowed Steve to play out this role. She would feign indifference to his advances at first but then allow herself to be seduced. This was a major turn on for Steve. It gave him a sense of control and made him feel powerful.

Now that his wife was gone, however, the problem for Steve was that the women he met most often did not require seduction. In fact, the women often initiated sexual talk and sexual activity. This made Steve feel out of control. In fact, Steve said that when a woman did not require seducing, it made him feel as if he had "lost [his] manhood." He was unable to just relax and enjoy the sex. In treatment, Steve eventually became conscious of an unresolved conflict that he had had with his very controlling mother. This was the source of his need to orchestrate and control his sexual encounters. Meeting a loving wife who indulged this need provided a 30-year accommodation to Steve's need to be in control. When his wife died, the neurotic side of this need rose to the surface and needed to be worked through, in order for Steve to function in the world in which he found himself after this accommodation ended.

Keep the Testosterone Levels Up

The alternative approach to sex after 60 is to refuse to accept any message that you may receive from your body indicating that sex is no longer a priority. This line of thinking emphasizes that sex is not only enjoyable but also good for you. Therefore the wisest course of action is to do what is necessary to make sure that you maintain your interest in having sex and your ability to have sex. Since the loss of sex drive in men over 60 is associated most strongly with lower production of testosterone, this approach emphasizes dietary and exercise strategies and the use of hormone replacement therapy in order to maintain the levels of testosterone in the blood that you had when you were younger.

   This approach is typified by the work of Shippen and Fryer, who argued
that men undergo a "male menopause" (or andropause) as the production of
testosterone gradually decreases.[11] These authors suggested that many people
do not accept the idea of male menopause, because the hormonal changes that
tend to occur in men are much more gradual than the corresponding changes
that occur in women during menopause. Whereas women's estrogen and progesterone levels fall quite rapidly at menopause, men's testosterone levels tend
to fall off slowly and steadily, decade by decade. Shippen and Fryer described
the female menopause as "virtually a two- or three-year hurricane that they
profoundly wish would go away."[12] In contrast, menopause in men "creeps in
upon them stealthily, until they reach a point where they can't help noticing
their muscles shrinking, their energy withering, their self-confidence crum-
bling, and their virility taking a tumble."[13] Shippen and Fryer noted that all
men are different, and there are some men whose testosterone levels stay at or
near youthful levels right into old age. These men tend to be the healthiest and
most vital individuals among men over 60. Shippen and Fryer therefore argued
that testosterone is one of the secrets of vitality among aging men.
   Shippen and Fryer also emphasized that the lowering of testosterone levels
in the blood is associated not only with loss of libido, but with other conditions that sap our strength and energy and give rise to a depressive change in
personality. This is because testosterone is more than just a sex hormone. It
is involved in the manufacture of the protein that is needed to form muscle.
It is also important in strengthening bones. It improves the body's ability to
use oxygen throughout the body, which results in greater energy. Testosterone
also helps to control blood sugar levels and to regulate cholesterol levels in the
blood. It helps with mental concentration, improves one's mood, and helps
to protect us from Alzheimer's disease. For all these reasons, these authors
recommended that as we age we should be mindful of the symptoms of low
testosterone levels, and they suggested that we should test for blood hormone
levels regularly.
   This testing involves measuring both the level of testosterone in the blood
and the level of estrogen in the blood, because as we age testosterone production tends to fall off, while the level of estrogen in the blood tends to increase.
Moreover, the symptoms of male menopause can result from either a reduction
in the overall level of testosterone in the blood, or from a shift in the ratio of
testosterone to estrogen in the blood. In young men, a testosterone to estrogen ratio of 50 to 1 is common, but in a man over 60 this ratio may well fall
to 7 or 8 to 1. Among the factors associated with increased levels of estrogen
in the blood in older men are: (1) age-related increases in the production of
aromatase, a substance that converts testosterone to estrogen; (2) impaired liver
functioning, which limits the ability of the liver to excrete excess estrogen from
the body; (3) zinc deficiency, since zinc inhibits levels of aromatase; (4) being

significantly overweight, since fat cells tend to store aromatase; (5) heavy use of alcohol, as the ingestion of alcohol tends to increase the level of estrogen in the blood; and (6) the use of certain prescription drugs, such as the diuretics used to control high blood pressure, since these drugs remove zinc from the body.

If testing reveals low testosterone levels or a low testosterone to estrogen ratio in the blood, Shippen and Fryer recommended that the patient first undertake the following steps: (1) begin taking supplemental zinc (approximately 50 mg twice a day); (2) get on a good diet and lose weight; (3) cut back on or eliminate alcohol intake; (4) consume soy protein, since soy protein contains isoflavons, which compete with estrogen for receptor sites in your body and stimulate the liver to excrete excess estrogen; and (5) check with your physician to find out if any prescription drugs that you may be taking tend to decrease testosterone production or increase estrogen production. If there are, try to find substitute medications that will have the desired positive effects without the side effect of reducing testosterone levels.

If these steps fail to restore normal testosterone levels and a normal testosterone to estrogen ratio, then it is likely that you have developed actual testicular incapacity, which is the inability of the testicles to produce sufficient quantities of the male hormone, no matter how much they are stimulated by the gonadotrophins released by the pituitary. At this point many experts argue that it is necessary to employ actual hormone replacement therapy in the form of injections, lozenges, skin patches, gels and creams, or pellets. The advocates of testosterone replacement therapy for men have cited research indicating that testosterone therapy may be beneficial for older men. There is evidence suggesting that testosterone replacement therapy may produce not only positive changes in sexual function but also improvements in body composition (e.g., muscle mass vs. fat ratio), increased strength, reductions in fatigue, improvements in mood, and increased bone density.[14]

As the evidence of the efficacy of testosterone replacement therapy has grown, members of the medical profession and medical professionals have become more aware of the potential benefits of hormone replacement therapy for men, and this has resulted in a substantial increase in the use of testosterone replacement therapy over the past decade. Rose reported that in 2002 more than 800,000 individuals had prescriptions for hormone supplements, an increase of 29 percent over the previous year. These patients were primarily men, and they included substantial proportions of men both under 60 and over 60 years of age.[15] The Institute of Medicine of the National Academies reported in 2004 that an analysis of U.S. census data revealed that the use of testosterone products among men over the age of 65 increased from 4.7 per thousand in 2001 to 5.6 per thousand in 2002, an increase of 19 percent.[16]

On the other hand, the Institute of Medicine of the National Academies has concluded that more research is required before we can be certain that testosterone replacement therapy reliably produces all of the positive outcomes that have been attributed to it. Moreover, some investigators have warned of potential adverse effects, including obstructive sleep apnea, enlargement of the prostate, and possibly prostate cancer. However, the evidence suggesting the relationship between testosterone replacement and these conditions is both weak and inconsistent.[17] Shippen and Fryer reviewed the research literature on the relationship between testosterone levels and prostate disease, and they concluded that "most current medical studies show a poor correlation between testosterone levels and prostate disease of any kind."[18]

On balance, it would seem that the argument for the use of testosterone replacement therapy as men grow older is becoming more widely accepted, and I would be remiss if I did not mention this option as something for you to consider if you are feeling discontented with your sex life, your mood, or your stamina. I use this course of therapy on a daily basis, and I also experience a strong cognitive benefit. I am tested regularly for any negative side effects, and I have great faith in the efficacy of this approach. However, both the initial decision to undertake such treatment and subsequent decisions regarding dosage, mode of administration, and the use of complementary treatments should be made in close consultation with a physician who is knowledgeable about male menopause and hormone replacement therapies. If you are not confident that your regular physician is sufficiently well-informed in this area, I would strongly advise you to see a urologist.

ERECTILE DYSFUNCTION

Erectile Dysfunction Defined

Erectile dysfunction (ED) is distinct from the loss of interest in sexual relations that characterizes male menopause. In erectile dysfunction, we feel like having sex, but we cannot. Erectile dysfunction is defined by the urology channel Web site as "the inability of a man to achieve or maintain an erection sufficient for his sexual needs or the needs of his partner."[19] Most men experience ED at some point in their lifetime, usually by the age of 40. It is usually transient, and an occasional occurrence generally has no serious negative psychological effect. However, some men experience chronic ED, either in the form of complete inability to achieve an erection, or in the form of only partial or brief erections. It has been estimated the 22 men out of every 1,000 men in the United States seek treatment for ED in any given year.[20]

Frequent ED can cause emotional and relationship problems, and it often results in diminished self-esteem. Sexual performance is often quite important to a man's self-esteem, so experiencing ED can not only mess up your sex life but also deflate your whole sense of personal identity and self worth. Often men with ED become unsure of themselves. They may avoid intimate situations with their partner so as to avoid the embarrassment of not being able to perform. However, avoidance behavior of this type may make your partner feel that you no longer love her or him, or that your partner is undesirable. Sometimes it makes partners wonder whether their men are having affairs. It may be very difficult to discuss ED with your partner, but you really need to let your partner know that this is the problem. After all, the problem affects your partner as much as it does you. Most people are extremely understanding and supportive when their partner has ED. Often the two of you will need to work together to respond to the problem.

In any case, it would be a tragedy if feelings of embarrassment prevented you from disclosing the problem to your partner and seeking appropriate treatment. In most cases the problem is physical in nature, and in almost every case it can be treated successfully. However, if you remain silent due to embarrassment, you will surely generate feelings of inadequacy and humiliation on the part of both you and your partner, and you will likely promote tension and distance between you. This can result in the development of a vicious cycle where physical problems become compounded by interpersonal stresses.

The urology channel Web site emphasizes that ED has many causes, most of which are treatable. This Web site also stresses that ED is not an inevitable consequence of aging.

The Etiology of Erectile Dysfunction

On the other hand, according to the Mayo Clinic Web site, ED is more common among men over 65 than among younger men.[21] It has been estimated that persistent ED affects approximately 5 percent of men in their 40s and approximately 15 to 25 percent of men by the age of 65. In order to understand why ED can occur in men of any age but is more common among older men, we must recognize that there are many causes of ED, some of which are age-related, and some of which are not. Nonphysical issues, such as psychological problems or negative feelings regarding your partner, and physical issues can both cause ED. Psychological causes include stress, anxiety, depression and/ or fatigue. Negative feelings toward your sexual partner may include anger or resentment over almost any relationship issue, from being a slob to spending too much money to disagreements regarding the raising of children.

There are also a broad range of physical problems that may contribute to ED, including: (1) nerve damage resulting from longstanding diabetes; (2) cardiovascular disorders, which can interfere with the blood supply to the pelvic region and to the penis; (3) the effects of some prescription medications, such as antidepressants, antihistamines, tranquilizers and sleeping aids, and medications used to treat high blood pressure, pain, and prostate cancer; (4) chronic use of alcohol, marijuana, or other recreational drugs; (5) diseases that affect the nervous system, including epilepsy, stroke, and multiple sclerosis; (6) surgery or traumatic injury that damages the nerves which control erections, including damage that occurs during surgery to treat bladder, rectal, or prostate cancer; and (7) hormonal disorders, including low testosterone level.[22]

Hormonal disorders has been generally considered to be a cause of ED in only a rather small percentage of ED cases. For example, the urology channel Web site states that "hormone disorders account for fewer than 5 percent of cases of impotence."[23] This is why I emphasized the distinction between ED, which involves wanting to have sexual relations but being unable to do so because of a failure to achieve or maintain an erection, and the loss of interest in sex that seems to accompany male menopause. On the other hand, however, Shippen and Fryer and the other clinicians and researchers who have advocated testosterone replacement therapy as a generally good thing would tend to give greater emphasis to the hormonal etiology of ED and to the power of hormone replacement therapy to relieve the problem.

Screening and Diagnosis of Erectile Dysfunction

Because ED can affect men at various ages and because there are a broad range of different possible contributing factors, men who are less than completely satisfied with their sexual performance should see a physician to determine the underlying cause of the ED problem and obtain recommendations regarding appropriate treatments. Men tend to view ED as a sign of personal inadequacy, weakness, or lack of virility, and they are often hesitant to report the problem to their doctor. But it is important to overcome any embarrassment that you may feel in this regard, because your doctor has many tools at his or her disposal to treat the condition successfully. Keep in mind that ED is a common problem, so you need not feel stigmatized. There also seems to be more and more public acceptance of the problem and more and more acceptance of seeking out solutions to the problem. This is clear from the many public personalities who have gone on television to promote the use of various pharmaceutical treatments for ED.

In assessing ED, your physician will probably begin by asking you questions about when and under what circumstances the condition developed. He or she will also ask questions about any physical conditions that you may have that could contribute to ED, as well as questions about any medications that you may be taking. In all likelihood your physician will order blood tests to screen for hormone levels and other potential problems, such as diabetes. All these initial steps are aimed at determining the etiology of the problem. Your physician will be attempting to determine if there is a physical cause for the problem, a psychological or emotional cause, or a combination of factors.

In some instances your physician might want to order one or more specialized tests. These include ultrasound examination to determine the adequacy of blood flow to the penis, a neurological examination to determine if your genital area has normal sensation, and/or cavernoscopy. The cavernoscopy is a test that measures vascular pressure in the corpora cavernosa, which are the chambers in the penis that become engorged with blood when we have an erection. If your doctor suspects that your ED issue may be more psychological than physical, he or she may ask you questions about whether you have erections during masturbation, with your partner, in the presence of other sexual stimuli (e.g., when you see a photo of an attractive woman), or when you sleep. Men typically have erections while they sleep that they are not necessarily aware of. For this reason, your doctor may ask you to wrap a special tape around your penis when you go to sleep. This tape will separate if you have an erection during the night. This result would suggest that the issue might not be physical but rather psychological in nature.

Treatments for ED

There are many treatments for ED. Which treatment or combination of treatments your doctor will recommend will obviously depend on the suspected etiology of the condition. If it seems that the problem is primarily psychological in nature, then your doctor might recommend that you begin some form of counseling. This could take the form of individual counseling, if it seems that the issue may be overwork, stress, or depression. It could also take the form of couples counseling, if it appears that there are underlying issues in your relationship that cause anger or resentment and leave you feeling ambivalent with respect to your partner. Your doctor might also recommend treatment by a professional who specializes in sex therapy, who can work with your and your partner to overcome inhibitions and/or expectations of impotence that may have arisen as the problem developed. Many men are reluctant to go to a sex therapist or to discuss issues of a sexual performance and behavior. But keep in mind that the folks who do this for a living are quite used to their patients' sensitivities and generally quite good at overcoming them.

If your problem appears to be physical in nature, the possible treatments include oral medications, hormonal therapy, penile injections, urethral suppositories, the use of vacuum devices, and surgical procedures. These are considered below.

Viagra, Levitra, and Cialis

These oral medications are selective enzyme inhibitors. They are most often used to improve partial erections and to increase the duration of erections. They do this by inhibiting an enzyme that facilitates the reduction of erections. In addition, these drugs increase blood levels of the chemical cyclic guanosine monophosphate (cGMP) which causes the smooth muscles of the penis to relax, enabling blood to flow into the penis to achieve erection.[24]

Although the three drugs all work in a similar manner, there are some differences among them. Viagra is absorbed and processed quite rapidly, and it is generally taken 30 minutes to an hour before intercourse. Although results vary somewhat based on the specific cause of the erectile dysfunction, most studies show that the medication produces satisfactory results in about 75 percent of those who use it. It has been shown to be effective with the majority of men whose ED is associated with diabetes (57%), spinal cord injury (83%), and radical prostectomy (43%). Levitra also works quickly and has been shown to improve sexual function in most men the first time they take it. Levitra has been shown to be effective in men of all ages. Cialis stays in the body longer than Viagra or Levitra. It promotes erection within 30 minutes of ingestion, but it continues to enhance the body's ability to achieve erection for up to 36 hours.

These drugs do have some side effects that you should know about. They sometimes cause headache, reddening of the face and neck, indigestion, and nasal congestion. In addition, Cialis may cause muscle aches and/or back pain, but these problems generally subside within 48 hours of ingestion.

Furthermore, not everyone can use these selective enzyme inhibitors. Men who are taking nitrate drugs that are used to treat chest pain and men who are taking alpha-blockers that are used to treat high blood pressure and benign prostatic hyperplasia should not use these drugs. Men who have had a heart attack within the past six months should not use these drugs. In addition, these drugs should not be used by men with medical problems that make sexual activity inadvisable. These conditions include uncontrolled high blood pressure, liver disease, and unstable angina. Finally, patients with kidney or liver disorders should use these drugs sparingly. Of course, these are all prescription medications, and your doctor should be aware of any contraindicating conditions.

Hormone Therapy

As I noted above, most specialists regard low testosterone levels or a low testosterone to estrogen ratio as a primary cause of erectile dysfunction in a relatively small proportion of the men who have ED. However, it is important to note here that the proportion may well be higher among men who have passed the age of 60 than among younger men. In addition, while low testosterone may not be the primary cause of your ED, it may nevertheless be a contributing factor. Therefore if you have ED, you should make sure that your doctor does the appropriate blood tests. If you find that your testosterone level is low or that your testosterone to estrogen ratio is low, then you would be well advised to undertake the steps outlined earlier in this chapter to try to rectify this hormonal deficit.

Please keep in mind that efforts to restore adequate testosterone levels in no way preclude the use of other approaches to the treatment of ED. The primary point that I am attempting to make here is that traditional treatment for ED has tended to regard hormone therapy as appropriate for only a very small proportion of the patients. In fact, recent evidence suggests that the application may well be broader. At any rate, you should be certain to discuss this issue with your doctor.

Other Treatments

If oral medication and/or hormone treatment do not produce satisfactory results, there are other treatments available. Some men find that self-injection of prostaglandin (Caverject, Edex) or phentolamine (Regitine) directly into the side of the penis and into the corpus cavernosum produces results similar to those of Viagra. These substances cause the smooth muscle in the corpus cavernosum to relax, and they cause vascular dilation. These substances have been shown to produce erections in 80 percent of the men who inject them. The erection begins in 5 to 15 minute following the injection, and it typically lasts for 30 minutes to several hours. The needle used is short and very fine, so there is little or no pain. It is recommended that these injections not be used more than once every four to seven days. There is some risk of priapism, which is an erection that lasts for more than six hours and requires medical relief.

It is also possible to use a urethral suppository containing prostaglandin (aprostadil). This method is known as MUSE, which stands for Medicated Urethral System for Erections. The suppository is inserted into the urethra through the opening of the penis by the patient using a hand-held delivery device. This method is well-tolerated and effective in approximately 60 percent of patients.

In addition to the use of medications, a vacuum device may be used to create an erection manually. In this method the penis is inserted into a plastic tube in which a vacuum is created. This draws blood into the penis creating an erection. Then the penis is removed from the tube and a soft rubber ring is placed around the base of the penis to keep the blood in and maintain the erection. This ring can be left in place for up to a half hour. This method tends to improve erections regardless of the cause of ED.

Finally, there are surgical treatments for ED. Penile implants may be used to create an erection, and in some cases men benefit from vascular reconstructive surgery to improve the flow of blood to the penis. These treatments are specific to particular physical problems and should be discussed with your physician if relevant.

The Age of Viagra

In an age when so many men with ED can be treated conveniently with Viagra or the other selective enzyme inhibitors, there appears to be a greater expectation on the part of our partners that we should continue to be interested in and capable of sexual activity well after our sixtieth year. This is important for us to appreciate, because the age of Viagra has perhaps rendered somewhat less tenable the position that we should simply "listen to our bodies" and gradually decrease our sexual activity if we feel no particular impetus to have sex. This may be very well and good for you, but if you have a wife or partner with whom you have been having sex for a good long while, you really need to check with her to find out the status of her sexual needs. If your partner still needs to have sexual intercourse, you may well need to ignore the signals that your body is sending you to shut down and start engaging in efforts to avoid shutting down. Whether these efforts involve Viagra or whether they involve hormone replacement therapy is a matter to be discussed with your partner and with your physician.

The point that I am trying to make here is that it is critical that we give consideration to the needs of our partners as well as ourselves in making these adjustments.

THE IMPACT OF AGING ON OUR PARTNERS

Finally, assuming that we are going to continue to engage in sexual activity as we move into and beyond the seventh decade of life, we are going to need to know something about the effect of aging on our spouse. Up to this point I have only talked about the effect of aging on the male sexual response, but it is important that we men be aware of the changes that affect our partners.

Just as men tend to experience age-related physical changes that affect our desire engage in sexual activity and our ability to do so, so do women. As the production of female sex hormones (estrogen and progesterone) declines, women undergo many internal and external changes that impact sexual activity. These changes were summarized by Masters and Johnson as follows: (1) older women take a longer time to respond to sexual stimuli than younger women; (2) lubrication takes longer and is generally less effective in older women than in younger women; (3) the vagina has reduced elasticity and expansive qualities, so it is more easily irritated; (4) the clitoris is reduced in size in older women, although it remains responsive to stimulation; and (5) orgasms are typically less intense and of shorter duration in older women than in younger women.

All of these changes mean that we men must *slow down*. The loving foreplay and the tender consideration that women want and need throughout the course of their sexual lives become even more critical as we and our partners age. We need to take things slowly. We need to take time to make love to our partners. We need to cuddle and kiss. If you and she like oral sex, now is the time to do it more. Now is also the time to give long full body massages and to use lotions and lubricants. You may very well find out that adapting your sex life in this way results in more satisfying sex rather than less satisfying sex.

Chapter Eight

THE MATTER OF ATTITUDE: OPTIMISM AFTER 60

In the last three chapters I have considered a number of circumstances associated with aging that can legitimately be viewed as stressful. None of us really looks forward to the biological changes that we typically associate with aging—the increasingly graying hair, the expanding waistline, the loss of visual acuity and auditory sensitivity, the sore muscles and joint pains, the loss of strength and dexterity. I have considered many of the steps that we can take to remain fit and healthy as we grow older, but sooner or later some of these biological changes will inevitably kick in, and we will not be able to do as much as easily as we have in the past.

I have also considered a number of sources of stress associated with changes in our social roles that occur as we grow older. Not only are our children grown up but the grandkids may well be grown up as well. Therefore, we are not needed by our families as much as we used to be. In addition, it may also seem that we are not needed as much by society as we used to be. We may be forced to retire from rewarding careers that have previously made us feel important or at least useful. If we are not forced to retire, we may be expected to assume a less prominent role at work. We may also worry about competition from a younger employee whom we expect to one day take over our job functions.

Even our hobbies may become a source of stress. Unavoidable physical limitations may hinder our ability to pursue our favorite long-time leisure interests. The inability to pursue these interests may have the additional effect of limiting our social interactions with peers who still engage in these activities. In previous chapters I have considered some of the steps that we can take to minimize the impact of these stressors, and in subsequent chapters I will consider other strategies that we can use to remain active, relevant, and productive.

But here I want to discuss another aspect of the process of coping with our advancing age. This is the question of *attitude,* the question of how we choose to subjectively interpret significant age-related challenges as they arise in our lives. The point here is that our attitude toward aging and age-related stresses may be even more important to our happiness after 60 than the changes themselves. Our attitude will determine whether we respond to age-related stresses by rolling over, giving in, and succumbing to depression, or whether we continue to take steps to maximize our health and our involvement in life. Our attitude will also determine whether we interpret age-related changes as an indication of personal irrelevance and worthlessness, or simply an indication that we must find new paths to fulfillment.

Let's consider briefly the importance of attitude in connection with the age-related physical and social changes I referred to above. With respect to physical changes, I want to make the point that our objective health is certainly important, but our subjective attitude toward our health and our concomitant ability to continue to engage in diverse activities is just as important. One man with a touch of arthritis may respond by curtailing his physical activity, while another may choose to continue to be active despite the occasional pain. The man who continues to be active does two things: (1) He still derives the pleasure associated with the activity; and (2) he most likely slows down the progression of the arthritis, which in turn enables him to continue this pleasurable activity even longer. This man will quite likely be satisfied with his life, even though he occasionally moans and groans about his sore joints.

Attitude is also critical with respect to the impact of changes in social, occupational, and leisure roles. The social roles we actually fulfill are important, but our attitude toward these roles and our capacity to adapt is even more important. One man whose children and grandchildren have all grown up and moved away dwells on his loneliness and wishes that some one would pay attention to him. He is miserable. Another goes out and becomes a volunteer reading tutor or a big brother or does hospital visits. He is feels useful, and he also enjoys meaningful social contact. One man forced into retirement from his lifetime profession simply sits around and does nothing. He is waiting to die. But another man forced into retirement becomes involved in another satisfying occupational role, goes back to school, or pursues an interesting hobby. Here again, the man who chooses to adapt not only derives satisfaction from the new activity but also opens up additional opportunities for productive and satisfying activities by meeting new people and letting them know that he is ready and able. Remember, the seventh decade of life is a time to open up new chapters in life, not a time to close the book.

CHOOSE OPTIMISM

The importance of how we choose to look at our lives has been pointed out by Martin Seligman in his book, *Learned Optimism*.[1] This book was written for people in general, not just for those of us approaching or past 60. However, Seligman's observations are especially relevant for men over 60 because Seligman was concerned primarily with teaching us how to respond to stress. Well, we have seen that we men over 60 do tend to experience a great many stressors as we grow older, and we have also seen that the manner in which we respond to these stressors will largely determine our psychological adjustment and our satisfaction with life. Therefore Seligman's ideas regarding the importance of maintaining an optimistic outlook are particularly important for us. At this point I would like to tell you a bit about Seligman's theory and then to encourage you to adopt the techniques that he recommends to maintain an optimistic outlook in the face of the stresses we experience.

HOW DO YOU EXPLAIN NEGATIVE EVENTS?

A key concept of Seligman's theory is that of "explanatory style." This term refers to the manner in which we explain to ourselves why events happen. Some of us have a pessimistic explanatory style, and others have a more optimistic explanatory style. According to Seligman, those of us who have a pessimistic explanatory style tend to view any negative life events that befall us as (1) permanent, (2) universal, and (3) internal. In contrast, those of us who have an optimistic explanatory style tend to view such events as (1) temporary, (2) specific, and (3) external. To explain these terms, I ask you to consider a 65-year-old man who has just experienced a negative life event. Although he greatly enjoys his work, he has been forced to retire due to a company policy establishing a mandatory retirement age.

A man with a pessimistic explanatory style would tend to interpret this event as *permanent*. He would tend to assume that since he has been forced into retirement and is now unemployed, there is probably very little chance that he would find new employment. He would assume that this is how it will be for the rest of his life. In contrast, a man with an optimistic explanatory style would tend to assume that his unemployment is *temporary*. He would assume that there are other employment options available, and as a result he would probably begin looking for new work or possibly go back to school.

In addition, a man with a pessimistic explanatory style would also tend to view his forced retirement as *universal*. He would tend to assume that if his company has this policy, then other companies in the same or similar fields probably have the same policy. Therefore, it would probably make little sense to him to begin a job search with other companies. In contrast, a man with an optimistic explanatory style would not assume that this mandatory retirement policy is universal. Instead, he would probably assume that the policy is *specific* to his firm. Therefore, he would make inquiries at other companies regarding the possibility of finding a new job. If he were not immediately successful in finding a new position, he might hire himself out as a consultant.

Finally, a man with a pessimistic explanatory style would tend to personalize the loss of his job. He would interpret his mandatory retirement as reflecting something *internal,* some personal characteristic or characteristics that really made him a nonproductive employee. Although he would recognize that the policy applied to all those employees who were reaching the age of 65, he would tend to assume that there is really something about being 65 that made him less valuable to the company, thereby justifying the policy of mandatory retirement. In contrast, a man with an optimistic explanatory style would tend to not interpret the company policy as reflecting any actual shortcoming of his own. He would tend to explain the event in one of two ways. He might assume that the company is simply wrong in establishing this policy, and that workers over the age of 65 are in reality at least as valuable as those under 65. Alternatively, he might assume that possibly some workers over 65 should retire, but he himself does not fall into this group. With either explanation, he would interpret the mandatory retirement as an event *external* to himself. He would not personalize the event. He would not interpret the event as indicating that he is washed up, and he would feel free to seek employment elsewhere. In fact, the man with the optimistic outlook would probably continue to seek new employment even if he finds that all the other companies in this field have similar mandatory retirement policies. Then he would know that he is not likely to be hired in the same field, but he would feel free to look into other industries that do not have mandatory retirement policies. If necessary, the optimist might even consider going into business for himself.

Seligman's research suggests that individuals with optimistic explanatory styles are less likely to get depressed than those with pessimistic explanatory styles. He also found that optimists tend to achieve more than pessimists, and that optimists tend to be healthier than pessimists, and that optimists manifest greater satisfaction with life than pessimists.[2] Again, he came to these conclusions with respect to people of both genders and all ages, but I maintain that these conclusions are particularly relevant to men passing the age of 60.

WHICH STYLE DO YOU HAVE?

Some of us are naturally optimistic, and others are naturally pessimistic. Many of you who are reading this book will have an optimistic frame of reference already. After all, if you went out to a bookstore or went online to find a book that would help you to get the most out of your life after the age of 60, that action in and of itself implies that you are at least somewhat oriented toward taking positive action aimed at improving your life. Much of the material that I have discussed in the book up to this point has been aimed at confirming the view that the future is bright. By reading this far you have already given yourself a good deal of information supporting the view that life after 60 can be a healthy, happy, and productive period. Furthermore, in the remainder of the book I hope to give you a good deal of advice regarding steps you can take to maximize your happiness with respect to a broad series of issues that many of us confront as we grow older.

On the other hand, some of you who are reading this book may have a more pessimistic view of life. Perhaps you have been feeling discontented and depressed, dreading the prospect of aging, yet you have not been doing anything significant to improve your health and happiness. Maybe you are one of those people who tend to accept life's adversities without doing everything in your power to minimize their impact. You may even have rationalized that accepting adversity is a sign of strength or stoicism. Maybe you didn't go out and get this book because you wanted a kick start on the road to greater happiness. Maybe you came across this book by accident, or maybe a friend gave it to you because he or she thought that you needed an attitude adjustment.

In any case, give some thought to the question of whether you are an optimist or a pessimist. If you think that you could have a better attitude toward achieving happiness as you move beyond 60, there are things that you can do to develop a more optimistic outlook.

DEVELOPING AN OPTIMISTIC EXPLANATORY STYLE

Seligman presented a series of specific techniques that we can use to cultivate an optimistic explanatory style. For example, he suggested that we learn to identify any pessimistic attributions that we assign to the adversities that befall us and that we think through the negative consequences of these pessimistic attributions. To this end, he suggested that we keep written records of the adversities that confront us and how we explained them to ourselves.

Keep Adversity Records

To sharpen the ability to identify pessimistic explanations, Seligman recommended that we *record* adversities as they occur and jot down our attributions and the consequences of these attributions. For example, if your physician tells you that you are overweight, you might say to yourself, "Well, I'm older now and my metabolism has changed." This is a pessimistic explanation that implies that your overweight status is permanent (since you will not be getting younger), and beyond your control (since it completely ignores specific steps that you could take to deal with the situation, like changing your diet and your exercise habits). Such a pessimistic explanation would most likely lead you to assume that there is nothing you can do about your weight and that you'll just have to live with it. As a consequence, you will not start a diet or exercise program aimed at losing weight. As a consequence of failing to change your diet and exercise, you will most likely remain overweight. As consequence of remaining overweight, you may well begin to feel inferior and unattractive, and you may feel that you must avoid potentially satisfying activities that require you to wear a bathing suit or exert yourself physically. In the end, all these outcomes may contribute to your feeling dissatisfied, unhappy, and depressed.

Seligman described the process of recording adversities, your beliefs regarding these adversities, and the consequences of your beliefs as "The ABCs," where the three initials stand for adversity, beliefs, and consequences.

The utility of keeping an ABC record is that by noting each adversity, your explanation for the adversity, and the consequences of this explanation, you will: (1) make the problem clear; (2) alert yourself to the possibility that you are using pessimistic explanations for the problem, and (3) come to understand that these pessimistic explanations may be causing you to respond to the adversity in an ineffective manner. Therefore the recording process will also make it clear to you that you need to substitute optimistic explanations for the pessimistic explanations that you may have been employing. Then you can instruct yourself to substitute more optimistic explanations for each adverse event, such as, "I have been eating too much and not exercising enough, and I since I can control these behaviors I can fix the problem of being overweight."

Learn to Argue with Yourself

Seligman pointed out that sometimes you may have to argue with yourself to dispute a pessimistic negative explanation for a stressful event and to substitute an optimistic explanation that implies a positive behavioral response. If your doctor tells you that you are overweight and your first response is to blame unavoidable changes in your metabolism, you may need to convince yourself that this is not a useful explanation. Of course, if you are a natural optimist you may not need to do this. But if you have any tendency toward a pessimistic explanatory style, you will probably need to learn how to convince yourself that it makes much more sense to view problems in terms of how much you can do to minimize their impact, rather than in terms of how unavoidable they are, or how badly they are likely to disrupt your plans and how unhappy you are going to be because of them.

Seligman instructed us that learning to argue with ourselves involves learning to routinely employ some very specific skills to our pessimistic explanations of each new adversity. These skills include: (1) *gathering evidence* to dispute pessimistic explanations of adversity and pessimistic beliefs regarding your ability to minimize or overcome adversity; (2) *developing alternative beliefs* to take the place of the pessimistic explanations; (3) *decatastrophizing* unavoidable negative consequences of adversity; and (4) *assessing the utility of pessimistic explanations* of adversity, regardless of the degree of credibility of such explanations. Let's consider each of these techniques.

Gathering Evidence to the Contrary

According to Seligman, the most convincing technique we can use to dispute a pessimistic explanation of an adverse event is to demonstrate that the belief is factually incorrect. Seligman also pointed out that it is often quite easy to muster factual evidence contrary to such negative explanations since a pessimistic individual tends to overreact to an adversity, interpreting the event in the most negative terms possible. Therefore, when you realize that you have attributed your weight gain to the unavoidable effects of aging on your metabolism, you need to make a conscious effort to determine whether this explanation is reasonable. You already know that it is not helpful because it justifies your inaction. But now you need to convince yourself that it is not true. So make it your job to get the information you need to reject this pessimistic explanation in favor of a more optimistic one.

Of course, reading books like this one is a step in the right direction. If you have read the previous chapters, you are already aware that we do not need to accept the fact that our metabolisms will slow as we get older and we will inevitably gain weight. As indicated in chapter 2, exercise can boost your metabolism. Diet also has an impact on metabolism. In my discussion of Syndrome X in chapter 3, I pointed out that reducing the consumption of alcohol and refined carbohydrates can help you to avoid the effects of the lower metabolism syndrome.

Beyond general efforts to learn more about aging, however, you need to inform yourself regarding each new adversity that comes along. When the doctor tells you that you are overweight, you can begin by asking him or her what you can do about it. You can follow up by going online when you get home and obtaining as much specific information as you can about aging and the metabolism. Even 10 minutes online will produce sufficient information to convince you that your pessimistic "aging metabolism" explanation is inaccurate.

Developing Alternative Explanations

The process of developing factual arguments against explanations of adversity that you have identified as pessimistic will also naturally lead you to develop alternative explanations. For example, when we research the topic of aging and the metabolism, the factual evidence that a sluggish metabolism is not a necessary concomitant of life after 60 consists largely of data to the contrary that suggest alternative explanations. The pessimistic explanation of the inevitably slowed metabolism explanation is belied by alternative evidence of the efficacy of exercise and diet in maintaining a healthy weight. Although this factual data is initially used to uncover and dispute the pessimistic explanation of the slowing metabolism, this data also constitutes the basis of an alternative set of beliefs that can be used to appraise the adverse event of being informed that you are overweight. Seligman is clear that it is very important for us to actually formulate and even record an alternative optimistic explanation for an adverse event that will take the place of the previous pessimistic explanation. Once you have clearly formulated the alternative beliefs, it will be easy for you to substitute them for the previous pessimistic explanation, should you ever find yourself thinking in that old pessimistic manner again. This is quite likely, because the attitudes we develop tend to become habitual, as do the explanations we assign to various adverse events in our lives. I frequently tell my patients that they should be mindful of their habits because your habits tend to become your behavior.

Decatastrophizing

Sometimes there are aspects of the stresses that we experience in connection with aging that are unambiguously negative, and there is no possibility of developing a totally optimistic set of beliefs surrounding the stresses. Let's say you have been having some problems with your vision and when you go for a check-up you are informed that you have pretty severe macular degeneration (SMD). As we have seen, this is a potentially serious problem that does not have an easy fix. You can use nutritional therapy and pharmacotherapy to delay the progression of the disease, and treatment may even result in the reversal of some vision loss. However, once SMD has progressed to a fairly advanced state, it is unlikely that your vision will be fully restored. This is indeed a source of stress since we rely heavily on vision to gather information about our surroundings and to go about our daily business.

Despite the fact that these circumstances would clearly comprise an adversity, you would still have it within your power to view the situation relatively more pessimistically or relatively more optimistically. The pessimist would tend to view the situation as a complete disaster. He might simply conclude that he will no longer be able to read, no longer be able to play golf, and no longer be able to drive. He would assume that the problem is going to radically alter his life, taking away most of the significant sources of joy that he has known. If he were to develop this most pessimistic set of beliefs, he would quite likely become fairly miserable in short order. However, the optimist would view the situation in less negative terms. He would acknowledge that he has permanent vision impairment, but he would focus on all the things that can be done to ameliorate this loss and maintain his ability to enjoy life. He would investigate the use of low vision devices that can enable him to continue to read. He would explore opportunities for individuals with limited vision to continue to play golf. He would find out what can be done in the way of glasses to allow him to continue to drive. If he learned that driving really was not feasible, he would explore alternative means of transportation.

In other words, when confronted with a truly negative event, you still have the option of viewing your situation in the most negative terms or in the most positive terms possible. Making a conscious choice to view the situation in the most positive terms possible will not only lift your spirits from the start, but it will also stimulate you to undertake positive coping behaviors that are likely to result in objective improvements in your situation. My late mother-in-law, a woman whose cup was always overflowing with optimism, used to say that "You've got to take the bitter with the better."

Evaluating the Utility of Your Explanations

Most important in the process of developing optimistic beliefs regarding adverse events is the idea that regardless of how difficult the situation may be, a more optimistic set of beliefs regarding the origin and likely consequences of the situation will be more useful than a pessimistic set of beliefs. In the case of the man who is told that he is overweight, there is an element of truth in the idea that our metabolism slows with age, and there is also much evidence that this reality does not preclude one from exercising and dieting to overcome the effects of one's slowing metabolism. Therefore the tasks of disputing pessimistic beliefs and developing optimistic alternatives can be a bit dicey. If you tend toward a more pessimistic outlook in general, you may be tempted at any point to give greater weight to the power of age-related changes in your metabolism, and less weight to the potential benefits of exercise and diet. In this situation, you can reinforce your motivation to view the situation from an optimistic perspective by simply asking yourself, "Which set of beliefs has the greatest potential utility?" If you have evidence supporting both pessimistic and an optimistic evaluations of your situation, the chances of adopting the optimistic view may well be increased if you recognize that choosing the optimistic explanation will be more likely to have positive outcomes than choosing the pessimistic explanation.

Of course, the most stubborn pessimists may argue that the evidence is the evidence, and it is less than fully honest to *choose* the more optimistic explanation of events, as opposed to the more pessimistic explanation, simply because the optimistic beliefs are likely to have greater utility. To this argument I respond by noting that subjectivity in our responses to the world is a key element of our personality and that the importance that we assign to different bits of evidence in any argument reflects who we are. I choose to be an optimist.

THE SUBJECTIVE ELEMENT

To illustrate the power and importance of the subjective element in determining our attitude toward life after 60, let's consider our attitudes toward our financial situation. Research has shown that our actual income level is important, but research also shows that whether or not we subjectively view our financial resources as adequate is even more important than the actual amount of money we have.[3]

Two men with exactly the same income may elect to view their situations in entirely different manners. One may choose to see his cup as half empty, beating up on himself because he has not achieved as much as he had hoped or as much as his friends or other members of his family. The other may choose to see his cup as half full, recognizing that he has what he needs and that his income is sufficient to enable him to participate in many satisfying and rewarding activities. These divergent views have nothing to do with whether he takes steps to increase his income. These differences reflect only his subjective evaluation of his situation. This is the difference between a man who has a houseful of material possessions but doesn't have the key to enjoying them, and the man who has far fewer possessions but an attitude that allows him to enjoy what he has.

ENHANCING WELL-BEING ACROSS OUR LIVES

This idea of maintaining an optimistic outlook and a perception that adversities can be confronted and overcome is a major theme that runs throughout the rest of this book. The chapters that follow provide guidelines regarding positive steps that we can take to deal with specific issues that often confront men who are moving past the age of 60. These include the question of religious involvement and spiritual development, the challenge of finding meaning in life as we grow older, and the question of how to handle such issues as retirement, dealing with adult children, grandparenting, and becoming caregivers. I also will also consider the approaches we can use to cope with specific problems that frequently impact men over 60, including substance use problems, addictions, differences with your spouse regarding your goals for the rest of your lives, losses and widowhood, remarriage, and age-related changes in lifestyle. In all cases the emphasis is on helping you to develop optimism, a sense of personal control, and a repertoire of effective response options.

Chapter Nine

RELIGION AND SPIRITUALITY

Leonard Rediscovers Religion

Leonard is 62. He retired from an executive position with a large corporation two years ago. His wife of 40 years passed away a year ago. Leonard is financially comfortable and in good health. He has four children and nine grandchildren who live nearby and visit him often. He likes to play golf and to fly fish, and he has a good number of friends with whom he shares these interests. He socializes regularly with members of his golf club. He describes himself as busy, highly satisfied with his life, and generally upbeat.

Just this year however, Leonard did something that surprised his friends and family. After nearly 50 years without setting foot in a church, he began attending church services each week. Leonard had discontinued attending church as a teenager, shortly after his confirmation. He had stopped attending church partly because he was simply "too busy," first with school and socializing, and then later with work and his family. However, he also acknowledged that there were aspects of the dogma of the Protestant denomination to which he belonged that he simply could not bring himself to believe, such as the biblical story of God's Creation of the world, the belief that Jesus was the Son of God, and the idea of a virgin birth.

Yet now, after so many years of comfortable uninvolvement, Leonard felt a strong impulse to reconnect with the church. He said that going to church made him feel "connected." He also embarked on an ambitious reading program that included the Bible (which he had never read cover to cover), as well as the works of a number of noted religious thinkers like C. S. Lewis, G. K. Chesterton, and Paul Tillich. Leonard had also begun psychotherapy.

When his family and friends asked Leonard about these incongruous new undertakings, he explained that in spite of his active and interesting lifestyle, sometimes late at night or early in the morning he found himself feeling lonely. At these times he became quite contemplative, and he had begun to ask himself questions that he had never considered before, perhaps because he never had the time to consider them before. He said that he found himself wondering whether his life has had any purpose. He asked himself what was the purpose of continuing to live now that his wife was gone and the children were all grown up and settled. He asked himself why he had outlived his wife and several of his good friends.

Leonard said that he wasn't sure why he turned to religion to address these questions. It just seemed natural to him. He said that his reading and introspection had not given him the answers to any of these questions but had made him much more comfortable with his uncertainties. He also said that with the perspective he had gained from 62 years of living, he no longer tended to view the doctrines of the church in such literal, black and white, "true or false" terms. He said that when he was a teenager, he could not bring himself to believe in miracles. Now, with the experience of a lifetime under his belt, he said that he sees miracles all around him every day.

WHY MANY MEN BECOME MORE SPIRITUAL AFTER 60

A good many of us have experiences similar to Leonard's during the years after 60. At this point in our lives, a number of factors come into play that foster the development of a more spiritual orientation toward life. Vaillant described some of these factors as follows:

> Aging slows us down and provides us time and peace to smell life's flowers. Aging simplifies our daily routine and facilitates the acceptance of things we cannot change. Aging banks our instinctual fires and increases our capacity to be internally quiet. Aging compels us to contemplate death and…focuses us toward becoming one with the ultimate ground of all being. Aging allows us to feel part of the ocean. The Hindu concept of life stages suggests that when we become grandparents, we should turn away from the world and take up spiritual interests. When devout Brahmins become grandfathers, they turn their worldly belongings over to their sons.[1]

In the case of Leonard, the need to address spiritual questions was fueled by an increase in the amount of time that he spent alone, due to his retirement from work and the death of his wife. The death of a spouse or the illnesses of close friends bring to the forefront of our consciousness the finite nature of life, and the heightened awareness of our own mortality leads many of us to ask whether our lives have had any purpose or meaning.

More than half a century ago, in his stage theory of human personality development across the life span, Erik Erikson suggested that the primary developmental challenge in the final stage of life was that of *ego integrity versus despair.*[2] Erikson defines ego integrity as pulling your life together, integrating the different parts of your life, and finding meaning in the whole life story. Those who achieve ego integrity are able to think back upon their lives with satisfaction. These individuals do not fear death but rather accept it as one of the many facets of our existence. Erikson suggests that despair develops among individuals who experience regret over unfulfilled and missed opportunities at a time when it is too late to begin again.

With the increase in life expectancy that we enjoy today, Erikson's formulation of ego integrity versus despair is in need of revision. Most of us now expect to live for a very long time after we pass the age of 60, so the achievement of ego integrity does not function primarily to prepare us to die but rather to prepare us to enjoy the considerable period of living that we still have ahead of us.[3] However, the finite nature of our life on earth remains a crucial factor motivating us to attempt to find meaning in our lives. Trafford summarized the paradox that we all face as we move past our sixtieth birthdays as follows: "In order to live fully in these extra years, you have to be ready to die."[4] Trafford explained:

> Certainly the urgency of death hovers over the bonus decades. Injuries occur and diseases come out of the blue, no matter how many miles you jogged or what food you ate or what books you read or how many people you loved. Still, the chances are you will survive an illness for many years. You may have a weak heart, a synthetic knee, a hearing aid. You may go for regular checkups to see if an artery has closed up or a cancer has come back. But you live…
>
> By this time, you've had little meetings with death—losses in health, setbacks in work, the end of relationships. You've experienced the deaths of loved ones—a parent, for example, or a close friend. You know that you are part of a long chain that stretches beyond time and place. But still, it is a sense of your own mortality that galvanizes your spiritual search.[5]

Note especially the last sentence in the passage from Trafford. It refers to the knowledge that you are "part of a long chain that stretches beyond time and place." Trafford stressed that recognizing how we fit into the universe is crucial to achieving ego integrity. She suggested that reviewing one's life, as we are apt to do when we finally have the time to do so, is an excellent way to achieve this recognition. Remembering those who came before us and those who will live on after us shows us how we are connected to the universe and where we fit in. Trafford suggested that discovering the meaning of our lives is "all about connections." Memories of loved ones who are older and those who are younger connect us with the time before us and the time ahead of us. These memories help us to see that we are part of an eternal human spiritual process, and it is in the knowledge of our connection to this transcendent process that we discover the meaning in our lives.

Of course, not every man passing 60 comes to question the meaning of his life, and not everyone experiences a need to find a spiritual connection with something that is universal. Some guys are perfectly happy working on their golf handicap, catching trout, and watching sporting events on TV. I am certainly not saying that anyone needs to "get religion" or be "born again" to be happy. But many of us do experience the need to ponder the meaning of our lives, and this need often expresses itself in religious involvement and/or efforts aimed at achieving spiritual development.

For this reason, if you should begin to wonder about the purpose of your life or your place in the cosmos, I urge you not to ignore these questions or push them aside in an effort not to "rock the boat." Instead, embrace your ponderings, and undertake whatever activities or explorations you may feel comfortable with to shed light on these questions. It is healthy for us as we enter our seventh decade of living to contemplate the course of our lives to this point and to review the things that we have done, the decisions we have made, and the relationships we developed.

This type of life review may lead you toward one or more of a whole range of different approaches to increasing your spiritual development and understanding. Some individuals find comfort in renewing or sustaining ongoing religious beliefs and observances. Other individuals are drawn to different forms of spiritual enlightenment or enrichment, such as meditation, yoga, or various forms of experiencing and communing with nature.

RELIGION AND SPIRITUALITY

Researchers have differentiated between religious social activities and personal spirituality. Religious social activities include attending religious services, participating in volunteer activities sponsored by or associated with your church or synagogue, and participating in social activities sponsored by the congregation. In contrast, personal spirituality is embodied in solitary activities such as praying, meditating, or bible reading, and by personal beliefs regarding the nature of God.[6] As you will learn later in this chapter, both extrinsic religious activity and intrinsic spiritual activity have been shown to be good for those who participate.

Unfortunately, there is a bit of a tendency on the part of some to regard religious activity as a developmentally less advanced undertaking than spirituality, and this bias has been reflected in both the professional and the popular literature on successful aging. For example, Vaillant writes:

> Religion involves creeds and catechisms. Spirituality involves feelings and experiences that transcend mere words. Religion is imitative and comes from without; religion is "so I've been taught." Spirituality comes from within; spirituality comes from "my strength, hope and experience." Religion is "left-brain"—it is rooted in words, sacred texts, and culture. Spirituality is "right-brain"; it transcends the boundaries of body, language, reason, and culture...
>
> Most religious beliefs involve dogma. Spiritual trust involves metaphor. So what is the difference between dogma and metaphor? Metaphors are open-ended and playful; dogma is rigid and serious. Metaphors mean "analogous to" and "as if"; dogma conveys "so I've been told" and "it's right there in the Bible (or in the Freud *Standard Edition*)." Metaphors allow the truth of our dreams to become clearer with

every retelling. In contrast, dogma may insist that heretics be executed. Metaphors add leaven to theory and to poetry, but dogma adds dead weight to Thomistic and Talmudic prose. Metaphors conceptualize; dogma enshrines. Dogma retards science; metaphors advance science. [7]

Vaillant also points out that developmental psychologists have determined that the cognitions of children evolve from concrete, literal operations into more complex, abstract, and metaphysical views of the universe. He equates religion with the concrete operations of children, and spirituality with the more advanced levels of cognitive development. He says that as children mature, they shift from blind obedience to the ten commandments based on obligation, judgment, and the threat of shame to "the more merciful and relativistic morality of the Golden Rule."[8]

To be fair, I should point out that Vaillant was quite aware that the distinctions he drew between religion and spirituality were perhaps "more black and white than they really are," and he acknowledges that "it is possible to be deeply religious [yet] very mature and to be 'spiritual' [yet] utterly self-absorbed."[9] Nonetheless, I believe that the bias against religion that is so widespread among academic and intellectual circles is unfortunate since it may inhibit our ability to act on an urge to reconnect with our religious roots, affiliations, and practices. Those of us who live among and socialize with highly educated secular academic types are well aware that to pursue various avenues toward spiritual development is generally accepted as an indication of intellectual superiority, awareness, and even enlightenment, whereas becoming more active in a specific church or temple may well be viewed as a sign that we have somehow lost our reason and "gone off the deep end."

The fear of being viewed as a religious nut and the concomitant reluctance to respond to an urge to resurrect or establish religious ties is unfortunate for at least two reasons. First, it is unfortunate because those who do get involved in religious activities tend to be more satisfied with their lives and less prone to psychiatric illnesses than those who do not. And second, it is unfortunate because those who are inclined to participate in religious observances and activities often experience those *"moments of peace and awe and wonder"* that constitute the very goal of man's spiritual search.[10] The two sections of this chapter that follow consider these two aspects of religion and spirituality.

RELIGIOUS BELIEFS AND ACTIVITIES ARE GOOD FOR YOU

There is a great deal of research evidence indicating that religious beliefs and religious activities are beneficial to our subjective well-being and our psychosocial health, both before and after 60. Koenig reviewed 350 research articles focusing on the relationship between religious activity and physical health, and he concluded that most of these studies indicated that individuals who were involved in religious activities were healthier than otherwise similar individuals who reported no such involvement.[11] He also reviewed approximately 850 articles on the relationship between religious involvement and mental health, and he concluded that more than two-thirds of these studies indicated that those who were religiously active scored higher on various measures of psychological adjustment. Matthews reviewed 325 articles on the relationship between religious involvement and physical health, and he concluded that more than three-quarters of these studies reported that religious participation was related positively to health.[12] Koenig and Lawson recently reviewed the literature on the effects of professing a faith in God on the overall health and sense of well-being of older individuals.[13] These authors concluded that individuals who attend religious services, pray, and engage in other forms of spiritual growth exercises live longer and healthier lives than those who do not.

More specifically, recent research suggests that individuals who have serious illnesses such as cancer are more likely to recover fully if they express faith in God and engage in prayer.[14] Faith and prayer have also been shown to be related to positive outcomes for patients being treated for substance abuse and for patients who are coping with chronic illnesses.[15]

There are a number of possible explanations for the positive effect that religious and spiritual activity has on our psychosocial and physical health. These include: (1) the social rewards and social supports associated with membership in a religious congregation; (2) the value of religious teaching that includes prescriptions regarding behaviors that elevate the individual and benefit the community; (3) the role of religious beliefs in helping us make sense of our lives and cope with adversities; and (4) the effect of religious and spiritual beliefs on our subjective assessment of our lot in life. In the next few paragraphs I'd like to discuss each of these explanations.

The Social Aspects of Religion

The social value of religion was recognized by Durkheim before the turn of the twentieth century.[16] Religion, as defined by participating in religious services, volunteer efforts sponsored by the church or synagogue, and participating in activities organized by the congregation, is clearly social in nature. Durkheim argued that religion has a beneficial effect on human social life and personal well-being because it regulates behavior and integrates the individual into a caring social circle. Membership in a religious community provides the individual with structured activities, stability and support, and a venue for sharing some of our more intimate and personal beliefs and concerns. Religious rituals are especially reassuring due to their predictability and the clarity of their shared meaning within the essential beliefs of the religion. Durkheim also noted that religious groups that manifest high levels of ritual in their public worship services and their private devotional practices tend to have very low suicide rates. These groups also tend to be characterized by very high levels of objective health and subjective satisfaction among the older members of the faith.[17]

Religious Prescriptions and Proscriptions on Behavior

Religions tend to urge or even command their members to behave in ways that are elevating. We are asked to love our neighbors as we love ourselves. We are encouraged to engage in acts of charity. We are urged to turn the other cheek. It is easy to be cynical regarding such basic behavioral prescriptions. Being instructed by the pastor or rabbi to obey such patently sensible rules makes some people feel like children. These people may feel that they are mature enough and wise enough to recognize the positive nature of such behaviors, and they don't need a preacher to explain these rules or remind them to follow the rules. In fact, these folks most often believe deep in their hearts that they are far brighter than the preacher anyway.

On the other hand, if we are really honest with ourselves, we must acknowledge that no matter how mature we are and no matter how intelligent we are, we sometimes fail to live up to the expectations implicit in these prescriptions. So it may just be that a full grown man, a man who has entered or passed the seventh decade of life, may need to be reminded of the things that he should do, just as a child needs to be reminded. The most important point is not who tells us to do good deeds. The point is that to the extent that we do engage in these good behaviors, we elevate ourselves. We feel better about who we are and why we are here.

Religious belief systems also typically contain prohibitions against antisocial behaviors like stealing and lying, as well as self-destructive behaviors such as excessive consumption of alcohol, gambling, and promiscuous sexual behavior. These proscriptions may also be viewed by some as infantilizing the members of the religion who follow the injunctions and restrict their behavior accordingly. However, to the extent that these proscriptions have the effect of lowering the incidence of anti-social and self-destructive behaviors among their members, they also have the effect of reducing the harm caused by the anti-social behaviors and the incidence of the diseases with which the self-destructive behaviors are associated.[18] Some of us are too proud to think that we need a set of prohibitions promoted by the church or the temple to keep us from doing things that are bad for us as individuals and damaging to the communities in which we live. However, to the extent that we can overcome our pride and simply comply with these simple, obvious rules, we will be better off.

I once had a rabbi in my practice who was unable to remain faithful to his wife. His struggle with this behavior led him to question his commitment to his faith, and he was contemplating giving up the pulpit because he could not accept the hypocrisy of his situation. He was so conflicted that he resorted to alcohol to dull the pain. This only made matters worse, and when he first came to see me he was thoroughly enmeshed in self-hatred. Long-term therapy enabled this patient to examine his motivations and choices in the context of his childhood and his relationship with his parents. He had come from a home that was big on religious observance but failed to measure up in terms of actual behavior. The rabbi realized that his own parents had not been faithful to each other, and he came to understand that his own choice of vocation was an effort to create in his own life what had been missing in his childhood. When he realized that his own failings were rooted in this childhood conflict, the rabbi was able to overcome his consuming self-hatred and ultimately to put his marriage back on track. In the long run, his first-hand knowledge of human frailty and its potential to do harm made him a much more powerful spiritual leader.

A Framework for Understanding

On a more cerebral and less direct level, religious beliefs provide us with a framework that we can use to help us understand the events that take place around us and the events that impact our own health and happiness. Berger refers to the elements of this framework of beliefs as "plausibility structures," and he argues that these structures give meaning to both the small events of our personal lives and the larger events of history.[19] Idler has argued that the sense of clarity that we derive from religious beliefs is conducive to good physical health.[20]

It is not surprising, therefore, that many of us turn to religion during times of trouble, such as a crisis involving serious illness. A belief in divine authority or a higher power can help us bear the travails that life brings our way without becoming sour on life in general. In *The Problem of Pain*, C. S. Lewis writes:

> Nor have I anything to offer my readers except my conviction that when pain is to be borne, a little courage helps more than much knowledge, a little human sympathy more than much courage, and the least tincture of the love of God more than all.[21]

Idler suggests that the impact of religious participation on our ability to cope with adversity is multidimensional. She argues that, in the language of the social sciences, religion provides us with a kind of emotional coping strategy, one that is particularly effective in restoring hope among the elderly and among those experiencing illness or loss.[22] Berger suggests that religious belief legitimates the marginal human situations of illness and death by giving them a place in a single sacred reality.[23] Koenig points out that religious faith, as exercised in private prayer, is a cognitive and emotional resource that is immediately accessible to the sick or disabled.[24] Pollner suggests that a member of a religious community who becomes sick benefits not only from the tangible social support that he may receive from other members of the congregation but from "social" support received from his acceptance of a higher spiritual power.[25]

Of course, no everyone has faith in the existence of a higher power. If you are an individual who does feel inclined to believe in a higher power who is there to support you in your struggles, you are very fortunate indeed. My purpose in this chapter is to help you to overcome any inhibitions that you may feel with respect to religious and spiritual pursuits, simply because you fear that some of your friends and family may view your efforts with skepticism. There are many who will not view your faith in this way.

Religion and Your Attitude toward Your Life

I made a big deal in the last chapter about your attitude toward your life, that is, whether you are an optimist or a pessimist, whether you tend to view the glass as half full or half empty. Well, your religious beliefs and the development of your spiritual self can have a major impact on your attitude toward life. Researchers who ask subjects the question, "Would you rate your health as excellent, good, fair, or poor?" have discovered that respondents base their answers on many factors other than simply their current disease status or even their overall physical shape.[26] Respondents have indicated that their answers to that question are influenced by the ability to work, their subjective feelings of distress, any good or bad health habits that they may have, comparisons of their current health status to their own health status in the past or to the health status of friends and family members, the extent to which they are experiencing pain or discomfort, their emotional well-being, the quality of their social relationship, and their ability to pursue activities that they have enjoyed in the past.[27]

Thus it is not too surprising that some individuals with fairly significant physical challenges may nevertheless view themselves as being in excellent health. Religious beliefs can help us to view our circumstances from the most positive perspective possible, emphasizing the areas in which we are strong and capable of deriving enjoyment from our lives. Affiliation with a religious community also adds to our social support networks, thus increasing the sources of gratification and joy that may be available to us, even if we have significant physical limitations.

Idler also suggests that our overall self-concept has both a physical component and a nonphysical component and that participation in religious and spiritual development activities will enhance the spiritual component. This can compensate for significant physical limitations. Nonphysical aspects of our self concept might include cognitive or intellectual abilities, aesthetic interests in music, literature, and art, membership in a professional group, and having satisfying social relationships. Charmaz argues that people who "define essential qualities of self as distinct from their bodies," especially those who are encouraged by others to do so, are more likely to transcend the situation of their illness. They have "defined a valued self beyond a failing body."[28] The development of an intact nonphysical sense of self would then be associated with positive global self-ratings of health, even in the face of significant illness.

I am reminded of a good friend who died recently at the age of 65 after a two-year struggle with Lou Gehrig's Disease (ALS). Over the course of this progressive illness Howard lost the use of his arms and had to be fed. Eventually he became completely paralyzed. However, he maintained a positive outlook and enjoyed his life to the end, because he had such a strong nonphysical self. He was an attorney, and he continued to work long past the point where he could write or even sit at his desk. He could still think, and he consulted with the members of his firm on various cases, even dictating briefs. He could also still hear, and one of the great loves of his life was gospel music. We made CDs for him to listen to, and we discussed our reactions to the various artists. Howard even commented at one point that in a strange way he was actually grateful that he had become ill, since it forced him to take time to listen carefully to all the great music that he had never heard before or never fully appreciated. Howard was not a religious man. He was a self-proclaimed agnostic. Nevertheless, I can't help but think that the last days of his life were made easier not just by the *music* part of the gospel music but by the *gospel* part as well.

Religious Beliefs and Activities and Satisfaction with Life

I pointed out above that there is considerable evidence that religious beliefs and participation in religious activities are associated with better physical and mental health among people in general and among older individuals in particular. There is also a substantial body of research indicating that religious beliefs and activities predict greater satisfaction with life.[29] For example, Hunsberger conducted in-depth interviews with 33 Canadian men and 52 Canadian women between the ages of 65 and 88.[30] The interview protocol included a number of measures of religious belief and participation, as well as a number of indicators of the respondents' satisfaction with their lives. The religious measures included a measure of the orthodoxy of the respondents' religious beliefs, a measure of the emphasis that had been placed on religion in their families when they were children, a measure of the perceived importance of religious beliefs, and a measure of the frequency with which the respondents actually attended religious services. The measures of satisfaction with life included self-ratings of happiness, adjustment, satisfaction with one's health, and the degree to which the respondent viewed life as exciting.

The results of the Hunsberger study showed that each of the measures of religious belief and religious involvement was related positively to the respondents' reports of how happy they were. Each of the measures of religious belief and involvement was also related positively to the respondents' self-reports of their personal adjustment. The respondents' self-reports of the importance of their religious beliefs were related positively to their satisfaction with their health. Both the importance ascribed to religious beliefs and the frequency of attendance of religious services were related positively to how exciting the respondents viewed their lives. Thus both religious belief and participation in religious activity were clearly associated with enhanced satisfaction with life among these Canadian seniors.

A study of 264 American blacks between the ages of 62 and 82 reported by Coke and Twaite examined a broad range of factors that might predict life satisfaction.[31] The predictors included not only self-ratings of the importance of religion and the frequency of participation in religious activities but also non religious predictors such as income, family role involvement, self-rated health, and level of education. Life satisfaction was measured by the five item Satisfaction with Life Scale.[32] This study included 144 males and 120 females, and the results were reported separately for the two genders. The investigators found that among the men studied, the number of hours of participation in religious activities was the strongest predictor of satisfaction with life. Frequency of participation in religious activities was a stronger predictor of life satisfaction than income, involvement with family, and even self-rated health. Frequency of participation in religious activities was also the strongest predictor of satisfaction among the women.

Thus one can speculate as to the primary reason why religious belief and participation is good for us, but the evidence is quite clear that it is in fact good for our physical health, our psychological adjustment, and our general satisfaction with our lives. Here again, I am not suggesting that readers with no inclination toward religion go out and find one. But I am strongly suggesting that anyone who does feel drawn toward religious belief should not hesitate to act upon it.

MOMENTS OF PEACE AND AWE AND WONDER

Regardless of whether you find yourself drawn toward a religion, the chances are pretty good that you will experience some form of "spiritual crisis" in the years after your sixtieth birthday. Trafford defined the spiritual crisis as the need to figure out the significance of life. "What is the significance of your life—of all life? [and] How do you grapple with fate's mysteries."[33] Trafford suggested that what we are looking for in our spiritual search are "moments of peace and awe and wonder—moments to break through the routine, to conduct your own life review and find new purpose. Moments where you give up control and let experiences flood in."[34]

This theme is prevalent in the literature on aging successfully. James Hollis describes a major task of the second half of life as "discovering a personal spirituality." He argues that "it is imperative that our spirituality be validated or confirmed by fidelity to our personal experience."[35] This concept of the personal nature of spiritual experiences is similar to Trafford's description of experiences involving "peace and awe and wonder." Hollis emphasizes that it is not enough to simple accept a spiritual tradition that is received from history or from family and makes no real difference in one's life. Only that which is experientially true is worthy of mature spirituality. This does not mean that one cannot find mature spirituality in religious practices, but it does mean that simply going through the motions of religious observances does not constitute mature spirituality. The religious experiences would have to resonate within you such that they provide moments of peace and awe and wonder. This is the beauty of spirituality.

It is only when we have such experiences that we can be certain that our souls are connected to a part of something that is infinite, and it is only when we feel this connection that we understand where our lives fit in to the universe. Thus Hollis argued that "whatever moves us deeply, occasions awe and wonder is religious, no matter through what venue it may come to us."[36] Such experiences enable us to transcend the barriers between the self and the universe, and in so doing come to understand our place and the purpose of our lives. Such experiences may come in a house of worship. They may also occur in the presence of nature, while gardening, gazing up at the evening stars, or walking in the woods at sunset. They may occur while playing or listening to music, while making love, or while meditating. Each of you will need to determine what path or paths toward spirituality resonate most easily with your soul. I can only say that when the spirit moves you to begin your spiritual explorations, you should heed its call. The exploration is a natural part of successful aging, and you will experience profound joy at the end of your chosen path.

Chapter Ten

FINDING AND MAINTAINING THE MEANING IN LIFE

Whether or not we feel an urge to discover or affirm our connection with the universe through religious observance or spiritual development, as we approach and pass our sixtieth birthday we are almost certain to begin to wonder whether our lives have any purpose or meaning. Most men have an instrumental orientation toward living, that is, we feel that we need to be doing something productive in order to justify our taking up space on the planet.

But as we pass 60 we tend to lose some of the roles in life that have made us feel useful. The kids have grown up. They may have moved away. They are (hopefully) no longer in need of our financial support, and they are most likely less in need of our advice. The grandchildren may even be reaching adolescence and becoming more independent. Our babysitting services may no longer be required. The grandsons may want to go surfing with their friends instead of fishing with grandpa. Our work and professional roles may be shrinking as well. We may or may not retire, but we are likely to feel less absorbed by our work. Most likely we have already achieved some success. We have a little financial cushion that reduces the need to work to simply to survive. Quite likely as well, we have thoroughly mastered whatever it is that we do for a living, so there is a sense of "been there, done that." Even if you're an incredibly skilled orthopedic surgeon, you may still come to feel that one knee replacement is pretty much the same as another.

These natural role reductions tend leave us wondering what we are doing here. We are healthy and have a long time left to live, but we may not be certain about what we are living for. Trafford describes this situation as being one in which we feel that we are too young to die yet too old to live.[1] The gravity of this issue is compounded by the increase in life expectancy. "Too young to die" may mean we'll be around for another 30 or more years. That's a very long time to wonder what it is that we are doing here.

So what can we do about this existential dilemma? It appears that there are both simple and complex answers to this question. The simple answer is to compensate for the lost or diminished roles by developing new ones or renewing the sense of joy and adventure in the old ones. Thus Rowe and Kahn suggest that continued "active engagement with life" is a critical component of successful aging.[2] They also suggest that active engagement with life can be fostered in two arenas: in close personal relationships with family and friends; and in continued involvement with productive activities.

FOSTERING CLOSE PERSONAL RELATIONSHIPS

I am going to begin my discussion of fostering close personal relationships with three case studies that illustrate very different paths we can take to fostering close personal relationships after 60. Morris focused on family. Jim focused on friends. David focused on new romance.

Morris's Family

Morris is a great big bear of a man with a full beard and twinkling eyes. He is 72 now. He was treated for a serious heart condition a few years back, but he is in pretty good shape right now. Morris is a Ph.D. social worker who had a busy analytic practice for his entire adult life. He has cut back substantially on his practice hours, but he still continues to see a number of his longer term patients.

Morris is a very happy man. His primary source of happiness is his family, including his wife Dora, his four children, and his 10 grandchildren. Dora is 65 and in good health. Morris describes himself as "hopelessly in love" with her. Dora was a teacher until she retired four years ago. Morris and Dora had three boys and one girl. Their sons are now 43, 41, and 39, and their daughter is 38. Morris told me that it was a good thing that the fourth child was a daughter, because they simply weren't going to stop having kids until they had a girl.

The children all live near Morris in the greater New York metropolitan area. Morris now lives on the upper West Side of Manhattan. He lived in Westchester while the kids were growing up, because "I wanted my kids to be in good public schools," and because "you need a backyard with kids." But he always loved Manhattan and moved back there when the last child finished college.

Morris was duly proud of his children. He had two sons who were investment bankers, one son who was a psychologist, and his daughter was a legal aid attorney. She is married to an attorney whom she had met in law school. The children had all been very good students and they had attended fine schools in various locations, but Morris "made sure" that they all came back to the New York area to start their careers and their families. Morris said that he had employed a variety of strategies to "be certain that they would all come home."

He said that from the time they were babies he and Dora had stressed the importance of family. They had always made a big deal about holidays and the importance of being together. Morris and Dora had always sent the kids money to get home for holidays, even though there were times when doing so strained the family budget. They also kept in close contact no matter where the kids happened to be at the time. Morris was completely unashamed about calling his kids several times a week when they were away at college. He said that his kids were among his best friends, and it was always good to keep in close touch with your best friends. When the children brought home their prospective spouses, Morris said he and Dora loved each new family member as one of their own. He said, "I love my child, so I love the person who my child loves."

Morris and Dora also maintained the practice of having family vacations even after the children went off to school, began working, and began to have families. They regularly rented a cottage (or two or three) at the beach or in the mountains and invited all the children and grandchildren to join them. These trips were often difficult to schedule, with everyone's different obligations. Sometimes he encountered resistance from some of the kids, but he was "relentless" in his efforts to get them to come. He said, "We always tried to anticipate the problems that they might have and do whatever I could to make it easier for them to come." Often Morris and Dora took a house for a whole month, and they had different combinations of the children come at different times during that month, whenever they could get away. Sometimes the grandchildren came for the whole month, and their children came on the weekends or for a week or two during the month. Several years ago, when Morris was sick, the kids all got together and took on the responsibility of making the arrangements for the family vacation. Now they have taken over this responsibility, delegating different aspects of the arrangements to different families.

Even during the routine, non-vacation periods of the year, Morris and Dora regularly arranged special outings and activities with as many of the children and grandchildren as they could. When the grandkids were young, these outings included trips to the zoo, to water parks, to sporting events, and to movies and theater. They were always available for babysitting. As the grandchildren grew up, Morris and Dora made sure that they were closely involved in the grandchildren's lives, never failing to attend their concerts, their soccer and baseball games, and never failing to call each grandchild on his or her birthday.

Morris knew the value of family from the start. When he married Dora, they knew that they wanted children, and they wanted their children to be the focus of their life. As Morris matured and entered the social work profession, Morris became acutely aware of the trend in America toward greater emphasis on the nuclear family and less emphasis on the extended multigenerational family. He knew or worked with many families in which the children moved away, got totally absorbed in their careers, and nearly lost touch with their parents. He knew grandparents who had never seen their grandchildren. He and Dora did not want that to happen to them, and they consciously made every effort possible to make their family life a joy for their children, so that maintaining the family bond would be an important factor in making decisions about marriage and career. Morris and Dora both unashamedly acknowledged that they would not hesitate for a moment to employ bribery, induce guilt, or do whatever they had to keep their children close to them. Morris simply said that there are some things that parents know best, and they had to have the courage to act on their convictions.

Given their close and continuing relationship with their children and grand-children, Morris never found himself with "time on his hands," even after he began to cut back on his professional practice. Dora said that she "hardly noticed" her retirement from teaching. Their family roles continued to give them joy and to make them feel that they had a reason to live.

Jim's Friends

Jim is 68. He lost his wife of 35 years eight years ago, just after his 60th birthday. He had been quite successful in his real estate business and was already retired when his wife died. They were very close and shared a variety of active outdoor hobbies, including sailing, golf, tennis, backpacking, and fly fishing. They had one child, a son, who was a marine biologist at Sea World in San Diego. Jim had two grandsons, and he visited them several times a year.

However, Jim's life is centered around a small group of close friends with whom he shares the activities that he loved and had formerly shared with his wife. He and a few of his sailing buddies became involved in yacht racing, and Jim eventually became the executive director of an organization that sanctions races. He spent a great deal of time with his friends planning and participating in races, and he also dedicated a great deal of time to expanding the membership of the sailing organization through public relations and fundraising activities. Jim also led his organization to become involved in sanctioning races for smaller sailing craft. In this way Jim hoped to introduce the sport of sail racing to a broader base of people, including many young people who might not be able to afford the time or the money required to become involved in yacht racing. Jim and several of his friends were instrumental in getting sailing adopted as a new varsity sport in a number of American universities and in improving the representation of the United States in international sailing competitions for various categories of sailboats.

Jim said that being a member of a racing team led him to develop extremely close relationships with his teammates, relationships that began with close teamwork under pressure and extended to long evenings discussing the stars, the universe, and the meaning of life. He said that his sailing buddies were like members of his family, with whom he could share his closest feelings, and on whom he knew he could depend if he ever found himself in a bad situation.

Jim also introduced some of his close friends to other activities that he loved. He organized backcountry camping and fly fishing trips for himself and his buddies. He said that the only thing that came close to watching the stars from a sailboat was sitting around a campfire with your best friends talking about the fish you had caught and the ones that got away. Jim clearly felt in tune with the universe in these shared activities.

Jim's story illustrates how we men can make conscious efforts to develop meaningful social relationships and roles to fill the void left by retirement and the loss of loved ones. Jim was fortunate that he had activities that he and his wife had enjoyed before her death, but after her death he made the extra effort to become involved in racing and to form a team with whom the development of even closer relationships was virtually assured. He also made the extra effort to become involved in and assume a leadership role in an organization aimed at making it possible for others to enjoy this activity.

The moral to be drawn from Jim's story is that those of us who have relatively little involvement with family and extended family can still create meaningful close personal relationships, if we are willing to take the steps required to develop such relationships. Jim had the advantage that he had a set of interests in place on which he could build rather easily, but even if you lack such interests, you can discover them and develop them. Get on the internet and explore different sports, hobbies, and activities. Shop around and pick out some activities that seem interesting. Locate the organizations that foster these activities. Get their literature. Go to an event or a meeting. See if the people there seem to be interesting and agreeable. There is an organization for almost every interest and activity, and most of these organizations are anxious to recruit new members. Get involved, and the friendships will follow.

David's New Romance

David was 67 when his wife died. He had been married twice, once when he was 23 for 7 years, and then again when he was 32 for 35 years. He had a son and a daughter from his first marriage, and two daughters from his second marriage. He had seven grandchildren. The children were spread all over the country, none of them within easy driving distance of David and his wife. He and his wife had visited each of his children about once a year over the last five years or so before her death. David loved his kids and he felt that he had "good" relationships with all of them. However, David was not close to his children in the same manner that Morris was close to his children, that is, like one big family. Most of David's visits to his children were for a weekend, and David and his wife did not stay with the children when they visited, preferring to stay nearby in a hotel and meet the kids and grandkids for some activities and for lunch and dinner during their stay. David said that he and his wife cherished their "privacy" and could take only so much of the noise that children made.

David had worked hard all his life, and he owned three hardware stores. At the time that his wife died, he had good managers for the stores, and he was able to take a good deal of time off. He and his wife had done a good deal of traveling, which they had enjoyed a lot. They had spent most of their time together, whether they were at home or off on a trip. When David's wife died, he was devastated. She was his best friend, his lover, and his traveling companion. When she died, there was a big hole in his life. He did not feel that he wanted to fill this void by becoming more active in his business. He had worked too hard to get it to the point where it was pretty much running itself. And he did not want to spend more time with his children or to go to live near one of them. He felt that they had good relationships now, and he didn't want to spend any more time with them than he had been over the last few years.

After the shock of his wife's death had worn off, David realized that he felt most comfortable in a one-to-one relationship with a woman. He wanted to continue to travel, and he needed someone to share this with him. He was also still interested in sex. So within three or four months of his wife's death, David was fully engaged in a search for a new wife.

David went back through his address book (and his deceased wife's address book) to remind him of people that they had met both at home and on their travels. He reasoned that since his own wife had passed on, there were probably some women whom he had met in the past who had lost husbands. He also reasoned that someone whom he had met while traveling would be a good potential mate, since she would presumably like to travel. He made a bunch of phone calls to catch up with these folks and find out their present status. When he contacted someone who was still happily married, he went a step further. He indicated that he was interested in meeting someone and asked directly if there was someone they knew who might be looking for someone like him. David went further; he took out an ad in a travel magazine explaining that he was a widower interested in meeting a mature woman who liked to travel and still had an interest in sex. He figured he might as well put all his cards on the table. He was on a mission with a purpose, and he did not want to waste time meeting women who would not fit his needs. On the other hand, David was not out of control.

In short order David was talking with and corresponding with, a number of women. He found that there was no shortage of eligible candidates. With the wisdom of age, he took it slowly, going out to dinner, getting to know quite a few women, and waiting for a spark. He made some new friends. He went on a few trips with some of his new friends. He had some sexual encounters. He was amazed at how frank and open he could be with the women he met. He described the women with whom became friendly with were "gloriously mature." They knew what they were looking for, and they seemed to understand what he was looking for.

Eventually David found someone very special to whom he felt very attracted. Laura was a widow who was a close friend to a couple whom David and his deceased wife had met several years before on one of their trips. When David called the couple to find out how they were doing and tell them where he was at, they immediately said that they had someone whom he had to meet. They invited David and their friend Laura to dinner at their house, and they hit it off right away. David and Laura dated for a long time, traveled together, and eventually began living together. They did not get married for quite a while, because Laura was somewhat apprehensive regarding the possible reaction of her children, with whom she was quite close. After several years together, however, once her children had gotten to know David quite well, they did marry.

David's story is not unusual. Many widowers find another woman to fill the void left by their deceased wife. The priest at David's wedding pointed out that such unions were sanctioned by the church, and he suggested that the deceased spouses of the bride and groom would want their surviving spouses to have comfort during the remainder of their lives here on earth. David and Laura each became comfortable talking to each other about experiences they had with their departed spouses and spending time with their new spouse's children. The home they had together had photos of the departed spouses and memorabilia from their previous relationships. These changes came slowly but naturally. David and Laura discussed these issues as they arose, but the issues were not a source of contention, and the discussions surrounding them seemed perfectly natural and normal.

So the idea of finding a new mate following the death of a spouse is both reasonable and feasible. But it does require an effort. David is perhaps somewhat unique because he was able to see through his grief and recognize that he still needed a partner, and because he was not the least bit embarrassed by his situation or afraid to communicate it to the world. Other men may harbor a lingering sense of apprehension that developing a new relationship is a manifestation of disloyalty to their departed spouse, or they may simply feel that they are no longer up to the task of meeting new people. They may feel that they have relatively little to offer. But in most cases they will have a great deal more to offer than they even realize. So if you have lost a partner, allow yourself to be open to the possibility of meeting new people. Socialize. If you have friends who want to introduce you to someone, don't be afraid. Assuming that you are meeting someone who is around your own age, you will likely find that she has a good idea of what she might be looking for and that she is realistic in her expectations. Therefore you can feel free to be open and honest about who you are and what you want. You have nothing to lose.

CONTINUED INVOLVEMENT IN PRODUCTIVE ACTIVITIES

The second course of action that Rowe and Kahn recommend to maintain our active engagement with life is continued involvement with productive activities. This does not necessarily mean that you should not retire from your lifetime career or cut back on the amount of time and energy that you put into your work. I am a firm believer in leisure time, relaxation, and doing things simply for fun. I also believe that after a lifetime of work a man is entitled to take time to enjoy life. However, I have already pointed out that we tend to be instrumental creatures, and we are likely to continue to feel some obligation to be productive, even during the last third of our lifetime.

This lingering feeling of a continuing duty to be productive may be a throwback to the earlier era of hunter-gatherers, when elders who could no longer contribute to the preservation of the tribe were necessarily put out to die. The need to be productive may also be an inherent aspect of human nature. It is widely believed that Freud defined mental health as the ability "to love and to work."[3] In fact, it is not clear that Freud actually made precisely this statement, but he states in *Civilization and Its Discontents* that "the communal life of human beings had, therefore, a two-fold foundation: the compulsion to work, which was created by external necessity, and the power of love."[4] The need to be productive has certainly been stressed by later developmental psychologists, including Erickson and Maslow.[5]

Of course, remaining engaged with life through productive activity is not synonymous with remaining on the job. Trafford argues that during the "bonus years" we can remain productive in a variety of different ways.[6] These include various forms of paid work, diverse volunteer activities aimed at "giving back" to the community, and new learning activities aimed at expanding the mind. Let's consider each of these possibilities.

Paid Work

First of all, if you are working at a job that you still enjoy and find challenging, maybe you should keep at it. If you are forced to retire by company policies or union contracts, it may be possible for you to perform the same or a similar function with another employer. If the nature of your work is conducive to it, you might even consider setting up your own shop.

If you are getting tired of the same old routine and do not want to simply keep working at exactly the same job, there are a number of other possibilities. Perhaps you should consider doing some advanced training in your field to bring you up to speed and open up possibilities for adding new elements to your work. I have a friend who is 71 years old who has been working as a psychologist for over 40 years. However, the work he is doing today is quite different from the work that he did when he began his practice. Over the years he has engaged in an almost continuous process of retraining, successively learning new technologies that can be applied to different psychological problems. Over the years he has helped patients using psychodynamic psychotherapy, behavior management techniques, cognitive restructuring, and most recently neurofeedback technology. He reports that each new treatment modality required training, that these different training experiences were all interesting and challenging, and that the mastery of each successive technology improved his rate of success with his patients.

Another approach to consider if you find that you are becoming increasingly bored with your profession is to apply your skills in another venue. If you have been teaching English literature at a prestigious university for 30 years and the students are all beginning to look the same and to follow a predictable sequence of development from freshman year to graduation, perhaps you could consider retiring from that position and taking a new teaching position at an inner city college, a community college, or an adult education program. In these different venues the students might present a different set of challenges that might well rekindle your enthusiasm. Or perhaps you could take a new teaching position at a university in another country. This would also present a different set of challenges and an opportunity to experience different perspectives on the works that you have been teaching.

Still another response to an increasingly humdrum career would be to consider retiring from your present job and taking a position in a different field related to your area of expertise. For example, our English professor reaching retirement age could enter the publishing industry as an editor or a literary agent, or he might sit down to do the creative writing that he had often considered but never had the time to actually do.

Some men will take an even bigger leap of faith in response to diminished enthusiasm for their lifetime careers. I have a friend who was a partner in a major New York law firm who retired from that job to become a professional photographer. He had been an amateur photographer for many years and had been told by many that he was talented, but he had always hesitated to leave the legal profession and the lucrative position that he had worked so hard to obtain. But then one day, at the age of 65, he realized that he really didn't need to make any more money. He also realized that staying at the firm would be easy, whereas trying to become successful as a photographer would be a new challenge. So he arranged an orderly transition at the firm, quit the law, and became a photographer. His social connections opened a few doors and helped him get shows, and he actually became quite successful. But more important, he felt like a kid again.

Obviously some of us are in better positions than others to make such decisions. But all of us have some room for creativity in the area of work. As we enter the seventh decade of our lives, we owe it to ourselves to ask whether our work is everything that we would want. If it is not, we owe it to ourselves to sit down and consider ways in which we can remain productive while engaging in work that is interesting and exciting.

Volunteer Work

Erikson talks about the developmental task of *generativity*. This term refers to the human need to give back, to reach out to help others. Volunteer work provides us with the opportunity to help others by sharing our skills, our knowledge, and our expertise. Many men become increasingly interested in volunteer work as they pass the age of 60, because we feel that we do have something to give, and because we feel that we have reached a position in life where we can afford to take the time to provide such assistance.

A friend of mine who has long since retired from a successful career as an entrepreneur now spends a substantial amount of time each week advising young people with entrepreneurial aspirations on how to put their ideas into practice. Another good friend of mine volunteers his time to run a fishing tournament for kids at a local lake in Westchester County. Others volunteer at museums, in schools, at the polls, and in nursing homes. All of these people report that their volunteer efforts make them feel good. They feel competent and productive. They feel that they are making a difference.

There is something about volunteer work that is pure. Because you are not being compensated for your time, your motives are unambiguously altruistic.

The people that you are helping know that your motives are pure, and you know that your motives are pure. We all have a tendency to harbor negative thoughts about ourselves and our behaviors. You may truly have become a physician because you wanted to help people who are hurting; but being a physician also brings significant compensation and respect, so the decision to become a physician cannot really be viewed as an act of altruism. In the same way, you may have become a teacher because you wanted to expand children's awareness of the world; but the short hours, long vacations, job security, and benefits may make you wonder whether there was a also a selfish aspect to this decision. But if you volunteer to help someone, there is simply no room to doubt your altruism. Often you will be doing work that demands more empathy than skill. You may in fact be performing work that requires much less expertise than what you did previously for a living. The only reason for volunteering is to give back. And it makes you feel great.

The research literature is very clear that volunteering is beneficial to your physical and psychological health. Morrow-Howell and associates studied 1,669 adults over the age of 60 for a period of nine years.[7] They found that volunteering was associated with better health and fewer depressive symptoms. Harlow-Rosentraub, Wilson, and Steele studied 275 adults over the age of 60 who volunteered for the first time.[8] They found that during the first year of volunteer work these adults demonstrated significant improvements in both physical and emotional health.

New Learning

Another activity that can keep us productively involved in living is new learning. It has been estimated that 41 percent of adults between the ages of 51 and 65 participate in some form of adult education, as do 22 percent of adults over the age of 65.[9] These adults are engaging in these activities for a variety of reasons. Some individuals simply engage in voluntary educational activities as part of a process of lifelong learning. These individuals may take courses on art, music appreciation, great books, or a variety of topics that are simply interesting. Other individuals are members of professions that require continuing education courses in order to renew professional licenses. Still others engage in educational experiences that are work-related. Such courses can be offered either in a university setting or under the auspices of an employer. Finally, many older men pursue a variety of educational experiences that introduce them to new sports or activities or help them to refine the skills that they already have in these areas. I have friends who have gone to spring training with professional baseball teams. I have other friends who have gone to school to learn how to fly fish or how to shoot sporting clays. I have friends who have learned how to backpack and climb mountains. I have friends who participate in workshops where they hone their skills with musical instruments or learn crafts like pottery or woodworking.

I feel that each of these forms of new learning is potentially valuable for keeping us old guys actively involved in the business of living. It is always good to explore new areas of learning in the arts, literature, and current events. Such experiences provide aesthetic enjoyment and keep us intellectually sharp. Continuing education related to our professions is essential to keep us up to speed in our fields, and these courses also help us to develop our networks of professional colleagues. We are reinvigorated by these courses, and sometimes we get ideas that we can employ to make our work more productive, efficient, and interesting. Learning about a new hobby or craft may simply represent an interesting diversion for a weekend or two, or it may become the basis of a passion that lasts for the rest of our lives. In addition to the leaning itself, all of these learning experiences involve social contact, and the potential for making new friends who can enrich our lives.

Living on Purpose

Remember earlier in the chapter I said that the existential question of "What am I doing here?" has a simple answer and a more complex answer. The more complex answer to the existential dilemma involves making a conscious effort to discover your purpose in life. Leider and Shapiro recently wrote a book entitled *Claiming Your Place at the Fire: Living the Second Half of Your Life On Purpose.* These authors state that

> To claim one's place at the fire means to live one's life on purpose. When we claim our place at the fire, we enter into the circle of vital elders who have been the source of wisdom in society since time immemorial. We do this by courageously reexamining and rediscovering who we are, where we belong, what we care about, and what our life's purpose is.[10]

This idea of "claiming our place at the fire" through a process of rigorous self-examination effectively unites the idea of maintaining an active engagement in living with the idea of spiritual development discussed in the previous chapter. Leider and Shapiro argue that in order to know our purpose in life we must carefully consider four questions. The first question is, "Who am I?" This question can only be answered by reviewing the story of our lives up to this point. This review constitutes the means by which "we rediscover and reinvent ourselves in the second half of life." The second question is, "Where do I belong?" Answering this question involves discovering our place in the community. The third question is, "What do I care about?" Answering this question determines how we stay connected to the world and how we mentor those who will take over after we are gone. The fourth question is, "Why am I here?" Answering this question tells us our purpose in living, which is the means through which we find creative expression and the make a difference in the lives of those around us.

Therefore, answering these questions is tantamount to figuring out how we are connected with something larger than ourselves, something universal, and something eternal. But figuring out this connection is tantamount to the definition of mature spirituality that I discussed in the last chapter. Moreover, answering these questions also dictates the nature of our connections to our family and community, as well as the nature of the productive activities in which we will engage to foster the well-being of family and community. In short then, the idea of finding our purpose in life spans the gap between our actions as individuals and our connection to that which is universal. The moral is clear. Regardless of the specific love and work roles in which we find ourselves, we should always strive to remain actively engaged.

Chapter Eleven

THE RETIREMENT QUESTION

We saw in the previous chapter that it is extremely important for men to continue to be engaged in productive and meaningful activities as they pass and move beyond their sixtieth birthday. We also saw that there are many ways in which this can be done, including both remunerative work and diverse forms of personal development involving volunteering, continuing education, and pursuit of enjoyable hobby and leisure activities. For all these reasons, the question of whether to retire has shifted from primarily a "yes" or "no" decision that is made at the age of 65 to a series of questions. These include, whether to ever retire, whether to retire completely or simply cut back a bit on the number of hours we work, whether to retire from one job and begin another, and when to make each of these decisions and to act upon them.

Ideally, none of us will ever retire from leading full and productive lives. However, we may well wish to retire from or even be forced to retire from a particular job. If we have the option of staying on at the same job or retiring from it, the decision is therefore one that we should base primarily on financial considerations. Even if you love your job, you may want to retire from that specific job and begin to receive a pension. You can probably find a very similar job at a different company and keep on getting paid for doing what you love, while receiving your pension from the last job.

Often these days men are offered the opportunity to retire from their current position early in exchange for a severance package that may be quite substantial. Here too your decision should be based on financial considerations. If you can take the early retirement option and still go out and find another job

that you will enjoy and that will pay you a decent wage, then the early retirement option may be your best bet. You will need to evaluate why the offer is
being made, what your future would be at the company should you decide to
stay, and what options are available for you outside. You will also need to see
how much savings you have and try to figure out how much you still need
to earn in order to guarantee a secure future. The point is that these days we
assume that you will want to remain active and engaged in meaningful and
productive work, but you may or may not need to make this work remunerative. You may need to continue to do work that is remunerative, but you may
not need to earn as much as you did in your previous job.

The main point that I would like to make in this chapter is that you need to
plan ahead, and this planning involves a number of variables. Many men have
jobs with retirement plans, and they assume that the future will take care of
itself. This is not always the case. Consider the example of Pat and Kathleen:

Pat's Aborted Retirement

Pat retired from his 30-year career as a police officer in a suburban village outside
New York City at the age of 57. He had been counting the days till he could "take it
easy" and devote full time to his primary leisure time activity, restoring vintage auto-
mobiles. Pat had a retirement plan through his employer, the township, that paid
him one-half of his yearly salary after 30 years of service. His retirement package
also provided lifetime health care coverage for him and his wife Kathleen. They had
home that was paid off and about $200,000 in savings. They also anticipated receiv-
ing Social Security payments beginning when Pat reached the age of 62. Pat and
Kathleen thought that they could afford to retire comfortably.

They sold their home in New York and purchased a new home on 15 acres just
outside of St. George, Utah. This is a popular retirement area, due to the climate
and the beautiful scenery. Pat and Kathleen spent most of the money that they had
received for their house in New York on their new home in Utah, a pool, and furnishings. In addition, Pat put up a large garage on the property to work on his vintage cars. He invested about $80,000 in equipment for his hobby, which he thought
would some day become lucrative. Once Pat and Kathleen were settled in to their
new home, they had about $60,000 left in their savings, and they had an annual
income from Pat's pension of about $38,000.

They found out fairly quickly to their great surprise that this was simply not
enough for them to live the way they wanted to. They loved their new home and the
new area, and they were very active in exploring Utah and the surrounding states. It
seemed that now that they had a lot of free time, it required a good deal of money to
engage in activities to fill up that time. Kathleen did a bit more shopping than she
had done before, simply because she spent a good deal of time in shopping malls. Pat
bought two vintage cars to restore and the parts and supplies needed to do the work.
Pat and Kathleen also enjoyed going to Las Vegas to see the shows there. But traveling around was expensive, as were the weekends in Las Vegas. They also wanted to
go back East several times a year to visit their children and grandchildren. These
trips were also expensive.

So they realized that after all was said and done, they had enough money to live,
but they did not have enough money to do the things they wanted to do. They knew

that their income would increase a bit when Social Security kicked in, but that would not happen for 5 years, even if Pat began taking payments at 62.

The solution to their problem was very clear. They needed to go back to work. Fortunately, the area in which they now lived was booming. Pat got a good job as the head of the security department at a new mall. Taking this job did not affect the pension that Pat was receiving from his former job in New York. Kathleen, who had worked only sporadically while Pat was a policeman, also took a job as a salesperson in a store that sells gourmet kitchen equipment. They planned to work for at least five years and to save as much as they could so that they would increase their nest egg. In this way they would be able to draw additional income from savings later on. In the meantime, Pat continued to restore cars in his spare time, and he did begin to make some additional money from this activity.

When Pat reached the age of 62, he did not quit his job. He kept on working. At this point he was enjoying both his job and his car restoration business, and he opted to wait to take Social Security so that he could continue to work and save. He also knew that waiting to take Social Security would increase the amount they would receive each month. Today Pat is 68 and he is still working. He has now put in 11 years as the director of security at the mall, and he has become vested in a second retirement program sponsored by his current employer. He now plans to retire at 70, because after 70 continuing to work will not increase his Social Security benefits. When he does retire, he and Kathleen will have more than enough money to do the things they want. They will have his two pensions, income from substantial savings, Social Security income, and income from the car restoration hobby business. Pat and Kathleen were lucky. They made a miscalculation about the amount of money they would need to live well in retirement, but fortunately they kept their health, and a favorable economy made it possible for them to go back to work and strengthen their financial situation.

Not everyone who retires without making adequate plans is as lucky as Pat and Kathleen. Many men are not as easily employable as Pat. If they realize after retiring that they really do not have enough income to live well, they may be forced to take relatively low paying jobs that only partially bridge the gap between the income they have and the income they would need to do the things they want. This is why, long before we consider retiring from our primary job, we need to obtain a realistic figure for the amount of income that we will require to live as we wish, and then make sure that the total of our retirement benefits, social security, income from savings, and whatever continuing remunerative work we wish to do will add up to an amount large enough to meet our needs.

WHAT YOU WILL NEED TO RETIRE

According to the AARP, people who retire typically need at least 70 to 80 percent of their pre-retirement income to be comfortable.[1] On the other hand, if you plan to travel extensively or engage in activities that are expensive, you could well need more. As we saw with Pat and Kathleen, filling up spare time with pleasurable recreational and or cultural activities can run into some serious money. Therefore you need to think long and hard about how you want to be spending your time and about the expenses that are involved in that vision of your future. In addition, life has a way of placing unexpected challenges in front of us. One can never tell whether some change in his health of the health of a partner might occur, necessitating increased medical expenditures. One can never tell when an adult child might experience a stressful situation requiring you to make a loan or to take on additional expenses. Therefore, it is wise to allow a margin for error in planning how much income you will need each year.

In determining how much you must save to feel reasonably comfortable, you can follow two approaches. You can plan to accumulate sufficient savings that the combination of any pension income you may have, your Social Security benefits, and income from all investments is sufficient to meet your anticipated monthly expenses. This would imply that you would live off these sources of income and not use any of the principal on your investments during your lifetime. This in turn would assume that you want to have something to leave to your children or to some other worthy person or cause. Alternatively, you may make an educated guess as to how long you may live, and at a certain point begin to spend a portion of the principal, so that by the time you and your spouse died there would be very little left. This has the advantage that it reduces the amount that you need to save in the first place.

Financial planners who opt for the strategy of spending down your savings as you grow older often suggest that you plan on living to at least 95, and that you plan to have approximately one-fourth of your savings still available to you at that point, in the event that you live longer. Under this strategy an individual who retired at 65 would begin taking some funds from principal at that point, but he would have saved a sufficient amount that his savings would still increase for some time after 65, reaching a peak value at around 75 and declining thereafter.[2] The specific amount that you will need to save each year to accomplish this goal is a function of many variables, including: (1) your anticipated need for income during retirement; (2) the age at which you begin to save; (3) anticipated sources of income other than savings (i.e., pension, Social Security income, annuities from any inheritances, and planned earnings from some level of continuing remunerative work, if that is applicable); (4) assumptions regarding the rate of return on your investments; and (5) assumptions regarding possible levels of inflation over the course of your retirement. Readers who are somewhat skilled at math can attempt to make these calculations themselves, or they can use computer programs designed for this purpose that are available on line, such as the *Retirement Planning Calculator*.[3] Given the complexity of these models and the number of assumptions that must be made, it is probably best to consult with a financial planner to develop an investment plan.

SAVING

One critical variable in retirement planning is the age at which you begin to save. The University of Iowa Extension Service notes in its publication on Retirement Planning that a man who begins to save at 20 needs to save only $5.48 per day in order to accumulate a nest egg of $1.5 million at the age of 65, assuming a 10% rate of return. Of course, most of the readers of this book are considerably older than 25, and most of them did not begin to save anything at all at the age of 20.[4] Nevertheless, even if you are 50 or 60 and you have not saved at all for retirement, you can still do a good deal to improve your situation if you begin saving *now*. Let's assume first that you are 50 and you are planning to retire at 65. Assuming a 10 percent rate of return on a tax deferred investment, you could accumulate $100,000 in 15 years by saving just $241 per month, or $1,000,000 by saving $2,410 per month.[5] Even if you are 60 now, if you saved $1,291 per month each month for the next five years and invested the money in a tax deferred investment at 10 percent, you would have $100,000 at 65.

Therefore it is literally never too late to start saving. This is particularly true since the level of income that we feel we need each month during retirement is for most of us only partly derived from savings and investments. A substantial proportion of this required income will likely come from retirement benefits and Social Security. In addition, with more and more men remaining healthy and active much later in life, the age of 65 is no longer the accepted point at which men retire.

CHANGING NORMATIVE RETIREMENT AGE

This is evident in the Social Security system. The earliest that an individual can begin to receive Social Security benefits is 62, but if you choose to draw benefits at 62, you will receive on 80 percent of what you would receive if you wait until "normal" or "full" retirement age. This age used to be 65 for everyone, but it is gradually shifting upward. It is now only 65 for individuals born before 1937. It ranges from 65 years and 2 months to 65 years and 10 months for individuals born between 1938 and 1942. It is 66 years for individuals born between 1943 and 1954. It ranges from 66 years and 2 months to 66 years and 10 months for individuals born between 1955 and 1959. And it is 67 for those born in 1960 of later. Moreover, individuals who wait until they are 70 to begin receiving social security payments will receive more than those who begin to collect at the normative retirement age.[6]

CONTINUING TO WORK

For all these reasons, therefore, more and more men over 65 are deciding to continue to work. A recent AARP survey found that 70 percent of mid-life and older workers believed that they would continue to work, at least part-time, during the period following 65 that has traditionally been viewed as the period of retirement.[7] Most of these respondents said that they expected that they would need to earn at least some money to make ends meet, but they also said that they liked working and wanted to continue to be productive.

Continuing to work may have implications for your Social Security benefits if you chose to begin receiving benefits before your full retirement age. Those who chose to receive benefits between the age of 62 and their full retirement age are allowed to earn only $12,960 (in 2007) before their benefits are reduced by $1 for every $2 earned over that amount. In the year that you reach your full retirement age, the earning limits increases to $34,400, and any benefits received in the months prior to your birthday month are reduced by $1 for every $3 earned over this limit. However, beginning in the month that you reach you full retirement age, you can have unlimited earned income and still collect full Social Security benefits.[8] These regulations tend to encourage healthy and active men over 62 to wait until at least their full retirement age to begin taking Social Security payments. Many wait until they are 70. Then you never need to worry about having benefits reduced because you earned too much money.

SUMMARY

More and more men are living longer and remaining active and healthy longer and longer. For most of us there is no need to retire in the sense of kicking back and sitting in the rocking chair. However, we may well have a pension plan that maxes out after 30 years or at a specific age like 60 or 65. We may also be in a job that has a mandatory retirement age. Or we may be offered an early retirement package. Under these circumstances, it may indeed be financially beneficial for a man to retire from the job he has held most of his life. However, retiring from that job does not in any way imply that he needs to retire from his field or from remunerative work in some other field that he finds interesting.

Given this flexibility, it is important that we remain aware of our options and determine the course of action that will be most beneficial financially, operating on the assumption that we are *not* under any circumstances going to be hanging out on the porch drinking iced tea and watching the traffic go by. Many men enjoy working out the costs and benefits of various strategies by themselves. However, retirement planning is a complex task, and you are well advised to get some professional help.

The matter of self-worth is a significant factor in the decision as to whether to retire. My father, a man in business for himself, went to the office every working day until shortly before he died at age 94. He always had a purpose in his days and a destination to go to. People counted on him, and this gave him a purpose and an identity. He did not fade away into mortality, but rather continued to interact with his family, his business associates, and members of the clergy. He had opinions regarding world affairs. He was a role model for me, as he should be for baby boomers who are looking at the potential of 30 more productive and creative years.

Chapter Twelve

SUBSTANCE USE AND ABUSE

Jack's Drinking Problem

Jack is 78 and in poor health. His is suffering from liver disease brought on by excessive alcohol consumption over the past 15 or 16 years. Jack was not a drinker during the better part of his adult life. He had grown up in a family with a history of alcoholism, and for this reason he had avoided drinking altogether during adolescence and early adulthood. At the age of 30 Jack began working in the hotel industry, and he modified his previous habit of refusing alcohol altogether to a pattern of accepting a drink if one was offered but then barely touching it. He felt that it would be bad for his professional image to be perceived as a "tea totaler." However, he was still very careful about drinking, partly because he remembered his family history, and partly because he felt that he needed to be mentally sharp and alert at any time that he socialized with colleagues and clients.

At 60, Jack retired. At this point, he did not feel that he needed to make the point that he was a good social drinker, and initially he stopped accepting alcohol when it was offered. However, Jack and his wife moved into a retirement community where "cocktail hour" at the clubhouse was a pretty big deal, so Jack once again resumed the pattern of accepting an alcoholic drink when one was offered but actually drinking very little of it. At this point in his life, however, Jack's lifelong strategy for dealing with alcohol did not hold up. For one thing, Jack no longer felt that he had to be quite so guarded in his socializing. He wanted to fit in with his new neighbors, but he didn't feel that he had to be totally in control at every moment, because he really didn't need to impress anyone, cultivate business relationships, or engage in any negotiations. In addition, Jack looked back on his life and saw that he never had a problem with drinking, as had other members of his family. Therefore he was a bit less concerned with the possibility that his drinking could get out of hand. Jack also experienced somewhat more pressure to drink from his new neighbors than he had from colleagues at work. It seemed like someone was always making a toast or asking everyone to drink up, and someone was always there to refill the wine glass. Finally, Jack's wife Beth had been a moderate social drinker for her entire life, and she had always thought that he worried too much about the possible dangers of alcohol. She thought that she liked him a little better after he "loosened up" a bit, and she told him so.

So at the age of 60 Jack actually began to drink alcohol for the first time. And he found that he liked it. It seemed to him that he felt the effects of the alcohol more than he had in the past. It helped him to relax and be sociable. He began to look forward to cocktail hour. He progressed from one drink to two or three. In time, he progressed further to having another drink or two when he and his wife returned home from cocktail hour. He got some positive reinforcement from his wife for his new zest for life, and a couple of times when the two of them were just a bit "high" they felt that they had better sex than they had before. So Jack continued with his social drinking, and for a year or so there did not appear to be any negative aspect of this new part of his life.

About a year and a half after they had moved to the retirement community, Jack had his first negative experience with the drinking. Jack's wife had gone off for a few days to visit with an old girlfriend. Jack didn't feel like going to the community cocktail hour alone, so he stayed home. He thought he would have a glass of wine. He sat down to watch TV and enjoy his wine. He remembers pouring a second glass. The next thing he remembers is waking up the next morning with a very bad headache. He was just trying to figure out what happened when his wife called. She had called the night before and gotten no answer, and she was worried. Jack said he wasn't feeling well and had simply gone to bed early. She asked why he hadn't called her before he went to bed. He couldn't think of anything to say except that he had had a glass of wine and just forgot. His wife was annoyed, and asked him if it was just one glass, or more. That was the first time that she or anyone else had questioned his drinking. He said maybe he had had more, and he would be more careful in the future. That satisfied his wife for the time being, and they hung up the phone. Jack then began to look around the house to clean up and get dressed. He was shocked to find not one, but two empty wine bottles. Apparently he had finished one bottle and opened another the night before, although he did not remember it. Jack was worried about this, because he remembered that his father would often drink and not remember anything that happened after a certain point in the evening.

So Jack made a promise to himself that he would be more careful in the future. The next few days he avoided drinking altogether, even though, for the first time he could remember, he really felt that he wanted to have a drink. His wife returned and they resumed their normal social activities, including cocktail hour at the club. He kept himself down to a drink or two for a while, and for a while he avoided further drinking at home after dinner. Over time, however, he resumed the second round of drinking after they came home. He began to drink more at night. Once or twice his wife suggested that he had had enough. On these occasions he sometimes stopped, but sometimes he took another drink surreptitiously. Sometimes he also stayed up after she went to bed to watch TV, but when he stayed up he also did some further drinking. In time, it got to the point that Jack would routinely find his way to bed some time after his wife, but in the morning he would not actually remember coming in to bed. Nor would he have any recollection of when he came to bed or what he had been watching on TV.

This pattern persisted for quite a while. Jack's wife was quite a sound sleeper, and she wasn't really aware of when he came to bed each night. However, she was growing increasingly annoyed that he did not come to bed with her, and she could tell that he was hung over in the morning. She suggested that he cut back and make it a point to come to bed with her each night. He knew that she was right and agreed to do so, but he found that he could not fall asleep, and he often found himself getting up after Beth had fallen asleep to take a drink or two to help him sleep. When this started, Jack was clearly wiped out in the morning, and he began sleeping later and later. This interfered with the activities that Jack and Beth had engaged in during the days, things like golf and walking. At this point Beth was really concerned and urged Jack to stop drinking. She said that she could not understand how someone who had gone through his whole life sober had become so dependent on alcohol. Jack agreed with her and tried to cut back on his drinking or to stop his drinking. But he could not. He went on this way for the next 12 or 13 years. He never got into trouble outside the home, like becoming disorderly or being arrested for drunk driving. But the quality of his life with Beth was clearly not what it should have been.

Then Jack's physical examination indicated that he had liver disease, and his physician questioned him carefully on his drinking. His problem was clear, and the doctor told him that he had to stop drinking, right now, or he would probably die very soon. This frightened Jack, and after some discussion with Beth and some friends, he decided to go to Alcoholics Anonymous. That was not helpful for him, however. He said that the people there were nice enough, but they were all so much younger. Many of them used other drugs besides alcohol, and many of them had been in serious trouble with the law. He said that he felt out of place among that particular group. So he stopped going. He didn't make any real efforts to find a group more similar to himself in terms of current age and the age when their drinking problem developed. He has cut down a great deal on his drinking because of the fear of dying, but he has not stopped. He does not think that he can stop, and each day that he tries to avoid drinking is "torture."

What we see in Jack is an example of late onset alcoholism, which is not uncommon among men in their 60s. I told Jack's story because I wanted to be sure to warn readers that this is a real possibility that you should be aware of and vigilant about. There are a number of factors that increase the likelihood of becoming dependent on alcohol as we grow older.

LATE ONSET ALCOHOL DEPENDENCY

Alcohol dependency develops over time. As we consume alcohol over time, we our bodies develop a tolerance to its effects. Over time we tend to need more and more alcohol to achieve the same state of intoxication. Therefore, our consumption tends to increase gradually. At the same time, our bodies tend to develop a need for the substance, so that discontinuing use can result in unpleasant sensations. This is why regular drinkers tend to experience a palpable craving for the drink or two after work. This is also why very heavy drinkers may experience serious withdrawal symptoms if they attempt to quit cold turkey. In people who are genetically predisposed to become dependent, the time period required to develop tolerance and withdrawal symptoms may be rather short in duration. For those who are not so predisposed, the period required to develop this dependency can be very long indeed. Thus individuals who are not particularly disposed to alcoholism may become dependent over a long period of time, and the negative indications of alcohol dependency may simply begin to emerge at around the time they hit 60 or so. On the other hand, individuals who have not been drinkers over the course of their lives, perhaps because they have alcoholism in the family, are vulnerable to develop dependency rather rapidly, should they begin to drink once they have passed the 60-year mark.

Physiological Changes and Alcohol

The simple effects of time are exacerbated by a number of natural age-related physical changes that occur as we grow older. For example, the amount of fat in our bodies tends to increase and amount of cellular fluids tends to decrease. These changes tend to increase the impact that alcohol has on our bodies. Our digestive processes tend to slow down somewhat, so the alcohol that we consume is not metabolized as quickly as it was when we were younger. For this reason, having three drinks over the course of two hours may have had little noticeable effect on you when you were 35 or 45, but it may make you quite drunk when you are 65. The increased potency of alcohol as we grow older has several negative consequences. First of all, to the extent that the feeling of being intoxicated is experienced as pleasurable, it increases our desire to consume alcohol. We like it, so we have it more often and in larger amounts. This increases our vulnerability to becoming dependent. In addition, being intoxicated is dangerous. Research has identified alcohol consumption as a factor that contributes to the increased risk of injury due to falling among older individuals.[1]

Changes in body composition and bodily functioning also increase the effect of prescription and over-the-counter drugs on older individuals. Furthermore, some prescriptions and over-the-counter drugs tend to potentiate the effects of alcohol. Since older persons tend to take more medications than younger people, both the direct effects of these medications and their interaction with alcohol can increase the magnitude and duration of the effects of alcohol. This leaves us still more vulnerable to developing a dependency.

Other physical issues include insomnia, which develops in some individuals as they grow older. Many people take a drink or two at bedtime to help them fall asleep. This works for some, but others find that they will wake up during the night and need to have another drink to get back to sleep. All in all, you will be much better off if you get some exercise and make yourself tired. You will also sleep better if you have a regular schedule that requires you to rise early each day. Many people cannot sleep at night because they have barely awakened during the day. Some of us experience chronic pain of various types and degrees as we grow older, and alcohol can also be used to cope with these aches and pains. Here again, there are better ways to handle the pain. If we are talking about mild muscle and joint pain, an occasional massage can help to relax you and loosen up your muscles. Acupuncture and stretching out with yoga exercises may also provide relief. Heating pads and topical analgesics are also useful. For debilitating pain, prescription medication is preferable to simply dulling the senses with alcohol, although obviously one needs to be careful with prescription pain medication as well.

Social Changes and Alcohol Use

In addition to these physiological changes, social changes may increase the tendency to use alcohol and thus the tendency to develop a dependency. We have already considered the question of retirement and the possible loss or reduction of professional roles. We have already mentioned as well the loss of family roles as children grow up and move away, and the losses associated with the deaths of friends and loved ones. All these losses can lead to loss of self-esteem, grieving, loneliness, and boredom. Many men who are experiencing these feelings self-medicate with alcohol. It numbs the pain. However, this is a poor coping strategy, because alcohol is also a depressant, and in the long run it is likely to leave us feeling more depressed and helpless, rather than less so.

On the other hand, as we saw with Jack, retirement can have the effect of removing previous restraints on alcohol consumption. We tend to socialize more with friends and neighbors who are also retired. We tend to travel and go on cruises. We tend to have celebrations. All of these activities produce opportunities for drinking and may result in peer pressure to drink. In addition, we tend to have fewer responsibilities and more free time. If you don't have to get up early to go to work, it's easy to rationalize staying up a little later and having one or two more drinks. This is certainly just one more good reason why it is so very important to remain actively engaged in life through productive activities of one type of another. If you know that your need to lead the boy scout field trip tomorrow morning at 7:00 A.M., you will have something to look forward to and an excellent reason for not staying up drinking tonight.

Recognizing When We Have a Problem

For a number of reasons, men past 60 who have a problem with alcohol dependence may have difficulty recognizing that there is a problem. We may be living alone, perhaps because we have lost a spouse. We may have retired. We may not be driving as much as we did when we were younger and we were working. These possibilities represent likely decreases in the chance that problem drinking would be detected by the most common routes, that is, by complaints from family members, by failure to perform work related functions efficiently, and by being stopped for driving under the influence. If we have been living with a partner for some time, there is a good chance that we will have similar habits when it comes to drinking. It is not unusual for both members of a couple to have a problem with alcohol later in life. However, the partners may rationalize the problem by viewing their drinking as normative, at least in relation to their drinking partner. Even if one partner has a problem and the other does not, the couple may have worked out an accommodation over the course of years. In the case of Jack described above, Beth clearly had concerns regarding his drinking and even pointed out that it was affecting their relationship. Yet she never really mounted a full assault on Jack's drinking. Perhaps she minimized the problem in her mind, thinking that even though Jack's drinking was certainly not good, it was not worth creating a war over. Perhaps she was generally satisfied with the secure life that they had in the retirement community and simply didn't want to rock the boat.

It is also the case that physical problems associated with excessive drinking may be misattributed to the aging process. Jack clearly suffered from insomnia when he tried to cut back on the use of alcohol as a sleep aid, yet many older men who do not have a drinking problem do experience difficulty falling to sleep. If Jack were to tell his doctor that he was having trouble sleeping, it is doubtful that the doctor would inquire about his drinking habits. On the contrary, it is more like that the doctor would prescribe a sedative, which might very well have a synergistic effect with the alcohol that Jack was consuming. It is also safe to suggest that most physicians are not looking out for alcohol abuse issues in their older male patients. It was only a serious situation with liver disease that prompted Jack's physician to ask about alcohol and recommend that he stop drinking.

Furthermore, many physicians steer clear of potentially embarrassing topics with their patients. Unfortunately, many doctors are predisposed to ignore the problem. I recently discussed this issue with a physician friend of mine, who felt that social workers and substance abuse workers worried far too much about the drinking habits of older patients. He told me a story of his great grandfather, who immigrated to the United States around the turn of the century and established a reputation in the family by becoming the head gardener in the White House under President Hoover. My friend told me that his great grandfather lived to be 113 years old, and that he worked in his grandmother's rose garden every day until he was well over 100. My friend also told me that his great grandfather's secret to long life was that every day at lunch time he ate a can of kippered herring and drank a pint of schnapps. So here was my friend the doctor telling me that he believed that alcohol dependence was overblown, because his great grandfather seemed to get along just fine. Although my friend was clearly making an unwarranted generalization from a single (and possible apocryphal) example, it is probably the case that many people who might be in a position to identify a man over 60 with an alcohol abuse problem are predisposed to overlook or misattribute the indications of the problem.

This really means that we had better take responsibility for self-diagnosis. Now this flies in the face of the caveats of substance abuse professionals, who stress the extreme likelihood of denial on the part of substance abusers in general, and who would appreciate the even greater potential for denial of the problem in a man who does not have to get up each morning and drive to work and back. So what I have done is to prepare a set of questions for you to answer to determine whether you might have some reason for concern regarding your drinking behavior.

THE DRINKING BEHAVIOR QUIZ

Please take a few minutes to answer each of the following questions. Just answer each question yes or no. Be honest.

1. In the last few years, have you used alcohol more frequently (e.g., more times per week) than you did earlier in your life?

    ___ yes   ___ no

2. Do you ever feel an urge to have an alcoholic beverage (e.g., at a particular time of day)?

    ___ yes   ___ no

3. Do you ever take a drink to help you fall asleep?

    ___ yes   ___ no

4. Do you ever have more than two alcoholic drinks on a single occasion?

    ___ yes   ___ no

5. Has a friend or family member ever suggested to you that perhaps you have "had enough"?

    ___ yes   ___ no

6. Has anyone ever told you that you act "differently" when you've been drinking?

    ___ yes   ___ no

7. Have you ever missed or had to cancel an appointment because you have felt "hung over?"

    ___ yes   ___ no

8. Have you ever attempted to limit or curtail the amount that you drink?

    ___ yes   ___ no

9. On the average, do you consume 7 or more alcoholic drinks during the course of a week?

___ yes   ___ no

10. Have you ever awakened and realized that you could not remember a part of what happened the night before?

___ yes   ___ no

11. Can you stop drinking after one or two drinks without experiencing any difficulty?

___ yes   ___ no

12. Have you ever gotten into a verbal or physical altercation when you have been drinking?

___ yes   ___ no

13. Has your partner, a good friend, or another family member ever suggested that perhaps you should cut back on the frequency or the amount of your drinking?

___ yes   ___ no

If you answered "yes" to any of the questions from 1 through 10, "no" to question 11, or "yes" question 12 or 13, you should consider the possibility that you are vulnerable to or possibly developing a dependence on alcohol.

Count the number of "yes" responses to questions 1 through 10, 12 and 13. Add a point if you responded "no" to question 11. If the resulting total is greater than 4, you may want to take some steps to curtail your drinking. If you answered "yes" to one or more of questions 5, 6, 7, 10, 12, or 13, you may be well on the way to a serious problem. In this case, you might want to consider discontinuing the use of alcohol altogether. The problem here is that the development of alcohol dependence is progressive, and the physical changes we experience as we pass 60 make us more vulnerable to the development of such dependence than we were when we were younger. In any event, attempting to discontinue the consumption of alcohol will provide a good test. If you can simply decide to stop and do so without experiencing any difficulty or discomfort, then you will·know that you do not have a problem. If you do experience difficulty or discomfort or find yourself unable to stop, then you will have additional evidence that perhaps there is a problem, and you might consider getting some help.

THE INCIDENCE OF ALCOHOL DEPENDENCE AMONG MEN OVER 60

Just to reinforce the point that alcohol is something that we need to be careful about as we get older, let me cite some statistics regarding the prevalence of alcohol abuse and dependence among men over 60. According to Marc Schuckit, the director of the Alcohol and Drug Treatment Program and the Alcohol Research Center at the San Diego Veterans Administration Medical Center:

> Among the people who come into the emergency room who are 65 and older, the rate of alcohol dependence pushes 15%...So if you are in a geriatric clinic some-place...it is likely that a substantial proportion of the older people coming to see you are alcohol- or drug-dependent...If you don't have a high index of suspicion, you are going to miss them.[2]

Schuckit notes that about 40% of individuals who experience alcohol dependence after the age of 65 developed the dependence after the age of 50, whereas 60% are people who have misused alcohol for many years but have been lucky enough to live to 65.[3] Rigler pointed out that late-onset alcoholics generally have fewer health problems and more social supports than elderly alcoholics who have long histories of alcohol abuse. For this reason, the prognosis of late onset alcoholics is better.[4]

Furthermore, the problem of late onset alcohol dependence and abuse is far more common among men past the age of 60 than women past 60. The federal Substance Abuse and Mental Health Services Administration (SAMHSA) estimates that 80% of those over 50 who sought treatment for alcohol addiction in 2003 were men.[5] It was also reported that many of the older men seeking treatment for alcohol addiction were first-time treatment participants. Charles Curie, a SAMHSA administrator, has stated that

> alcohol abuse among older adults is something that few want to talk about, and a problem for which even fewer seek treatment on their own...Too often, family members are ashamed of the problem and choose not to address it. Healthcare providers tend not to ask older patients about alcohol abuse if it wasn't a problem earlier in their earlier years. That may help explain why so many of the alcohol-related admissions to treatment among older adults are for first-time treatment, even though we know that treatment works well at every age.[6]

So the potential for late onset alcohol dependence is significant in men past 60, and there is a good chance that it won't be identified by family members or by your physician. That's why I included the Drinking Behavior Test in this chapter. The National Institute on Alcohol Abuse and Alcoholism has issued low-risk guidelines for elderly men.[7] The guidelines are strict: No more than one drink per day on the average; and a maximum of two drinks on any drinking occasion.

TREATMENT OPTIONS FOR ALCOHOL DEPENDENCE AND ABUSE

If you do think that you might have a problem with alcohol, you should see your physician and seek a referral for treatment. Seeing your physician is important, because you will need to assess the severity of dependence. If you have a substantial dependency and you simply quit drinking "cold turkey," you may experience withdrawal symptoms that can be quite severe. These symptoms include sweating, elevated heart rate, hand tremors, insomnia, nausea, hallucinations, agitation, anxiety, and even seizures.[8] According to the Surgeon general, in older adults these symptoms can even be life threatening.[9] For this reason, the detoxification of older adult patients ideally should be done in an in patient setting. Schuckit usually recommends the use of long-acting benzodiazepines such as Valium to help with the symptoms of withdrawal.

Beyond the issue of detoxification, men over 60 who are seeking to discontinue alcohol use may seek the support of a group such as Alcoholics Anonymous (AA). In selecting a meeting group, however, you would be well advised to shop around to find a meeting whose members are fairly similar to you in terms of age and background. Particularly if you are attempting to deal with late onset alcohol dependence and you have never really experienced such problems as violent behavior, trouble with the law, or concurrent use of illicit drugs, there will be some meetings where people will be talking about a lot of experiences that you really cannot relate to, and this may make you feel somewhat disconnected. This was Jack's experience when he attended an AA meeting. If you are living in an area in which there are a reasonably large number of people who are over 60, the chances are pretty good that you will be able to find a group alcoholics who have experiences that are similar to your own.

PRESCRIPTION, OVER-THE-COUNTER, AND ILLICIT STREET DRUGS

The Special Committee on Aging reported that individuals over 60 are three times as likely as younger persons to use prescriptions drugs,[10] and the use of over-the-counter medications by those over 60 is even more extensive.[11] The most commonly prescribed psychoactive medications for older adults are the benzodiazepines (e.g., Valium), antidepressants (e.g., Elavil), and opiate/opioid analgesics (e.g., Codeine, Oxycontin). These drugs do have the potential to be abused. Schuckit notes that all these drugs cause an intoxication similar to that associated with alcohol, and they have a withdrawal syndrome that is similar to that of alcohol as well.[12] These drugs all tend to potentiate the effects of alcohol. In addition, both prescription and over-the-counter drugs have the potential to be misused inadvertently, simply because patients misread directions. Although the abuse of prescription medication appears to be more common among older women than among older men,[13] the National Household Survey on Drug Abuse concluded that older men were more likely than women to report the use of sedatives, tranquilizers, and stimulants.[14]

Both men and women are at risk of abusing analgesics, some of which are highly and rapidly addicting.[15]

Given the potential for abuse of prescription and over-the-counter medications, I would advise readers to be cautious in using these drugs. Be particularly careful to follow the directions for prescription medications and to follow any instructions to avoid the use of alcohol when taking these drugs.

In contrast to alcohol and prescription medications, men over 60 are less likely to use illicit street drugs. The Epidemiologic Catchment Area Study indicated that less than 0.1 percent of adults over 60 met the DSM-III criteria for drug abuse/dependence on illegal drugs. As a point of comparison, the proportion of individuals in the 18- to 24 year-old age group who met these criteria was 3.5 percent.[16] There may be some change in these figures as those of us in the baby boomer generation enter our 60s, as we are now doing in greater and greater numbers. We were in the generation of the flower children, and our use of illegal drugs like marijuana and LSD was far more prevalent than that of the generation before us. Many of us outgrew pot a long time ago and never went back, and yet many a social setting will have the occasional joint being passed around, and the old attraction to that familiar smell may still pertain. As with everything else, my advice is restraint and moderation.

SUMMARY

As we mature and become emotionally and financially settled, we can afford to relax in some areas where we have had to struggle over the course of our lives. Looking after our health is not one of these areas. We must be careful with diet and exercise, have regular medical care, *and be extremely careful with drugs.* For many reasons that I have noted in this chapter, we become more vulnerable to substance dependence and abuse as we enter the seventh decade of life. Alcohol is particularly problematic, because it is socially acceptable to drink, and because we are likely to think that we are entitled to "kick back and have a drink." You are entitled. But be careful. Alcohol is a powerful drug and a depressant. It is also addictive, and the longer you live and drink, the more chance you have to develop a dependence. It also interacts with other drugs that you may be taking for good medical reasons. Remember the questions in the Drinking Behavior Quiz, and heed the warning signs.

Chapter Thirteen

DEALING WITH OUR CHILDREN AND OUR PARENTS

This chapter was originally titled, "Dealing with Our Adult Children." However, in the course of thinking about the issues that we men over 60 experience in relation to our adult children, it became very clear to me that the increase in life expectancy has added a new and interrelated set of issues that arise in relation to our older parents, who are very likely to be still alive and well. In fact, Trafford has observed that it is not really appropriate at this point in history to talk in terms of the three-generation family.[1] Today it is much more appropriate to think of four generations of family members interacting in complex patterns. Typically, these four generations would include dependent children (our grandkids), adult parents (our kids), grandparents (us), and our parents, whom Trafford refers to as "Centenarians." In America these four different generations typically have frequent contact, and occasionally they all live in the same house. To give you an example of such a family and an idea of some of the complexities associated with multiple generations interacting, consider my friend Brad.

Brad's Four-Generation Family

Brad is a 61-year-old neurologist. He lives with his wife of 10 years, Sarah, in a large Victorian home in an affluent suburb of New York. Sarah is 60, and she is a psychologist. Brad and Sarah are both engaged in full-time private practice, which they run out of offices in their home. Also living in the house with them is Sarah's mom, Caroline, who is 81, and Sarah's son, Brian, who is 25.

Sarah's mom came to live with them about two years ago, when her (second) husband, John, to whom she had been married for 25 years, suddenly decided to divorce her and move to France. John is 83 and just a little bit nuts. Caroline did not want to get divorced. She was aware of and unhappy with his erratic and unpredictable behavior, but she had settled into life with him and she was very comfortable with her lifestyle. Together John and Caroline had been comfortably retired for some time, and they had lived in a nice home in a suburb of San Francisco. Caroline really loved the home, but she could not keep it when they divorced. They sold their home and split all their assets. This left Caroline with her own retirement fund of about $750,000. She did not feel that she had enough money to enable her to buy another residence and still have enough money left over to live comfortably. She was also emotionally devastated and felt that she needed the support of her closest family members. Therefore, she opted to come east and live with her daughter and son-in-law. This would make her finances manageable, and she would also be close to Sarah's children and grandchildren, all of whom lived with or close by to Sarah.

Sarah has three children, including two daughters aged 35 and 37 from her first marriage, both of whom are married and have children of their own, and Brian, her son from her second marriage. Brian is very smart and very personable, but he is not a hard worker. Brian went off to the state college after high school but flunked out and moved back home. Then he went to a technical school to learn about computer network security. He did well there, and now he is building a business servicing the network security and electronics needs of individuals and small businesses. He appears to be doing quite well, but he has not yet determined that he can afford to move out of the house into his own place, at least not without cramping his lifestyle. Brian has a steady girlfriend who stays overnight at the house several times a week.

Further complicating this multigenerational family constellation are Sarah's two daughters and their families. The older daughter, Rebecca, lives within blocks of Sarah in the same town. She has two sons, Stuart and Ron, aged 6 and 3. Rebecca and her husband Mike have a relatively modest income. (Really they do quite well in comparison to the population in general but not that well in comparison to the typically affluent residents of the upscale town in which they live.) Accordingly, Sarah and Brad help them out a bit by allowing their housekeeper to provide daytime childcare services for Stuart and Ron, by frequently babysitting themselves, by buying the kids toys and clothing and paying for various forms of entertainment, and by taking everyone out or having the whole family over to dinner several times a week.

Therefore, on most days, at dinnertime Brad and Sarah's house is filled with the two youngsters who are 6 and 3, Sarah's 25-year-old son who has not quite separated, her 30-something daughter and son-in-law, the 60-something couple themselves, and Sarah's 81-year-old mom.

Sarah's younger daughter Ellie lives in another suburb about 40 minutes away. Ellie is married to Sam, who is a very successful investment banker about 10 years older than Ellie. Sam had been married once before but had no children from that marriage. Ellie and Sam have three sons, Sam Jr., Justine, and Jack, aged 6, 4, and 2. They live in another upscale suburb about 40 minutes away from Brad and Sarah. Ellie, Sam, and their kids are generally present at Sunday dinners and on holidays, further increasing the complexity of the intergenerational family interactions (as well as the noise level).

Brad's family constellation may seem somewhat unusual, but in fact it illustrates a number of demographic trends that have tended to affect men over 60 in their relationships with their families. First of all, the increase in life expectancy and health is clear in the presence of four generations in the same household. Second, the prevalence of divorce in our society is illustrated by Brad and Sarah, each of whom has been married before, as well as by Sarah's mom Caroline, who exemplifies the increase in the number of older individuals who are getting divorced. As you will see later in this chapter, divorces at every generational level can have a significant impact on intergenerational family interactions and conflicts. The experience of Caroline in coming to live with her daughter and son-in-law after her divorce illustrates one of circumstances that frequently leads parents to come to live with their adult children. Widowhood is another such circumstance.

Brian's return home illustrates the ever increasing phenomenon of "failure to launch" and the impact that this can have, even on couples over 60, if the child in question was born after the parents were 30 or 35. In Sarah's case, this issue is compounded by the fact that both her mother and her older daughters tend to offer unsolicited advice on how to solve the "Brian problem." This advice typically involves insisting that he move out or pay rent, which Sarah and Brad are not prepared to do. This issue is exacerbated by a number of factors. First, Sarah is a psychologist who prides herself on advising people how to solve their problems, so she finds it difficult to be advised about her own issues (especially by her mother and her daughters). Second, Sarah feels a bit guilty because she divorced Brian's dad to be with Brad, and on some level she suspects that this divorce may have contributed to Brian's academic difficulties. Brad keeps quiet because he is in the stepfather position and does not want to rock the boat.

The circumstances of Sarah's two adult daughters illustrate the complexities that can develop when our children are either less successful than we are or more successful than we are. If they are less successful we may feel that they requiring financial assistance. In this case, helping them can make us feel useful and valuable, but it can also make us a bit resentful, when we recall that "nobody ever did this stuff for me." Relating to adult children who are more affluent than you are can also raise questions. Thus Brad notes that "it feels funny when your son-in-law picks up the check for dinner." Ellie and Sam and their kids spend two weeks each year at a very exclusive beach and golf resort in South Carolina, where they rent a house for an amount that Brad perceives as a small fortune. This past year they asked Sarah and Brad to join them there for one of these two weeks. They all had a great time, but Brad noted that it definitely required some cognitive adjustments on his part. Brad said that he didn't know whether to be grateful or embarrassed. At one point Brad thanked Ellie and Sam for being so nice to them, and he told them that now he understood "why parents want their kids to be successful." That remark seemed to be well received, for Ellie and Sam were happy to be acknowledged for their accomplishments and for doing something nice. At another point Brad remarked to them that this was a very special vacation, because he never would have been able to spend a week at such a nice place. This time Brad was not so sure that he had said the right thing, since he thought that they might have interpreted it as a criticism for spending too much money. The point is that all these differences between generations have implications for the interpersonal dynamics of the family.

I will say more about each of these issues as we move along in this chapter. At this point, I would like to describe the nature of the relationships that most men passing their sixtieth birthday tend to have with their adult children and with their own parents.

RELATIONSHIPS WITH OUR ADULT CHILDREN AND OUR PARENTS

In their book, *Intergenerational Communication across the Lifespan,* Williams and Nussbaum argue that although the popular media tend to depict the family as a defunct social institution that has disintegrated beyond the point of repair, the fact of the matter is that most children maintain enduring relationships with relationships with their parents, and "the adult child–elderly parent relationship has the added bonus of two mature adults interacting within a relationship negotiated through many years of both joy and pain."[2] According to Nussbaum and colleagues, the child-parent relationship remains strong across as many as 70 years because: (1) the participants tend to be in consistent contact with each other; (2) they show high levels of affection toward each other; (3) they tend to help each other out when help is needed; (4) they tend to reach a consensus on the most basic values, beliefs, and opinions; and (5) they learn how to avoid expressing hostile thoughts.[3] The idea of family consensus on basic values and the idea of avoiding the expression of hostile thoughts implies the working of a familial accommodation process. Both parent and adult children tend to exercise a form of accommodative censorship that "protects the solidarity of the relationship." So we tend to remain close to both our adult children and our own parents.

Having a close relationship does not necessarily mean living together in the same home. Only about 15 percent of Americans who are over the age of 65 co-reside with adult children.[4] When adult children and their parent(s) do co-reside, the parents are as likely to live with an adult son as with an adult daughter. The majority of elderly parents who live with an adult son or daughter live with a child who has either never been married or has been married previously but not now. Thus it is somewhat uncommon for a child's spouse to be living in the same home as the child's parent(s). There are many circumstances that occasion co-residence. It is commonly believed that ill-health on the part of one or both parents typically necessitates that they move in with an adult child who can care for them. However, research suggests that this reason accounts for co-residence in fewer than half of the cases where co-residence occurs. Older adults often move in with adult children following the death of a spouse. In addition, adult children often move back into their parents' home in response to the financial setbacks of a divorce. Thus coresidence may result from circumstances that affect either the older parent or the adult child. An older parent may move in with his or her adult child; or an adult child may move back in with his or her parents.

In the more frequent situation where an older parent does not co-reside with an adult child, they are nevertheless likely to live relatively near to each other and to have relatively frequent contact. A national survey commissioned by the American Association of Retired Persons indicated that more than half of adult children live within a one-hour drive of their parents.[5] The survey also showed that 69 percent of adult children have weekly contact with their mothers; and 20 percent have daily contact with their mothers. Similarly, a National Survey of Families and Households indicated that 40 percent of adult children have face-to-face contact with their parents once a week or more.[6] The frequent contact of adult children with their parents also means that grandparents tend to have frequent contact with their grandchildren. Coke and Twaite note that nearly three-quarters of both white and black grandparents reported that they had seen their grandchildren within the last two weeks.[7] The frequent contact between grandparents and their grandchildren adds to the complexity of intergenerational relationships because this contact invites grandparents to make observations and comments on how the grandchildren are developing and how the parents are performing their parental role.

Although there is no general consensus among researchers on the best way to measure relationship quality, there is general agreement that adult children and their parents typically feel that they are emotionally close to each other.[8] Typical of this extensive body or research is the Interpersonal Linkages Survey conducted by Lawton, Silverstein, and Bengston. These investigators concluded that 80 percent of adult children interviewed in a national survey reported "emotionally close" relationships with their parents.[9]

Research also indicates clearly that adult Americans and their parents typically engage in extensive and continuous exchanges of assistance, which may take the form of advice and emotional support, tangible help with household chores, shopping, child care, or financial assistance. Most often this reciprocal exchange of support and assistance occurs during the course of stressful life transitions, such as the illness or death of a spouse or other family member, a divorce, or the loss of a job.[10] These stressful life transitions may impact either an adult child or an elderly parent, so the direction of the assistance may be from adult child to parent, from parent to adult child, or (most likely) both ways. The reciprocal nature of the adult child and parent relationship is not simply normative. Researchers have suggested that the exchange of resources, including companionship and affection as well as tangible help and financial assistance, is a powerful incentive to maintaining close intergenerational family relationships and frequent contact.[11] This implies that if we wish to maintain good and close relationships with our adult children, we should be prepared to both give and to receive various forms of support and assistance and that we should strive to maintain the mutuality of these exchanges. I consider this delicate and complex balance in the next section of this chapter.

OBLIGATION, AUTONOMY, AND MUTUALITY

The reciprocal exchange of support and assistance that characterizes relationships between adult children and their parents is founded on two sets of entrenched cultural norms that may sometimes appear to be in conflict. These are the norms of obligation and autonomy.[12] On the one hand, society tells us that adult children and their parents should assist and take care of each other over the course of their lives. But on the other hand, our society places great emphasis on independence. Adults are expected to assume responsibility for their own well-being. Closely related to the social expectation that individuals should take care of themselves is the view that nuclear families should maintain themselves independently of wider their kinship networks, and also the view that those outside the nuclear family, including kin, should respect the privacy of the nuclear family. The tension inherent between the norms of obligation and independence requires that relationships between adult children and their parents maintain a delicate balance. Both adult children and their parents want to know that they have someone to offer emotional and tangible support when needed, yet both adult children and their parents also want to maintain their individuality and autonomy. Therefore, we can and should help and allow ourselves to be helped, but we should not help or be helped so much that we take over the lives of those we are helping or allow our own lives to be taken over by those who are helping us.

This balance between obligation and autonomy is most easily maintained when things are going well for both the adult child and the older parent. The tension between obligation and autonomy tends to become more salient if the adult child has serious problems that require elderly parents to assume more responsibility than they can comfortably handle, or if the aging parents are in need of high levels of support that threaten the independence or the lifestyle of the adult children. Clark and Anderson express the issue of conflicting norms as follows:

> It would appear that in our culture there simply cannot be any happy role reversals between the generations, neither an increasing dependency of parent upon child nor a continuing reliance of child upon parent. The mores do not sanction it and children and parents resent it. The parent must remain strong and independent. If

his personal resources fail, the conflicts arise. The child, on the other hand, must not threaten the security of the parent with requests for monetary aid or other care when parental income has shrunk through retirement. The ideal situation is when both parent and child are functioning well. The parent does not depend on the child for nurturance or social interaction; these needs the parent can fulfill by himself elsewhere. He does not limit the freedom of his child nor arouse the child's feelings of guilt. The child establishes an independent dwelling, sustains his own family, and achieves a measure of the hope the parents had entertained for him. Such an ideal situation, of course, is more likely to occur when the parent is still provided with a spouse and where high socioeconomic status buttresses the parent and child.[13]

Of course, Clark and Anderson are describing an "ideal" situation, and we do not all live in ideal situations. There is a bit of a catch-22 involved in saying that we can balance obligation and autonomy when things are going well, because it is precisely when things are not going well for either the adult child or the aging parent that support and assistance may be needed. But there are some guidelines that we can use to help to keep the tension between obligation and autonomy within manageable limits. Consider these suggestions:

1. Don't give so much your adult child (or to your parent) that you will ruin your own life. Don't give so much financial support that you will place your own financial future in jeopardy. Don't take on so much babysitting and so many chores that you don't leave yourself time to nurture your relationships with your wife and your friends, or enough time to pursue your own leisure activities. If you feel that you are being asked to do so much that you are beginning to resent the request, you must learn to set limits and to say no if necessary. This may be a skill that you have had difficulty with over the course of your entire lifetime. Generally those of us who have been able to say no when necessary all along will also be able to say No now. In addition, those of us who have been able to say No all along will probably be less likely to be asked to provide unreasonable levels of assistance or support.

2. By the same token, don't ask for forms or levels of support from your adult children that will require them to disrupt their lives and lose their autonomy. If you do need to ask for help, try to give the request a limited and specific time frame.

3. *Do not* assume that because you are doing some babysitting or kicking in a little money for the kids' mortgage payment that you have the right to tell them how to live their lives. One of the great sources of conflict surrounding efforts to help is the idea that some parents have that their help entitles them to an equal vote or even a veto in making the important decisions of the nuclear family. This is clearly threatening the autonomy on the adult child and his or her family. If the kids are in need of help, they are probably already a bit insecure about their ability to be independent. They will resent any conditions that you attempt to place on your assistance; and they will most likely even resent your well-intentioned advice and suggestions. You must provide assistance because you want to help not because you want to control. You must tread very lightly here.

4. Conversely, if you find yourself in a position where you are receiving some help from your children, you must nevertheless be willing to stand up to protect your own autonomy and independence. Suppose you are retired and living alone on

a modest income in a small and somewhat run-down home in the country. You are comfortable, but limited in terms of discretionary income, and in terms of where you can go and what you can do. Suppose further that your grown-up son wants you to come and live with him and his family in his big house in the suburbs. He says he'll feel more comfortable knowing that you're right there. He says you'll have a much nicer place to live and the security of knowing there is always someone around. He says that there is plenty for you to do around the house, and you can help to take care of the kids. You are apprehensive because you value your privacy and your time alone, and you are not at all sure that you want to sign up as a full-time handyman and child care specialist. Well, if that's how you feel, you need to be able to say no. You need to be able to tell your son what you want out of your life and how you feel you can best achieve it.

5. Therefore, above all, work hard on developing intergenerational communication. You need to be able to talk about these issues with your children and with your parents. You have known them for a long time, and you have probably developed a pretty well-entrenched pattern of communication (or non-communication). The chances are that if you are close to them and you are already giving and/or receiving some forms of support and assistance, you are able to communicate openly and honestly. But this is not necessarily the case. If changing circumstances have recently led to more frequent contact and greater provision of support and assistance, you may not know how to communicate. If this is the case, you may need to make a special effort to develop these crucial communication skills. You may even want to seek some professional help in developing these skills, as well as in negotiating the parameters of mutual support.

There is one other point that needs to be made here relevant to Clark and Anderson's contention that a high socioeconomic status is predictive of good intergenerational relationships. They contend that being affluent contributes to harmonious intergenerational relationships, because affluence means that neither the adult children nor the older parents will need to become too dependent on each other. Well of course it is always better to have more money than less money, but it is also true that everything in life is relative, and affluent families often face very much the same issues as less affluent families. Looking back on Brad and Sarah's family, we see that even though Caroline is probably better off financially than the typical retiree, her perception of her financial limitations nevertheless played a part in her decision to move into her daughter's home. We also see that differences in income levels between Sarah's two adult daughters added a noteworthy dimension to the intergenerational issues, even though in objective terms and relative to the nation as a whole both daughters were doing rather well. We also see that money is a potential source of tension between Sarah's older daughters and her younger son. Even though they were all sent off to college without having to apply for scholarships, the daughters still feel just a touch of resentment because "he got more." And Brian, having grown up in an affluent world, actually believes that at this point in his life he cannot afford to live in his own place, because then he would not be able to afford to live in the style to which he has become accustomed, which means he would have to cook and clean up for himself, and he might not be able to afford his cars and vacations.

Therefore you should be aware that having money is not a panacea. It may even complicate intergenerational dynamics, if adult children are jealous of each other and worried about what they have coming to them.

Having described in a general way some of the intergenerational dynamics that we must be aware of if we wish to maintain close and rewarding relationships with our adult children and our older parents, I would now like to consider a series of specific issues that frequently prove problematic to men in their sixties. These include childrearing issues, intergenerational differences in values and lifestyle, the "son-in-law" problem, issues associated with divorce and reconstituted families, and unresolved childhood problems.

CHILDREARING ISSUES

This is a significant problem for many older guys who have grandchildren. Of course your adult children are less effective parents than you were. Even though they are grown up now, they are still your kids, and you must know more than they do. You have had more experience raising kids, and you have the benefit of hindsight. You know what a parent should do to make his kids turn out well. You have been through it all. So naturally you want to tell them how to do it right. *Right?*

But *be very careful* here. You must remember that your adult children need to be independent and autonomous. They need to fulfill their parental role and to feel competent in performing that role. If you insist on telling them how to feed, educate, entertain, and discipline their kids, they will resent the intrusion, and it will damage your relationship with your adult children. My advice on this issue is simple. *Don't offer unsolicited advice.* If you are asked for your opinion, it's certainly OK to give it. *But make sure that you have a discussion.* Don't give them a general lecture on "how to raise kids." Instead, listen carefully to the questions they ask about how to deal with the *specific* problems that they are having with their kids. Validate their concerns by acknowledging that the problems are significant and that the problems are difficult to handle. Share your feelings regarding each problem, and if you can throw out some suggestions regarding how you might approach the issue. Always be clear that you are suggesting approaches that they might consider, rather than telling them how to do it correctly. If you want to maintain a good relationship with your adult children, there will be times when you will need to bite your tongue.

The issue of whether to offer advice to your adult children regarding childrearing is complicated in the multigenerational family by the phenomenon that Williams and Nussbaum refers to as "sandwiched communication."[14]

Whether or not the four generations are living under the same roof, representatives of the different generations will be likely to be around each other a great deal. Therefore, conversations that might otherwise take place between a parent and a child alone are likely to include the child's grandparents as well. Therefore, if you are the 60-year-old grandfather of an adolescent, you may not always have the option of excluding yourself from family discussions in which childrearing issues arise. You may be included simply by virtue of your being there.

Now add to this multigenerational picture the normal adolescent striving for independence and autonomy and the normative conflict that occurs between adolescents and the parents who are attempting to limit these strivings and to protect the adolescent from himself. It is easy to see how an adolescent might attempt to enlist your assistance in his efforts to negotiate the limits that his parents are trying to place on him. He might ask you whether you allowed his parent to do the things that he wants to do now when they were his age. This can happen quickly and you can be drawn into the power struggle on one side or the other before you really even know it.

We have all made jokes about how satisfying it is to see our children put through the wringer by their children, just as our children put us through the wringer when they were kids. Fine, it's OK to sit back and be amused, but try not to be drawn into the struggle. Again, if your adult children ask for your advice, then it is all right for you to offer your views. But always be aware of the potential for being drawn into the parent-child power struggles. To the extent that you allow yourself to be recruited by one side or the other, you can be sure you will be resented.

Of course, situations can arise where you might need to intervene. If your adult child has a substance abuse problem or is otherwise mistreating your grandchildren, or allowing them to be mistreated, you may have to make the decision to confront your child or even go to the appropriate authorities. But this would only be in extreme circumstances where your child had clearly failed in his or her parenting role. Otherwise, you must always remember that your children are the parents of your grandchildren, and they are ultimately responsible for raising their own children.

INTERGENERATIONAL DIFFERENCES IN VALUES AND LIFESTYLE

One of the things that tend to promote close relationships between parents and their adult children is the tendency to share similar values.[15] We all hope that in the course of parenting we will instill good values in our children. We employ our schools and our religious institutions to assist us in this process, but mostly we transmit our values through the example of our own behavior.

And generally our kids turn out to be quite like us. On the other hand, social values do change from generation to generation. Certainly those of us who are just turning 60, the baby boomers who became young adults during the 1960s had very different ideas about drug use and premarital sex than our parents. And just as certainly these differences were a source of conflict between us and our parents. Political views also tend to differ from one generation to the next, as suggested by Churchill's famous remark that "if you're not a liberal at twenty you have no heart [and] if you're not a conservative at forty you have no brain." Many a family dinner has become acrimonious when the discussion turns to politics.

But by the time we reach the seventh decade of life, we really ought to be able to put differences of this nature in the proper perspective. One of the crucial characteristics of the intergenerational family that fosters closeness is the ability of members in each generation to not lose sight of the basic shared values of kindness and mutual respect and the corresponding willingness to overlook or accommodate some areas of disagreement. Teenagers may lack the perspective necessary to make such accommodations. Their youth is their excuse. You and I are older and more experienced. We have no such excuse.

THE SON-IN-LAW ISSUE

One relationship that is particularly difficult for men with married daughters is the relationship with the son-in-law.[16] Fathers typically expect their wives to assume the major responsibility for their daughter's development, but fathers typically believe that it is their responsibility to protect their daughter, and they take this responsibility very seriously. Therefore sons-in-law are typically carefully scrutinized and judged harshly. From the father's point of view, it is close to impossible for a son-in-law to be recognized as supporting his daughter adequately or treating his daughter in the manner that she deserves.

This issue is naturally hardwired into us as dads, and it is probably not possible to turn off the tendency to regard our son-in-law critically. But it wouldn't hurt if you at least tried to keep in mind that you are very likely judging him harshly. Nor would it hurt if you went a little bit out of your way to develop a relationship with him in his own right. In the final analysis, your daughter will be happier if you and your son-in-law get along than if you don't.

ISSUES ASSOCIATED WITH DIVORCE
AND RECONSTITUTED FAMILIES

As we saw with Brad and Sarah, divorces can occur in any of the adult generations of the multigenerational family. Divorces are stressful life events which have major emotional and financial repercussions. Divorces can lead to an 81-year-old moving in with her daughter and son-in-law, as it did with Caroline. Divorces can also occur among our adult children, and this can lead to their moving back into our homes or at least to an increase in the level of support and assistance that we provide. Divorces and remarriages also complicate the family constellation and generally necessitate a delicate renegotiation of arrangements for family holidays and traditions.

UNRESOLVED CHILDHOOD ISSUES

Hollis laments that "few parents are able to give…unconditional love to their children, having not received it themselves."[17] He notes that the young people who are making babies now are often still trying to separate from their own parents. They are flooded by the dynamics of their families of origin and overwhelmed by the tasks of taking on both domestic and professional lives. Hollis points out further that grandparents can provide much to these young parents, because "they have been able, over the decades, to come closer to themselves, achieve their maturity, and may offer example and affirmation to the grandchild. [However] other grandparents, having not taken on the journey, remain narcissistic, demanding as always, and are shocked to find themselves unwelcome in their children's homes."[18]

What Hollis is saying here is that if we are to develop close and meaningful relationships with our adult children, we must be able to allow them to take charge of their own lives. We cannot confuse our own development with their development. We cannot insist that our children attend the school we would like them to attend, enter the profession that we desire for them, marry the person we choose for them, or tell them how to raise their kids. We can only become truly close to our adult children when we treat them as adults and allow them to make decisions for themselves.

In addition, we must be able to confront our failures as parents. We must be willing to discuss the ways in which we may have harmed our children through our own parenting ineptitude. If we have harmed our children, if we have abused them or allowed them to be abused, we must be willing to acknowledge these wounds and try to make amends. We may need to seek professional help to identify areas of past dysfunction and improve our capacity to communicate meaningfully and on an adult level with our children. These steps may be difficult to take, but the payoffs can be enormous.

Chapter Fourteen

GRANDPARENTING

In this chapter I will be discussing issues that men approaching and past 60 frequently encounter in connection with their grandchildren and great grand-children. Those of you who have read through this book from the beginning to this point may be wondering if these issues have not already been covered. Indeed, to some extent they have. In chapter 6, I noted that retaining family involvement and family role responsibilities can be an important way of continuing to feel useful and productive. As grandparents, we can perform important services for both our grandchildren and for our children who are their parents. To the extent that we all need to be needed, performing these roles can help us to feel satisfied with our lives. In addition, in relation to the topic of finding or continuing to find meaning in our lives, I described in some detail in chapter 10 how Morris endeavored to strengthen intergenerational relationships within his family, in order to guarantee that he and his wife would be always be involved in the lives of their children and grandchildren.

Then in chapter 13, in discussing the dynamics of intergenerational relationships, I cautioned readers that it is very important for those of us who are grandparents to recognize that we must allow *our* children to parent *their* children. There I suggested that we cannot presume to tell our children how to raise their kids, for if we do our children will surely resent us. In that chapter I also described the desirability of maintaining mutually supportive relationships between us and our adult children, and I specifically warned that we should not undertake to give so much support and assistance to our children and our grandchildren that we wind up resenting the constraints that such support and assistance impose on our own aspirations regarding what we want for ourselves during the remainder of our lives.

All that having been said, there is still a great deal to be considered when it comes to appropriately managing our roles as grandparents. We are all different with respect to the resources that we have to give as well as the nature and the extent to which we wish to interact with our children and grandchildren. Therefore, I will give you some ideas on how you can go about determining what you want your role as grandparent to be, as well as some advice on how to communicate your wishes and negotiate your grandparenting role with your children. I will also give you some pointers on how to deal with some of the more common grandparenting issues with which many of us will need to deal.

Finally, I will consider a special set of circumstances that occur relatively frequently today, in which grandparents actually assume the role of primary caretaker for one or more of their grandchildren. When grandparents are caretakers, we have a very complicated situation that can be quite stressful on the grandparents involved.

HOW INVOLVED WITH YOUR GRANDCHILDREN DO YOU WISH TO BE?

You have probably not given much thought to the question of how involved you want to be with your grandchildren. Most of us develop assumptions regarding what grandparents do and how grandparents behave, based on the experience that we have with our own grandparents. If your grandparents were frequently present in your life and you had close relationships with them, you will likely expect to have similar relationships with your grandchildren. Similarly, if your own grandparents were less available or more distant emotionally, it might not occur to you that you have the option of taking on a much more active role. But you do have options. There really is no general consensus in our society regarding the appropriate amount of contact that grandparents should have with their grandchildren, about the things that grandparents should do for their grandchildren, or about the degree to which grandparent-grandchild relationships should be relatively close and intimate, or relatively more distant and formal.[1]

Experts on grandparenting have identified five different "styles of grandparenting," which include the formal grandparent, the funseeking grandparent, the surrogate parent, the reservoir of family wisdom, and the distant figure.[2] *Formal grandparents* are those who like to provide their grandchildren with special treats and indulgences, but who also maintain a clear distinction between the grandparenting role and the parenting role. These grandparents leave parenting strictly to the parents, their children. These grandparents maintain a constant interest in their grandchildren; but they offer no advice. *Fun seeking grandparents* are playful and informal with their grandchildren. When they are with their grandchildren, they strive to have a good time and make sure that their grandchildren have a good time as well. Grandparents who assume a *surrogate parent* role are those who provide all-day child care for grandchildren whose parents both work all day. Grandparents who see themselves as *reservoirs of family wisdom* see themselves as possessing special skills or resources that their children do not have. Therefore, they expect their adult children to assume a subordinate position with respect to decisions regarding how the grandchildren should be raised. Finally, *distant figure grandparents* have contact with their grandchildren only on holidays and special occasions. At other times they are distant and remote from the grandchildren's lives. Of course, these categories are much more distinct in theory than they are in real life. In actuality, we as grandparents may represent one of these categories in the extreme, or we may exhibit aspects of several of the grandparenting categories. Nevertheless, the categories are useful when we think about the grandparenting roles that we might choose to assume, because they highlight dimensions along which the nature and intensity of our grandparenting roles can be defined and described.

So how do you want to define your role as grandparent? It must be pretty obvious to the reader by now that I personally would opt for more rather than less involvement when involvement is feasible. However, this is a decision that each individual must make for himself, and what I would like to do here is to make you aware of the pros and cons of greater involvement.

Arguments in Favor of Greater Involvement with Grandchildren

The main argument in favor of your assuming an active role as a grandfather is that your involvement will almost certainly be of great value to your grandchildren. Grandparents often assume the primary responsibility within the family for passing on values, traditions, and culture.[3] We as grandparents are in a unique position to pass on values and traditions to our grandchildren, because we occupy a special place in the multigenerational family constellation. According to Trafford, from the perspective of the grandchild

a grandparent is timeless. There is adoration and absolute trust—by virtue of a grandparent's status in the family hierarchy, much like the professional trust a physician commands over patients.[4]

Because of our special status within the family, then, grandparents are likely to command respect. We do not have difficulty getting the attention of our grandchildren, whether they are youngsters or adolescents. In addition, if we have allowed our adult children to assume the primary responsibility for structuring and disciplining their children, we as grandparents are not likely to be involved in the same power struggle as that which invariably characterizes the relationship between parents and their adolescent children. Although our adolescent grandchildren may be predisposed to ignore or reject almost everything their parents say, they may well be willing to listen to us. Therefore, if we tell them stories that make it clear how much we value having the family together for holidays, we are much more likely to get our adolescent grandchildren to show up than would a direct parental request to come home. To the extent that we as grandparents take responsibility for maintaining religious traditions and lead by example, we are likely to pass these traditions on.

The same can be said of cultural traditions. I have a friend whose extended family has a long tradition of going hunting each year. He had been trying to get his adolescent son to join in this tradition for several years, with no success. His son had other interests, and because of his involvement in the adolescent struggle to separate, his son was predisposed to reject pretty much any suggestions that his dad had regarding possible activities they could engage in together. In addition, father and son were competitive toward each other in almost everything they did together, and the adolescent son was clearly apprehensive lest his father "show him up" at hunting camp.

However, when the young man's 62-year-old paternal grandfather got wind of the situation, he made short work of the problem of getting the boy to come along and join in. Granddad had always taken the boy camping and fishing when he was younger. He had always tried to teach him how to do things, and he had never competed with the boy. He had always made a fuss when the boy caught a fish or built a fire, and as a result the young man had developed a considerable sense of pride in his ability to get along outdoors. So one day grandpa sat down with the boy and said, "I wonder if you would do a favor for me. You know I'm getting a little slow of foot, and I don't want to be a burden on any of the other guys at the hunting camp. So I was wondering if you might have time to come along with me this year and help me out with some of the work…and maybe at some point we could even hunt together."

And of course, put that way, the boy happily agreed to come along. He felt respected by his grandpa because he was actually being asked to help out in a meaningful way, and he loved and respected his granddad enough that it never occurred to him to say no. And in the end the boy ended up both helping grandpa and hunting himself. And he enjoyed it; and he was successful; and he received a lot of positive feedback from other folks at camp. And the tradition continued.

And of course there are other ways in which our involvement with our grandchildren can help them develop. When they are little we can baby-sit for them, giving their mom and dad a bit of respite from child care responsibilities.

We can read to them, transmitting our love of books and giving them a leg up in school. As our grandchildren grow up, we can help them out with their school work. We can tell them things about history, about events that we have lived through and they have not, and about things that we have seen that they have not. We can take them to zoos and museums. We can take them on vacations with us, to the Caribbean or to Europe. When they are ready to go to college, perhaps we will be in a position to give them some financial help with their tuition or their books. And, like Morris, we can pay their fare to come home for holidays.

And here's something that you should know. I'm not just assuming that being closely involved with their grandparents is good for grandchildren. There is plenty of solid research data that shows us this is true. Kornhaber's Grandparent Study suggests that grandchildren who feel close to at least one grandparent tend to: (1) feel accepted for who they are; (2) be emotionally secure; (3) feel that they have an emotional sanctuary available to them during periods of stress; (4) have positive feelings toward older individuals in general; (5) show respect for their own parents; (6) have a superior understanding of world events, based on what they learn from their grandparent(s); and (7) feel that they are part of family that roots to the past and a sense of "family ego."[5]

Other reasons favoring relatively frequent and close involvement with your grandchildren are the positive impact that your involvement may have on your adult children (their parents), and the positive impact that your involvement may have on you yourself. Obviously, with more and more dual-career families out there, your grandchild's mother and father are both likely to be pursuing careers, and they will be hard pressed to give their children as much time and attention as they might like. To the extent that you can spend time with your grandchildren and let them know how much you love them, you will be helping to make up for any deficit in parental attention that may exist. You will be giving your adult child and his or her spouse some much needed respite time. That respite time is not only important to the adult children but it may also reduce their stress and make it easier for them to give quality time to your grandchildren when they are together. Remember from the last chapter that the mutual exchange of support and assistance between the generations in the multigenerational family is an important contributor to family solidarity. Your helping out your children by giving your love and your time to your grandchildren can benefit everyone. (Just remember not to try to take over the parenting function; and don't do so much that you become resentful.)

The potential benefits to you of close involvement with your grandchildren include the knowledge that you are in fact making life better for both your adult children and your grandchildren, and the resulting sense of usefulness and self-efficacy. In addition, involvement in activities with your grandchildren may help to keep you active and help to make you feel young. Finally, you may well find that some of the activities that you plan and undertake because you think that your grandchildren may like them are in fact a lot of fun for you as well. My friend Brad, whose mutigenerational family I described in the last chapter, once took his entire four-generation family to a nearby dairy farm for a weekend "family farm vacation." He did this because he thought that the grandchildren would enjoy the animals and learn about where food comes from—from an actual farmer. And they did. But the surprise was that the adults also enjoyed the experience immensely. They enjoyed the outdoors, the animals, sitting around an evening bonfire, seeing shooting stars, and hearing coyotes. In fact, some of the adults saw shooting stars and heard coyotes for the first time in their lives. The grandkids talk about going back to the farm all the time, and each time they do all the adults unashamedly agree that they had a great time there.

Arguments for Placing Some Limits on Your Involvement with Your Grandchildren

So with all the good reasons I have given you for maximizing your involvement with your grandchildren, what arguments could there be for placing some limits on these relationships? Well, there are two possible reasons that you might consider. The first is simply that some men over 60 are not into doing things with children and adolescents. Maybe they are heavily invested in other activities that children and adolescents would not be interested in; or perhaps they are simply not sociable. I am not endorsing or condemning such an orientation. I am simply noting that it does exist. If you are one of these individuals, you might want to guard against the possibility that family pressures will lead you to spend more time than you want to with the grandkids, doing things that you find boring, and wishing that you were somewhere else. If you spend time with your grandchildren because you don't know how to get out of it, the grandkids will see right through you, and they won't be that fond of you anyway.

The second reason has to do with competing demands for your time and resources. Some of us like our grandchildren just fine but still want to set some limits to our involvement. We enjoy spending some time with them, and we may even enjoy doing some of the things that make them happy. But we like doing other things as well, and we feel as if there is just not enough time to do everything that we would like to do. This perception is very common among grandfathers in their sixties, because many of us are still very much involved in our professional lives as well as our interests and hobbies. We may have made plans to travel and to accomplish certain goals in life, and we may therefore feel that we simply do not have the time that would be required to spend limitless amounts of time babysitting, entertaining grandchildren, going to soccer and baseball games, and taking grandchildren on vacation with us. I have already noted in the previous chapter that intergenerational relationships tend to be best when the exchange of support and assistance is mutual and that we should strive to avoid situations in which we are giving so much of our time or our money that we are jeopardizing important personal goals. It is easy for this situation to develop, and it will certainly generate resentment and bad feelings, first of all on your part, but eventually on the part of your adult children and your grandchildren as well.

But the caveat I am stating here is just a bit more general than that embodied in the warning, "Don't do so much that you will ruin your own life." In the last chapter I was really talking about situations like giving so much financial assistance to your adult children and grandchildren that you cannot afford to retire at all, or you cannot afford to take the vacation in Europe that you have always dreamed of. Here I am talking more about smaller, but more commonplace sacrifices. For example, consider a situation where you are sitting at home on Sunday afternoon watching your favorite football team, and the grandchildren arrive. They will demand your attention, and they will want to watch "Dora the Explorer" instead of the football game. So the question is, "When this happens, does your happiness at their arrival make you forget the game, put on Dora, and happily give them your time, or would you honestly rather just keep watching the game?"

There is no "right" or "wrong" answer here. Forget social desirability and what you think you ought to say. If you admit that deep in your heart you would really rather continue to watch the game, then you need to build this emotional reaction into your ideas regarding the amount of time that you wish to spend with your grandchildren, as well as the specific circumstances under which you want visits to occur. You are not a bad person if you feel this way. Some of us are just more people- and family-oriented than others, and you cannot be what you are not.

How to Decide and Negotiate How Extensive You Want Your Relationship with Your Grandchildren to Be

Therefore, if you are still employed and/or otherwise heavily invested in a set of activities that require your time and do not include grandchildren, you must acknowledge this reality and accept that it may mean that you will want to be somewhat less involved with your grandchildren than some of your contemporaries might be. Ask yourself some hard questions: How much do my adult children, my wife, and other members of the family want me to baby-sit and help with the chores related to raising the grandchildren? How much would this require me to alter my lifestyle? What do I really want to do? How do my overall goals and interests compare to my available resources and the amount of time that I have to spend to pursue these goals and interests?

These are not easy questions to answer. Ultimately, you will need to decide how you wish to allocate your scarce resources and your scarce time between your grandchildren and the other things that you value in life. Then, once you have decided upon how you would like to arrange this allocation, you will need to discuss and possibly negotiate your wishes with your spouse, with your adult children, and in the case of older grandchildren, perhaps with the grandchildren themselves.

This discussion is very important because research has shown that it is very important that grandparents and their adult children are on the same page as far as what the grandparents are willing to do and expected to do. Most grandparents want to have a significant role in the lives of their grandchildren, and they are willing to make some sacrifices in order to do so. However, we grandfathers tend to resent strongly any tendency that our children may exhibit to take our support and assistance for granted. We don't like it if our children assume that we will spend open ended amounts of time caring for the grandchildren, and we also become annoyed if our adult children assume that we will provide financial assistance beyond that which we have discussed and agreed to explicitly.[6] An AARP survey of grandparents showed that grandparents who provided babysitting or respite care for their grandchildren on a regular basis were especially resentful when the parent of the grandchildren arrived late to pick them up or simply failed to show up, assuming that the kids would be fine with their parents.[7]

SOME SPECIFIC GRANDPARENTING ISSUES

At this point I would like to make the assumption that the typical reader does want to have close relationships with his grandchildren and has made the decision that he will balance this goal against other competing priorities in his life. If you are this typical reader, therefore, you will probably need some help with (1) managing your time; (2) how to give advice to your adult children regarding how to raise the grandchildren (already considered in the context of the intergenerational family in chapter 13); (3) what you need to do when the grandchildren arrive for a visit; (4) what you need to know about temporary power of attorney during the times when you are caring for your grandchildren; (5) how to relate to the other grandparents of your grandchild(ren) (i.e., the parents of your son-in-law or your daughter-in-law); (6) what you should do if the parents of your grandchildren should divorce; (7) what to do if you and your spouse should divorce; (8) how to handle the step grandparents that your grandchildren will acquire if one or both of their divorced parents remarries; and (9) what you need to know about giving money to your children and grandchildren.

Managing Our Time

Fulfilling our responsibilities at work, pursuing important outside activities, and looking after our personal needs, while at the same time fostering a close relationship with our grandchild(ren) can be a formidable task. So how do you cope with this task? First of all, you must accept that fact that it might just not be possible to find enough time to do everything that you would like to do on each of these fronts. You can only do so much. Don't forget the "looking after our personal needs" part of the equation. These needs include sleep and downtime. Many men our age have been "burning the candle at both ends" for a lifetime. To the extent that this has become a habit, the grandfather role can simply become another excuse to burn ourselves out.

Faced with this dilemma, we must engage in conscious time management planning. Sit down with a calendar of the week and a calendar of the year. Start with the calendar of the week. Mark off the times of the week when you are *committed to be somewhere.* How many hours are scheduled? Think about that number. Is it too large? Start to think about the importance of each of the scheduled hours? Are they all crucial to your life, or are some less important to you?

Now take a piece of paper and write down four headings: (1) work; (2) out-side activities; (3) personal needs/downtime; and (4) grandchildren. Under each of these headings, write the scheduled times that appear in your weekly calendar that apply to that heading. Now add up the number of hours each week that apply to each of the four headings. Which of the areas consume the largest amounts of your time that are already scheduled? Are you happy with the breakdown?

Now go back to the weekly calendar and add in the various times of the week when you *typically* find yourself involved in a certain activity, although this activity is *not really a formal commitment.* How do these time periods fall out into the four categories? Now add up the number of hours that pertain to both your *scheduled commitments* and your *typical activities* each week. Now which of the areas take up the greatest amount of time? Are you surprised at the amount of time that is going to each of these areas? Are you happy with the breakdown now? To which areas would you like to give more time? To which areas do you feel you may be dedicating too much time? Are there specific activities during the week that you could just as soon do without?

Now that you have given some time to thinking about where your time actually goes, you may have a sense of where you would like to do more and where you feel you might be able to cut back. I can't tell you how to allocate your time each week. You must decide that for yourself. But if you follow the steps outlined above, you will have a better idea of where your time is going and how you might like to modify your schedule. Once you have gone through this exercise for your typical week, you can use a similar procedure to consider your year. This will help you to see how many weeks each year you are dedicating to professional meetings, leisure and recreational activities, relaxing vacations, and extended periods of time spent with grandchildren. This exercise may also help you to recognize areas to which you would like to dedicate more time, as well as areas that are less important to you.

Of course, once you have examined your actual allocation of scarce time and come to some conclusions regarding how this allocation might be modified to better fit your own interests and priorities, you will still need to negotiate any changes that you contemplate with all of the family members who are affected. If you decide that you would really like to spend a week each year camping with your grandchildren, but you think that in order to accomplish this goal you may have to give up the Caribbean vacation with your wife, you will have some discussing to do.

Giving Advice

I have already discussed the issue of giving advice to your adult children on how to raise their grandchildren in the context of the multigenerational family and the need to foster our relationships with our adult children. I suggested that we grandfathers need to recognize our adult children's need to parent their own children and that we should avoid offering *our children* unsolicited advice on how to raise *their children* correctly if we hope to avoid alienating our own children.

Here I would simply like to make the point that following this advice not only respects and nurtures our relationships with our adult children but also benefits our grandchildren. Your grandchildren need to see their parents as parents, just as your children need to be their parents. Your job is to support their efforts to nourish, structure, and discipline their children. If you give them unsolicited advice on "how to do it correctly," especially if you do so in front of the grandchildren, you are likely to give your grandchildren the idea that their parents know nothing and can be ignored. If the grandchildren are adolescents, they probably tend to feel this way anyhow, so your well-intentioned advice may simply exacerbate the fundamental issue that your adult children and their children are working through.

When the Grandchildren Visit

This section contains real practical advice. When they come, expect them to take over and run amuck. If you need to see something on TV, have them come at a different time or record the program. They will want to put on a different show; and once they have done that they will go off a play somewhere else. That does not mean that you can put your show back on. The grandchildren will come back to the TV every so often just to make sure that their show is still on. And what show is on doesn't matter anyway because you will need to follow them to make sure that they don't hurt themselves or destroy the house.

Speaking of safety and destruction, you must child-proof your home before the grandchildren arrive. This means making sure that they cannot get into the caustic agents that live under the sink, and it also means that you need to move the Steuben crystal sculptures that you have been displaying proudly around the house. If there are rooms that you don't want them to get into, you must lock the doors, because the fact that you don't want them in there will only make it imperative to them that they find out what mysteries you are trying to hide from them inside.

If young grandchildren are present, forget sit-down fancy dinners. If the grandchildren are under 15, they probably will not want to eat anything that you would want to eat anyway, and they probably won't sit at the dinner table either. The most likely scenario is that you and a few adults will be eating at the dinner table, and the grandkids will be in the family room eating a completely different meal, supervised by one of their parents, who is thereby denied the opportunity to have dinner with the other adults. So why not save the formal dinners for a different time when the young grandchildren are not present or after they have grown up a bit? Why not go with buffet serving, and with both adult- and child-friendly foods? And let everyone take their food to the family room, where those that really want to eat can eat, and those who would rather just play can play? That way, you will be able to eat and watch the grandkids play at the same time.

Temporary Power of Attorney

If your grandchildren are going to stay with you while their parents are away for the weekend or a two week vacation, you need to have a document granting you temporary power of attorney to care for the grandchildren. This document will authorize you to make crucial medical decisions on behalf of the grandkids. If the grandchildren are hurt and require emergency medical attention, the failure to have such a document could prevent your grandchild from getting appropriate and timely medical care. It could create a life-threatening situation.

The document granting power of attorney does not require that you hire an attorney but in most states it does need to be witnessed and notarized. The parent(s) must state in the document that they are naming you as their attorney and granting you authority to consent to all medical care that may be necessary for the child(ren's) health. Both you and the child(ren) must be named explicitly. The parent(s) must be named explicitly, and the form must be signed and dated by each parent. The power of attorney should have an expiration date.

Regardless of the expiration date, some states require that such documents be renewed periodically, like every six months or every year. It is probably wisest to draw up such a document and at least run it by an attorney and/or your physician to make sure that it will serve the intended purpose.

Suppose Your Grandchildren's Parents Divorce

I have already noted briefly that divorce in one generation or another is an extremely common phenomenon in today's multigenerational families such as Brad's four-generation family, described in the last chapter. In that context I simply observed that divorces tend to complicate the family constellation and place greater demands on the grandchildren's time, particularly when remarriage introduces additional individuals who will most likely want to be spending some time with the grandchildren. I pointed out that all of this means that we grandparents may have to accept spending somewhat less time with our grandchildren, and in any case we will probably have to renegotiate how family holidays will be spent.

But of course, when your grandchild(ren's) parents divorce, there is a great deal more to think about than where the grandchildren will be spending Thanksgiving. If your daughter divorces her husband and becomes the custodial parent, you may find that you are called upon to provide her with a great deal more emotional, physical, and financial support than you provided before. She may even move in with you for a time. So it is possible that you may actually be spending a great deal more time with the grandchildren than before. On the other hand, if your child is not the custodial parent, or if either parent remarries and other grandparents become more involved with the care of the grandchildren, you may find that your grandparenting role become more limited. To minimize this possibility, it would be best for you to try to maintain a relationship with your child's ex-spouse and his or her parents. This will certainly be particularly difficult for a father who feels that his daughter or son has been treated poorly by the ex-spouse, but to the extent that you and your child can handle it, it will be beneficial to the grandchildren, and it will increase the probability of continuing to have frequent contact with them.

Beyond the issue of minimizing blame and trying not to take sides, grandfathers also need to remember that when your adult child divorces, your grandchild(ren) may well feel that the divorce was somehow their fault. You need to focus as much attention as you can on the grandchild(ren), reassuring them that it was certainly not their fault that their mom and dad could not get along and needed to get divorced. You also need to be aware that children tend to feel insecure about the future when the nuclear family that they have known is breaking up. You can help the grandchildren a great deal with this by making it clear to them that you will always be there for them. Emphasize this point by requesting that your adult child and his or her divorcing spouse make a provision in the divorce agreement for you to see your grandchild(ren). You can also reassure your grandchild(ren) that their parents still love them, in spite of the fact that they are divorcing.

Suppose You and Your Spouse Get a Divorce

If you and your spouse should get divorced, you must realize that it has implications for your grandchild(ren) as well as for your adult children. Of course, from the perspective of the grandchildren, your getting divorced will not be as threatening as their parents' getting divorced would be, but there are still some steps that you should take to ease the transition. You need to explain to your grandchild(ren) that both you and grandma will continue to love them and to spend time with them. You also need to tell the grandchildren that they may not always see you and grandma together all the time, but they will certainly see each of you separately.

Above all, regardless of the circumstances of your divorce, you must avoid doing anything that would threaten the relationship of your ex-wife to either your adult child or the grandchildren. You might feel mightily tempted to try to justify your decision to divorce to your adult child and perhaps even to your grandchildren, if they are older. But you should avoid saying anything negative about their grandmother. If the circumstances of the divorce are such that they can be explained without reflecting poorly on your ex-spouse, then go ahead and explain. But remember that your grandchildren love both of you, and you must avoid saying anything that would put them in a position of having to decide who is right and who is wrong.

Dealing with Your Grandchildren's Step-Grandparents

If your divorced adult child remarries, and/or if his or her ex-spouse remarries, there is the possibility that your grandchildren will acquire a new set (or two new sets) of step-grandparents. These would be the parents of your adult child's new spouse, and or the parents of the new spouse of your adult child's ex-spouse. (I realize that this is getting complicated, but that is precisely the point that I am trying to make. Divorce and remarriage at various levels of the multigenerational family further complicates the already complicated family dynamics, and we need to consider these complications from the perspective of serving the best interests of our grandchildren.)

When step-grandparents appear on the scene, we grandfathers are likely to think of them as "less related" to our grandchildren than we are. Well, I guess that's true. They are not flesh and blood. But that does not mean that they should be given short shrift within the extended family constellation. Think of the situation *from the point of view of your grandchildren*. They are now living in the household of a parent (who might be your son or daughter or might be the ex-spouse of your son or daughter) and a step-parent. To the extent that the step-parent will want to visit with his or her own parents, your grandchildren are quite likely to be spending a good deal of time with these new step-grandparents. Particularly if your adult child was a son and his ex-spouse has custody of the grandchildren, these step-grandparents may well be spending more time with your grandchildren than you are.

The situation can be extremely complicated and extremely difficult, and obviously it is not possible here for me to give you advice about how to act in each individual set of circumstances that may pertain. However, I can give you a good rule to follow: Always think first about the situation from the perspective of the grandchild(ren) that you love. Ask yourself what you can do to make the situation easiest for them. This may require that you be nice to people with whom you are not particularly friendly. It may require that you accept social arrangements that afford you much less time with your grandchildren that you would really like. But it may well be better for the grandchildren to spend a bit less time with you than you would like, if it avoids conflict with ex in-laws and step-grandparents who take up bigger spaces in the lives of your grandchildren than you do.

You can make do with the contacts that you do have, make sure that these are all positive, send birthday gifts and e-mails, and wait for the grandchildren to grow up enough that they will be able to decide for themselves to spend more time with you than may have been feasible when they were younger.

Providing Financial Assistance and Gifts to Your Grandchildren

Whatever the nature and extent of our relationships with our grandchildren, we may very well be able to and want to give them some financial assistance. According to the AARP Grandparent Survey of 2002, nearly half of all grandparents provide some financial assistance to help with the living expenses of their grandchildren, and more than half of all grandparents provide financial assistance to help their grandchildren with educational expenses. You may also wish to simply give some money to your grandchildren so that they have something to start their lives. I am not a financial advisor, and I would urge you to consult with an advisor regarding these issues. However, I would like to just take a few paragraphs to let you know that there are ways to make these provisions that can save you and your grandchildren money on taxes.

As far as helping with college goes, you should be aware of the existence of the Independent 529 Tuition Plan. This is a prepaid tuition plan that enables you to begin paying for your grandchild's college tuition now. The payments that you make to an Independent 529 Tuition Plan are free of federal tax. You can also get discounts that enable you to pay less than current tuition rates for your grand-child's tuition. The amount of tuition that you purchase now doesn't change, no matter how much tuition rates might increase in the future. The value of your prepayment also compound between the time when you make the purchase and the time that it is used. Your grandchild does not need to pick a college now. There are over 200 colleges and universities participating in this program, and he or she can go to any one that he or she chooses. You may contribute a maximum of $137,500 per grandchild to an Independent 529 Plan.

Another way to help with college is to open an Education IRA or Coverdell account for your grandchild. This allows you to contribute up to $2,000 per year for each grandchild. The earnings on these accounts are free from fed-eral tax.

You may also use the Uniform Gifts to Minors Act to make irrevocable gifts to your grandchildren that are placed in an investment account. You may be the custodian of that account, or you may appoint someone else, like your financial advisor. The grandchild assumes control of the account when he be-comes an adult (generally at 18). If you want to retain control over money that you have given to a grandchild to avoid the possibility that he will take it all when he becomes 18 and spend it, you can set up a trust. However, this requires a lawyer and has the attendant expenses.

THE CUSTODIAL GRANDPARENT

You Might Be Called Upon to Raise a Grandchild

More than 10 percent of the grandparents in the United States have assumed the primary responsibility for raising one or more of their grandchildren for a period of at least six months at some point in their lifetime.[8] More than half of these so-called custodial grandparents cared for one or more grandchildren for a period of three years or more, and one-fifth indicated that they had cared for at least one grandchild for 10 years or more. It has been estimated that five percent of all American children under the age of 18 are living in their grand-parents' homes at any one point in time.[9] Currently approximately four million children are being raised in grandparent-headed households.[10]

In approximately one-third of these households, neither parent is present. Perhaps they have been killed in an accident. The other two-thirds are house-holds in which a grandparent or grandparents lives with one or more grandchil-dren and the father and/or mother of the grandchildren. In these households, the parents of the grandchild(ren) may have divorced, and the custodial parent may have moved in with his or her parents because he or she does not have the financial resources to establish a household of his/her own. Or perhaps one of the parents is seriously ill, in a hospital or in a rehabilitation facility, and the other parent moves in with the grandparents because it is the only way that he or she can manage. There are many different paths leading to the situation where a grandparent must assume the primary responsibility for raising a grandchild, but the figures suggest that it could happen to you.

It Can Be Stressful for Grandparents to Raise Their Grandchildren

Social scientists have suggested that individuals function under specific social expectations regarding the roles that they will assume at various stages during their lifespan. When we find ourselves performing roles that are neither typical nor expected for individuals of our age, the disparity between social expectations and the reality of our lives is inherently stressful for us.[11] A 60-something grandfather who finds himself play the role of father to an adolescent granddaughter (or perhaps an infant great grandchild) may well find this role difficult.[12]

The reason why such a time-disordered role is likely to be stressful are pretty obvious. A 60-something grandfather may well have been looking forward to some form of retirement, and to spending some quality time with his wife. Assuming responsibility for the care of their grandchild(ren) may well disrupt or even destroy this dream.

To make matters worse, the circumstances requiring grandparents to assume the caregiving role are likely to have been stressful. Perhaps it was an adult child's divorce, or perhaps it was the adult child's drug dependence or incarceration. Perhaps it was the death of both parents in an unexpected and tragic accident, or perhaps it was the death of an adult child due to AIDS. It may have been an unplanned pregnancy of a young daughter or granddaughter. Many grandparents blame themselves directly or indirectly for what has happened to their child that has precipitated their assumption of the parental role. Such beliefs may subject them to further stress and increase the likelihood that they will experience impaired psychosocial functioning.[13] Several investigators have linked the caretaking role to depression among grandparents, warning additionally that a depressed grandparent may become vulnerable to alcohol abuse or dependence on tranquilizers.[14]

Grandparents raising their grandchildren may also experience increased levels of stress because the grandchildren for whom they care are more likely than comparably aged peers from nuclear families to manifest behavioral and psychological adjustment difficulties.[15] Several observers have noted that self-blame characterizes not only grandparents who are raising their grandchildren but the grandchildren as well.[16] These investigators asserted that grandchildren who are being raised by grandparents often blame themselves for what has happened in the family, and as a result of this self-blame they too may suffer from poor self-esteem and depression. The children of mothers who have been substance abusers are more likely than other children to experience developmental disorders.[17] Other psychosocial adjustment problems that are represented disproportionately among this population of grandchildren include sleep disorders, eating disorders, regressive infantile behavior, excessive clinging, angry acting-out behaviors, defiance, and school-related problems.[18]

Certainly the presence of any of these problems in a grandchild would be expected to increase the demands placed on the person or persons who are responsible for looking after that grandchild. If you become the individual primarily responsible for raising a child with one or more of these issues, you will have to learn about the nature of the grandchild's disorder(s) and assume responsibility for providing appropriate remedies. This additional responsibility may represent both an intellectual and a financial challenge for grandparents.

Furthermore, grandchildren whose parents have been in and out of rehabilitation facilities and those whose parents have been in and out of prison may experience shame and embarrassment among peers and family members alike. Members of the community as well as school and social service professionals may adopt negative stereotypical attitudes toward these children, assuming that they are the products of so-called bad seeds.[19] This may require you, as the responsible adult, to assume the role of advocate for their grandchildren, a task which many of us would consider daunting.

For many custodial grandparents, dealing with the educational system on behalf of their grandchildren is particularly problematic.[20] Many grandparents who are raising their grandchildren lack formal legal custody, and school systems sometimes fail to recognize the grandparents as the legitimate caretakers responsible for consultation with school staff and for granting permissions for various school activities.[21] In addition, grandparents may feel that time has passed them by and they are out of the loop. They may be unfamiliar with such educational innovations as the new math, and they may not be computer literate. They may feel embarrassed or even threatened by school personnel who are not particularly helpful and who speak unintelligible technical jargon while providing little effort to explain.[22]

Given all these factors, it is not surprising that grandparents who are raising their grandchildren tend to experience elevated levels of stress and associated negative affect. Over time, such stress may also result in the emergence of specific psychological symptoms including depression, anxiety, interpersonal sensitivity, hostility, paranoid ideation, obsessive compulsive, and somatization.[23]

The Rewards Grandparents May Derive from Raising Their Grandchildren

Of course, the existence of all these stresses associated with the assumption by grandparents of the primary responsibility for raising one or more of their grandchildren must be balanced off against aspects of the role which may be perceived as positive or rewarding by grandparents. The majority of caregiving grandparents report that the experience of raising one's grandchildren gives one a greater purpose for living; and Kelley suggests that caring for their grandchildren helps many caregiving grandparents to feel young and active.[24]

Researchers have significant positive relationship between measured life satisfaction and self-reports of the number of roles that grandparents perform for their children and grandchildren.[25] They interpreted this finding as supporting traditional social science theories that maintain that satisfaction with life is in part a function of the sense of self-efficacy and self-esteem that is derived from perceiving oneself as being useful.

Other investigators have argued that raising a grandchild gives grandparents a chance to raise a child differently, to nurture family relationships, to continue family histories, and to continue to receive love and companionship from their grandchild.[26] These authors have concluded that to many of the grandparents who are raising their grandchildren, rewards of this nature make all their sacrifices worthwhile.

Grandparent Peer Support Groups

One form of social support that deserves special mention in the context of grandparents who are raising their grandchildren is the peer support group. Small peer support groups can be extremely beneficial to such grandparents.[27] The members of these groups share information and advice on such topics as problem-solving strategies, parenting skills, obtaining legal representation, and being assertive with professionals. Group members can also share their thoughts and feelings about the stigma and isolation they experience, the guilt and anger they feel toward their adult children who placed them in the position of having to care for their grandchildren, and the difficulties they may experience at their grandchildren's schools. These group discussions let participants know that they are not alone in their struggles.

Some of these groups are informal, often run out of a grandparent's home, whereas others are sponsored by a health or social service agency, church, school, or other organization. Those sponsored by community organizations typically involve the participation of a part-time professional staff member such as a therapist or social worker. Groups in the latter category tend to have a formal psyhoeducational component, generally led by the professional staff member. You can easily locate an organization sponsoring such groups on the internet. You may find an existing group that you can join; or you can obtain assistance in establishing such a group.

Chapter Fifteen

WHEN LATE LIFE GOALS OF SPOUSES DIFFER

Bob and Ellen

Bob and Ellen are 65 and 62, respectively. Bob retired last year following a 35-year career as a science teacher, and Ellen expects to retire in three years from her position as a senior buyer for a major department store chain. Bob and Ellen live in White Plains, New York, in a home that they purchased 24 years ago. Twelve years ago, they bought a summer and weekend home located on 21 acres in the Pocono Mountains in Pennsylvania. Since they purchased their weekend home, they have spent most weekends and all their vacations there.

Bob and Ellen came to my office seeking counseling. They were contemplating divorce because they had just realized that they had entirely different ideas about what their life would be like when Ellen joined Bob in retirement. Bob had assumed that they would be selling their home in White Plains and moving full time out to the house in the country. He planned to become a "gentleman farmer." He wanted chickens and pigs, and he wanted to plant vegetables. He felt that in order to do this properly he would need to be living at the country home full-time, to keep the foxes out of the chicken coop and the deer out of the garden.

This plan horrified Ellen, who felt that weekends were more than enough time to spend in the country. She loved the theater and planned to spend a great deal of time in New York City after she retired. She had even thought that they might sell the house in White Plains and use the money to buy an apartment in Manhattan. However, Bob had absolutely no interest in moving into Manhattan. When she realized how adamantly opposed Bob was to moving into the city, Ellen was willing to drop this idea. However, she was certainly not willing to give up her home in White Plains, which at least allowed her relatively easy access to the city by car or train for day trips to museums and plays.

Furthermore, Ellen wanted to travel when she retired. She felt that they had spent almost all their vacation time up to retirement at the house in the country, and she wanted to see the rest of the United States and to tour Europe. This was something else that Bob had little or no interest in doing. He also felt that he could not be away from "the farm" for extended periods of time, as would be required for such trips.

The thing that I found most amazing about this couple was the fact that they had managed to get into (in the case of Bob) or near to (in the case of Ellen) retirement without ever sitting down together to have a discussion about what they wanted to do with their lives. The discrepancy in their plans only became clear when Bob mentioned casually one day that he would be wanting to build a new barn and put in some expensive fencing in the country home and that he would be glad when they had sold the house in Westchester because it would give him the extra money that he needed to make the place "a real farm." When Ellen objected to selling their home, Bob felt that all his plans for the farm would be impossible to achieve.

Fortunately, with me acting as a facilitator and a mediator, Bob and Ellen were able to work out their discrepant goals. With some effort they negotiated a series of compromises that enabled them to avoid divorce. They ended up selling the house in White Plains and buying a small apartment in the same town. This apartment was right near the train station, so Ellen could get into and out of the city easily, either with or without Bob. She did not mind downsizing in this way because the kids had long since gone off and they didn't need a big house. Nor did they need to maintain and pay the taxes on the big house in the suburbs. They took the money left over from the sale of the house after they bought the apartment and used it to set up the farm in the country the way Bob wanted to.

They compromised on how they spent their time as well. Once they had both retired, they spent four days each week in the country and three days in White Plains. Bob was able to hire a man who lived by their house in the country to come in to feed and water the animals on the days that he wasn't there. Bob went into the city with Ellen quite a bit; and Ellen also went into the city on other occasions with her daughter or with her women friends. Bob agreed to take two weeks off each year to travel with Ellen, again hiring his neighbor to cover for him on the farm. Ellen took this two-week vacation with Bob; and she also took several other vacations each year with her daughter or her friends. These vacations without Bob were often cruises, which Ellen enjoyed but Bob did not.

Although I found it difficult to believe that this couple had never discussed their goals for retirement, the fact of the matter is that Bob and Ellen represent the majority of couples at or approaching retirement age rather than the exception.

An online survey of 489 couples over the age of 50 conducted by the Scotiabank of Canada indicated that fewer than one-fourth of the participants reported that they had ever had a thorough discussion of their later-life/retirement options with their spouse or partner.[1] More than one-half of the responding couples indicated that they had no more than a "rough idea" of how each other feels about the issue. Nearly 60 percent of the couples surveyed actually *disagreed* as to whether they were looking forward to retirement. In many cases, one spouse indicated that he or she expected their partner to retire, although the partner expected not to retire. In addition, the couples often disagreed with respect to their ideal location and type of residence they wanted for their later years. In many instances one spouse had in mind a move to a warmer climate, while the other was happy to stay where they were presently living. In many instances also, one spouse had in mind a move to a smaller, low-maintenance dwelling, such as a town home or an apartment, while the other felt comfortable right where they were living at the time of the survey. Spouses also tended to disagree with respect whether they expected to spend most of their time during the later years of life with each other only, or whether they planned to spend a great deal of time with family and friends.

The obvious conclusion to be drawn from the case of Bob and Ellen and from the findings of the Scotiabank survey is that couples should make it a point to share and discuss their respective goals for the years after 60. Of course, you may well be thinking that couples should share their aspirations and plans throughout the course of their marriages, and you are correct. However, sharing goals as retirement age approaches is particularly important because if one or both spouses does in fact retire, new options tend to open up as far as where to live and how to spend time and money. It is very easy for two spouses who are both heavily invested in their careers to fall into a regular day-to-day, week-to-week routine, focusing on the here-and-now and not giving a second thought to the long-term. We may not even give much thought to what we want *individually* for the years after 60. But if we are not developing ideas individually, then we are certainly not likely to discuss our dreams for the future with our spouses. Nevertheless, it is very easy to develop vague assumptions about what you will most likely do with the years after 60, based on your personal interests and preferences. Thus Bob assumed that they would be living on his little farm in the country, whereas Ellen assumed that they would be using their greater free time to pursue cultural interests in Manhattan.

I have already given you some ideas on finding and maintaining meaning in your life in chapter 10. I stressed the importance of living our lives with a purpose and finding the aspects of life that resonate deep within us. For many of us, finding this purpose and this resonance will lead naturally to the development of plans for where to live and what to do. For example, if you remember Jim the sailor from chapter 10, the resonance that he felt in sailing determined where he spent much of his time (on the water in a sailboat) as well as the people with whom he spent most of his time (his sailing teammates and the members of the sailboat racing organization that he headed up). But Jim was not married. He did not need to communicate his goals to a spouse and take into consideration what gave her life meaning. However, Bob and Ellen were a couple, and in order for them to stay together and still get what they each felt they needed out of life, it was necessary that they each articulate and share with each other both their passions and their ideas regarding the conditions under which they could fulfill these passions. Then it was necessary that they negotiate and agree upon a plan for the future that accommodated their respective needs.

COMMUNICATION AND NEGOTIATION

I recommend that couples schedule regular weekly discussion sessions throughout the course of their relationship. These discussions should occur at the same time each week, and when something comes up that makes it impossible to have the scheduled discussions at the regular time, the discussions should be rescheduled for the same week. It is easy to slip into a routine that does not involve sharing each others' aspirations and plans for the future. We all have pressing demands and deadlines associated work, family, and even our leisure activities. These pressures will conspire to keep us from engaging in forward planning. But failing to share our evolving interests and goals is a prescription for drifting apart and late life divorce. Therefore, if you want to remain happy with your partner over the course of your lifetime, you simply must make time to share.

Your weekly discussion sessions should include, but not necessarily be limited to, the following questions:

1. What ideas, events, or activities have engaged your interest this week? Are there areas of interest that you would like to pursue further?
2. What aspects of your life would you like to change over the next five years?
3. Where would you like to be living when you are 60? How about 70?
4. To what purposes would you like to be devoting your energy to when you are 60? How about 70?
5. What do you want your social schedule to be like when you are 60? That is, with whom do you wish to spend your time, and what activities do you want to engage in?
6. Are there places that you want to see or particular things that you want to make sure that you do during your lifetime?
7. What are your financial goals for the next 10 years?

You and your partner should respond to each of these questions, and then share your respective reactions. Following this routine should guarantee that you and your partner will be aware of each other's hopes and aspirations. It will help you to identify areas in which your goals may be diverging, and this in turn will enable you to discuss possible differences and make plans that will enable you to accommodate each other's desires. Failure to discuss these issues regularly could ultimately lead you to the type of relationship-threatening divergence of dreams that we observed in the case of Bob and Ellen.

If you discover that your goals are tending to take different directions, try to negotiate a compromise like Bob and Ellen did. If you need to, employ a professional counselor and/or mediator to facilitate your negotiations. You will quite likely find that both of you can accomplish your objectives without splitting up.

BE AWARE OF YOUR MANY OPTIONS

In conducting your negotiations with your spouse regarding the future, keep in mind that you have many options with respect to living arrangements. It is not required that married couples do everything together, nor is it required that married couples reside under the same roof 365 days a year. Couples who have very different interests are free to pursue their respective goals separately, while still sharing those activities that they both enjoy. It has become much more acceptable for a married man to engage in social and recreational activities with friends other than his spouse. Most often these are same-sex friends, but it is not necessarily regarded as inappropriate at this point in time if we pursue some of our interests in mixed sex groups or even with a friend of the opposite sex. Of course, it is imperative to make sure that you make sure that your spouse is open to such arrangements; and it is important to be scrupulously honest and open about such activities.

In addition, couples are free to spend part of each week and/or part of each year living in different parts of the country, or even in different countries, if that's what they need to do to follow their dreams. Many couples split their schedules to accommodate each other's needs. In the past it was much less common to see couples spend substantial periods of time apart. But in an age when people routinely travel across the country for a long weekend, these arrangements are much more feasible and much more common. Here again, you need to be clear with your spouse about the parameters of such arrangements. Being apart for extended periods invariably presents the temptation to socialize with other women, and the potential for having an affair is increased. Of course, some couples may be OK with that as well. I am not trying to tell you how open or monogamous your relationship should be. I am trying to tell you that there are an infinite variety of living arrangements, and that you and your partner must reach an agreement regarding what arrangements will be most satisfactory for both of you.

In addition, advances in communication technology may well make it easier for spouses to pursue their goals without separating for extended periods of time. The internet makes it possible for us to pursue many of our interests at a distance. For example, in the past a spouse who sought to earn a degree might need to spend most of the year away from home to be at a particular university. Spouses often did not see each other for long periods of time, and the stresses on the relationship were significant. Now, many external degree programs are available that enable students to do much of their work at home, either taking courses on the internet or earning credits at a local university, while spending limited amounts of time away at a distant campus.

THE DIVORCE OPTION

There are circumstances when spouses have grown so far apart or have otherwise alienated each other to the extent that divorce, even after many years of marriage, appears to be the best course of action. Deirdre Bair has recently described the phenomenon of late-life divorce as "almost an epidemic" throughout Europe and among certain communities in the United States.[2] She described the findings of a recent AARP study of divorce in mid-life and beyond that attempted to determine why so many older couples are divorcing:

> Husbands and wives may be facing the death of a parent or the last child leaving home—or, in a growing number of cases, children moving back in, sometimes after their own divorces and often with children of their own. These couples may have reached the age and stage of life where they begin to worry about growing old, or if they are already older, they may think about how the years are flying by and their mortality is catching up with them. Not surprisingly, if they look at their mate and see someone with whom they have not communicated for years, they may ponder what their lives have been and what they still might become. Into these volatile situations, events both major and minor trigger life-changing decisions, and more and more frequently, older couples in long marriages see divorce as the answer.[3]

I have already noted that a late-life divorce can be painful not only for the divorcing couple but also for their adult children and even their grandchildren. In addition, there are many practical reasons why couples who find themselves with different dreams should nonetheless consider remaining married. First of all, getting divorced can be very expensive. In addition, divorce may result in the loss of retirement benefits, including medical insurance.

A mature couple who have been married for many years should be able to sit down together and consider all of the pros and cons of a potential divorce. They should also be able to negotiate an understanding regarding living arrangements that will enable them to pursue their respective individual goals while maintaining a relationship that allows them to do those things together that they both enjoy. The range of options is limitless. A couple may spend most of their time pursuing different interests and only a relatively small amount of time doing things together. The spouses can have some friends individually and other friends as a couple. They may even choose to live in different parts of the country for a part of the year or even most of the year. One of the best parts about growing older is that we are free to live as we choose.

Chapter Sixteen

CAREGIVING

Russ and Glenna

Russ and Glenna are retired college professors. Russ is 66 and Glenna is 64. They have been married for 37 years. For most of their marriage, they were quite independent. Each of them was exceedingly devoted to their careers. They met each other at a professional conference. At that point they were both new PhDs. Russ was teaching at Columbia and Glenna was teaching at SUNY Buffalo. Although they fell madly in love, and married shortly after they met, neither of them was willing to give up their academic appointment so that they could live in the same town. Therefore they had a "long distance relationship" for the first five years of their marriage. Russ lived in New York and Glenna lived in Buffalo. When school was in session, they saw each other only twice each month, for long weekends. They alternated with the traveling. For one weekend Russ would fly to Buffalo, and for the next Glenna would fly to New York City. Toward the end of the fourth year of this arrangement, Glenna became pregnant. When she gave birth to their son, she remained in Buffalo and Russ remained in New York. For nearly one year Glenna had virtually the sole responsibility for child care, aided by a mother's helper. Although Russ was not happy spending so little time with his infant son, he was not about to give up his teaching position to move to Buffalo.

Eventually Glenna was able to obtain a teaching appointment at Fordham, and from that point on they were able to live together full-time. However, they remained quite independent. Russ and Glenna were in the same field (sociology), but they had quite different research interests. They each had their own set of professional colleagues with whom they communicated regularly. Each of them dedicated most of their time to their research and their publications. In addition, they both traveled extensively to attend professional conferences and to do consulting work. Although they occasionally went to a conference together, they did much more of their work-related traveling separately. Even after they retired from their teaching positions, they continued to attend professional conferences and seminars related to their respective areas of expertise. They loved each other very much and enjoyed the time that they did spend together, but they definitely had separate and independent identities.

Then three years ago, Glenna had a stroke. As a result of the stroke, she has substantial physical weakness on the left side of her body, and she has lost much of her short-term memory. She finds it difficult to retain new information. Sometimes she forgets things that have just been said. As a result, it is somewhat difficult for her to have normal conversations. She often needs to be reminded of what is being discussed and where the conversation has led up to now. This is not too difficult for Russ to deal with, but Glenna's limitations have led her to cut way back on her outside activities. She still does some writing, but she has stopped doing consulting work and traveling. In fact, her physical limitations make it impossible for her to drive or to get around easily.

Russ has become Glenna's caretaker. He drives her wherever she needs to go, from her physical therapy appointments to the hairdresser to stores. Russ also does all of the household chores that they had previously shared. In addition, he goes out each day with Glenna for a walk, which her physical therapist strongly recommends to strengthen her body.

Assuming the caretaker role has also led Russ to alter his activities. He no longer travels extensively, because he does not feel that he can leave Glenna alone for long periods of time. Their adult son and his wife visit once or twice a week and provide Russ with a little respite time, but long trips are not possible. Russ is philosophical regarding the changes that have occurred in their lives. He notes that even though he has had to give up some things that he enjoyed doing, he has gotten a lot in return. He says that the stroke has brought him closer to Glenna, and he cherishes the time that they spend together. Russ also derives a great deal of satisfaction from the fact that he can be there for his wife and make her life easier.

This couple is typical of many couples who have moved beyond their sixtieth birthdays. In the majority of couples where caregiving is required, it is the wife who provides the care to her husband.[1] There are a number of reasons for this disproportionate representation of wives relative to husbands among spousal caregivers. We men tend to seek medical care less regularly than women, perhaps because we regard illness as a sign of weakness or loss of control. But our lack of diligence in terms of preventive medicine can leave treatable illnesses undetected, thus increasing the chance that the illness will become a serious problem. In contrast, the greater diligence of women with regard to health care tends to help them live longer than their husbands and be healthier than their husbands. Thus our wives are more likely than we are to find themselves caring for their spouses. However, there are still many men past the age of 60 who find themselves providing care for a wife in the same way that Russ cared for Glenna. Therefore it is important for us to know something about the circumstances under which caregiving becomes a necessity, the ways in which caregiving affects both our marriage and our lives as individuals, the steps that we can take to reduce the stresses associated with providing care, and the options we have under different scenarios regarding the health status of our spouse.

LONGEVITY AND THE NEED FOR CAREGIVING

The situation in which one spouse provides care at home for the other is increasingly common. As longevity has increased, so has the number of older individuals who have some form of chronic physical condition that requires some degree of care. According to Lillian Hawthorne,

> The increase in longevity had not only changed how long people were living but also how they were dying—and therefore how they lived until they died. So now, in the early twenty-first century, people are dying later in life and of illnesses people never had before because they did not live long enough to get them. And, for the most part, people are not dying suddenly, or all at once, but over time and after periods of extended treatment or chronic illness.[2]

In short, the medical advances that have lengthened our lives have also increased the possibility that during our longer lives we may experience different kinds of health problems. Older individuals are more likely to experience the skeletal deterioration associated with osteoporosis, loss of vision due to macular degeneration, neurological impairments from Parkinson's disease, or loss of mental faculties resulting from Alzheimer's disease. Research also indicates that the likelihood of developing some form of cancer increases substantially after the age of 65. This may be for no other reason than the fact that living longer allows time for slow-growing cancers to develop.

In addition to the simple fact of increased life span, medical advances are also allowing many more older individuals to survive illnesses that previously would have killed them. The proportion of individuals who survive heart attacks and strokes has increased, as has the proportion of individuals who survive for considerable periods of time following a diagnosis of cancer.[3] People are not suffering fewer illnesses because they are living longer. Rather they are suffering different kinds of illnesses and they are surviving these illnesses for longer and longer periods of time. Statistics indicate that three-fourths of all individuals over the age of 75 have at least one chronic health problem, and many of these individuals have more than one such problem. These health problems often require some level of caretaking, although they are not immediately life threatening.

FORMS OF CAREGIVING

Within the context of the multigenerational family, caregiving can take many forms. In this chapter I have chosen to focus on the care given by a husband to a wife, but much caretaking is done by adult children (usually daughters) for their parents. In addition, even those of us who are in our 60s may very well have one or more parent still living and requiring our care. A recent survey conducted in a suburb of New York City indicated that three-fourths of caregiving relationships were between a child and his or her parent, parent-in-law, grandparent, or grandparent-in-law.[4] Obviously, some of the dyads in this category would be comprised of men over 60 caring for a parent or parent-in-law who is in his or her late 70s or 80s. Approximately 10 percent of all caregiving dyads consisted of spouses or partners. Four percent of caregiving dyads were comprised of siblings, and the remainder of the caregiving dyads were comprised of individuals who had some other form of relationship to each other.

Although most caregiving relationships are between individuals from different generations (referred to as *vertical* caregiving relationships), it has been argued that it will be more and more common for caregiving relationships to include the caregiver and the recipient of care to be from the same generation. This is referred to as horizontal caregiving, and into this category fall caregiving relationships between spouses or partners. According to Hawthorne, these social and economic shifts in society are currently resulting in a decrease in the proportion of vertical caretaking relationships and an increase in the proportion of horizontal caregiving relationships. For example, family sizes have tended to decrease over the past half century. This leaves fewer children who can be called upon to provide care for parents. In addition, increased geographical mobility tends to find children living farther away from their parents than they used to, leaving them unable to provide continuous care for their parents. Further, more and more families are two-earner families. In the past many women were homemakers, which made it possible for them to seamlessly integrate the tasks of caring for an elderly parent into their schedule. But now most wives are working along with their husbands, leaving no one at home to provide convenient care for a parent in need.

Further, Hawthorne suggests that social values influence the extent to which adult children feel obligated to provide care for their older parents. She writes:

> Today's older generation has long taught and sought independence, both for themselves and for their children. They did not want to depend on their children or impose on their lives as their own parents may have done on them. So, in a sense, they intentionally freed their children from the burden of parental obligation that they themselves had endured. During their own younger or adult years, this was not difficult and was even satisfying. But when they reached their older years and began to feel or expect the need for care, they also began to feel some regrets about the lessons of freedom from responsibility that they had taught and their children had learned so well![5]

I personally feel that Hawthorne may have overstated her case that adult children do not feel compelled to provide care for their older parents. The figures clearly indicate that the majority of caretaking for older parents is in fact provided by their children. Nevertheless, it is the case that many couples who have been married for a long time become their own and one another's care-takers. In many cases there is no other option. In other cases, such as that of Russ and Glenna, the spouses may receive some caregiving assistance from children but rely in large measure on each other.

THE ROLE OF THE CARETAKER

Providing care for a spouse typically has two primary components: (1) actually providing your wife with the assistance that she needs to manage her medical condition effectively, including providing food, making sure that medications are taken as ordered, help with bathing and other activities of daily living if necessary, and providing emotional support in the form of comforting and encouragement; and (2) assuming responsibility for those chores and roles that your spouse had handled previously, before she became less able to function independently. Most men involved in providing care for their wives find that the additional household chores represent more of a burden than providing their spouse with the various forms of direct care that she may need. This is because most men have not involved themselves much in food shopping, cooking, doing laundry, and cleaning. And we are used to feeling competent about what we do. Therefore we may very well be apprehensive regarding our ability to carry out these functions adequately. And of course, some of us would rather not acknowledge our lack of preparedness by asking for instruction or assistance.

In addition, men who take responsibility for caring for their wives may also need to assume the role of family social coordinator. In most couples, it is the wife who arranges the social schedule and social activities. If she is unable to do this, the burden will fall on the husband. But many men are so out of the loop when it comes to social activities that they are afraid to pick up the phone and make a date with friends. Such discomfort will likely be exacerbated if aspects of the wife's medical condition are imposing greater limitations on what she can actually do now in comparison to what they did before.

On the other hand, some experts on spousal caretaking have noted that many men are pragmatic and instrumental by disposition, particularly if they have been working at careers that have involved management functions. When these men assume the caregiving role, they are likely to employ a problem-solving approach, perhaps the same instrumental approach that they employed previously on their jobs, in order to meet the challenges associated with providing care.[6] Adopting an instrumental coping style has been viewed as allowing these male caretakers to utilize available sources of support and assistance and to set limits on caregiving activities. These tendencies in turn have been viewed as not only improving their ability to meet the needs of their spouse but also affording them some protection from becoming burned out with the caregiving role.[7]

The message here is clear. *If you are assuming the role of caretaker for your spouse, be prepared to face challenges that you might not have anticipated.* Some of the new functions that you will be performing may not be nearly as trivial as you might have expected, and you may need some help. If you need to learn how to cook, take a cooking course or ask a friend or an adult child to come over and show you how. If you can afford to get some paid help with household chores or even with caretaking activity, do so. Regard the new role as a new challenge that you can meet with greater efficiency or with less efficiency, and then choose greater efficiency.

THE STRESSES ASSOCIATED WITH CAREGIVING

There are many significant sources of stress for men who provide care to their wives. Despite the instrumental approach to caregiving that researchers have attributed to men in general, it is still true that some men who provide care for their spouses have difficulty asking for help, thinking that they really should be able to handle the job without outside assistance.[8] Coe and Neufield have observed that some men caregivers seek assistance only as a "last resort."[9] These men consider asking for help to be a sign of dishonor and a violation of their own sense of pride as well as their family's privacy. These men may place unnecessary burdens on themselves, and they are likely as well to become isolated socially. Both of these aspects of their situation are stressful. Thus it is not surprising that researchers have shown that husbands who provide care for a spouse are two to four times more likely than similarly aged husbands who do not provide care to as spouse to suffer from clinical depression.[10]

It has also been argued that men who provide care for their spouses are likely to feel that their work is unappreciated.[11] This feeling can lead to conflict with both the spouse herself and with other members of the family.[12] These possibilities further exacerbate the stress experienced by the male caretaker. Russell observed that "caregiving is basically a solitary activity, carried out in social locations predominantly occupied solely by care receiver—care giver dyad."[13] Slotkin observed that care work is largely an invisible enterprise carried out in the very private context of the home, and he concluded that for this reason a major predictor of the amount of stress a man will experience in connection with caring for his wife will be the changes that may take place in his social network and social activities.[14]

Research suggests that men who are providing care for their wives tend to experience losses in freedom such as the ability to leave the home at their discretion and free time to pursue social activities that take place outside the home.[15] The lack of time may impact several areas of the caregiver's life, limiting his social contact and contributing to isolation from friends and activities.[16] Of course, to a substantial degree the lack of freedom experienced by the caregiver will be a function of his own attitudes and values. Some men will view concerns with their own needs as selfish.[17] Although the utilization of outside assistance or respite might allow caregivers the opportunity to leave their homes and engage in social activities, it has been reported that many men caregivers believe that it would be wrong for them to turn the care of their spouse over to someone else, even for a short period of time.[18]

Here again the message is clear. *You need to recognize your limitations, and you need to take care of yourself as well as your wife.* She will not benefit if you burn yourself out. Use all the resources that you have available to you to facilitate your caregiving role. Don't be ashamed if you are not superman.

THE IMPORTANCE OF SOCIAL SUPPORT AND ACTIVITY

Let me state unequivocally right here that if you should find yourself in the position of providing care for your spouse, *you absolutely must allow yourself to have some social activity outside the home.* If you allow yourself to become totally isolated and you become miserable as a result, you will eventually come to resent your spouse, and the time that you spend together with her will not be good time either. This will leave you with nothing in your life that is reward-ing, and you will be asking to join the ranks of the clinically depressed caregiv-ers. You and your spouse need to be able to discuss how much time you need to get out and have some fun, and how much time she feels comfortable being alone or spending with someone else.

The research is quite clear that when caregivers seek out social connections and maintain socially supportive relationships, the level of stress that they report experiencing goes down, and their psychosocial adjustment and subjective well-being go up.[19] White male spousal caregivers have been reported to be more likely to receive emotional support from their adult children, and more likely to receive practical assistance from agencies and other formal sources of support.[20] Men caregivers benefit greatly if they can establish several well-defined support networks.[21] Friends constitute one social group who can provide emotional sup-port and social integration. Political, civic, and charitable organizations represent other possible venues for social contact. Religious institutions provide another source of emotional, social, and spiritual support.[22] Informal or formal support groups that meet regularly and workshops for caregivers that are one-time events can also be extremely helpful. Such groups and workshops allow caregivers to share their experiences, validate their feelings, and exchange practical advice and suggestions on how to handle specific caregiving issues. These groups and workshops also provide an opportunity for meeting and developing friendships with other men and women who share the experience of caregiving.

With respect to both participation in caregiver support groups and the de-velopment and maintenance of social networks in general, gender is a big issue for men who are caring for their spouses. Most men who seek social contact will seek contact with other men, because they want to avoid any appearance of over-familiarity with women other than their wife. This is understandable but unfortunate, since many potentially rewarding opportunities for socializing involve members of both sexes. How you might feel about this issue is of course a matter of personal opinion. Clearly the feelings of your spouse need to be taken into consideration in deciding what is and is not permissible with respect to social activity. I simply note that many social activities will include both male and female participants. This would be true of membership in a political party, the chamber of commerce, and the bridge club, and it would also include most book, film, or theater clubs. Of course you could confine your social activities to sports or fishing, where you would tend to find primarily men. But it seems to me a shame to allow an excessive concern for socially scripted gender roles to eliminate possible avenues for social interaction. All I can say is that you need to be very open and honest with your wife about what you are doing and with whom. After all, if she requires that you care for her, then she is by definition in a position of heightened vulnerability, and she may well tend to be more jealous of social contacts with women than she would be under other circumstances.

Another issue arises with respect to the gender composition of support groups. Since we men do tend to be somewhat more pragmatic and instrumental in our orientation toward the caregiver role than do women caregivers, it could be frustrating to be in a group in which the men were substantially outnumbered by the women. Here again, this is a matter of personal opinion. I am simply saying that some men will likely feel more comfortable in a group comprised primarily or entirely of men, while others would do just fine in a group consisting mainly of women. I have had a number of men caregivers as clients, and I always try to get them connected with some kind of caregiver support group or caregiver workshop. In many instances, they sometimes feel a bit out of place when heavily outnumbered by women. They complain that too much of the interaction in the group consists of emotional catharsis and not enough of the interaction represents the exchange of useful information. Fortunately, there are quite a few such groups available, and you are free to shop around until you find a place where you feel comfortable.

THE SPECIAL CASE OF ALZHEIMER'S

A recent survey of caregivers in New York State indicated that approximately 15 percent of all caregivers provide care to a recipient who has Alzheimer's disease or some other related form of dementia.[23] Although no precise data are available with respect to the proportion of men over 60 who are providing care to a spouse with Alzheimer's, Cahill has concluded that research conducted in the United States, the United Kingdom, and Australia suggests that "there are many male caregivers in the over 60 year age group...including husbands caring for cognitively impaired wives."[24]

Alzheimer's disease represents a special situation for caregivers. The progressive and degenerative nature of this disease results in cognitive, physical, and emotional deficits that markedly increase the patient's dependency on caregivers.[25] Those who provide care to Alzheimer's patients often must dress, feed, bathe, and toilet their loved one.[26] Moreover, Alzheimer's patients often require 24-hour supervision, because they tend to remain awake through the night and they often wander.[27] Caregivers must also contend with troublesome cognitive symptoms that include confusion, forgetfulness, disorientation, and mood swings.[28] In the advanced stages of Alzheimer's disease, patients often fail to recognize their caregivers.[29] DeLongis and O'Brien have observed that "perhaps most devastating for caregivers is that they are providing care for family members who are increasingly unrecognizable as their former selves."[30]

What is particularly difficult for spouses who care for Alzheimer's patients is that the caregiver experiences a gradual but inexorable loss of many of the previously supportive aspects of the relationship with the spouse at the same time that the demands of caregiving are increasing.[31] The caregiving husband faces the loss of his lifelong partner, companion, and confidant. Previously enjoyed leisure and social activities can no longer be shared, and sexual relations are typically disrupted or diminished.

Another aspect of Alzheimer's disease that is especially difficult concerns the need to make decisions regarding the type of care that the patient will require as the disease progresses. Many caregivers ultimately decide that it is necessary to place their spouse in a nursing home. This is obviously a very difficult decision. It can be a source of conflict among family members. A husband may wish to continue to care for his wife at home, but his adult children may see the toll that the caregiving is taking on him, and they may push very hard for mom to be placed in the home. Disagreements among family members regarding such decisions are particularly difficult, because a potential source of emotional support becomes still another source of stress. The decision regarding whether and when to place the Alzheimer's patient in a nursing home is also complicated by the expenses that are involved. While placing the patient in a nursing home facility may alleviate the caregiving burden and provide the caregiver with some additional time to engage in recreational and social activities, the financial burden may present an additional problem.[32]

It is not at all clear that placing a spouse with Alzheimer's in a nursing home represents an unmitigated benefit to the caregiver. Research on the effects of nursing home placement has yielded contradictory findings. Several studies comparing caregivers who did place spouses in nursing homes to those who did not have indicated that the caregiving spouses who do decide on a nursing home placement benefit from greater free time and greater opportunity to engage in social and recreational activities.[33] Other studies have suggested that caregivers who decide to place the Alzheimer's patient in a nursing home report greater satisfaction with social and leisure activities.[34]

On the other hand, placing a spouse in a nursing home can itself be a stressful, even traumatic, event that engenders emotional distress.[35] This view was supported by a study of caregivers that showed that approximately one-half of caregivers who placed a spouse in a nursing home had elevated levels of mental health symptoms following the placement.[36] Another study indicated that nearly one-half of caregivers who placed a spouse in a nursing home facility met the criteria for clinical depression one-month following the admission.[37] On the other hand, several longitudinal studies have indicated that depression experienced by those caregivers for spouses with Alzheimer's either decreases marginally or remains unchanged following the admission of the patient to a nursing home.[38] These studies suggest that the caregiving spouses are quite likely depressed before the decision to place the patient is made and that the decision itself has relatively little impact on the caregiver's depression.

Of course, the research findings speak to caregivers in general. If your spouse is diagnosed with Alzheimer's disease, you will need to make decisions according to your own ideas about what is best for the both of you. What I want to do here is to give you the information that you need to make informed decisions, balancing your values and attitudes against what others have done in similar circumstances. It is clear that if there are adult children in your family, they will most likely need to be involved in the decisions that are made. You will need their emotional support and perhaps their tangible assistance with caregiving as well. Even if you are the primary caregiver and the person most affected by your spouse's condition, you need to try to keep the family together at this time. You also need to accept the fact that you are not superman and that you may need to seek help. Caregivers with whom I have worked have struggled with the decision to admit their spouse to a nursing home, only to find that the decision that they feared would separate them from their spouse actually made it possible to enjoy her company and to look forward to seeing her.

Feelings of guilt can be alleviated by discussing possible long-term options with your spouse *before* the disease has progressed to a point where discussions cease to be meaningful. Most spouses who face chronic diseases that will eventually require virtually full-time care will not want their spouse to bear that burden alone. The two of you can probably come to an agreement as to when it might become appropriate to consider various types of accommodations, including nursing home placement. Obviously this may be the most difficult discussion you and your spouse have ever had, yet it may bring you closer than you could have ever imagined.

ALTERNATIVES

In addition, there are some alternatives to nursing home care that can be employed to ease the caregiver burden while maintaining the life that you have known together to the greatest extent possible for the longest period of time that is possible. Downsizing your home or moving to a senior residential community can be of some help, since the amount of effort and energy that needs to be put into home maintenance will be reduced, freeing you for other role responsibilities. Moving to an assisted living facility can provide an even greater level of assistance while allowing you and your spouse to continue to live together in the same home. Moving in with or closer to one's children is also a possibility, if all agree. I would only point out that arrangements of this nature require considerable effort to carry off smoothly, since all the complexities of the multigenerational family will be operating, along with the additional concerns associated with your spouses medical condition.

In-home care is also a possibility for those who can afford it. Having someone come in to your home, even part-time, to lighten the caregiving load and/ or to help out with household chores can be immensely helpful. However, keep in mind that step means that a stranger will be coming into your home and "taking over" for part of the time. It can be difficult to adjust to this stranger and to accommodate your relationship with your spouse to his or her presence.

None of these decisions is easy, but it is important that you know that there are a variety of approaches that can be used to make coping with a spouses chronic medical condition more manageable.

GETTING HELP

There are places where you can get help making these decisions. There is a Web site designed to provide information regarding Alzheimer's disease (www.alzheimers.org) as there are for stroke (www.stroke.org), Parkinson's disease (http://www.apdaparkinson.com), and macular degeneration (www.eyesight.org). You need to be proactive, unashamed of your spouse's condition, and you need to be willing to accept help. You also need to be free from guilt. You can do as much as you can do. It is not a mark of weakness to allow others to share the load.

Chapter Seventeen

GRIEF AND BEREAVEMENT

A Widower's Story

James is 65. His wife Mary died from breast cancer about nine months ago. She had been diagnosed four years before her death. At the time of her diagnosis, she had a radical mastectomy and follow-up radiation treatments, and for two years it appeared that she would remain cancer free. However, the cancer recurred. From that point on the course was downhill; Mary had several rounds of chemotherapy and radiation treatments, which only temporarily slowed the progression of the disease. She was hospitalized several times in the last year, but during the last two months of her life she was at home under the care of a hospice organization.

James acknowledges that Mary had all the care possible under the circumstances. They recognized that her illness was terminal some time before her death, and they made the best possible decisions regarding changing the focus of her treatment to palliative care. Hospice was called into the case in a timely manner. James and Mary had time to reflect on their lives together, and Mary did not suffer very much at the end. James has read a good deal about dying over the past several years, and he is firmly convinced that Mary had a "good death."

However, nine months after Mary's death, James describes himself as "not in a good place." He attended a cancer support group before Mary's death, and he attends a bereavement group now. So he knows that he has been doing what he should to get support. But he feels as if he hasn't been able to come to grips with Mary's absence and with the changes in his life now that she is not around. He doesn't cook and "the house is always a mess." He has three adult children, but none of them live close by, and they haven't really been all that close over the last 10 or 20 years. James doesn't really have a close group of friends either. Throughout most of his life Mary had arranged the social contacts, and James' only independent source of social contact was at work. James values the social contacts that he has in his bereavement group, but in a way he feels like his participation in the support group actually serves to keep him focused on his loss, maybe even making it more difficult to move on and "start living a life."

James owns a delicatessen, and he has not retired. He had cut way back on his personal involvement in the business even before Mary became ill, and he cut back still further during the course of her illness. Now he sometimes fills up his time by going in to the delicatessen to work, but he feels like "an extra wheel" there now. He still likes to have the social contact with his employees and with the customers, but he doesn't feel the same enthusiasm for the business that he did when he was younger. James also expresses concern for his own mortality. He wonders whether he will succumb to a serious illness as his wife did, and he wonders whether he will have "gotten settled in a life" before he dies.

James's situation illustrates several aspects of modern life that have great impact on the experience of bereavement among those of us who are over 60. These include the changed manner in which death tends to occur, the availability of effective palliative care, the availability of support groups for surviving spouses, the major changes in the activities of daily living that confront men following the loss of their partner, and the need of the surviving spouse to transition into a new life without the departed partner.

THE CHANGING WAY WE DIE

As life expectancy has increased, the manner in which we typically die has changed. It used to be that most people died quickly as a result of an acute or infectious disease. But now death typically occurs as a result of a chronic disease that we develop rather late in life, such as cancer or heart disease.[1] "Death is now a process rather than an event."[2] Because most deaths take place at the end of long, debilitating, progressive illnesses, the dying patient's last weeks are often spent in a hospital or a nursing home facility, and at least some life sustaining technologies are typically employed. Patients tend to live their final years with at least some physical symptoms. They may experience shortness of breath, loss of appetite, lack of mobility, and diminishing cognitive functioning.[3]

THE IMPACT OF CHRONIC ILLNESS
ON THE SURVIVING SPOUSE

It has long been believed that unexpected and sudden deaths are more troublesome for surviving spouses than anticipated deaths resulting from chronic illnesses or diseases.[4] Experts on death and dying have assumed that individuals who anticipate their spouse's death will be able to use the time they have left to prepare psychologically and practically for the transition to the new status of widower (or widow).[5] It has been suggested that the period of forewarning can be used to resolve any conflicts that may have existed between the dying spouse and the surviving spouse, and it has been argued that couples who use this time between diagnosis and death to resolve unfinished emotional business may find that their relationship is greatly enhanced during their final days as a couple.[6] Finally, the couple can use this time to make practical plans and arrangements that will impact the surviving spouse's financial and social adjustment.[7] However, a good deal of research has been done on the effect of forewarning on the psychological adjustment of widows and widowers, and this research is not conclusive. There are studies that suggest that the sudden death of a spouse is associated with poorer adjustment outcomes for the survivor, but there are also studies that suggest precisely the opposite.[8] Studies have also been reported in which no relationship was found between the amount of forewarning spouses had and the adjustment of the surviving spouse following the death.[9]

I believe it is important for a dying partner to give encouragement to her husband to re-partner, should he choose, and to make this known to her children. This statement of intention and approval is important for children should their father choose to introduce a new partner to the family constellation.

It is certainly true that long periods of decline prior to dying can have stressful aspects. Protracted illness is very expensive, and the longer an ailing individual lives before succumbing to a chronic disease, the more expensive her care is likely to be. These expenses can make a huge dent in savings that the surviving spouse might need to ease the financial stresses that he may face over the remainder of his life. In addition, as considered in the last chapter, a long period of chronic illness prior to dying places the spouse in a caregiver role. This is a difficult and stressful role to assume in itself; and the assumption of the caregiving role also limits the caregiver's capacity to work and earn needed income, thus exacerbating the financial stress that he may be experiencing. In some instances the death of one's spouse following a long period of debility can represent a liberating event. Remember the case study of Mark that I presented in chapter 6 on social connections after 60. His wife Bella died after an extended period of disability during which Mark was a devoted caregiver. Everyone in the family assumed that he would die soon after her. But Mark surprised everyone by taking advantage of his new found free time to resurrect old friendships and visiting old friends for the first time in years.

NEGATIVE PSYCHOSOCIAL OUTCOMES AMONG SURVIVING SPOUSES

There is a great deal of evidence that older spouses whose partners die tend to experience significant psychosocial adjustment difficulties. Bereaved partners tend to experience both physical health problems and emotional disorders, particularly symptoms of depression and anxiety, during the months and years following their loss.[10] Bereaved spouses experience more frequent illnesses than non-bereaved spouses of the same age.[11] They report experiencing more frequent and severe pain than that reported by non-bereaved spouses.[12] The bereaved spend more money than the non-bereaved on medical care.[13] Bereaved spouses consume more alcohol and smoke greater amounts of tobacco than non-bereaved spouses.[14] They also take more prescription medication than non-bereaved spouses.[15] Bereaved spouses tend to experience disturbed sleep, compromised immune systems, and higher mortality rates than non-bereaved spouses.[16]

WHY LATE-LIFE BEREAVEMENT CAN BE PARTICULARLY DIFFICULT

Nearly one million people each year become widows or widowers in the United States.[17] Approximately three-quarters of these individuals are over the age of 65. Thus the loss of one's spouse is a nearly universal experience among older persons. The only way to avoid bereavement is to die first.[18]

Because it is perceived as normal to become a widower or a widow at some point in the latter part of one's life, it is often assumed that the loss of a spouse at an older age is somehow less stressful than the loss of a spouse in early adulthood or during the midlife period.[19] Thus Neugarten argues that the death of a spouse among the elderly is "rehearsed, the 'grief work' completed, the reconciliation accomplished without shattering the sense of continuity of the life cycle."[20] It has also been suggested that because there are so many older individuals who have lost a spouse, widowers and widows have the opportunity to interact with and receive emotional support and advice from many peers who have gone through the same experience. In contrast, a younger widower or widow will not find nearly so many peers who share their experience of loss.[21] Some experts have even argued that older persons are better able to cope with bereavement than younger persons, simply because they have learned from experience how to adapt to life's stresses, and they can apply this experience to the process of coping with the death of a spouse.[22]

However, in reality there are many reasons why bereavement in the latter part of one's life may well represent a greater challenge to one's coping ability than the death of a spouse earlier in the life span. For one thing, older individuals tend to experience other losses in their lives besides the loss of their spouse. They may have retired or had to cut back on their work, possibly resulting in a loss in self-esteem due to the perception that one is no longer as productive a member of society as one once was. In addition, the kids are gone, so we no longer have the gratification associated with making sure that they have all they need. This again cuts into our sense that we are needed. We may also have lost friends and family members other than our spouse. Even the loss of a pet can be difficult. The fact that older individuals tend to have many losses pile up around one point in the lifespan has been termed "bereavement overload."[23] It has been argued that this overload of stressors can deplete the coping resources of the bereaved individual, increasing his vulnerability to developing physical and psychosocial difficulties.

Another factor that may make bereavement difficult for older persons is the tendency of one's social network to shrink as we grow older. Retirement may cut us off from social contact at work, and problems with our health may tend to limit the extent to which we can get around to engage in community and social activities. Therefore we may have less readily available sources of social and emotional support than younger bereaved spouses might have.

I should also point out that when couples have been married for many years, they tend to grow more and more interdependent.[24] Older spouses simply tend to be highly dependent upon each other for companionship. For this reason, loneliness has been identified as one of the most important difficulties faced by bereaved older spouses.[25] In addition, older spouses may be highly reliant on each other to get all the household chores done. When one spouse dies, the bereaved survivor may very well have to figure out how to do a large number of chores that he has never before had to deal with. He may not know how to do some of these chores and may require help to learn how to do them.

WHY BEREAVEMENT IS OFTEN MORE DIFFICULT FOR MEN THAN FOR WOMEN

Although bereavement is more common among women than among men, there is evidence that bereavement may be more difficult for men than for women. There are more widows than there are widowers, primarily because women live longer than men, but also in part because men who are widowed are more likely than women to remarry. Among Americans who are 65 years old or older, 46 percent of the women are widows, whereas only 14 percent of the men are widowers.[26] This discrepancy becomes more and more extreme as we consider older age cohorts. Among individuals 85 and over, there are 14 widows for every widower.[27]

Most of the recent research comparing widowers and widows with respect to physical health and psychosocial adjustment suggests than men have greater difficulty with bereavement than women do. Widowers are more likely to experience debilitating physical conditions and limitations following the loss of a spouse than widows are.[28] Widowers are more likely than widows to experience clinically significant levels of depression during bereavement.[29] Widowers tend to score lower than widows on measures of psychological well-being.[30] In addition, widowers are more likely than widows to die shortly after their spouses die. A recent study showed that 18 months following the death of their husband, only about 5 percent of women had themselves died. In contrast, over the same

18 month period, 18 percent of widowers had died.[31] Among women, there is no difference between those who are widows and those who are still married in terms of the risk of suicide. Among men, the risk of suicide is five times greater among widowers than among men who remain married.[32] Some investigators have argued that these differences in physical and emotional outcomes for widows and widowers indicate that "bereaved husbands lose their sense of meaning and purpose, give up hope, and lose the will to live."[33]

A number of explanations have been offered for the fact that bereavement appears to have more devastating consequences for men than for women. One explanation is that women tend to have stronger support networks than men do.[34] It has been argued that "women typically have many more close social relationships than men and are likely to be the ones to nurture and sustain the couple's social relationships with others."[35] Therefore, when our wives die, we tend to be left up in the air, uncertain whether we want to engage in social activities and out of practice with respect to the normal behaviors undertaken to maintain and strengthen friendship relationships. In addition, many men are heavily dependent on their wives for emotional support, because their wives are often their only real confidants.[36] When a man loses a long-term partner, he is likely to be very lonely indeed.

Another explanation for the relatively more serious effects of bereavement on men is that men are more dependent on their wives for practical help than women are on their husbands.[37] By practical help I mean things like shopping, taking care of the house, and paying the bills. Although it has become more common for wives to work and for husbands to participate meaningfully in household chores and child raising activities, it is still the women who perform the lion's share of the household tasks.[38] According to the results of a recent poll of American households, nearly 60 percent of women report that they do most or all of the household chores.[39] Moreover, men who are today approaching 60 or beyond the age of 60 tend to have been less involved with these traditionally female roles than are younger men. Thus the loss of a wife results not only in the stress associated with the loss of one's friend, lover, and confidant but also in many cases the stresses associated with figuring out how to keep the household together.[40]

Finally with respect to the more negative outcomes experienced by widowers than by widows, research suggests that women are generally more health conscious than men.[41] Wives often take responsibility not only for their own preventive and health producing behaviors but also for those of their husbands. Therefore, if a wife dies, it is quite likely that her husband will "stop taking care of himself." He won't think to take his vitamins or to schedule regular physical examinations, and he certainly won't think to schedule a colonoscopy. In addition, researchers have shown that bereaved men are more likely than bereaved women to increase tobacco use and alcohol consumption.[42]

For all these reasons, therefore, it is important for widowers to be aware of the factors that impact the severity of the stresses they are likely to experience following the loss of a spouse. Of course we will experience loneliness and grief when we lose the partner with whom we have spent much of our lives. These feelings are natural, and in a sense they are the price that we pay for a lifetime of companionship. But we can do much to keep ourselves from falling apart totally when we lose a wife or partner.

THINGS WE CAN DO TO KEEP US FROM FALLING APART

We can do much both before and after the death of our spouse to help us cope with our grief and keep from falling apart as we make the transition to a new way of living. If there is forewarning due to a chronic progressive disease process, it is important that we strive to repair any emotional damage that may exist in our relationship with our spouse. Freud and Bowlby both argue that conflict over the course of the marital relationship and particularly ambivalent feelings toward a dying spouse tend to be associated with greater distress on the part of the surviving spouse.[43] More recent research has called this argument into question, suggesting that bereaved individuals who had the happiest marriages tend to experience more intense and prolonged grief.[44] However, it seems clear that regardless of the level of marital conflict that existed over the course of a lifetime, working through unresolved emotional difficulties before the death of our spouse will eliminate at least one potential source of stress during bereavement, that due to self-recrimination and the perception that we did not do as much as we could to "make things right" before the end.

As noted above, another thing that you can do during your partner's last months is to make whatever decisions that need to be made with her before her death in order to make your life following her death more manageable. These may include such practical issues as making sure that her will is in order and making decisions regarding the disposition of personal property among the children. You do not want to be put in the position of having to decide after your wife's death which daughter ought to get mom's favorite necklace or earrings. Your wife needs to work this out with you and with them before she goes.

Spiritual support in the form of religious belief and spiritual reflection can help you cope with your spouse's illness and death, and with your new mode of living following her death. Belief in an afterlife can be reassuring. So can the belief that the two of you will meet again someday in a better place. Obviously, if you do not hold these beliefs, you cannot really force yourself to believe in anticipation of your partner's death. However, many men have not really given much consideration to these issues before the reality of their spouses impending death becomes clear. If you are one of those who have neglected or ignored the spiritual side of life, it would be good to reconnect at this time.

Reconnecting with your religion can also have the added benefit of making you aware of the availability of pastoral counseling and bereavement support groups that may be sponsored by your church or temple. Several empirical studies have shown that religious beliefs tend to ease our grief, help us to find meaning in our loss, and help us move on with life.[45] Research has also suggested that individuals whose religious beliefs include a personal relationship with God are more likely than those with no such relationship to be maintain secure attachments following the death of the spouse, providing them with a continuing sense of safety and security despite the loss of their partner.[46]

When the death of your spouse actually occurs, the two most important predictors of adjustment are: (1) availability and utilization of social supports; and (2) your personal psychological outlook. With respect to social support, it has been shown that social support can lessen the effects of many stressful life events, and there is widespread agreement among experts on bereavement that men who have lost a partner should strive to maintain and develop social contacts in an effort to prevent negative outcomes of bereavement such as poor physical health and depression.[47] Of course I would agree in urging any bereaved man to make whatever efforts he can to maintain contact and activities with friends and family, as well as efforts to develop new friendships and interests. Nevertheless, it is only fair to point out that even though the support of friends and family is important, it is rare indeed that such contacts completely fill the void left by the lost partner.[48] Even men with substantial support networks are likely to experience great loneliness following a spouse's death.

With respect to your personal outlook, the key word is *optimism*. You may remember that in chapter 5, I considered Seligman's theory of learned optimism, arguing that individuals who have an optimistic explanatory style are better able than those with a pessimistic explanatory style to cope with the various stressful events that are typically associated with growing older. Well, bereavement is one of the most important of these stressful events, and maintaining an optimistic outlook is critical to how you will adjust to the loss of your spouse. Research has shown that bereaved individuals who score high on a personality trait known as dispositional optimism were less depressed following the death of a partner than those with a less optimistic personal point of view.[49] The optimists were also more likely to find meaning in their spouse's death. If you are thinking now, "All that is well and good, but you can't teach an old dog new tricks," remember that Seligman gives us specific techniques that we can use to become more optimistic. He tells us that we should evaluate each event that occurs in our lives in terms of its positive and negative aspects and then emphasize the positive. Therefore, if you have recently lost your partner after a long illness, try to emphasize the positive aspects of the situation. Consider the fact that she is no longer in pain. If you can, think of her as being in a better place. Consider how fortunate you are to have had her as a life partner, and cherish the memories of her that you will always have. Think about your options for the future with anticipation. Now that you are free from the obligations of caregiving and dealing with doctors and nurses, you can contemplate new directions, new interests, new activities. Don't feel guilty about these thoughts. Your partner loved you, and she certainly would feel better knowing that the remainder of your life here on earth will be rewarding and productive.

Another area related to optimism involves giving your life a continuing source of meaning by undertaking good works. Volunteer. Giving your time and energy to others is a sure way to take your mind off your own difficulties and a sure way to make you feel productive and worthwhile. Volunteering also typically involves developing a new network of social contacts, which further enriches your day to day experience.[50] One recent study showed that providing support for others was a significant factor in reducing the risk of mortality among both widowers and widows.[51]

PATTERNS OF GRIEVING

So far in this chapter we have seen that the death of a spouse is stressful for many reasons other than just the emotional devastation of losing one's longtime partner and confidant. We have also seen that the stresses of bereavement are present regardless of whether our spouse's death occurs suddenly or (more likely these days) at the end of a long period of chronic progressive illness. We have seen why the loss of a spouse can be even more difficult for persons over 60 than for younger individuals; and we have seen why the loss of a spouse is often more difficult for men than for women. And we have considered some of the steps that we can take to mitigate the impact of this most stressful life event and keep us from falling apart. These points made, the question remains, "What can I expect to experience when my partner dies?" No matter how much forewarning we have or how well we attempt to prepare ourselves, we never really know how we will respond when the moment of death occurs.

Grieving has been defined as "a painful yet necessary process that facilitates adjustment to the loss."[52] Grief may involve feelings of depression, anger, guilt, anxiety, and preoccupation with thoughts of the lost partner. Grief reactions may also involve somatic complaints. These may include upset stomach, shortness of breath, feelings of muscular weakness, and insomnia. Related to the emotional distress associated with losing a wife, men often experience confusion, disorganization, and forgetfulness.[53]

Grief reactions are highly variable with respect to both the severity of the symptoms experienced and the duration of the reaction. For a long time, experts presented a picture of the "normal grief reaction," which was typically described as a period of intense distress immediately after the loss of the loved one which gradually subsides over time. According to this model, bereaved individuals are likely to experience some distress and depression for up to 18 months before recovering from the loss and returning to normal functioning.[54] This period was viewed as necessary for the bereaved individual to work through his feelings and review his relationship with the deceased partner.

In contrast to this so-called normal grief reaction, some individuals experience *chronic* or *complicated* grief, which is typically described as a grief reaction that: (1) persists for more than 18 months following the death of the loved one; (2) involves "serious impairments in work or family roles," and (3) is characterized by continuing intensive symptoms of separation distress, such as intrusive thoughts of and yearning for the deceased.[55] Those who experience chronic grief reactions tend to experience difficulty accepting the reality of the loved one's death. They become detached from life and perceive life as without meaning. They tend to describe themselves as lacking purpose and feeling as if a part of the self has died.[56] It has been estimated that between 15 and 20 percent of bereaved individuals manifest a pattern of chronic or complicated grief.[57]

The research regarding the factors that might predict a chronic or complicated grief reaction is limited, but the research that exists suggests that the reaction is most common among those who were heavily dependent upon their spouse prior to her death, and among those who are characterized by insecure adult attachment.[58] Individuals who have a history of experiencing a major loss during childhood, such as the loss of a parent, appear to be more vulnerable to complicated grief following the death of a long-term partner.[59] Regardless of the origins of chronic grief, it is clear that individuals who experience chronic grief are in need of assistance. In some instances bereavement support groups can be helpful in resolving this state. Individual psychotherapy is often indicated, since the chronic or complicated grief reaction is often tied to dysfunctional adult attachment patterns that may have their roots in early childhood experiences. In such cases therapy may be required to identify the pathogenic experiences and remediate the insecure attachment patterns that are exacerbating the normal grief reaction. The bottom line here is that for anyone experiencing such a reaction to the death of a spouse, it is important for that person to seek out professional help. There are many mental health practitioners who specialize in treating this condition. I have worked with many men who have experienced chronic grief following the death of a partner, and the therapeutic experience is typically enormously helpful.

Some men experience relatively little distress or depression following the death of their partner. In the past, experts on bereavement considered this response to be maladaptive, based on the idea that the surviving spouse was denying the reality of the loss and failing to engage in the necessary process of grieving. A response to bereavement involving little or no grieving was viewed as a ticking time bomb that might result in very serious difficulties down the road. However, this view has been questioned recently. In the first place, the proportion of individuals who experience minimal or mild distress following the death of a spouse is far greater than was previously believed.[60] A recent study of bereaved older men and women showed that over 45 percent of these individuals showed little depression immediately prior to the loss of the spouse, and continued to report very few symptoms during the 18 months following the death.[61] Given that up to 20 percent of the bereaved experience chronic or complicated grieving, it is therefore quite likely that there are more bereaved spouses who fall into the group who experience minimal distress than there are who fall into the so-called normal grief reaction group.

Rather than describe these spouses who experience minimal distress as denying reality and failing to engage in grief work, therefore, it has become more fashionable among experts in bereavement to refer to these individuals as "resilient copers."[62] Research supporting this view of bereavement includes evidence that individuals who report little difficulty do not appear to have been maladjusted or disengaged from their spouses prior to the death, and evidence that these individuals do not appear to be avoidant or in denial following the death of the spouse.[63]

Therefore, if you lose your wife or partner and you do not fall apart, do not assume that there is something wrong with you. If you are able to go on with your life, adequately perform the activities of daily living, continue to engage in rewarding social contacts and activities, do not let anyone tell you that you have a problem or that you need help. If you have prepared for the impending death of your spouse, you may simply be exhibiting good coping skills and resilience toward the stresses that confront us as we grow older. You must be the final judge as to how you are doing and whether you need to seek help following bereavement. You should not feel obliged either way. You need to know that there are many sources of help available if needed; and you need to know that you may not need them.

Chapter Eighteen

REPARTNERING FOLLOWING DIVORCE OR BEREAVEMENT

Whether you have divorced or your long time partner has passed away, you will need to decide whether you wish to seek out a new companion. If you do want to establish a new relationship, you will need to be clear about what you are looking for. Do you want just companionship? Do you want a sexual relationship? Are you looking to find someone to live with, or do you value your privacy and prefer to maintain a separate residence? Do you seek to re-marry? Regardless of the answers to the previous questions, you will also need to decide on the timing of your efforts. Will you feel ready to date quite soon after your divorce? What about after the death of your spouse or partner?

MEN ARE MORE LIKELY THAN WOMEN TO SEEK A NEW RELATIONSHIP

Older guys seem to need a partner more than older women. Among both divorced and widowed individuals over the age of 60, a substantial body of research suggests that men are more likely to become involved in a new romantic/sexual relationship than women, and that men are also more likely to remarry. The gender discrepancy is somewhat less dramatic among individuals who are divorced than among those who are widowed. In addition, among both men and women over 60, those who are single due to a divorce are more likely to initiate a new relationship than those who have been widowed.[1]

Among a large sample of divorced individuals that included both baby boomers in their 50s and individuals over 60, Bair found that the great majority of respondents of both sexes reported that they were either involved in a sexual relationship or that they could have one if they wanted to.[2] However, the majority of the women in this group reported that it was easier not to get involved in such a relationship than it was to get involved. The women suggested that it was simply too much work to establish and maintain intimate relationships. This was not true of the men. Most of the divorced men over 60 either had or were seeking to develop new romantic and/or sexual relationships.

There are several possible reasons why men and women over 60 who are widowed are less likely to seek out a new romantic partner than men and women in the same age group who are divorced. First, widowed individuals may experience substantial conflict regarding a possible new relationship. Some bereaved individuals express the view that entering into a new relationship would somehow be disloyal to the memory of the departed spouse. My experience has shown that those men and women who experienced happy and fulfilling relationships and have had that taken from them through death will look to repeat their success, and that more often than not they do so.

It is also certainly the case that some individuals who divorce even after the age of 60 do so primarily because they are dissatisfied with their sex life with their spouse. Some even get divorced because they are already involved with or at least interested in another sexual partner. Even among the widowed, however, a substantial number of individuals will seek out a new relationship, and the research indicates that this proportion is greater among men than among women.

A recent study indicated that among men over 65 who are widowed, 31 percent become involved in a new sexual relationship within two years of the death of their spouse, and 25 percent remarry. In contrast, among women over 65 who are widowed, only 7 percent become involved in a new romantic relationship, and only 5 percent remarry within the same two-year period.[3] Another study showed that widowed women who do remarry take twice as long to do so as widowed men who remarry.[4]

Another factor that impacts the likelihood of a divorced or widowed person seeking out a new romantic relationship is the age of the individual at the time of the divorce or the death of the spouse. The older one is, the less likely a widowed person is to seek out a new partner.[5] This appears to be true of both men and women.

WHY MEN ARE MORE LIKELY THAN WOMEN TO SEEK A NEW PARTNER

There are both practical and emotional reasons why men are more likely than women to seek a new partner following divorce or bereavement. Among the practical reasons are the demographic realities and gender and aging.

Women live longer than men, and even among people over 60, there is still a tendency for the male member of a couple to be older than the female. For this reason, there are great many more women available to each man than there are men available to each woman. It has been estimated that among those over 60 there are at least five available women for every available man.[6] Moreover, this ratio increases with age, rising to 15 to 1 among individuals over 85. The relative scarcity of available men may make some women reluctant to seek out a new partner. In contrast, men over 60 who are divorced or widowed may find themselves to be the object of the attention of several women, making it relatively easier for men to pursue relationships and find an appropriate new partner.

On the other hand, it has also been argued that men need a partner more than women do. In the last chapter I discussed the practical and emotional reasons why bereavement is typically more difficult for men than for women. Practically, men tend to depend on their wives to run the household. Emotionally, men tend to have few close relationships other than the relationship with their wife, and they therefore tend to be more reliant on their spouse for emotional support than women are. Davidson has argued that men may seek to remarry for either or both of these reasons.[7] Recent evidence suggests that the need for emotional closeness may be the most important factor that motivates men over 60 to seek out a new partner. Based on a study of bereaved men, Carr reported that men who had been emotionally reliant on their departed spouse were most likely to seek out a new partner and eventually to remarry.[8] In contrast, among widows, women who had been most emotionally reliant on their husbands were less interested in developing and pursuing new relationships. Carr also found that bereaved men who reported receiving social support from friends and family were much less anxious to find another woman than men who reported receiving less support.[9] The latter finding suggests that it is the emotional support of a partner that men cannot do without, and if this need can be filled through friends and family, the felt pressure to find a new romantic partner is considerably lessened.

Thus we have seen that men are more likely than women to seek out and develop new relationships following a divorce or bereavement, and we have concluded that the most powerful reason for the male need to find a new partner is probably the need to have someone with whom we can have a close emotional relationship. Sex may or may not be an important element in this relationship. Similarly, the need to find someone to help keep the household running smoothly may or may not be a major motivating factor. All this is important because it should give you, the reader, a sense that it is all right to want to find another partner. A good number of men your age who have divorced or who have lost a spouse do develop a new relationship, and many of them remarry. You may or may not feel this need, but if you do, there is nothing wrong with you. Nevertheless, if you are thinking that a new relationship would be nice, there are some things that you should take into consideration. I would like to consider these issues now, beginning with the question, "Are you ready?"

ARE YOU READY TO SEEK A NEW PARTNER?

Both divorce and bereavement can be traumatic, and time is often necessary to recover sufficiently to even contemplate the possibility of a new relationship. Of course, in either divorce or bereavement, there is a wide range of issues and circumstances that impact when one might be ready for a new partner, and there is a broad range of possibilities regarding reasonable time periods. Under some circumstances, the issue of recovery is completely irrelevant. Under other circumstances, it may be paramount.

If you are a man who was in a bad marriage for some time, fell into an affair, and initiated a divorce to be with your new love, then the chances are good that you will not be needing to recover and you will be anxious to begin a new life with your new love as soon as possible. It is often said that unhappy spouses tend to pick out and reserve their next mate before divorcing, so as not to be alone. If you were in a marriage that satisfied neither you nor your spouse and the two of you agreed mutually to end it and move on, but there was no extramarital affair involved, then you may well be anxious to find a new partner, but you may need some time to build up your courage and your social skills repertoire before you can actually enter into the dating scene. If this is the case you might well benefit from the support of friends who can encourage you and perhaps include you in social events where you might begin to meet new women. On the other hand, if you were left by a spouse because she found someone else, you will likely be hurt, and you may well be bitter and resentful. These bitter feelings against your ex may generalize, and you may feel that you will never be able to trust another woman. In this case, you may need a good deal of time and the support of friends and family. Professional help may also be required to resolve these feelings and reinforce your efforts at socializing.

The same kind of continuum applies to the situation of bereavement. I once had a patient who met someone new and developed an intimate relationship before his terminally ill wife died. At first glance this probably seems to you to be unseemly at best, heartless at worst. Yet the circumstances were such that this behavior was in fact not at all unreasonable. Here is the story:

Ed's Story

Ed is a 72-year-old retired banker. His wife Amanda, began to manifest the symptoms of Alzheimer's disease when Ed was 59 and she was 57. At the time she was diagnosed, they had been happily married for 34 years. They had three adult children, all of whom were married and had children. Amanda's illness followed a rapid down-hill progression over a period of 12 years before she died at the age of 69.

For the first 6 years of her illness, during which she retained some awareness of who she was and who he was, Ed cared for her diligently in their home. In order to do this he retired early from his banking career. He was a full-time caretaker. At first Ed was content with this role. He loved his wife, and he felt that taking care of her gave his own life a purpose. Over this six-year period Amanda lost more and more of her memory and her cognitive awareness. Eventually she was unable to recognize Ed or any of her children. She required constant supervision, and she needed to be fed and toileted. Ed was overloaded with the caregiving responsibility. He could not participate in any of the activities that he had enjoyed over the course of his lifetime, and he had virtually no social contact. He was lonely and depressed.

Finally, when Amanda had lost all sense of who Ed was and where she was, Ed felt that he had no choice except to place her in a nursing home. He continued to visit her there, although she did not recognize him and seemed to have no interest in his visitation.

Following his decision to place Amanda in the nursing home, Ed began to emerge from his depression and reclaim a life of his own. He returned to the golf club where he had not played for years. He resumed old friendships. Then Ed met a woman who enjoyed playing golf. Meeting Elaine was a godsend. She was an attractive 60-year-old who had been widowed three years previously. They had both been lonely too long, and they became sexually involved almost immediately. This caused Ed some feelings of guilt, since Amanda was still alive in the nursing home. But every time he was together with Elaine he felt like he had been given a new life. Elaine liked everything that Ed liked—not only sports but also traveling and dining. At the age of 66 Ed's life turned around.

At the time the Ed met Elaine, Amanda had been in the nursing home for al-most a year. He knew that her condition was irreversible and terminal, but he also knew that she could linger for years, which in fact was the case. He was spending more and more time with Elaine, more and more nights together. They wanted to live together, but they were "old fashioned." They wanted to get married. They did some research and found that under these circumstances it was not unusual for the spouses of advanced Alzheimer's patients to obtain a divorce for the purpose of remarrying. They discussed this possibility, but they were apprehensive about the reactions their respective children might have.

After a good deal of soul searching and some helpful pastoral counseling sessions with the minister at Ed's church, they were able to make a very difficult decision. They consulted with their children and obtained approval for Ed to obtain a divorce. Ed and Elaine were pleasantly surprised that all of their children understood the situation and supported their decision. Ed made appropriate financial arrangements to guarantee Amanda's continued nursing home care, and he got his divorce. Ed and Elaine were married almost immediately. It was nearly four years before Amanda succumbed to her illness.

Ed still has fond memories of Amanda and their life together. He also has a very happy and rewarding life with Elaine. Ed describes the decisions that he made with respect to Amanda as requiring introspection, prayer, and the support of Elaine, his children, and his pastor. Today, Ed and Elaine are happy with each other and at peace with themselves.

The point here is that Ed was clearly ready for a new relationship. He had more than adequate time to process his loss of Amanda during the extended period of caregiving. He recognized that the relationship with his wife was over. Although she had not yet died, she was effectively dead to Ed. First he made the difficult decision to place her in a nursing home, which gave him back his life and precluded the very real possibility that he would become resentful of his caregiving role and bitter toward Amanda. Then he made the difficult decision to obtain a divorce and remarry. He did not make this decision quickly or rashly. He sought the counsel of his pastor, thought long and hard about his needs and responsibilities, and discussed the issue thoroughly with Elaine and with their respective children. He made a good decision.

Some bereaved men rush into a new relationship too quickly. Consider the story of another patient of mine, Jack, who came to me for counseling following his divorce at 67 following a second marriage that lasted less than a year.

Jack's Story

Jack was 66 when his wife Jackie was killed in a motor vehicle accident. He and Jackie had a very traditional marriage. Jack was the executive in charge of quality control officer at a large pharmaceutical company until his retirement at the age of 65. Jack had met Jackie in college, and they were married a week after his graduation. Jack took a position in the pharmaceutical firm immediately after college, and he earned an MBA through a company-sponsored program during the first few years of his service to the company. He was a loyal and hard working company man for 43 years. Jackie was graduated from college on the same day as Jack, but she never sought employment outside the home. Their first child was born less than a year after their marriage, and they raised five children together. Actually, a more accurate description would be that Jackie raised five children with Jack's financial support. It wasn't that Jack didn't love the children. He did. But his idea of his role in the family was to be the breadwinner. He never attended a parent-teacher conference or a high school sporting event. He came home late most nights, and he interacted with his children primarily on holidays and vacations.

Jackie was contented with their life together. She had complete discretion with regard to managing the household. She had more than enough money to work with, and she enjoyed taking care of everyone. She picked out the suburban home in which they raised their kids. She did the decorating, paid the bills, made sure that Jack and the kids were appropriately dressed, arranged for the kids to get to their various activities, and planned the family vacations. She did it all, and she enjoyed it. She socialized with female friends at the country club, and she became a member of the school board. And Jack loved her for it. Although he worked long hours, he was always happy to come home to her. Each night she would bring him up to date on the kids, and he would share his experiences at work with her. She often provided helpful advice on how to handle certain situations at work, and she was a great corporate wife. All of Jack's associates at work enjoyed coming to parties at their home. Although their respective roles were highly compartmentalized, the time they had together was very good indeed. They had a good sex life, and they were completely faithful to each other over the entire course of their long marriage.

Their children all went to college and launched successfully. They were scattered about the country and engaged in various occupations ranging from teacher to physician. All five were married, and all had children. Jack and Jackie visited them occasionally, but as long as Jack worked there was not really enough time for them to visit extensively. Jackie could have visited for longer periods on her own, but she really didn't like to travel without Jack, and he really didn't like it the few times that she was away. When Jack retired, he and Jackie moved from their large home to a retirement community in the same geographic area. They were just beginning to settle in there and become acquainted with their neighbors when Jackie was killed.

Jack was devastated when Jackie was killed. He was lost, almost catatonic. He didn't have a clue about what to do or how to behave. He didn't even think to call the children to tell them what had happened. They found out from the police, who recognized that he would need some help dealing with the situation. One of Jack's daughters flew in from the West Coast to arrange for the funeral. She stayed on for a few weeks to see if she could get Jack back to a condition in which he would be able to take care of himself. Finally she concluded that she would not be able to do this, and she arranged for a housekeeper to come in to take care of the house and make sure that Jack was fed. She also contacted as many of her mother's friends as she could to let them know how difficult a time Jack was having and to request that they keep in contact with him and invite him over for dinners and parties. Then she had to go home.

To their credit, Jack's family friends stepped up to the plate. They visited. They had him over to dinner a lot. They got him to go out to shows and sporting events. He moved in a daze, but he did move. Jack recognized that these friends were looking out for him, and he was more than willing to go along with their suggestions. He had always allowed Jackie to take care of the details of his social life, and in her absence he allowed their friends to do the same thing.

So Jack had a housekeeper to feed him, clean the house, and make sure that he had clean clothes. And Jack had friends to keep his social calendar in order and make sure that he wasn't spending his entire life squirreled up in his house.

The problem came when Jack was alone. When he got back from dinner at the home of a friend, he was lonely. He had always been able to share with Jackie—to share his problems at work, to share his frustrations and his victories, to share the important events of her life. They were confidants. They were also lovers. He missed her physical presence in the house and in his bed. He missed the way she smelled. He missed sex, and he missed snuggling. He missed having coffee with her each morning. Jack's life was not empty, and he took advantage of what was there. But there was a huge hole.

Then one night about two months after Jackie's death, a couple of well-meaning friends invited Jack to dinner to "meet someone." They had decided that Jack needed a new wife. They felt that he had been a lot more fun when Jackie was still alive, and they even felt a bit uncomfortable having him come over without a mate. (Couples are used to relating to each other as couples, and they will often go to great measures to restore the status quo before a bereavement.) So here was this woman. Her name was Anita. She was a widow. She was quite attractive. She was extremely sympathetic with regard to Jack's recent loss. She was soft. She smelled good. They had some wine with dinner. Jack remembered sex. Jack offered to drive her home. He spent the night.

The experience for Jack was magical. The sex was great. They had both gone too long without it. Maybe even more important, at least for Jack, was spending the night together. There was someone there, someone to touch, someone to ease his pain and loneliness, and someone to wake up with. It seemed to Jack that the long nightmare of loneliness was over. They married within the month.

They divorced in less than a year. As it turned out, they had nothing in common except their mutual loneliness and their need for a sexual partner and a confidant. They disagreed about where to live. Anita wanted them to live in her apartment in the city, and Jack wanted them to live in his home in the retirement community. They disagreed about what to do for fun. Anita liked parties, dancing, television, and cruises. Jack liked reading and long walks in the country. They disagreed about pets. Anita had two little lap dogs that she adored, and Jack had no interest in animals. They disagreed about politics and about religion. They disagreed about money. Anita liked to spend money, and Jack did not. They disagreed about how much time to spend with Anita's children and grandchildren, who lived close by. Anita wanted to spend a great deal of time her family, and Jack just wanted to spend time with her.

Fortunately, Jack and Anita were both smart enough to see that they had made a mistake, and when they found themselves bickering they were mature enough to discuss it and decide to divorce amicably. They still bump into each other occasionally and they can laugh about their mistake.

But Jack and Anita were very lucky in regard to correcting their mistake. Bereaved men who run precipitously into new relationships are often not this lucky. They may find that they are unhappy yet remain in the new marriage, leading to a life of unfortunate comparisons of their current dissatisfaction to the previous happy marriage. They may end up divorcing, but the divorce may be a difficult one with great emotional and financial costs.

Therefore, if you are a bereaved spouse and you are feeling lonely, you need to be very careful about seeking out a new relationship. You must make sure that you do not rush headlong into a relationship based on an urgent need to "have someone there." In this regard, I would advise bereaved men not to consider marriage before they have achieved a degree of social and emotional support from sources other than a new love. We can get a great deal of support from contact with male friends. Often during our marriages we come to rely on our wife as our only real confidant. We may have some male friends that with whom we play golf or go fishing, but we don't talk to them about our feelings, our loneliness, and our pain. Men are often uncomfortable hearing about a friend's pain and sadness. This is where a therapist can help. We can also get support from our children or from other family members. Even if they are far away, we can communicate by telephone and e-mail. You might be surprised at how helpful a grown child can be, and at how willing they are to be helpful. In addition, bereaved men can get support from self-help and professionally run support groups for those who have lost spouses. These groups can be particularly helpful because you know that the members share the experience of bereavement and the struggle to regain emotional equilibrium. If you tell the members of such a group that you have found someone to fill up the empty spaces in your sex life and your need for emotional closeness, someone in the group will certainly tell you to be careful.

The point is that when we are seeking a long-term relationship, we must have sufficient control over our needs that we are able to look beyond a woman's sexual attractiveness and sympathetic ear to consider the entire package. Contemplating marriage at 60 involves pretty much the same set of criteria that it involves when we are 20 or 30. After all, if you are only 60 and you get married now, you may be with this woman for another 30 or 40 years. So make sure you get it right. You need to consider your respective values, interests, and goals for the future. You need to make sure that you are compatible not just sexually but also intellectually and psychologically. Do you share interests? Can you and your prospective mate give each other the space that you might need to pursue independent interests? Are you compatible with respect to how neat you need the house to be? Are you a slob while she is a neat freak? Can you live with her china figurines? Can she live with your stuffed bass and trout? All these things should enter into the decision to remarry. And you can't consider these issues adequately if you are still hurting so bad from loneliness that all you can think of is having someone to wake up with.

So take as much time as you need to get back on an even keel and to develop a social and emotional support network of your own *before* you seriously contemplate getting remarried. You can date, but if you're not able to evaluate a relationship in a comprehensive and somewhat objective manner, just back off. If you are dating someone and having sex with her she may pressure you to get married. Don't be afraid to put on the brakes. Show her this chapter. If she cannot understand why you need to take some time to get your feet under you and get to know her better, then she is probably not the right one anyway.

Having said this, I would now like to consider some of the issues that divorced and bereaved men over 60 should be sure to consider when contemplating a new long-term relationship. These include your basic values, the need to balance independence and togetherness, maintaining your other friendships and involvements, lifestyle compatibility, views on finances and spending, the amount and nature of contact you each desire to have with your respective children and grandchildren, religious differences, and sexual compatibility.

BASIC VALUES

It is important that you and a potential long-term partner are compatible with respect to basic values. This does not mean that you have to agree upon everything. It does mean that you must not find a potential partner's values repugnant and that you must be able to respect and tolerate her values in areas where you disagree. How much disagreement a couple can reasonably tolerate will vary from couple to couple. But here are some disagreements that present problems:

If you are an entrepreneur and your prospective partner is a genuine socialist, you had better look elsewhere. You really might have a hard time discussing with your spouse the latest round of labor negotiations down at the plant. If you believe firmly in the right to self defense and you keep a loaded firearm in your house, you might not want to marry an individual who is firmly committed to complying with the demands of a robber and would never commit an act of violence, even in self defense. You wouldn't want to save the family from an intruder and be condemned for your action. If you believe that "charity begins at home" and have never made a contribution to any cause, you might reconsider marrying someone who insists on giving large contributions to charities with questionably high overhead percentages (unless she is independently wealthy).

Of course, I have painted these disagreements in rather stark terms. This is because differences of this magnitude are truly relationship threatening. The same areas of disagreement might be acceptable if the level of intensity of your respective beliefs were lower. For example, you could be an entrepreneur and your prospective partner might be sympathetic to labor, as long as she understands that your job in management is to keep labor costs down, and you acknowledge the right of the workers to bargain in their best interests. Then you may be able to "agree to disagree" and perhaps not discuss the issue extensively. Similarly, you and a prospective spouse might disagree on the advisability of using force in self defense, as long as mutual respect exists.

The point is that these questions need to be discussed. You need to get to know someone really well before you get married. It takes time to get to know someone's values, and it takes time to determine whether the differences in basic values that we discover fall into the level of acceptable differences that we can live with, or whether they are deal breakers. Remember, when we marry in our 20s we are still growing and changing. When we are in our 60s our personalities and habits tend to be much more deeply entrenched.

BALANCING INDEPENDENCE AND TOGETHERNESS

Over the course of our long lives we have grown accustomed to a certain level of independence. Men who were married for a long time before a late life divorce or bereavement have most likely reached an accommodation with their former spouse with respect to the balance between independence and togetherness. The primary exception to this principle consists of men who divorced because they were unable to reach such an accommodation. Men who have had long and good marriages have certainly worked out this balance with their spouse, and they have come to take for granted the freedom they have assumed with respect to that portion of their life that is independent of their spouse. They have also developed expectations regarding the amount of time and the nature of the activities in which they will engage together with their spouse. Because these assumptions and expectations are so well established during a long marriage, men who are bereaved often fail to consider this issue when they seek out a new partner. In fact marriages vary substantially with respect to the level of independence with which the spouses are comfortable, and with respect to the extent to which the spouses do things together. Therefore, when you meet someone new and begin to think she might be someone with whom you would like to develop an intimate relationship and perhaps even marry, you need to discuss your mutual expectations regarding independence and togetherness.

I have a good friend whose marriage involves a very substantial degree of independence. Both he and his wife have interests that they share as well as interests that they do not share. He is away from home for up to two months each years engaging in his favorite passions of backpacking, hunting, and fishing. His wife has zero interest in these activities. When he participates in these activities, he does so either alone or with friends who share the interests. His wife has a similar level of interest in antiques, which he does not share. So she does her antiquing with friends of her own. They have learned to coordinate their schedules so that they can have their fill of their respective avocations and still be together for family holidays and for activities that they both enjoy, like the philharmonic and the theater. Both spouses have both male and female friends, and they often find themselves pursuing their independent interests in mixed gender groups. Neither of them has an issue with this. They are both completely faithful to their spouse, and they each expect fidelity in return. They respect each other's need for independence without feeling personally threatened.

On the other hand, I know other folks who would never consider going away from their spouse to engage in independent recreational activities, even for a day, let alone for weeks at a time. These couples would feel uncomfortable either leaving or being left, and they could not tolerate the thought that their spouse might be happily participating in enjoyable activities along with members of the opposite sex.

There is no right or wrong answer to the question of balancing independence and togetherness. What works for some folks is wrong for others. The point is that when you contemplate a new relationship, you cannot assume that the balance you and your former partner found comfortable will automatically work with a different individual. This is something that needs to be discussed in detail. You need to be specific in these discussions, and you need to find out the motivations behind the position your prospective mate takes.

If you have made it a habit to spend two months each year away from home in the woods, you need to tell you prospective new partner and ask if she can deal with it. And you need to state your intention not in an abstract, general manner, but by giving her specific time frames. For example, you need to say that each July you spend a week in the Northwest Territories fishing for arctic char, during September you go elk hunting in New Mexico, in January you spend a week bonefishing in the Bahamas, and each year there will be a few trips that change from year to year.

You need to find out whether she might be interested in sharing any of these activities with you. Just because your former spouse wasn't interested in them, it doesn't necessarily mean that you new partner is disinterested. Perhaps you can share some of the trips. For those trips that you need to do on your own, you must find out how your prospective new partner feels about your being gone *at the particular times* you will be away. You need to ask whether she will be able to occupy herself and be contented while you are gone. You need to determine whether she is telling you that the trips are OK because she really is OK with this level of independence in the relationship, or whether she is just making a concession because she feels that she must in order to keep you. If you suspect that the latter may be the case, you need to discuss the matter further because over time she may become less accommodating. She may discover that she thought it would be OK, but in fact she is miserable when you are gone. She may ask for a renegotiation. You want to try to avoid or minimize this possibility. So talk it through now. You should also be candid with her if there is possibility that there may be mixed gender groups involved in some of your activities. You need to discuss expectations regarding fidelity explicitly.

MAINTAINING INDIVIDUAL FRIENDSHIPS
AND INVOLVEMENTS

Closely related to the balance between independence and togetherness is the question of maintaining the friendships and involvements that you have had prior to re-partnering. Many new partners assume that you will be spending all your time with them and that your old friends will become relatively inconsequential in your life. This assumption really mirrors the prevailing social pattern among married couples in our society, where the husband has only his wife as a true confidant, and the wife takes responsibility for arranging the couple's social schedule. However, you may not have fit into this pattern in your previous marriage, and if you have recently gone through a divorce or a period of bereavement, you may well have developed a network of social and emotional support consisting of various same and opposite sex friends and family. The chances are that the members of this network are important to you. Therefore, men considering repartnering are likely to place greater value on outside friendships and involvements than men who have not had the experience of losing a spouse through divorce or death.

If you have dear friends who are important to you, you had better be clear with your prospective new partner that they are part of the package. You had better make certain that you new partner likes your other friends or at least that she can tolerate your relationship with them. The same goes for organizations to which you belong and community activities in which you participate. Here again, the best situation would be the one where she genuinely likes your friends and wants to join you in your organizational affiliations and activities. If this is not the case, then you need to discuss in some detail how your independent friends and involvements can be accommodated within your new partnership.

LIFESTYLE COMPATIBILITY

In the same way that individuals differ with respect to how much independence they require, individuals differ across a broad range of aspects of the lifestyle. Some of us are neat, and some of us are sloppy. Some of us are always on time, and some of us are never on time. Some of us read *GQ* and buy our clothes at Barney's, and some of us read *Popular Mechanics* and shop at Wal-Mart. Some of us like the city, and some of us like the country. Some of us drive a hybrid, and some of us drive an SUV. You get the picture.

These are things that everyone needs to consider when they are developing a new relationship This is as true of 30-year-olds as it is of 60-year-olds. However, a 60-year-old man who has lost a spouse and is desperately lonely may tend to overlook these obvious important issues. Even if you feel that you have gotten back on your feet, you should make a special effort to take the time to discuss these lifestyle choice with a prospective new partner. Go slowly, spend some time together to see if you are compatible in these lifestyle habits. You might want to live together for a time before committing to remarriage, just to be on the safe side.

FINANCES AND SPENDING

Finances are a big issue. This is true regardless of whether you are rich or poor. It is true regardless of whether your prospective new partner is rich or poor. I'm not saying that money doesn't help. It does. If you are rich certain aspects of your life will be easier. Having the money to hire people to take care of a range of chores can be very helpful in coping with some of the lifestyle differences between you and your prospective new partner that I discussed above. For example, having a housekeeper can go a long way toward taking the edge off the problem of having a new spouse who is a slob. Having money can make it easier if you find that your new partner has rather more expensive tastes in clothing and household furnishings than you do.

If *both* you and your prospective partner are comfortable financially, so much the better. This happy circumstance may lessen any concern that you might have that she wants you "for your money." It might also alleviate similar concerns on the part of your children, who are looking forward to inheriting your estate. On the other hand, having a lot of money also means that there is more to worry about, raising the possibility that you and you new partner will have to consider prenuptial agreements and provisions to make sure that your children are properly taken care of.

The bottom line here is that whether you have a lot of money or only a little money, finances need to be discussed with your prospective new partner. And this is true even if you are only planning to live together. You will need to consider each of the following questions:

1. Will your finances be completely pooled, kept completely separate, or will you make some specific arrangement somewhere in between? Many couples place a portion of their income into a joint account for joint expenses and keep the rest of their income separate. This has some advantages because the individual spouses can spend their own money on whatever they want or not spend it at all. It eliminates the husband going nuts if the wife buys a $1,000 handbag or the wife going nuts if the husband buys "another" new set of golf clubs. It also means that if you give your wife a Christmas or birthday present, it really is a present since the money has come from your individual funds. Of course, you still need to decide which expenses are joint and which are individual. Vacations taken together are typically paid for from joint funds, unless the trip is a gift from one spouse to the other. Just keep in mind that when the expense becomes joint and joint money is used to pay for it, then you and your partner must agree on the expenditure. In some ways, the more things that are kept separate, the less negotiation is required.

2. Who will actually manage the money? Who will pay the bills, get the estimates for repairs, and make decisions regarding whom to hire? Someone must have the ultimate responsibility for making sure that bills get paid on time. It is most common in our society for the woman to assume this task, but this is by no means universal. You simple need to come to an agreement and then stick to it. Of course, if one of you is much more conscientious than the other, it may be best for that person to take charge. That way the phone won't be getting turned off because someone lost the bill. However, managing the family finances is a job that involves substantial time and effort, and if you are the more conscientious member of the dyad, you will need to avoid getting saddled with doing all the chores of this nature.

3. How will you resolve disagreements regarding joint expenditures on which you cannot agree? What if you are happy with a $30,000 car, but your spouse wants an $80,000 car? Joint expenditures require joint decisions, and you and your prospective spouse will need to agree upon a method of working out differences of opinion. Here again, you need to keep in mind that the patterns you developed

and followed with your former spouse will most likely not simply translate over into the new relationship. Every relationship is different, and you need to discuss these matters.

RELATIONSHIPS WITH CHILDREN AND GRANDCHILDREN

This is also a common source of discord among couples who have formed later in life following divorce or bereavement. You may recall that in chapter 14 on grandparenting I pointed out that grandparents differed greatly in terms of the level of involvement they wanted with their grandchildren. I also discussed different grandparenting styles, including the formal grandparent, the fun seeking grandparent, the surrogate parent grandparent, the reservoir of family wisdom grandparent, and the distant grandparent. You and the woman you are considering for a partner may have very different views on grandparenting. You may differ greatly with respect to how often you wish to baby-sit, whether and how often you want to participate in activities with the grandchildren, whether you want to go on vacation with the grandchildren, and how much you want to spend on the grandchildren's birthday presents.

If you do differ substantially on these questions, then you have an issue, because each of you has already formed a relationship with your respective grandchildren, and the grandchildren (and their parents) are going to expect you to be consistent with the way you treated them before. Thus, when Jack married Anita and discovered that she wanted to spend a great deal more time with her grandchildren than he did, this was not simply something that she could easily change. She and her grandchildren were both used to spending a good deal of time together, and it would not have been fair to the grandchildren to simply cut back on Anita's involvement.

The reality of your existing relationships with your respective grandchildren makes the issue of grandparenting involvement a particularly important one to discuss with your prospective new partner. In addition, assuming that you do have a reasonably substantial relationship with your grandchildren, it is very important that your prospective new partner meet your grandchildren and spend some time with them before you remarry.

RELIGIOUS DIFFERENCES

Even today, religious differences between you and your prospective partner can be a problem or even a deal breaker. In the extreme case, either you or your partner may be so religious that marrying a person of another faith is not a possibility. This is rare, but it does happen. In a way such a dramatic problem is a blessing, because it will break the deal early on, before anyone gets hurt.

However, many of us do not feel that a union between two people of different faiths is impossible or even unusual.

First of all, many people today have drifted away from active participation in our religion of birth. If you haven't been in a church or a synagogue in years and are not planning to get started now, religious differences may be a non-issue. On the other hand, if you are still participating in religious observances but you do not feel that your religion requires you to partner with someone of the same faith, then there are certain issues that you will need to consider.

For example, who goes to which house of worship when? If you are Presbyterian and your prospective partner is Jewish, and if both of you are serious about attending weekly and holiday services, then you are either going to be spending a lot of time together in your respective places of worship, or you are going to be attending separately. The former possibility may be problematic for two reasons. First of all, you may find that you are just spending more time at worship than you need to or want to. Secondly, you may find yourself having too little free time to engage in nonreligious activities. If the two of you wish to continue in the observance of your faith, you will likely need to compromise. Your church one week and her temple the next, or some similar arrangement. You will also need to compromise when it comes to holidays. Many homes today have both a Christmas tree and a Menorah. Most folks can respect differing beliefs and even enjoy the customs and traditions of other religions. But you should discuss with any prospective partner your religious views and practices and hers. Of course conversation is the obvious resolution.

SEXUAL COMPATIBILITY

Earlier in this chapter I pointed out that the latest research suggests that men over 60 who are divorced or widowed are more likely to seek out a new partner because they need emotional closeness than because they wish to have a sexual partner. The same is probably true of older women. This doesn't mean that older men and women are not interested in sex. We saw in chapter 7 that some older men and women are very interested in sex. We also saw that good sex is still possible later in life, if we take things slowly, allow nature to take its course, and if necessary, employ such aids as medications and lubricants to compensate for some of the natural effects of aging on our sexual responses.

However, the particular woman that you are considering as a new life partner may be either more or less interested in sex than you are. Therefore, you both need to be very clear about what you want and need from your partner. At 60 plus I would hope that you would be able to discuss sex with a prospective new partner, and hopefully before you remarry you will have been intimate and figured out the forms of sexual expression with which you are comfortable and whether you are both satisfied with the sexual relationship that you have. I would urge you to be open and honest about your feelings and to communicate openly with your partner about your needs and hers. I would also urge you to experiment with new techniques, and with sex aids as necessary. If you need Viagra, get some. If she needs a ton of lubricants or an assortment of vibrators, get them and use them. At this point in your life, you have nothing to prove except your dedication to pleasing her.

HOW TO FIND A NEW PARTNER

Finding a new partner is easier for men over 60 than for women over 60, because we have a favorable sex ratio. However, that doesn't necessarily mean that it will be an easy task to find someone whom you will find interesting and someone with whom you will be compatible. In addition, we have seen that men who have been in long-term marriages prior to a divorce or to bereavement frequently find that whatever social skills they may have possessed have gotten rusty. Therefore, it is probably a good idea to accept all the help you can in meeting women who are appropriate candidates for a new long-term relationship.

There are a great number of resources available to assist you. Friends are generally only too willing to introduce you to someone they know, and often this is a good way to meet new people. The fact that you're meeting someone who is a friend of a friend increases the likelihood that you will be compatible in terms of background and interests. Also, your friends probably know both of you well enough that they would screen out someone who would be clearly inappropriate for you. On the other hand, when friends fix you up, they tend to have an interest in the success of the match. Therefore you will need to be on your guard against the possibility of forcing yourself to like this new person in order to please the friends that fixed you up. For this reason, it is best if these meetings take place at parties where multiple guests are present, so that you are not really fixed up with a date but rather you simply have the opportunity to meet and talk. In that way, you will not feel obligated, and if there is no chemistry the woman in question will not feel rejected.

Along the same lines, you can meet women at senior centers and during activities for seniors, at social groups run at the church or temple, at various organizations for people who share recreational interests, and at community and local political events. Each of these venues has the advantage that you will be there to engage in an activity, and you will meet women in the course of pursuing the activity. This will take the pressure off the meeting, and it will give you something to talk about naturally. In addition, meeting women at any of these natural venues will increase the probability that you will be compatible in one or more areas. If you meet at a church social you will probably have the same religion. If you meet on a cycling trip, you will have that interest in common. And if you meet at a political fund raiser, then you will most likely share a common political orientation.

Of course, there are singles groups, dating services, personal ads, and the internet. These sources can be useful. These resources are very popular worldwide. At least you know that someone you meet in this manner is also looking for a partner. In addition, there are services that enable you to narrow the choices to individuals with whom you share certain characteristics. There are Jewish dating services and Christian dating services. If you place a personal in *New York Magazine,* your ad will be read by a particular group of readers who tend to be well-educated, literate, and intellectual. You can even use a computer-based service that will find individuals who match you on background, interests, and aspects of you personality. I have a very dear friend who has been widowed for six years. She lived in Israel. She is glamorous, outgoing, funny, and smart. And she is 76. She went onto J-date, an international Internet dating service, and there she met a 75-year-old gentleman from England. They met several times, and today they are living together in South Florida, happy as can be.

So these resources can be useful. The only caveat is that when you place an ad or go online, you do open yourself up to a large world of strangers, not all of who are well-meaning. Therefore, if you do use such sources, be careful, move slowly, and get to know the people you meet before you get too heavily involved.

ANOTHER OPTION

I would be remiss at this point if I did not also point out to you that some older men choose not to re-partner following divorce or the death of a long-time partner. If this is how you feel, that is OK. Some men feel that they have had the love of their life, and they choose not to embark on another long-term relationship. Some men enjoy their own company and the independence associated with living alone. This choice allows one the freedom to decide on his own where he will live, when he will go out and come home, where he wants to go on vacation, and whether and with whom he wishes to socialize. You might decide to live abroad for a while, or you might choose to take up some new activity with an entirely new set of acquaintances. You may meet someone along the way with whom you want to spend time, but in the meantime you are free. Be happy. Expand your horizons. Now is the time.

Chapter Nineteen

CHANGES IN LIVING ARRANGEMENTS

Russ and Margie

For 40 years Russ ran a garage and auto repair business in Pelham, New York. Over the years he brought his two sons into the business and expanded so that together they had three locations and they employed eight additional full-time mechanics. Russ was very successful, and he was a well-known and popular figure in the community. Russ and his wife lived for 36 years in a house a block away from his first place of business. Their home was pretty small when they bought it, but over the years they bought the lot next door and they put several additions on the home to make it larger and nicer. They had a gourmet kitchen, a workout room, and a home theater. They also added a pool and planted some beautiful landscaping. Looking back later, Russ and Margie had very fond memories of this home, where they had Sunday dinners with their sons' families, and where they celebrated Christmas each year with their family and their extensive network of friends.

Russ worked long hours. He enjoyed work, especially the contact with the customers and suppliers. But it was hard work, and over the years he developed arthritis and bad knees. He and Margie talked a lot about retiring to Florida. They thought a change in climate would help his arthritis. Russ thought that he might learn to play golf, and they both dreamed about being able to just kick back and relax in the warm sunshine. When Russ hit 60, he was ready to hand the business over to his sons. He and Margie bought a retirement home in an upscale retirement community designed for "active adults" who were 55 and over. Their oldest son bought their home in Pelham, and he in turn sold his home to his younger brother. There was enough room in the big house that Russ and Margie could comfortably stay there when they came back to visit the children and grandchildren, which they thought they would do each year in the summer.

So off to Florida they went. They stayed just under one full year before they moved back to Pelham. It turned out that they didn't like Florida or their new community.

The first problem they encountered was with the community associations restrictions on the property. When Russ arrived, he put up a flagpole. He and Margie also brought down from the home in Pelham a wishing well that they had owned for 30 years. They thought that it brought them good luck, and it reminded them of home. But no sooner had they made these additions than the property owners association sent them a letter stating that the flagpole and the wishing well were not in compliance with the association rules and would have to be removed. This immediately put them in conflict with their new neighbors, and Russ was stubborn enough to complain and resist the association, which enabled him to keep the offending improvements for as long as they lived in the community.

Then there were the people in the community. To Russ and Margie, they seemed standoffish and stiff, "like they thought they were better than us." Whether the dispute with the association had anything to do with this attitude was not clear. Russ and Margie went to some of the social events that the community sponsored, but they never met any people with whom they felt comfortable. Russ said that he had always tried to avoid seeing doctors and lawyers and had never been too fond of teachers, but now the only people he met were doctors and lawyers and teachers. Although he had always been gregarious and popular among his neighbors at home, Russ felt uncomfortable with the people who lived in the community. He felt that he had little in common with them and nothing to talk about. He said that the first time he went to get a haircut he asked a fellow customer if he would "take the Giants and four points on Sunday," and the man had no idea what he was talking about. Russ took golf lessons but he never actually played, because it seemed that everyone in the community had been playing for their entire lifetime, and Russ did not want to get put in a group in which he would slow everyone down.

In addition to this sense that the members of the community looked down on them, Russ and Margie perceived the majority of the residents as "much older than us." It made them feel older than they were. And there were no children. One of the things that Russ had always loved was having the local kids come into his gas station to get air in the tires of their bicycles. Russ would adjust their seats for them and make minor repairs for nothing. The he would talk with the kids about the little league and what was going on at the school and how their parents were doing.

Then there was the physical layout of the community itself. There were no sidewalks and no places to just "hang out." Russ had been used to walking around town in Pelham, saying hello to the shopkeepers and neighbors along the way. He socialized at his gas station, in the luncheonette on the corner, and in the local pub. But in the retirement community there was no place to walk to and no sidewalks to walk on. Everybody drove everywhere. There was no luncheonette, diner, or deli right near their home. Russ had to go out of the community to the mall down the road to get a slice of pizza or a cup of coffee, and this was no fun because the people at the mall were never the same. There was no group of folks that Russ knew would be there for coffee each day. There was a fancy restaurant and a bar at the golf club in the community, but Russ didn't feel comfortable there and could not understand why it cost six dollars for a beer.

The there was the weather. Florida was not warm. It was hot! Too damned hot! It was only cool enough to be comfortable outside during the winter, and then it rained a lot. During the summer you could not leave the air conditioning.

For a month Russ and Margie tried to convince themselves that they were happy in their new home. After a month they recognized and acknowledged that they had made a mistake, but they continued to hope that they would "settle in" and get used to the new environment. They thought about the time and the money they had invested in the property, the move, and the new furniture that they had bought for the house, and they were reluctant to call it quits. However, when they came back to Pelham for what was supposed to have been their first visit back with the kids, they realized what they had been missing: their children and grandchildren, their friends, their neighborhood. They realized that these were the things that they loved and the things that made them happy. They called the realtor in Florida and told her to put their home on the market. They went back only to gather up their important personal possessions, including the wishing well.

Their ill-fated experience with the retirement community ended up costing Russ and Margie about $70,000, but they regarded the loss as an "educational expense." They bought a town house in Pelham, only about four blocks from the home of their younger son. Their new house was close to the village, and it allowed them to visit their friends and their children easily and frequently. Russ could go in to the garage to help out whenever he wanted, and he could hang out for hours at the luncheon-ette. Russ and Margie still had Sunday dinners with their family at "the big house." The only difference now was that their daughters-in-law now did more of the cooking, and Margie did a little bit less.

This experience is not at all uncommon. For a long period of time, the idea of retiring to a community in the sun where life would be easy was the normative American dream for couples approaching retirement age. But many folks bought into this dream "hook line and sinker," without giving the move due consideration. It is important to weigh a warmer climate against the rewards associated with continuing to live in our own community, among our friends and family, and close to the places you have grown to love. As you will see in this chapter, it is quite possible to arrange our living situations in such a way as to gain many of the best aspects of life in a retirement community, without leaving our home neighborhoods. It is extremely important that we give adequate thought to where we wish to live as we approach 60, because the choice of living environment is one of the most important factors that determine how satisfied we are likely to be with the rest of our lives.

THE IMPORTANCE OF ENVIRONMENT

Next to our spouse, where we live is the single most important element in determining the happiness of people over 60.[1] By "where we live," I am referring to more than just a house. Happiness is not determined by the number of square feet in your house, the Jacuzzi in the bath, the six-burner cook top in the kitchen, or the pool in the backyard. All these things are nice, but living in a nice home is neither a necessary nor a sufficient condition for satisfaction with our living environment. Research shows that broader aspects of the environment are just as important. These include such factors as: (1) the proximity of the home to family and friends; (2) the accessibility of shops, services, and recreational activities; (3) the accessibility and usability of transportation; (4) the congeniality of the surrounding environment, including both the physical attractiveness and the accessibility of the neighborhood. The latter element involves such issues as the cleanliness of the neighborhood, the availability of pedestrian paths and adequate street lighting, and the safety of the neighborhood.[2] These aspects of the neighborhood have been shown to be related to high levels of social interaction with neighbors, friends, and relatives.[3] Social interaction is related directly to our level of satisfaction with our lives.

Of course, different men have differing levels of need for social interaction. There are those among us who require rather little such interaction, men who are engrossed in some particular solitary intellectual activity, and there are men who are happiest when they are walking alone in the country watching birds. What is important for you in making the decision as to where you will live is to consider the activities that give you the greatest pleasure in your life, and to then evaluate alternative living situations in terms of how well each option facilitates your access to and engagement in these activities.

THE DEMANDS OF YOUR LIVING ENVIRONMENT

Another factor that we must consider in deciding where to live as we approach and pass our sixtieth birthday is the level of demand placed upon us by our living arrangement. Although most of us will remain healthy and continue to live independently for many years after 60, we may very well want to cut down on the amount of labor involved in keeping up our homes. I have a 61-year-old friend George who lives in the country and places great value on self-sufficiency. He heats his home with wood stoves, plants a large garden each year, and even keeps goats and chickens. He is still very healthy and active, but even he has begun to take steps to ease the burdens associated with maintaining his home and lifestyle.

When he was younger and had just moved to his small farm in the country, George cut, split, and stacked all his own firewood. He was intensely proud of the fact that he could do all this and that he had virtually no expense for heating his home. He has several very large chain saws that he has used to fell trees. He has a small tractor that he has used for gardening but also to drag logs to a place behind the barn where they can be cut up. He has a gasoline powered hydraulic log splitter. He built two very large woodsheds, which he has full almost all the time. He uses the wood from each shed on alternate years. In that way all the wood can age for a minimum of one year before being burned. He has large wheelbarrows to haul the split wood to the sheds where it can be stacked to dry.

As George has gotten a bit older, he has learned that he can cut back a little on the work that he does personally each year to prepare his firewood. First, he stopped cutting down trees himself, partly because he nearly killed himself a couple of times. Now he has loggers come in to cut trees. They take the main section of each trunk to a mill to be cut into lumber, and they drag down all the larger branches to the spot behind the barn where they are cut up, split, and stacked. George still does some cutting and splitting, but now he hires a couple of local high school kids to do the heaviest of this work. It just got to be too hard on his back to do it all himself.

In other words, he has begun to accommodate to his changing physical capabilities by hiring people to do some of the things that are just too difficult. To the same end, my friend now has a man with a tiller come in each spring to prepare his garden for planting. This is the most labor intensive aspect of home gardening, and the small investment he makes each year in having the tilling done is more than worth it in terms of the wear and tear on his body.

Now because this particular friend has a real rural lifestyle, complete with difficult and even dangerous work, the need to accommodate to the effects of aging probably manifested itself to him at an earlier age than might be the case among men with less strenuous lifestyles and living arrangements. Most of us do not routinely perform really hard physical labor, and we may not find that any particular aspect of our daily activities is becoming difficult for us until quite a bit later in life. Nevertheless, the principle remains the same. Different living arrangements place differing levels of demand on us, and at some point we need to consider the steps that we can take to insure that the demands do not overwhelm us and possibly lead to injury or exhaustion. We need to see to it that the demands match our capabilities.

With respect to this match of demand and capability, we have a very broad range of choices, ranging from staying where we are and adapting in ways like George has done, all the way to living in continuing care retirement facilities, where virtually all of the chores of day to day living are done for us, and we also have 24-hour access to skilled nursing care, should such care be necessary. The sections of this chapter that follow below described some of the different possibilities we might someday consider in selecting our living arrangement for ourselves, or for a parent or other relative.

STAYING PUT

The most straightforward option may be to stay right where we are, at least for a good long time. Many of us will be perfectly healthy for years after we pass the age of 60, and we can easily handle the work associated with keeping up our residence and performing all the necessary activities of living. In making this decision, you need to ask yourself whether the things that you need to do each day and each year can still be accomplished with a reasonable effort, or whether they are becoming increasingly difficult or tiring. Obviously the answer to this question is a function of both the living situation and your personal state of health and energy. Keep in mind that a certain amount of work is good for us. If we have everything done for us we are likely to become bored and not know what to do with ourselves. However, if you find that you are just too tired to get everything done or too sore each night to fall asleep, then it may be time for an accommodation.

Accommodation does not necessarily mean "move." As we saw with George, it may simply involve getting some help. In the case of George and his firewood, having people come in to help ended up costing him nothing, because the income obtained from taking the lumber to the mill more than paid for the boys to come in and help cut and stack the wood. For individuals who are getting a little older and find that they are more and more strained by routine home maintenance and household chores, hiring a handyman and/or a part- or full-time housekeeper may provide sufficient assistance to allow you to remain in your home for a good long while.

As we saw with Russ and Margie, there are many reasons why it can be good to stay where you are. If you are close to friends and family and you enjoy your home, there is no reason to disrupt your life before you have to. Your current friends and family comprise a vital support network, and you should think twice before you simply get up and move away from them. Depending upon how much money you can afford to spend on various forms of household help, you may very well never need to move if you don't want to.

ACTIVE ADULT COMMUNITIES

The terms *active adult community* and *senior community* generally refer to retirement developments where individuals who are past a certain age can purchase homes, town homes, or apartments. Typically the age requirement is that at least one person in the household must be 55 or over.[4] In this case there may be someone younger in the home. In other cases, a minimum age of 62 is specified, and everyone in the household must be over this age. Obviously any community can establish whatever minimum age requirement it wishes, and the community may or may not allow someone below the minimum age to live in the dwelling along with the qualified older adult.

These communities typically feature low demands for maintenance on the part of the residents. Typically the grounds are kept and maintenance on the dwellings is incorporated into the cost of the unit and/or the association dues. In many of these communities there are recreational facilities such as a golf course, tennis courts, a pool, and a health center. There may or may not be planned activities supervised by the community association.

The caveats associated with such adult communities are: (1) They can be relatively expensive, particularly if there are substantial amenities and recreational programs. (2) There are typically no children in residence and few visiting at any one time. If you like children, if you like to work with them or even just hear them at play, this can be a problem. Also, there will be few young adults around, except for members of the staff. Lots of men over 60 enjoy social contact with younger people. It keeps us feeling young. So if you want mixed age social contact, this might not be the type of community that you would like. (3) Many of these communities have strict association rules regarding the maintenance and decoration of your home. Russ and Margie got into trouble because of their flagpole and their wishing well. Other members of such communities have been at odds with the association over the color they wanted to paint their home, the display of a Christmas tree or a Menorah at holiday time, the display of political placards for local politicians, or owning a pet.

Some folks say that retired people tend to have too little to keep their minds occupied, and therefore they like to concern themselves with relatively trivial aspects of other people's lives. I hope that after reading this book you will not be one of these retired not-so-busy bodies. But your neighbors might be. At any rate, if you are a golf nut and you want to move to a community where you need to worry about nothing else, this type of arrangement might fit the bill. However, make sure you know the people who are living there already, and make sure that you are aware of all the restrictions that you may be buying into.

CONGREGATE HOUSING

In Congregate Housing (sometimes also referred to as Continuing Care Retirement Communities or CCRCs) individuals live independently in their own homes or apartments, as they do in active adult communities. Also, residents generally have the opportunity to share in activities with other residents. In fact, congregate living communities may be difficult to distinguish from active adult communities. However, in congregate housing, there are additional levels of care that residents may take advantage of as the need arises. In addition to the services provided by most active adult retirement communities, such as home and landscape maintenance and security, continuing care retirement communities will offer in the same community increasing levels of care, including assisted living, skilled nursing care, and even Alzheimer's care. Having all these options present in one community obviates the necessity for residents to move as they require greater levels of assistance with the chores of daily living.

ASSISTED LIVING

In Assisted Living (referred to in some states as Residential Care for the Elderly or RCFE) residents live in separate private living units, but they have a number of additional services including meals, reminders of medical appointments and transportation to these appointments, reminders to take medication when needed, housekeeping services, provision of linen and laundry services, and if necessary assistance with bathing, dressing, and eating. This level of care is generally appropriate for individuals who are physically capable but have a mild cognitive impairment, and for persons who are mentally capable but have physical problems with motor activity or balance. Most states require that Assisted Living facilities be licensed. Assisted Living services are not covered by Medicare.

NURSING HOMES

Nursing Homes (or Skilled Nursing Facilities) offer 24-hour-a-day care for individuals who are unable to live independently. Trained staff members assist residents with personal and daily activities such as getting out of bed, bathing, eating, using the bathroom, and monitoring medications. Medical professionals are available to provide specialized care. Many nursing homes have a staff physician who visits regularly to monitor the residents' health. All nursing homes have a physician available 24 hours a day in case of emergencies. Nursing homes also have procedures in place for hospitalizing residents if this becomes necessary. A registered nurse will be on hand at all times to supervise the nurse's aids and assistants who help residents with such tasks as bathing, dressing and eating. Most nursing homes also have a physical therapist on staff.[5]

Regular skilled nursing facilities are not appropriate for individuals who have advanced Alzheimer's disease, as Alzheimer's patients sometimes exhibit erratic or dangerous behaviors. There are nursing homes that specialize in the care of Alzheimer's patients. These facilities have staff members with specialized training to cope with such behaviors.

If you have a parent or another relative who requires nursing home care, there are some specific questions that you should ask in deciding on the right facility. Of course, location is important. You need to know that you will be able to visit often, and that you will be able to take the resident out of the home for visits or for other activities. Obviously the ambiance is important. You want the facility to be clean and to smell fresh. You want the facility to have private baths for the residents, and comfortable (preferably adjustable electric) beds. You want the facility to be nicely decorated, and the grounds to be clean, safe, and well landscaped. Obviously you want a facility that has a reputation for having friendly staff who like working with older persons. You should feel free to inquire about these issues from current residents and the relatives of current residents. You need to make sure that the food is both nutritious and appealing. Many nursing homes have a dietician. Does this one? What kinds of activities are available to the residents? Do the residents enjoy them and actually participate? Does the facility have volunteers who come to visit residents? Do the residents have an opportunity to interact with persons of various ages? How about people who come in with their dogs to visit? Many nursing home residents look forward to visit from the "pet therapy lady" more than any other activity. Are religious services available? Are there provisions for physical therapy? Is there a psychologist or psychiatrist available for consultation on a regular basis? Do residents have access to hairdressers, barbers, masseuses, and similar services?

OTHER OPTIONS

The living arrangements described above represent the standard options that we think of typically when we envision a spectrum of care ranging from independent living through skilled nursing care. However, there are certainly a large number of other possibilities, both for us and for our parents.

Hotels and Senior Apartments

I remember reading a book that considered the lives of some low-income senior citizens who were living in single-room occupancy (SRO) hotels.[6] Far from the negative image that we tend to conjure up when we think of SRO housing, the book concluded that the great majority of older individuals living in this arrangement were extremely happy with their situations. They had their private space in their rooms where they could go when they wished to be alone, and they had the common area of the hotel lobby where they could socialize with other residents at virtually any hour of the day or night. In addition, since most of these hotels are located in cities, the residents had convenient access to various forms of shopping and services, as well as to a variety of cultural events. The principle of living in a hotel or a boarding house where one has private space in addition to a common area for socializing applies across the socioeco- nomic status continuum. More affluent seniors might have a suite in a very nice hotel and still benefit from the social interaction with other residents that takes place in the common areas. This is a wonderful idea for men who find them- selves alone in the later years. Hotel living affords security, familiarity, domestic care, and independent living. I especially recommend it for men who wish to be pampered and still maintain their privacy. There are also apartment buildings in many cities that have been designed specifically for seniors, and most of these feature common areas where residents regularly get together.

Shared Homes and Board and Care

Some older persons, particularly single individuals, share homes or apart- ments with housemates. This saves money and provides social and emotional support and interaction. Although we think of this type of arrangement as occurring among individuals who are similar in age, this does not have to be the case. An older individual may share his home with a younger person, perhaps adjusting the expense sharing arrangement in exchange for taking care of some or all of the household chores. The internet and local newspapers are good resources to use to find such arrangements.

Along similar lines, some older individuals take advantage of what is generally referred to a *board and care,* which is a group living situation in which 2 to 10 seniors will share a converted or adapted single family home, generally under the supervision of a younger adult or couple who may own the home. This arrangement can provide a family-like atmosphere, while still providing the resident with private space in his or her own room. Some of these group living situations are designed specifically for individuals with a particular issue, such as Alzheimer's. Others simply tend to take individuals who require a similar level of care.

Multigenerational Homes

And of course, we can live in multigenerational homes with our family members. This arrangement is perhaps not as common as it used to be, but it can be an extremely good situation for family members of every generation. The oldest generation (great grandparents) and the next oldest generation (grandparents) have the advantage of regular contact with their children and their grandchildren. This contact keeps us young. The middle generation (the parents) have a built in source of babysitting, as well as someone to help ease the burden of helping the kids with their homework. The children have the advantage of hearing from the elders about things that happened before they were born. They might learn about World War II, Korea, and Vietnam. They might learn about the world before the Civil Rights Movement or the Women's Movement. They might learn about the days before computers and video games.

As I discussed in chapter 14 on grandparenting, the intergenerational family dynamics of multigenerational families can be a challenge. Everyone living together in one house is not for everyone. It requires the ability to tolerate a busy and sometimes noisy environment, and it requires the ability to set boundaries and say no on occasion, as in "No, I cannot baby-sit on Saturday night, because your mother and I are going out to dinner," or "I would, but we are going to the movies." However, among families who are close and really love each other, families composed of mature individuals who are not afraid to negotiate giving and taking, multigenerational living can also be extremely rewarding.

When our parents or our children do live with us (or we live with them), it is highly desirable to have a home that is large enough and laid out in such a manner as to afford the various generations their own private space. Two- or three-family homes are ideal for this, as are homes with special mother-in-law apartments. (I don't know why they call them *mother-in-law* apartments and not *father-in-law* apartments. Maybe it's because women tend to live longer than we men and are therefore more likely to end up living with their children.) At any rate, we all need some privacy. We need a space where we can have things that the children might break if they could get at them. We need a quiet space where we can read or listen to music when the children are downstairs watching TV. We need a space where we can make love to our wives or have our own guests over at any time of day without fear of being interrupted. In this regard, many communities that have strict zoning for single family occupancy have special provisions and/or exceptions to the regular zoning restrictions specifically for the purpose of accommodating multigenerational families.

One more point that I need to make in connection with multigenerational living is that if you do find yourself with a parent living in your home, or if you find yourself living with your children, you should know about senior centers and particularly about senior day care. Senior centers provide a great way for older persons to get out of the house each day, socialize, and participate in a range of activities. Often the senior center will make available free of low cost transportation to a from the center. Going out each day gives the members of the different generations residing in the home a chance to get away from each other for a part of the day. It gives the attending senior a "life of his own" outside the family itself.

Senior day care is more for older adults who have become frail, or physically or cognitively impaired. Senior day care will provide not only an opportunity for activities and social interaction but also physical, occupational and/or speech therapy and help with some of the activities of daily living. For an individual providing care in the home to a frail parent, Senior day care can be a real blessing. It may allow the caregiver to work outside the home while the senior is at the senior center, and it will certainly provide a respite from care giving on a 24-hour basis.

In many areas there are also social and recreational centers that serve specific groups. For example, in many urban areas there are community centers that provide a venue for social gatherings and psychological support for members of the gay community. The nation's oldest and largest social service and advocacy organization, SAGE, is dedicated to members of the gay, bisexual, and transgender community. This organization was established in New York City with a view to providing a place for older members of the gay community to socialize other than the gay bar. For many older gay men in New York, this organization has come to take the place of a family.

Chapter Twenty

SOME FINANCIAL ISSUES TO CONSIDER: DOWNSIZING, INHERITANCES, ESTATE PLANNING, AND HEALTH INSURANCE

Martin

Martin's wife died five years ago, when he was 65. They had retired five years earlier after selling the small clothing manufacturing business that they had run for many years. They sold the business for $1.2 million, and the income from this money was sufficient to provide them with a reasonably comfortable lifestyle in retirement, though by no means a luxurious one.

At the time that Martin's wife died, they were living in a beautiful older home outside Cleveland. They had lived in this home for most of their lives, raising there four children there. It was a very large home on an eight acre piece of property in an affluent community. They had given much thought to relocating to a smaller home, for two reasons. First, staying in their present home was very expensive. It seemed as if something always had to be fixed or replaced. One year it was the roof, the next year it was the windows, and the year after that it was the plumbing. These were major expenses. The home was also expensive just to heat and light. And they really could not keep the place looking nice without a cleaning lady and expensive landscape and gardening services. Second, the neighborhood had gotten very upscale over the years. Their taxes were astronomical because of the large piece of property they owned. At the same time, their property had appreciated tremendously, and they knew that they could sell the property to a developer for a small fortune. In fact, a friend of theirs in the real estate business suggested to them that if they sold the home and bought a smaller one in a different area, they would realize a net profit that would, at an absolute minimum, double their present retirement nest egg. This would give them a really substantial retirement income, one that would enable them to do a good deal of traveling and do a lot for their children and grandchildren as well.

In addition to these purely financial considerations, Martin and his wife had also considered moving to the West Coast. Three of their four adult children and six of their seven grandchildren were living in Southern California in the San Diego area. They would certainly like to be closer to the kids, and they also thought that they might prefer the climate there to the chilly winters in the Cleveland area.

However, they never got around to moving while Martin's wife was still alive. There were many reasons for this. One was simple inertia. It was easier not to do anything than to make plans and take action. In addition, they really loved their old home, and they were very close to their neighbors, so they resisted the logic of their own thoughts about downsizing and moving, and they simply kept on postponing any action.

When Martin's wife died, however, he began to view things differently. He felt lonely in the big house. He lost the desire to keep track of what needed to be done to keep the house in good shape, and he lacked the energy to deal with the trades people who needed to be hired and supervised. He began to spend a good deal of time visiting with his children, and the house outside Cleveland sat unoccupied for weeks at a time. Finally, Martin's children sat him down and convinced him that he really needed to take some action. He knew that they were right. They loved his visits, but he couldn't go on staying in the spare room at the home of one or another of the kids. It was too disruptive to the kids' households. Clearly, the fact of the matter was that Martin really needed to get a place of his own in San Diego, near to the children, but not on top of them.

So Martin went back to Cleveland to put the house on the market. He thought that he would sell the house and use some of the proceeds to purchase a small home near the children. In that way he could pay cash for the new home, which would give him a better bargaining position. He thought that he would take the things that he needed from the old house and put them in storage until he had purchased a new home.

Now all of this so far seems quite reasonable. However, Martin was not able to execute the plan in a manner as reasonable as the plan itself. When he returned to the house in Cleveland and began to consider what furniture and personal items he would want to take to California, he suddenly realized that everything in the home, from the swing on the porch to the quiche pans in the kitchen, had a memory attached to it. He felt as if giving up any of the furniture or any of the memorabilia would be like giving up a part of his departed wife. He felt as if giving up these things would require him to grieve his wife and his former life all over again.

To make matters worse, when he made inquires with furniture dealers regarding selling some of the pieces, he was shocked to learn how little money they would pay him. He sat in the house and tried to sort through the various items to determine the things that he really had to keep and the things he could let go. He sat. He could not decide. He was paralyzed. At the same time, he was embarrassed to call the children to tell him what a difficult time he was having getting this job done. He could not bring himself to admit, even to himself, that he needed some support and some help in making these necessary decisions. He sat for several days. Finally, he called a moving and storage company up and had the entire contents of the home packed up and taken to a storage facility in San Diego.

This hasty decision enabled Martin to sell the home in Cleveland, but it also created an expensive problem. When Martin got back to San Diego and he began looking for a home, he had 13 rooms worth of furniture and all the contents of a very large house in storage. On a conscious level, Martin knew quite well that he was looking for a nice one- or two-bedroom apartment or town home, but he kept thinking about all of the things he had from the old house. So as he looked for places to live, he kept finding places that were far bigger than what he really needed. When he would mention one of these places to his children, they would remind him that the place was much bigger than what he needed, much more money than he needed to spend, and much more work to maintain than he wanted to get involved with. And Martin would know that they were right. He would not go ahead and buy a place that was too big, but he would not bite the bullet and buy a more appropriate place either.

Finally, after three months of procrastination (during which Martin was back living in one of the kids' the "spare rooms" and paying a small fortune to store all that furniture), his oldest daughter suggested that maybe Martin ought to get some therapy. She hypothesized that he had not yet worked through his feelings regarding the loss of his wife and that this failure was keeping him from moving on with his life. Reluctantly, Martin agreed to seek treatment with a therapist who specialized with bereavement issues, and she confirmed what Martin's daughter had suspected. After some discussion with the therapist, Martin and his children planned together what pieces of furniture he could keep comfortably in a two-bedroom home. In addition, the children took some of the furniture into their respective homes. They did the same with the books, art work, photos, and other personal items from the home in Cleveland. Then they hired a broker to consign the remaining items for auction.

It was much easier for Martin to accomplish this downsizing with the support of a therapist who told him that his feelings were not unusual and he did not need to be embarrassed. The support of his children helped a great deal, as did their willingness to take some of the items into their homes, where they would continue to remind everyone of his wife and the family life they had known in Cleveland.

A combination of factors make downsizing a sensible step for many men who are approaching and passing their sixtieth birthday. The kids are grown up and gone. You don't need all that space anymore. You don't need to tire yourself out keeping a big house up and running. And you don't need the expense. You don't need to pay a lot of money to maintain the home, and you don't need to pay the high taxes on a home in the town that you chose because it had the best school district for your kids (and therefore the highest property taxes).

But the downsizing issue is just one of a series of issues related to finances that frequently confront us as we age. Other issues of this nature include dealing with inheritances. Many of us receive an inheritance when we are in our 50s or 60s, due to the death of a parent. While an inheritance is, on balance, a good thing, receiving an inheritance does require us to make decisions. We need to know how to deal with this situation responsibly. Another issue that we need to confront is how to dispose of any money that we expect to have when we die. We have already noted in the chapter 11 on Retirement that some men are able to live on the income from savings during retirement, in which case they will likely have a substantial sum to leave to others when they die. Other men draw down their savings during the latter part of their lives, leaving less money to dispose of. However, whether you plan to die with a lot of money or with just a little, you need to plan on how to distribute it. Therefore you need to know about wills, estate planning, gift giving, and powers of attorney. Finally, with life expectancy increasing with advancing medical technology, you are likely to live for many more years, but you are also highly likely to spend a great deal of money on medical treatment. Therefore, you will need to know some things about health insurance, long-term care insurance, Medicare and Medicaid, and prescription drug benefits.

DOWNSIZING

Although downsizing is a logical step for many good reasons, it is nevertheless a difficult step for many of us. Here are some reasons why downsizing is logical and expected: (1) We no longer need the big home; (2) we don't need the work associated with maintaining the big home; (3) we don't need the unnecessary expense of the big home; and (4) we may well wish to relocate anyway, either to be near our children or to live in a better climate that is more conducive to the activities we enjoy.

On the other hand, downsizing is difficult for many reasons as well. (1) Downsizing involves the recognition that we have not been as successful as we could have been. Even if we have been quite successful, it is nevertheless true that if we had limitless resources there would be no need to downsize. We could simply keep the big home and hire all the help we needed to maintain it. We would not need to sell the big home in order to buy another place near the town where the kids live; and we could travel all we want to visit all the kids, wherever they are. (2) Downsizing symbolizes the realization that we have given up the ambition to conquer the world, and we have accepted the fact that we have achieved about as much as we are going to achieve, at least financially. This does not mean that we cannot continue to lead meaningful lives, but it does mean that the focus of our activity is no longer on acquiring property and expanding our sphere of influence. Instead it means that our focus is on contraction. (3) Downsizing may involve giving up activities and possessions that we love. If we move from a large piece of property to a smaller one, we may have to give up our vegetable garden or the ability to go hunting right behind the house. If we move from a larger dwelling to a smaller one, we will have to give up some of our physical possessions. This is difficult for some people, particularly for men who are bereaved and who are reminded of their lost spouse by the household articles that they both loved and used together. It can also be difficult for individuals who have extensive collections of art, books, antiques, or whatever that must be sold because they simply will not fit into a smaller dwelling. (4) Finally, downsizing can be difficult simply because it is a good deal of work to sell off or give away a bunch of stuff, as it is to go through the steps necessary to sell one residence, buy another, and move.

Okay, it's difficult. But here are some things that you can do to make it easier. First of all, emphasize the positive reasons for the downsizing rather than the negative ones. Keep in mind that just because your new dwelling will be smaller than your old one, it may very well be nicer and more desirable. If you are moving into a small home in an active adult community, emphasize the convenience of the golf course, the tennis courts, the pool, and the health club. These amenities will make it more convenient for you to participate in a variety of enjoyable and healthy activities. Emphasize the fact that all the yard work will be done for you. This will give you time to do more things that are fun. Emphasize the security of the community in contrast to the lack of security associated with most larger private homes. If you are relocating to a better climate and/or to be closer to your children, emphasize all you can do in the new area and/or all the activities you can pursue with the children and grandchildren.

If you are one of those people who feel an emotional connection to physical possessions, think of the downsizing exercise as a form of personal growth therapy. In chapter 9 of this book, I considered the need that most men experience to develop their spirituality as they approach the last third of their lives. Getting over the need to own pretty things that one can fondle and gloat over is a step toward spiritual development. You need to strengthen your attachments to people and get over your attachments to things. Silas Marner, sitting alone in his cottage counting his coins, is not a model for mental health. In chapter 10 of this book, I considered the need men have to find and maintain meaning in life. In the final analysis, meaning is derived from being useful to our family members, our friends, and our fellow citizens. It is not derived from acquiring things or from keeping things. It lies in relationships.

IF YOU INHERIT MONEY

Inheriting money is nice, provided you don't lose your head and act stupid. Inheriting money is sufficiently problematic for the baby boomer generation that the AARP has a set of guidelines on inheriting in the Financial Planning section of their Web site.[1] According to the AARP, about 35 percent of boomers will receive some form of inheritance before they die, and the average amount of these inheritances will be $64,000. Therefore it is reasonable to conclude, in the first place, that most of us will not receive any inheritance, and most of those who do will not be receiving an amount of money that will be life transforming. Therefore, rule number one regarding inheritances is, don't count on one. Whether you eventually inherit any money or not, act as if you will not. Do your own saving to secure your future.

If you do receive an inheritance, here are some bits of advice from the AARP:

1. *Don't do anything immediately.* We inherit money when someone dies. Losing a family member can be very stressful, even if they were very old, and even if their passing was not unexpected. Therefore, you would be really smart to just take your inheritance and park it somewhere, in a savings account or some other stable, liquid investment instrument, until you feel that you are ready to do some serious planning. Take some time to grieve and adjust to the loss before you attempt to make any serious decisions about spending or investing.

2. *Don't blow the money.* There is a tendency to view inherited money as a free gift that is in a different category from any other wealth that you may have amassed. If the inheritance is substantial, you may feel rich. You may feel entitled to spend the money on something completely frivolous, something on which you would never spend your "own money." This is really not a sensible way to think about inherited money. You will only have so much income over the course of your lifetime, and money you earn is no different from money that you inherit. Therefore, you should consider what to do with the inherited money in the context of your overall financial situation. This would imply that at least a substantial portion of any money that you inherit should be used to contribute to your future. You can spend a bit of the money on frivolous purchases, but please consider using the bulk of it to pay off any debts you may have, pay down your mortgage, or add to your long-term investments.

3. *Seek competent professional advice.* Receiving a substantial inheritance can have significant tax implications, and you will want to consult with an expert to make a plan that will minimize the cost to you. If you inherit an IRA, for example, it is often possible to continue to take advantage of tax deferred savings. However, the rules are different for spouses who inherit from the rules that apply to children who inherit, and it is important to check with a professional who will be able help you make the correct decisions.

ESTATE PLANNING

On the other side of the inheritance question, all men need to have a will and a plan for the disposition of any estate they may leave behind. Men who are approaching or who have passed their sixtieth birthday in particular need to give some thought to where our money will go after we die. Although I have stressed over and over again that men who are in good health at the age of 60 may well expect to live for many, many more years, there are no guarantees. You might get hit by a bus or perish in a plane crash. So take the time to consult with a professional to develop an appropriate estate plan. Even if you do not have a great deal of wealth, you still need to have a basic estate plan in place.[2]

There are three essential elements of an individual's estate plan. These are: (1) a will; (2) the assignment of power of attorney; and (3) a living will or health care proxy (also known as a medical power of attorney). In addition, many men will want to establish a trust. Begin the process of developing an estate plan by taking an inventory of your assets, including your investments, retirement savings, insurance policies, and real estate and business interests. You need to decide who you want to inherit these assets. However, you also need to decide who you want to handle you financial affairs in the event that you become incapacitated, and you need to decide who you want to make medical decisions for you if you become unable to make them for yourself.

Your Will

Everyone needs to have a will. If you die without a will (intestate) the state will determine who gets what. If you leave behind a spouse and children, in most states the law requires that you assets be split between them. At the same time that you have your will prepared, you should review the beneficiary designations on your investments, including your 401K retirement plan, IRA, pension, and life insurance policies. These accounts are typically transferred automatically to your beneficiaries.

Power of Attorney

Hopefully you are healthy today and you will remain healthy and in possession of your full mental faculties for your entire lifetime. But you cannot be certain of this. Should it come to pass that you become unable to handle your personal financial affairs, you will need someone whose judgment and integrity you trust to take charge of paying your bills, managing your investments, and making financial decisions. When you have decided who this person should be, you grant him power of attorney to manage your financial affairs if you become unable to do so. The individual designated as your agent through the legal instrument of the power of attorney is empowered to sign your name and is obligated to be your fiduciary, that is, to act in your best interests and in accordance with your wishes.

There are two different types of power of attorney. The *springing power of attorney* is often used in estate planning. The springing power of attorney only goes into effect under a particular set of circumstances that you specify. These circumstances typically refer to your becoming incapacitated. With this type of power of attorney, your designated agent typically needs to provide the court with letters from your physician(s) to verify that you have become incapable of making decisions for yourself. It is also possible to execute a *durable power of attorney*, which becomes effective immediately and does not require your agent to furnish any proof of your incapacity prior to signing your name. Under most circumstances individuals who are currently healthy would opt for the springing power of attorney, but it would be a good idea to check with your personal attorney to make this decision. In any event, the individual who you designate to become your agent should be trustworthy, competent, and willing to assume this responsibility. In most cases this individual will be a friend or family member, and you will not need to worry about paying the individual for taking on this responsibility. If no suitable individual is available to you, it is possible to name an outside agent, such as a bank or an attorney. In this event you will need to negotiate compensation for this service. Compensation may be based on an hourly fee for service basis, or it may be based on a percentage of your assets paid annually. In either case, these fees can be quite high.

If you become incapacitated and you have not assigned power of attorney, the court will appoint one. This is generally undesirable, since the process will cost your estate money, and you cannot be certain that the person who is appointed is someone whom you might have selected.

Living Will

The living will (also referred to as an *advance medical directive*) states your wishes with respect to the use of life-sustaining medical interventions in the event that you are terminally ill and unable to communicate your issues.[3] Living wills are tricky. There may be state laws that restrict the medical interventions to which these documents apply, and medical personnel may disagree on how to interpret your instructions. For this reason, advance medical directives are sometimes not followed. You can increase the chances that your actual wishes will be followed if you designate a medical power of attorney. This is an individual you trust who will be able to make medical decisions on your behalf if you cannot do so for yourself. Any individual that you would consider to take this responsibility should be sufficiently informed that he or she will be able to understand the medical issues involved, strong enough to make difficult decisions under stress, and completely committed to your best interests and your wishes.[4]

Trusts

Although many believe that trusts are only for the wealthy, the National Association of Financial and Estate Planning has suggested that trusts may be important estate planning tools for individuals with net worths of as little as $100,000. A trust can benefit individuals who fall into any of the following groups:

1. Individuals who want to have some control over money they leave to their heirs. You might not want to leave a large sum of cash to your children, for fear that they will immediately go out and spend it foolishly. A trust will enable you to place conditions on the distribution of assets. For example, you can divide the money to be left to each heir into several portions, to be made available when the heir reaches specific ages. You might also stipulate that the inheritance will be received only after certain specific conditions are met, such as graduation from college.
2. Individuals who wish to secure the interests of both a spouse and their children. Men who have divorced and remarried often want to make sure that their wife

will be taken care of as long as she lives, yet they want any residual assets to go to the children they had during their first marriage. This can be accomplished through the use of a trust.

3. Individuals who want to help a relative on Medicaid. If you have a relative who is disabled and on Medicaid or some other form of government assistance, a trust can be used to enable you to provide that individual with some financial assistance without disqualifying him or her from the programs from which they are benefiting.

4. Individuals who seek to minimize taxes. Trusts can be used to reduce taxes on gifts and estates.

5. Individuals who seek to avoid probate. Probate court is expensive. It may cost five to seven percent of your estate, and it is likely to take a long time before assets are distributed. In addition, probate court records are public, and you might have concerns for the privacy of your heirs. A trust can be used to avoid these difficulties.

Trusts may cost up to $3,000 to establish, possibly even more if the terms of the trust are particularly complex. If you go to an attorney who has expertise in estate planning, you should be able to negotiate a single fee for drawing up your will, power of attorney, living will, and trust. In addition to these elements of your estate plan, you may also want to consider making gifts to your beneficiaries before you die.

Gifts

You can give up to $12,000 annually in cash or assets to anyone you like without incurring a tax. There are substantial taxes on gifts exceeding $12,000. In addition, you can pay an unlimited amount to cover the educational or medical expenses of another person, provide that you send the money directly to the service provider. You may also reduce the size of your estate (and your estate tax) by making charitable contributions. There are some pretty complex rules governing gifts that are made within three years of your death. It is best to obtain expert advice on gifts and contributions as part of your comprehensive estate planning.

HEALTH INSURANCE

Most men under the age of 65 have health insurance through their job or their spouse's job. Most men over 65 get their primary health insurance from Medicare. Insurance that you get through your job is called *group health insurance*. Often your employer pays most of the premium for such insurance, and you pay the rest. If you don't have group health insurance, you may buy individual health insurance for you and your family. Group health insurance is cheaper than individual health insurance, and for this reason you want to keep any group health insurance you have for as long as you can.

However, people under 65 who have group health insurance may lose their coverage for a variety of reasons. They may be laid off or fired. They may quit their job. If they are insured through their wife's job, they may lose coverage if their spouse loses her job, or if she dies, or if they divorce. Some men also lose their health coverage if they retire before the age of 65 from a job that does not offer retiree health insurance benefits, and they are still too young for Medicaid. If this happens to you, you need to investigate several different possibilities.

You may be able to get COBRA benefits (COBRA stands for the Consolidated Omnibus Budget Reconciliation Act of 1985). This federal law may enable you to keep your group health insurance for 16 months after you leave a job. If you are moving from one job to another, you should investigate HIPAA. This acronym stands for the Health Insurance Portability and Accountability Act of 1996. When you move from one group plan to another or from a group plan to an individual plan, HIPAA may protect your right to insurance. You may also check with your group health insurance provider to see if they offer a conversion to an individual policy. If these steps do not enable you to continue your health insurance coverage, you may want to investigate group plans available through other organizations to which you may belong, including professional, fraternal, and social organizations.

Another concern of men who are approaching or past the age of 60 is that of long-term care insurance.[5] Long-term care refers to many services beyond medical care and nursing care that may be used by individuals who have disabilities or chronic illnesses. Longer life spans imply that there is more time during the typical lifetime in which there is a risk of serious health problems that require intensive care. Such care can be extremely expensive, as in the case when a patient requires 24-hour a day nursing care. Such intensive care over a long period of time can dissipate you life savings. Long-term care insurance helps you to pay for these services. Also, the younger you are when you get long-term care insurance, the cheaper it will be.

Long-term care insurance typically covers the cost of: (1) help in your home with daily activities like bathing, dressing, cleaning and cooking; (2) adult day care; (3) assisted living services provided in a residential setting other than your own home, including health monitoring and help with the activities of daily living; (4) visiting nurse services; and (5) care in a nursing home.

Of course, human nature being what it is, most of us do not think about getting long-term care insurance until we are old enough to recognize that we might some day need it. Generally, this is too late in life to get the insurance at an affordable rate. According to the AARP, the best time to get long-term care insurance is during middle age, during your 40s or 50s. At this time you will be most likely to be able to obtain coverage and least likely to have to pay exorbitant premiums.

SUMMARY

In this chapter I have attempted to cover a number of topics related to our financial situations as we approach and move into our 60s. Most of these issues have both emotional and financial repercussions. Recognizing the advisability of downsizing, sensibly investing inherited money, engaging in the process of estate planning, and securing long-term health care insurance are all steps that we should take as we grow older. The problem is that each of these sensible steps also involves the recognition that we are, in fact, getting older. I hope that by this point in this book I have convinced you that passing 60 is in fact not the end of the world, and I hope that knowing there is much healthy and productive living left to do will empower you to take the steps that you need to take to secure your financial future. Paradoxically, recognizing that we are growing older and taking the steps implied by this recognition is precisely what we need to do to maximize our ability to truly enjoy the last third of our lives.

Chapter Twenty-One

CONFRONTING AGEISM

Ronnie

My friend Ronnie just turned 51. He is a regional sales manager for a company that markets T-shirts and novelty items to individual stores and chains of stores throughout the nation. Ronnie's title is the regional manager for the Northeast Region. He has anywhere from six to nine salesmen working under him. Each of them has a territory within the region, they work for commission, and Ronnie likewise receives a percentage of their sales. In addition, Ronnie personally handles some of the larger accounts in the region, particularly the sales to chains of stores. Over the years Ronnie has made a very good living with this company. Last year his commissions exceeded $300,000.

Ronnie does most of his work out of an office in the basement of his home. He also travels quit a bit to schmooze with the bigger customers. He has always given his salesmen quite a bit of freedom in how they do their work, operating on the assumption that since they are working for commission, it is in their best interest to work as hard as possible and sell as much merchandise as they can.

Recently I asked Ronnie how he was doing, and he responded, "Not that well." He said that his boss, the director of sales for the company, had recently adopted a bunch of new policies, like requiring all salesmen and regional sales directors to make detailed accountings of how they spent their time. He had also reorganized the territories within the various regions, giving each salesperson smaller territories so that more salesmen could be hired to get "better coverage." When the salesmen complained that they were having established accounts taken away from them, the director proposed taking the larger accounts from the direct control of the regional sales managers and redistributing them among the salesmen. Ronnie said that as near as he could figure this change would cost him about one-third of his earnings. Ronnie said that he and the other regional sales managers had complained about the new plans, but they were given no relief.

Ronnie said that between the new accounting guidelines and the almost certain cut in earnings that would result from the proposed changes, he was about ready to quit. Unfortunately, however, his initial inquiries among friends and colleagues within the industry suggested that similar changes were taking place in other companies as well, and it was not at all clear that Ronnie would be able to find a new position that matched the one he had, even assuming that the proposed changes went through and he suffered a substantial cut in income.

Ronnie said that maybe it was inevitable and that this business was simply not what it used to be, since so many of the larger stores were now purchasing directly from overseas manufacturers and even telling these manufacturers what products they wanted and how these products should be made.

I suggested to Ronnie that he might want to view his situation somewhat differently, as an example of age discrimination. Ronnie looked puzzled and said, "Wait a minute here, I'm only 51." But I pointed out to Ronnie that his seniority had carried him to a place where he was really earning a lot of money, and that if he and the other regional sales managers were all doing the same, their whole level within the company was costing an awful lot. Therefore it would really be in the best interests of the company to either cut their compensation or to force them out. Also, it seemed that the company was hiring new sales people who would command a great deal less compensation.

When he thought the situation through, Ronnie acknowledged that my idea made sense. He decided to discuss the situation with the other regional sales managers, and together they took their case to management, with the implied threat that they might seek relief from the Equal Employment Opportunity Commission. As a result, a compromise was reached, and life became a bit easier for the regional managers.

This example shows clearly that *ageism* or *age discrimination* can be as relevant to a 50-year-old mid-career manager as it can be to a 65-year-old. The Age Discrimination Act of 1967, which is currently the law of the land with respect to age discrimination, applies to all workers *40 years of age and older*. If you are 50 years old and you still think of yourself as young, if you cannot imagine how the effects of ageism could impact you, try applying to medical school.

AS OLD AS WE FEEL, OR AS OLD AS SOCIETY MAKES US FEEL?

I began this book with a chapter on "The Myths and Realities of Life after 60." The reason that I started with that topic is that I know from my practice that most men who are approaching the age of 60 have very negative views regarding the prospect of getting older. These views are rooted in ageist attitudes that exist within our society. These attitudes suggest that men over 60 are nonproductive, forgetful, and slow to learn new things. The problem is that we tend to internalize these views, which only makes us depressed and keep us from engaging in the types of behaviors and activities that will have the effect of keeping us healthy and making our lives enjoyable and satisfying.

Because of ageism, I felt that I needed to convince even my 50-year-old readers that life after 60 can be good. I felt that unless I convinced you that ageist stereotypes were inaccurate and life after 60 *can* be good, it wouldn't make much sense for me to describe all the things that we can do to *make sure* that it will be good. The reason why many men need to be convinced that there is life after 60 is that they have unconsciously accepted the negative stereotypes of aging that characterize our society. In short, most of us internalized ageist attitudes.

AGEISM

The term *ageism* was coined in 1969 by Robert Butler, who was the first director of the National Institute on Aging.[1] Butler defines ageism as

> a process of systematic stereotyping of and discrimination against people because they are old...Old people are categorized as senile, rigid in thought and manner, old-fashioned in morality and skills...Ageism allows the younger generation to see older people as different from themselves, thus they subtly cease to identify with their elders as human beings.[2]

Butler argues that ageism is no different from racism or sexism, in that it involves making assumptions about individuals based on stereotypical attitudes regarding the characteristics and behaviors of a class of people defined on the basis of a single characteristic, in this case their age. Another pioneer in the field of gerontology, Erdman Palmore, describes the characteristics of stereotyping in his book, *Ageism*.[3] Palmore suggests that:

1. The stereotype gives a highly exaggerated picture of the importance of a few characteristics.
2. Some stereotypes are invented with no basis in fact, and are made to seem reasonable by association with other tendencies that have a kernel of truth.
3. In a negative stereotype, favorable characteristics are either omitted entirely or insufficiently stressed.
4. The stereotype fails to show how the majority share the same tendencies or have other desirable characteristics.
5. Stereotypes fail to give any attention to the cause of the tendencies of the minority group- particularly to the role of the majority itself and its stereotypes in creating the very characteristics being condemned.
6. Stereotypes leave little room for change; there is a lag in keeping up with the tendencies that actually typify many members of a group.
7. Stereotypes leave little room for individual variation, which is particularly wide among elders.

Robert Griffith, a physician who specializes in geriatrics and a leader in the movement to eliminate ageism, argues that due to stereotyping, as soon as a person is described as *old*, most people, including most health care providers, automatically assume that the person is: (1) of little value; (2) a burden on society; (3) slow to accept change; (4) unable to look after himself; (5) slow, deaf, or stupid; and/or (6) child-like or sweet.[4]

THE MANIFESTATIONS OF AGEISM

Negative stereotypical attitudes held with respect to older individuals are manifested in our society in many ways, including: (1) jokes; (2) the manner in which older individuals are portrayed in literature, in birthday cards, and on TV; (3) the terms used to describe older individuals in the language; (4) the manner in which older individuals are treated on daily basis by their family, friends, and associates; (5) discrimination in the workplace; (6) discrimination in the delivery of medical and dental care; and (7) discrimination in the consumer market.

Jokes

A survey of 84 individuals aged 60 and up that was completed in 2001 indicated the most frequent manifestation of ageist attitudes experienced by the respondents were jokes that made fun of older people. The respondents reported that the jokes made fun of old people's lack of sexual attractiveness, their lack of sexual desire (in the case of women) and ability (in the case of men), their absentmindedness, their generally crotchety nature, their inability to drive a motor vehicle safely or to find a particular destination, and their various physical complaints, ranging from constipation to joint and muscle pains. Remarkably, 58 percent of those surveyed reported that they had actually *been told* one or more jokes of this nature during the month immediately preceding the survey.

To get a perspective on what these data mean, consider how shocked you would be if you learned that 58 percent of African American respondents had been told a racist joke, or that 58 percent of Christians reported that they had been told a joke making fun of a biblical story of Jesus' ability to perform miracles. Most of us would be shocked and angered to hear that member of a particular ethnic or religious group was told *right to their face* a joke that could only be construed as insulting. We would think that even if a person thought such a joke was funny, he would at least avoid telling it in front of a member of the group being made fun of. Yet with older persons this is apparently not the case. We can tell jokes about old people's foibles and frailties with impunity. Even older persons themselves tell such jokes.

This is just an indication of how pervasive and widely accepted the negative stereotypes of older people are in our society.

How Older Individuals Are Portrayed in the Media

In testimony before the U.S. Senate Special Committee on Aging delivered in 2006, Yale University Professor of Public Health Becca Levy argued that the media's negative portrayal of older adults is a major vehicle through which young people are socialized to accept negative stereotypical attitudes toward the elderly.[5] At the same hearings, actress Doris Roberts, who plays Raymond's mother in the sitcom *Everybody Loves Raymond*, complained about the negative manner in which older individuals are depicted on TV:

> My peers and I are portrayed as dependent, helpless, unproductive and demanding rather than deserving…In reality, the majority of seniors are self-sufficient, middle-class consumers with more assets that most young people, and the time and talent to offer society.[6]

While Roberts was decrying the negative characteristics imputed to seniors in the media, Professor Levy noted that the value the media places upon youth and youthfulness may well explain why so many senior citizens are seeking cosmetic surgery, which generally has no medical value, but does have risks of complications and a very high price tag.

Birthday cards really rub it in. I suppose one could argue that it's good to be able to laugh at ourselves, but I personally do not need to get hammered with a lot of messages telling me that I am washed up, over the hill, impotent, fat, and forgetful. I am none of these things, and I don't appreciate when I get a card that says I am. In fact, with my 60s came a new confidence that is based on experience, maturity, and a very positive attitude toward living.

The Language

Why is it that there are "dirty old men" but no "dirty young men?" Why is it that there are "old curmudgeons," but no "young curmudgeons"? There are "old goats," "old geezers," and "old fogeys." But there are no "young goats," "young geezers," or "young fogeys"? (What is a fogey, anyway?)

Or look at the other way. Why is it that there are "dashing young pilots," but no "dashing old pilots"? Think about it. The negative stereotypes surrounding older people are so ingrained in our society that they have become thoroughly incorporated into the language. You can't teach an old dog new tricks. Old soldiers never die. There are at least some "young fools" out there, but "there's no fool like an old fool."

How Older Individuals Are Treated

Older men are also treated differently from younger men under identical circumstances. Barrie Robinson has listed a number of ways in which older individuals are treated differently from younger persons:[7]

1. If an older individual should falter for a moment because he is unsure of himself, people immediately assume that he is "infirm." This may precipitate an unnecessary effort to come to his assistance or a criticism that he should know better than

to attempt to do "things like this" by himself. The example that comes to mind here is the Boy Scout who feels obligated to help the old man across the street, whether he wishes to cross the street or not. Similarly, if an older person pauses mid-sentence in search of the proper word, you can rest assured that someone will feel compelled to fill it in for him. I hate that!

2. If an older individual forgets someone's name or forgets what he was looking for when he came into the room (i.e., the "hereafter" phenomenon, as in "What am I here after?") people automatically assume that he is senile. This is really annoying, because I assure you that young people forget names, and they too sometimes forget why they came into the room, just as we older men do.

3. People assume that older individuals are incapable of expressing themselves clearly enough to take care of themselves. Therefore, well-meaning relatives and friends (and sometimes even strangers) may intercede on our behalf in interactions that we are perfectly capable of handling by ourselves. For example, if a younger adult overhears you attempting to explain what you want to a particularly dense clerk in an electronics store, the younger adult will may very well assume that your age has rendered you inarticulate, and he or she may very well begin to attempt to translate for you. In this case the interloper thinks that he or she is being helpful, but in reality he is only being insulting.

4. People expect that older individuals will "act their age" and confine their conversation to topics that are appropriate for "seniors." God forbid we mention sex. Someone will feel the need to smile in a condescending and patronizing manner and explain, "He really is a horny old goat," or even worse, "Pay no attention to him. He's really harmless."

5. If an older person asks a younger person to repeat something, the younger person will assume that the older person is stone deaf, and he will repeat the remark at the top of his lungs while at the same time mouthing each word in an exaggerated manner so that the older person can read his lips. It doesn't matter that a subway train was going by the first time. If you're old, they assume you're deaf.

6. If an older individual has the temerity to register a complaint about anything, younger people assume that he is just a "cranky old curmudgeon." There is no chance that an older individual might have a legitimate complaint. Old people are simply miserable by nature. We enjoy complaining.

This type of assumption regarding how older individuals should be treated is particularly insidious, because it often manifests itself in a behavior that seems to be considerate, even charitable. Therefore it is difficult for the older individual, the person who is being stigmatized and patronized, to register a complaint. To do so would seem ungrateful and would only confirm the stereotype that old men are cranky.

Discrimination in the Workplace

Have any of the following ever happened to you?

1. Your employer demanded that you retire when you reached a specific age.
2. Your employer gave you an undeserved poor work performance evaluation and then used your supposed record of poor performance to justify firing you, demoting you, or not promoting you.

3. Your employer failed to give you a promotion for which you feel that you were in line. Instead he hired a younger individual from outside because management says the company "needs new blood."
4. The company was barely making a profit, so your employer fired you in order to keep younger workers who were earning less money.
5. Your boss did not allow you to take some training courses because he felt that you would probably retire before the company would recoup its investment in your training.
6. Your boss assigned a specific job responsibility to someone younger because he felt that a "younger-looking" individual would be more likely to be successful.
7. You interviewed for a job, but the prospective employer hired someone younger than you because the employer felt that the other person represented a better "long-term" investment for the company.[8]

If any of these things ever happened to you, you may well have experienced age discrimination in the workplace.

According to the U.S. Equal Employment Opportunity Commission (EEOC), the Age Discrimination Act of 1967 (ADEA) protects individuals who are 40 years of age or older from employment discrimination based on age.[9] The ADEA's protections apply to both employees and to job applicants. Under the ADEA, it is unlawful to discriminate against an individual because of his or her age with respect to any term, condition, or privilege of employment, including, but not limited to, hiring, firing, promotion, layoff, compensation, benefits, job assignments, and training. It is also unlawful to retaliate against an individual for opposing employment practices that discriminate on the basis of age, or for filing an age discrimination charge, testifying, or participating in any way in an investigation, proceeding, or litigation under the ADEA. The ADEA applies to any business with 20 or more employees, including the federal government and state and local governments. It also applies to employment agencies and to labor organizations.

For many years after the ADEA became law, relatively few complaints were lodged. However, as the baby boomer generation began to approach their sixtieth birthday, the public began to be more aware of age discrimination. As a larger and larger proportion of the population began to be aware of age discrimination and to realize that they were potential victims of age discrimination, the shifting age mass of the body politic has resulted in greater utilization of the provisions of the ADEA. According to Harvey Stern, the Director of the University of Akron's Institute for Life Span Development and Gerontology, the EEOC reported a 24 percent increase in the number of age-discrimination complaints filed in 2003, compared to 2001.

Discrimination in Health Care

In the medical care industry, older individuals are routinely treated differently from younger individuals.[10] Older patients tend to receive less aggressive treatment than younger patients with the same symptoms. Studies have shown that: (1) senior citizens with cancer are less likely than younger patients with cancer to receive radiation and chemotherapy; (2) senior citizens with diabetes are less likely to receive all the recommended blood tests, physical examinations, and other screening devices that are employed to monitor the disease; (3) senior citizens with heart disease are less likely than younger individuals with the same condition to receive anti-clotting treatments that have been shown to reduce the risk of death; and (4) senior citizens are under-treated for mental health issues.[11]

There are many reasons why older individuals are discriminated against in the health care system. Many physicians prefer to use their skills to cure acute illnesses rather than to manage chronic diseases. Because chronic conditions are more common among older individuals than among younger individuals, health care providers trained to focus on discrete causes of diseases and their cure may ignore the opportunity to task action to improve the quality of life of older patients. An additional related issue is that many physicians still adhere to a traditional view of aging as a continual process of decline. Therefore they may consciously or unconsciously operate on the assumption that fixing a particular problem in an older individual is futile.

Medical students rarely receive special training in managing the multiple and complex medical problems of older adults. A study of physicians reported by West and Levy indicated that the typical physician in the United States has a level of knowledge of aging that is approximately the same as that of the typical undergraduate. Furthermore, medical students are not taught to treat older patients with respect and to avoid being patronizing. There is a shortage of geriatricians, physicians specializing in the unique health problems of older adults.[12]

Health professionals also tend to share the negative stereotypical attitudes of the society regarding the cognitive capability and mental health condition of older individuals. When they are confronted with a patient complaining of symptoms like problems with memory, disorientation, or confusion, they tend to assume that these problems are simply an inevitable part of the aging process.[13] This may lead them to fail to identify these symptoms as possible indicators of a treatable disease entity. The same is true of symptoms of mental illnesses such as depression, anxiety, and dementia. Health care providers often think that mental illness in old age is untreatable. They may even believe that symptoms of mental illness are a normal aspect of aging.[14]

Age Discrimination in the Consumer Marketplace

Ageism also manifests itself in the consumer marketplace. Senior citizens may be denied a credit card simply because of their age. They may find that they are unable to purchase automobile liability insurance or that they are being charged a higher rate than a younger individual, even though they have an unblemished driving record. They may be discouraged from joining certain health clubs that are attempting to present a certain image as a meeting place for the young, the beautiful, and the athletic.

In the same way, older individuals may find that their travel agents tend to steer them away from certain resorts, acting on the belief that the destination tends to cater to a "younger crowd" or specializes in activities that are appropriate for younger individuals. Agents engaging in such behavior may not even be consciously aware of what they are doing. If they are aware that they are steering older clients to specific places because of their age, they may honestly feel that they are doing so for the clients' own good. Nevertheless, the result, that is, the older clients' options are limited, is the same as if the agents had bad intentions.

Older patrons may find that they are seated in a specific area of the restaurant, particularly when they go to particularly so-called trendy places. Even those restaurants that have special reduced rates for senior citizens may engage in a form of age discrimination by offering these specials at certain times of the day (i.e., the early bird special). This practice may seem innocuous or even appropriate, given the tendency of seniors to go to bed early. But the idea that seniors go to bed early is itself a stereotype. In reality, any practice that tends to divide older customers from other customers simply on the basis of age can be viewed as a form of discrimination. Similarly, older customers may also find that they are ignored or given only half-hearted service in certain types of stores, such as high-end electronics and computer stores.

Senior citizens may also be discriminated against by institutions of higher education. Although many colleges and universities are attempting to attract senior citizens to continuing education programs and even to undergraduate and masters level degree programs, there is still age discrimination in admissions to prestigious graduate and professional schools, such as medical schools, law schools, and prestigious programs in business administration.

THE EFFECTS OF AGEISM

Melissa Dittman of the American Psychological Association has argued that ageism is not only hurtful to older individuals but the effects of ageism may actually shorten their lives.[15] The logic behind this argument is that exposure to negative stereotyping and discrimination has a negative impact on the self-perceptions of older individuals, and negative self-perceptions are related to decreased life expectancy. One long-term longitudinal study of individuals over the age of 50 indicated that individuals who had positive views of aging and older persons when they were 50 years old lived an average of 7.5 years longer than individuals who had negative views of aging and older persons when they were the same age.[16]

Butler writes:

> Ageism, like all prejudices, influences the self view and behavior of its victims. The elderly tend to adopt negative definitions of themselves and perpetuate the very stereotypes directed against them, thereby reinforcing society's beliefs.[17]

Palmore argues similarly. He suggests that the consequences of ageism are the same as those associated with attempts to discriminate against other groups, that is, the members of the group who are the victims of prejudice and discrimination tend to internalize the dominant group's negative image and behave in ways that conform to that negative image.[18] What's worse, when the members of the stigmatized group begin to behave the way that they are expected to behave according to the negative stereotype, their own behavior reinforces the stereotypical thinking. This vicious cycle can be represented by the flow diagram presented in Figure 21.1.[19]

Figure 21.1
The Vicious Cycle of Dependence

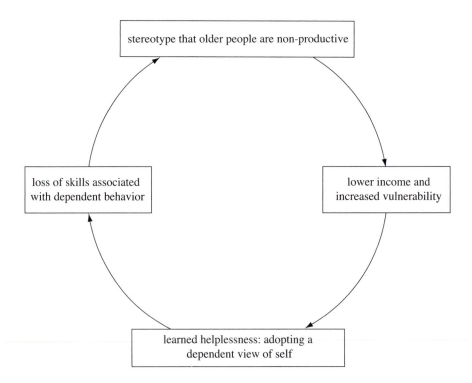

In our society, the elderly are expected to be "asexual, intellectually rigid, unproductive, forgetful, happy, enjoy their retirement, and also be invisible, passive, and uncomplaining."[20] An older individual who has internalized these expectations may "act old," even though this behavior may be totally out of keeping with his personality and his previous behavior. But "acting old" may involve stopping or cutting back on social and recreational activities, failing to seek appropriate medical treatment, failing to be assertive in business and personal interactions, accepting forced retirement, and even accepting an impoverished lifestyle. These changes can have a negative impact on one's physical health and one's psychological adjustment. They can promote even further loss of self-esteem, in the extreme manifesting in self-hatred, serious depression, and even suicidal thoughts or behaviors.

Many older men simply accept the negative stereotype of the elderly hook, line and sinker. These men dutifully behave as old men are expected to behave. As a result, they begin their downward course toward invisibility and ultimately toward death. Other men respond to ageism with denial. That is, they reject their status as an older person. These are the men who have hair transplants and cosmetic surgeries so that they can pass for being younger. They may even lie about their age. They socialize with younger people, and they seek out younger women. They drive red convertibles and take up sky diving. Well, I have made the point that it is good to stay active and keep fit, so I really can't state unequivocally that each and every one of these behaviors of denial is dangerous and foolish. However, most of these behaviors have the potential to make you look foolish, particularly if you start to believe that you are younger than you are. This can lead you to avoid getting necessary medical screenings and procrastinating with respect to retirement planning and estate planning. The key is that you need to accept the fact that you are growing older, but reject the negative stereotypes of aging that cause you to deny that you are growing older.

Still another response to ageism is avoidance. Some men seek to avoid being exposed to ageist discrimination by isolating themselves. If they feel that they will not be welcomed in a particular trendy restaurant, they will simply not go, even if they really would like to try the food. If they feel that they might be rejected for a job because they are too old, they will simply not apply. If they feel that their doctors really don't care as much about them as they do about their younger patients, they may give up going to the doctor. Some older men isolate themselves in another way. They retreat into the world of substance abuse, staying at home drinking or taking drugs. The ultimate technique for avoiding ageism is suicide.

But there is an alternative to accepting the role of the old man, denying that you are an old man, or avoiding any situation in which you might be exposed to age discrimination. The fourth response to ageism is to confront it. We can learn to recognize when we are being subjected to discrimination based on our age, and we can make a fuss. I consider this alternative in the following section of this chapter.

CONFRONTING AGEISM

There are three strategies that we can employ to confront ageism and avoid the negative outcomes described above. These are: (1) point out examples of age discrimination when they affect you; (2) join and become active in advocacy groups that lobby for the interest of senior citizens; and (3) make your own life a model of productive engagement that will demonstrate by your example that older men can and do make a contribution to society and should be accorded the status in our society commensurate with their contribution.

When Age Discrimination Impacts You Personally

This is a no-brainer. When you feel that you are being discriminated against, say something. Don't worry about your image as an affable and compliant senior. Assert yourself as an adult who is entitled to he same treatment as any other adult. If someone tells you a joke that makes fun of an old person, tell that person that the joke is offensive. Tell him that you would appreciate it he would not tell jokes like that to you in the future. If the joke teller was himself an older individual, explain to him that his telling the joke is an indication of the fact that he has internalized negative stereotypes and that in the long run buying in to these stereotypes will be harmful to him, as well as to the people to who he is telling the jokes. If the joke was told in the presence of younger people, tell the individual who told the joke that he is contributing to the creation of negative stereotypes of the elderly among the younger generation.

When you see an older person depicted as crotchety, dependent, or demanding in the media, complain. Don't just complain by yourself, but get others to join with you in your protest. If you have influence with your children and grandchildren, point out the problem to them and suggest that they stop reading the offending newspaper or stop watching the offending radio or television show.

When you feel that someone has treated you in a demeaning or patronizing manner because you are older, tell them how you feel. You don't need to be rude, but you do need to let them know what the effect of their actions has been on you.

If you think you would like to continue to work or go back to work past the age of 65, do so. Don't be intimidated. If you think that your employer has discriminated against you on the basis of age, call your state Equal Employment Opportunity Commission and file a complaint. If you think that you have been turned down for a job for which you are qualified simply because you are older than some other applicants, do the same.

If you experience discrimination in connection with health care, say something. Ask your doctor if he would make the same recommendations for diagnostic tests and treatments if you were younger. Remember that he works for you. If you feel that you are not getting the right answers to these questions, find another doctor and get a second opinion. Find a geriatrician, or at least a primary care physician whom you know to be competent with respect to the health problems of older adults and who is ready to treat you with the same degree of value and respect that he or she would give to any other patient.

Similarly, if you experience discrimination or a lack of sensitivity from a maître d', a travel agent, a hotel keeper, or a sales clerk, make a fuss. If you feel that they haven't given you the same level of service that they might give to a younger person, or you feel that they have been condescending or patronizing, then give them a good reason for wanting to get rid of you. Make a scene.

Join and Become Active in Senior Citizen Advocacy Groups

There is strength in numbers, and the best way to develop political power to combat ageism is to join and become active in senior advocacy groups. On a macro scale, this refers to lobbying organizations such as the AARP, but I am not referring solely to national organizations. Organize groups of seniors in your town to press for the implementation of policies aimed at confronting ageism and fostering the interests of seniors. Be politically active. If you are affiliated with a particular political party, organize the seniors who are members of the local political organization to become a united voice in favor of pro-senior policies. Make elected officials and party officials aware of your group and its goals. Back up your lobbying activities by showing that you can be useful in turning out the vote.

Be a Positive Role Model of Active Involvement

Get involved in useful and productive activities that benefit others, including members of your family, friends, neighbors, and the community at large. Be the keeper of wisdom for your grandchildren. Tell them about the historical events that you remember. If you have a hobby or pastime that you love, share it with them. Take them fishing. Take them to ball games. Show them by your example that older men can be healthy, vibrant, vital, and interesting.

Do the same in the community. Volunteer. Be an umpire for the Little League. Help out in community charitable events. Assume leadership positions. Take responsibility. Help other seniors to do the same. Let them know that they can be role models as well. In this way you will not only be doing things that will make you feel good about yourself but you will also be showing everyone in town that just because a man is past 60, it doesn't mean that he can't be a productive member of society and a strong leader in improving the community. And don't be afraid to mention that there are lots of folks your age who are just as competent and capable as you who need to be included in community activities. After all, look at our national leaders. There are baby boomers out there with great track records and apparently many good years ahead of them. President Bush the elder was just shown on TV making his fifth or sixth skydive, and President Clinton is keeping fit and doing speaking engagements all around the world.

Chapter Twenty-Two

PUTTING YOUR LIFE
IN PERSPECTIVE

Keith

Keith is 57. He is a partner in a large New York law firm. He has a seven-figure annual income. He has been happily married for 30 years to Jenny, who is 52. They met shortly after Keith finished law school. Jenny had just graduated from college and she was working as an administrative assistant at Keith's law firm when he joined the firm. They married within a year, and Jenny quit work to start a family. Now they have three grown children, all of whom are independent, successful and happily married. They have four grandchildren so far.

Keith and Jenny make a very attractive couple. They live in Chappaqua, New York, in the home where they raised their children. They also have an apartment in New York City. They are very active socially. They entertain a great deal, and they are active politically. They regularly attend the philharmonic, ballet, and jazz concerts at Lincoln Center. Keith is at a point in his career where he no longer needs to work 70 hours a week. Jenny went back to graduate school 16 years ago. She became a social worker, then a psychoanalyst. She has a private practice that she limits strictly to 20 hours per week. So they are both working productively, yet they have time to have fun. They travel a good deal, both in the States to visit their children and overseas.

Keith began psychotherapy with me two years ago. His presenting issue was a pervasive sense of "emptiness." He said that everything was "OK" but "just OK." Nothing seemed to mean very much to him, and he couldn't understand why. After all, he was about as successful as a man could be. He was still in love with his wife. They liked being with each other, and they still had a good sex life. They had interesting friends and they did lots of fun things. It seemed to Keith that everything had worked out just the way it was supposed to work out, and he should be proud of his accomplishments and happy with his life.

Keith said that he was not unhappy, but he was not really all that happy either. Although everything in his life was right, somehow it just didn't feel "right." Keith said he was perplexed and confused, and he wondered if there wasn't something wrong with him for not appreciating how well his life had worked out.

Sadly, I see quite a few men like Keith in my practice. They are men in their 50s and 60s who have "gone through the motions" and dutifully performed the roles that were expected of them but have not really given much thought to why they were performing these roles. It is as if they have lived their life playing out a script that someone else wrote. And as they get to the second half of life, they begin to think about their lives. They reach a point, as Keith did, where it is no longer necessary to work 70 hours a week. They begin to wonder what it all means. It is then that they began to sense that they have been playing a role. Their lives are not bad, but they are not really *their* lives at all. They are lives that were assigned by parents, teachers, and the culture in which they grew up.

Now I will make a confession. In writing this very book that you have been reading, *I may well have contributed to this problem.* Much of this book has been given over to advice on how to maintain your good health and remain active and involved as you approach and pass your sixtieth birthday. In giving you this advice, I have endorsed and perpetuated a relatively new but increasingly powerful cultural value, the preoccupation with maintaining our physical health and our satisfaction with living for longer and longer periods.

Although there is certainly nothing wrong with health and happiness, the idea that we can extend them almost without limit can be problematic with respect to the goal of discovering the purpose of our life. Go back for just a minute and think about Keith. He followed a script through life. He studied hard, went to college and law school, worked hard at the firm and became a partner. He found a good woman and raised a good family. All of these things are good, except that he was not really living his own life, but rather the life that his family and his culture had laid out for him. Think back to chapter 10 of this book, on "Finding and Maintaining the Meaning in Life." Think back specifically to the section on "Living Your Life on Purpose." This is what Keith had failed to do.

And what I am saying now in my confession is that I truly hope that you *do not simply accept* the prescriptions of this book for health, long life, and active involvement as still another script that you should follow in order to be successful. I do not want you to feel that now, after you have worked hard in school, accomplished much professionally, and successfully raised a fine family, you need to follow another set of prescriptions that will make you as successful in the years after 60 as you were in the years before 60. Get past other people's prescriptions for success and find out for yourself what is real and meaningful for you.

And here's another thought. To what extent does preoccupation with health and fitness and looking good enable us to deny the reality of our own mortality?

I work out regularly and I enjoy it a lot. I often think about the possibility that I will reach 90 or 100, and I will still be going to the gym. We read about medical advances making a life span of 150 a real possibility in the near future. Perhaps through cloning, we will someday be able to defeat death and live forever... maybe... someday. But until then, we must be mindful lest our obsession with health serves to distract us from the awareness that in fact our lives are transient, and it is our personal responsibility to infuse these brief lives with meaning. Thus James Hollis argued that

> The avoidance of our mortal, transient condition is pathological. To be mindful of our fragile fate each day, in a non-morbid acknowledgement, helps us remember what is important in our life and what is not, what matters, really, and what does not. It has been my experience that those who handle aging and mortality least well are those who fear that they have not been in *this* life, that they have not been *here*, that they have not lived the life that they were called to live. Those most preoccupied with appearance are typically those most resistant to the task of inner authority, for they continue to seek validation from the world out there.[1]

This has been my experience in my practice as well. Patients like Keith come to therapy because it provides them with a venue in which they pause and get a perspective on their lives. Therapy enables us to consider the influences of our parents, our teachers, our authority figures, and our culture on who we are and what we have become. By recognizing the forces that have led us to where we are now, we may come to realize that much of our life has been determined by others, and that we have done little to enact our own personal vision of who we are and what we consider meaningful. For many, this is the crucial first step in taking back responsibility for our lives.[2]

LIFE REVIEW AND GENERATIVITY

Erkson stated that the primary developmental task of the mid-life period was the development of generativity, achieving a sense of productivity and creativity, as opposed to stagnation. He stated further that the primary developmental task of the late-life period was the development of ego integrity, achieving a basic acceptance of one's life as having been appropriate and meaningful, as opposed to despair. The chances are that as you read this book you are moving along toward the latter part of the mid-life period, and that reading this book has made you stop to think a bit about the late-life period. So where do you stand with respect to this question of generativity? Do you feel productive and creative? And how do you expect you will fare with respect to ego integrity as you grow older? Do you feel that your life up to this point has been appropriate and meaningful?

How do you suppose Keith would have answered these questions when he came into my office trying to figure out why everything seemed empty and nothing really seemed to matter all that much to him? Was he productive and creative? Certainly his family, colleagues, and friends would have seen him this way. But did Keith see himself this way? No, he certainly didn't. He came in saying that he felt like he *should* feel that way, but in fact he did not. Maybe he would give himself a little credit for productivity, but none at all for creativity. And what about ego integrity? Did Keith see his life to that point at appropriate and meaningful? Most likely he would acknowledge that his life had so far been "appropriate," but he certainly did not view his life to that point as meaningful. Keith came into treatment to sort out these issues. But there are other ways to approach them.

Gerontologists have long advocated the process of "Life Review Therapy" to help senior citizens with the task of achieving ego integrity.[3] In life review therapy an individual reflects back on his past life and attempts to gain perspective, seeking to understand the complex array of influences that have led him to do the things that he has done and to become the person that he has become. It is often said that the goal of life review therapy is to help the individual accept who he is now as the inevitable outcome of these influences. Hayslip and Panek argued that the benefits of life review include "resolving internal conflict, improving relationships with family, making decisions about success and failure, resolving guilt, clarifying values, and simply 'getting out' feelings about painful past experiences."[4] The process of life review among the very old is viewed as preparation for a good death. Life review allows us to accept who we are so that we can die with the knowledge that we have "done the best we could" under the circumstances into which we were born. It is a means through which we can achieve peace of mind.

Keith's therapy with me was a form of life review as well, but Keith was only 57 and had not even begun to consider his mortality. Keith's therapy with me was a life review conducted while he still had time to find and achieve his purpose in life. It was a life review aimed at helping him to achieve generativity during his lifetime and not simply ego integrity in preparation for death. As we reviewed his interactions with and his responses to his parents, his teachers, his peers, and his social milieu, he began to understand how much of his life had been controlled by the expectations of others. He realized that his outwardly successful life seemed empty and unimportant to him because it was largely not his own life but a life lived to satisfy others. This recognition allowed Keith to engaged in some serious soul searching and introspection that enabled him to discover experiences and goals that were really important *to him*, while he still had the time to have these experiences and accomplish these goals.

Of course, you may argue that therapy undertaken at any point in the lifespan is an effort to understand how we got to where we are and why we are not satisfied with where we are. And you would be right. Some individuals become sufficiently miserable early in their lives that these questions demand answers; however, most of us who have functioned rather well by society's standards have been too consumed with succeeding to notice whether we were miserable or not, too wrapped up with work and raising a family to notice the emptiness or the lack of importance that we may later experience in our accomplishments. Most of us begin to be aware of these nagging questions only after we have begun to slow down a bit, as Keith did after he had established his position at the law firm. When this happens, toward the end of mid-life or the beginning of late life, we begin to wonder if our lives have had meaning, and it is then that many of us seek guidance from a therapist, or a clergyman, or a guru.

What I am saying here is that you must be receptive to these questions as they arise. In fact, you should not wait until you begin to feel that life is empty and without meaning in order to consider questions regarding the purpose, direction, and meaning of your life. Leider and Shapiro called on us to ask ourselves regularly who we are, where we belong, what we care about, and what is our life's purpose.[5] Hollis instructed us to seek out "whatever moves us deeply [and] occasions awe and wonder."[6]

Each of us will address these issues at some point in our lifetime. I am saying that sooner is better than later. If you are approaching 60 today, you have much time to find the answers and thus discover the purpose of your life.

But you do not have forever.

NOTES

CHAPTER ONE

1. Kart, C. S. (1990). *The realities of aging: An introduction to gerontology* (3rd ed.). Boston: Allyn and Bacon, p. 8.
2. Kart (1990), p. 9.
3. Rowe, J. W., & Kahn, R. L. (1999). *Successful aging.* New York: Dell, p. 14.
4. Kart (1990), p. 9.
5. Rowe & Kahn (1999), p. 16.
6. Rowe & Kahn (1999), p. 19.
7. Hayslip, B., & Panek, P. E. (2002). *Adult development and aging.* Malabar, FL: Krieger Publishing Company, pp. 23–24.
8. Whitbourne, S. K. (1998). Physical changes in the aging individual: Clinical implications. In I. Nordhus, G. VandenBos, S. Berg, & P. Fromholt (Eds.), *Clinical geropsychology* (pp. 79–108). Washington, DC: American Psychological Association.
9. Scientific American. (1998). Dogma overturned. *November,* pp. 19–20.
10. Bondareff, W. (1986). The neural basis of aging. In J. E. Birren & K. W. Schaie (Eds.), *Handbook of the psychology of aging* (pp. 157–176). New York: Van Nostrand Reinhold.
11. Kart (1990), p. 12.
12. Merz, B. (1992, October). Why we get old. *Harvard Health Letter,* 9–12.
13. Verwoerdt, A., Pfeiffer, E., & Wang, H. S. (1994). Sexual behavior in senescence. *Journal of Geriatric Psychiatry, 2,* 163–180.
14. Rowe & Kahn (1999), p. 32.
15. George, L. K., & Weiler, S. J. (1981). Sexuality in middle and late life: The effects of age, cohort, and gender. *Archives of General Psychiatry, 38,* 919–923.
16. Abeles, N. (1997). *What practitioners should know about working with older adults.* Washington, DC: American Psychological Association.

17. Matthias, R. E., Lubben, J. E., Atchison, K. A., & Schweitzer, S. O. (1997). Sexual activity and satisfaction among very old adults: Results from a community-dwelling Medicare population survey. *The Gerontologist, 37,* 6–14.

CHAPTER TWO

1. USDA. (2007, February). Physical activity. Retrieved from http://www/health.gov.

2. Rowe, J. W., & Kahn, R. L. (1999). *Successful aging.* New York: Dell.

3. Rowe & Kahn (1999), p. 100.

4. Rowe & Kahn (1999), p. 101.

5. U.S. Department of Health and Human Services. (2002, June). *Physical activity and older Americans: Benefits and strategies.* Agency for Healthcare Research and the Centers of Disease Control, p. 1. Retrieved from http://www.ahrq.gov/ppip/activity.htm.

6. U.S. Department of Health and Human Services (2002, June), p. 1.

7. U.S. Department of Health and Human Services (2002, June), p. 1.

8. Simon, H. (Ed.). (2002, March). Exercise. Retrieved from http://www.reutershealth. com.

9. Rowe & Kahn (1999), pp. 108–111.

10. U.S. Department of Health and Human Services. (1996). *Promoting active lifestyles in older adults.* Atlanta: CDC, National Center for Chronic Disease Prevention and Health Promotion. Nutrition and Physical Activity. Retrieved from http://www.cdc.gov/nccdphp/dnpa/physical/recommendations/older_adults.htm.

11. U.S. Department of Health and Human Services. (2001). Increasing physical activity: A report on recommendations of the Task Force on Community Preventive Services. *Morbidity and Mortality Weekly Report, 50*(RR-18), 1–14. Retrieved from http://www.cdc.gov/mmwr/preview/mmwrhtml/rr5018a1.htm. According to USDHHS, Only 16 percent of individuals aged 65 to 74 reported that they engage in at least 30 minutes of moderate physical activity on 5 or more days a week, and only 12 percent of those aged 75 or over. Vigorous physical activity, that is, activity that causes heavy sweating and/or large increases in heart rate, is better than moderate physical activity. Even fewer older Americans reported participating in vigorous physical activity for at least 20 minutes at least three times per week: only 13 percent of those between the ages of 65 and 74; and only 6 percent of those 75-years-old or older.

12. U.S. Department of Health and Human Services (2002, June), p. 5.

13. National Heart, Lung, and Blood Institute. (2001, December). *Clinical guidelines on the identification, evaluation, and treatment of overweight and obesity in adults.* Retrieved from http://www.nhlbi.nih.gov/guidelines/obesity/ob_home.htm.

14. Colditz, G. A. (1999). Economic costs of obesity and inactivity. *Medical Science Sports Exercise, 31*(11 Suppl), 663–667. According to Colditz, every year, fall-related injuries among older people cost the nation more than $20.2 billion. By the year 2020, the total annual cost of these injuries is expected to exceed $32.4 billion. An inactive 75-year-old male can expect to have annual medical costs that are twice as great as those of an active 75-year-old male.

15. Pollock, M. L. (1989). Exercise prescriptions of the elderly. In W. W. Spirduso & H. M. Eckert (Eds.), *Physical activity and aging.* American Academy of Physical Education Paper No. 22. Champaign, IL: Human Kinetics Books, pp. 163–174.

16. Simon, H. (Ed.). (2002, March). Exercise. Retrieved from http://www.reuters health.com.

17. Simon, H. (2007, May). Moderate exercise: No pain, big gains. *Harvard Men's Health Watch, 11*(10), 1–5.

18. Heath, G. W. (1988). Exercise programming for the older adult. In S. N. Blair, P. Painter, R. R. Pate, L. K. Smith, & C. B. Taylor (Eds.), *American College of Sports Medicine resource manual for guidelines for exercise testing and prescription.* Philadelphia: Lea and Febiger.

19. Berg, R. L., & Cassells, J. S. (1992). *The second fifty years: Promoting health and preventing disability.* Washington, DC: National Academy Press, p. 232.

20. Wheat, M. E. (1987). Exercise in the elderly. *Western Journal of Medicine, 147,* 477–440.

21. Pollock (1989).

22. Heath (1988).

23. Simon (2002, March).

24. Petot, G. J. (2005). Food for thought…and good health. In M. L. Wykle, P. J. Whitehoue, & D. L. Morris (Eds.), *Successful aging through the life span: Intergenerational issues in health* (pp. 87–100). New York: Springer Publishing Company.

25. Petot (2005), p. 90.

26. Jacobsen, D. W. (1998). Homocysteine and vitamins in cardiovascular disease. *Clinical Chemistry, 44,* 1833–1834.

27. Clarke, R., Smith, A. D., Jobst, K. A., Refsum, H., Sutton, L., & Ueland, P. M. (1998). Folate, vitamin B12, and serum total homocysteine levels in confirmed Alzheimer disease. *Archives of Neurology, 55*(11), 1449–1455.

28. Rowe & Kahn (1999).

29. Meydani, M. (2001). Antioxidants and cognitive function. *Nutrition Review, 59*(8, II) S75–S82.

30. Petot (2005), p. 90.

31. Halliwell, B. (2000). Why and how should we measure oxidative DNA damage in nutritional studies? How far have we come? *American Journal of Clinical Nutrition, 72,* 1082–1087; Martin, A., Youdim, K., Szprengel, A., Shukin-Hale, B., & Joseph, J. (2002). Roles of vitamins E and C on neurodegenerative diseases and cognitive performance. *Nutrition Review, 60*(11), 308–334.

32. Englehart, M. J., Geerlings, M. I., Ruitenberg, A., van Swieten, J. C., Hofman, A., Witteman, J.C.M., et al. (2002). Dietary intake of antioxidants and risk of Alzheimer disease. *Journal of the American Medical Association, 287*(24), 3223–3229; Morris, M. C., Evans, D. A., Bienas, J. L., Tangney, C. C., Bennett, D. A., Aggarewal, N., et al. (2002). Dietary intake of antioxidant nutrients and the risk of incident Alzheimer disease in a biracial community study. *Journal of the American Medical Association, 287*(24), 3230–3237.

33. Connor, J. R., & Beard, J. L. (1997, May–June). Dietary iron supplements in the elderly: To use or not to use? *Nutrition Today, 32*(3), 3–7.

34. Connor & Beard (1997, May–June), p. 1.

CHAPTER THREE

1. Kart, C. S. (1990). *The realities of aging: An introduction to gerontology* (3rd ed.). Boston: Allyn and Bacon, p. 111.

2. Rowe, J. W., & Kahn, R. L. (1999). *Successful aging.* New York: Dell, p. 41.

3. Quoted by Lavine, G. (2007, January 9). Is it high time for a checkup? *The Salt Lake Tribune,* p. 7.

4. Barrow, K. (2005, June 8). Men's Health: The what, when and why of men's health screenings. Retrieved from http://www.healthology.com/mens-health/article 971.

5. Anderson, H. (2002, October 21). Physical exams and medical tests for older adults. Retrieved from https://www.healthforums.com/library/1,1258,article.

6. University of Texas-Houston Medical School. (1997, July 27). Benign prostate hyperplasia (BPH). Retrieved from http://medic.uth.tmc.edu.

7. Life Extension Foundation. (2006, July 18). Blood testing protocols. Retrieved from http://www.lef.org/LEFCMS/aspx.

8. American Cancer Society. (2007). Colon and rectum cancer. Retrieved from http://www.cancer.org.

9. Worldnow. (2007). Prostate cancer. Retrieved from http://www.whas.com.

10. Dollemore, D., & Raymond, C. (1997). *Disease-free at 60-plus.* New York: Rodale.

11. Barrow (2005, June 8).

12. Dollemore & Raymond (1997).

13. Quoted in Dollemore & Raymond (1997).

14. Worldnow (2007).

15. Henkel, J. (1995, July–August). Conditions men get, too. *FDA Consumer Magazine.* U.S. Food and Drug Administration. Retrieved from http://www.fda.gov/fdac/features/695.

16. Quoted in Henkel (1995, July–August).

17. Orwell, E. (1999, Summer). Strategies for osteoporosis. *Osteoporosis report.* National Osteoporosis Foundation. Retrieved from http://www.nof.org/men/strategies_men.htm.

18. Orwell, E. (1999). *Osteoporosis in men.* New York: Academic Press.

19. National Cancer Institute. (2005, August). Understanding skin cancer. Retrieved from http://www.cancer.gov./cancertopics/wyntk/skin.

20. Buhle, E. L. (2007). An introduction to skin cancer. Retrieved from http://www.maui.net/~southsky/introto.html.

21. The Skin Cancer Foundation. (2007). Melanoma. Retrieved from http://www.skin cancer.org.

22. National Cancer Institute (2005, August).

23. The Skin Cancer Foundation (2007).

24. National Cancer Institute (2005, August).

25. Penn State University. (2007, January). Carotid artery disease and stroke. Retrieved from http://www.hmc.psu.edu/healthinfo/c/carotidartery.htm.

26. National Center for Health Statistics. (1994). Annual summary of births, marriages, divorces, and deaths: United States. *Monthly Vital Statistics Report, 42*(13). Hyattsville, MD: Public Health Service.

27. Centers for Disease Control. (1992). Cerebrovascular disease mortality and medicare hospitalization—United States, 1980–1990. *MMWR 41,* 477–480.

28. Penn State University (2007, January).

29. Favrat, B., Pecoud, A., & Jaussi, A. (2004). Teaching cardiac auscultation to trainees in internal medicine and family practice: Does it work? *BMC Medical Education, 4*(5), 4.

30. Chambers, B. R., & Norris, J. W. (1985). Clinical significance of asymptomatic neck bruits. *Archives of Neurology, 35,* 742–745.

31. Ouinones-Baldrich, W. J., & Moore, W. S. (1985). Asymptomatic carotid stenosis: Rationale for management. *Archives of Neurology, 42,* 378–382.

32. Mayo Clinic. (2007). Diagnosis of carotid artery disease. Retrieved from http://www.mayoclinic.org/carotid-artery-disease/diagnosis.html.

33. National Diabetes Information Clearing House. (2007). Diabetes overview. Retrieved from http://diabetes.niddk.nih.gov/dm/pubs/overview/index/htm.

34. National Diabetes Information Clearing House (2007).

35. Kendall, P. (1997, October 22). Syndrome X and insulin resistance. Colorado State University Cooperative Extension. Retrieved from http://www.ext.colostate.edu.

36. Syndrome X Association. (2007, January 25). What is metabolic Syndrome X? Retrieved from http://syndromexassoc.org/Home.asp.

37. Organon. (2002). What is andropause? Retrieved from http://www.andropause.com.

CHAPTER FOUR

1. Seip, R. (2006, August 4). Aging and longevity: Use it or lose it: Maintain your competitive edge as you age. Retrieved from http://www.selfgrowth.com.

2. Rowe, J. W., & Kahn, R. L. (1999). *Successful aging.* New York: Dell, p. 125.

3. Rowe & Kahn (1999), p. 126.

4. Hayslip, B., & Panek, P. E. (2002). *Adult development and aging.* Malabar, FL: Krieger Publishing Company, p. 163.

5. Storandt, M., & VandenBos, G. (1994). *Neuropsychological assessment of dementia and depression in older adults: A clinician's guide.* Washington, DC: American Psychological Association.

6. Politt, P. A., O'Conner, D. W., & Anderson, I. (1989). Mild dementia: Perceptions and problems. *Aging and Society, 9,* 261–275.

7. Heston, L. L., & White, J. A. (1991). *The vanishing mind.* New York: Freeman.

8. Gatz, M., Kasl-Godley, J., & Karel, M. (1996). Aging and mental disorders. In J. E. Birren & K. W. Schaie (Eds.), *Handbook of the psychology of aging* (pp. 365–382). San Diego, CA: Academic Press.

9. Alzheimer's Disease Association. (1995). *Is it Alzheimer's?* Chicago, IL: Author.

10. Rowe & Kahn (1999), p. 127.

11. Schaie, K. W. (1990). The optimization of cognitive functioning in old age: Predictions based on cohort-sequential and longitudinal data. In P. B. Baltes & M. M. Baltes (Eds.), *Successful aging: Perspectives from the behavioral sciences.* Cambridge: Cambridge University Press. Also Rowe & Kahn (1999).

12. The Fitness Habit Web site. (2005). Mental fitness. Retrieved from http://www. hence-forth.com/Fitness_Habit/6_mental_fitness.htm.

13. Boggan, B. (2003). Alcohol, chemistry, and you: Effects of ethyl alcohol on organ function. General Chemistry Case Studies. Retrieved from www.chemcases.com.

14. Alcohol Abuse Prevention Program of Virginia Tech University. (2007). Alcohol's effects on the brain and body. Retrieved from http://www.alcohol.vt.edu/alcoholEffects/brainBody.htm.

15. National Institute on Alcohol Abuse and Alcoholism, U.S. Department of Health and Human Services. (2004, October). Alcohol's damaging effects on the brain. *Alcohol Alert, 63.* Retrieved from http://www.niaaa.nih.gov.

16. National Institute on Alcohol Abuse and Alcoholism. (1995). *The physician's guide to helping patients with alcohol problems.* Rockville, MD. U.S. Department of Health and Human Services, Public Health Service, National Institutes of Health (NIH Publication No. 95–3769).

17. Petot, G. J. (2005). Food for thought…and good health. In M. L. Wykle, P. J. Whitehouse, & S. Morris (Eds.), *Successful aging through the life span: Intergenerational issues in health* (pp. 87–100). New York: Springer.

18. Christen, Y. (2000). Oxidative stress and Alzheimer's disease. *American Journal of Clinical Nutrition, 71*(Suppl), 621S–629S; Greenwood, C. E. (2003). Dietary carbohydrate, glucose regulation, and cognitive performance in elderly persons. *Nutrition Review, 61*(5, II), S68–S74; Tangney, C. C. (2001). Does vitamin E protect against cognitive changes as we age? *Nutrition, 17*(10), 806–808.

19. Diamond, M. C. (2001). Successful aging of the healthy brain. Paper presented at the Conference of the American Society on Aging and the National Council on the Aging, New Orleans, LA.

20. Weil, A. (2005). *Healthy aging: A lifelong guide to your physical and spiritual well-being.* New York: Knopf.

21. Rowe & Kahn (1999), p. 134.

22. Weil (2005), p. 225.

CHAPTER FIVE

1. NIMH. (2005). *Men and depression.* (NIH Publication No. 05–4972). Retrieved from http://menanddepression.nimh.nih.gov/infopage.

2. Gatz, M., Kasl-Godley, J., & Karel, M. (1966). Aging and mental disorders. In J. E. Birren & K. W. Schaie (Eds.), *Handbook of the psychology of aging* (pp. 365–382). San Diego, CA: Academic Press.

3. Beekman, A.T.F., de Beurs, E., van Balkom, A.J.L.M., et al. (2000). Anxiety and depression in later life: Co-occurrence and communality of risk factors. *American Journal of Psychiatry, 157,* 89–95; Wetherell, J. L., Maser, J. D., & van Balkom, A. (Eds.). (2005). Editorial: Anxiety disorders in the elderly: Outdated beliefs and a research agenda. *Acta Psychiatrica Scandinavica, 111,* 401–402.

4. Beekman et al. (2000); Schovers, R. A., Beekman, A.T.F., Deeg, D.J.H., Jonker, C., & van Tilburg, W. (2003). Comorbidity and risk-patterns of depression, generalized anxiety disorder and mixed anxiety-depression in later life: Results from the AMSTEL Study. *International Journal of Geriatric Psychiatry, 18,* 994–1001; van Balkom, A.J.L.M., Beekman, A.T.F., de Beurs, E., et al. (2000). Comorbidity of the anxiety disorders in a community-based older population in the Netherlands. *Acta Psychiatrica Scandinavica, 101,* 37–45.

5. Le Roux, H., Gantz, M., & Wetherell, J. L. (2005). Age at onset of generalized anxiety disorder in older adults. *American Journal of Geriatric Psychiatry, 13,* 23–30.

6. Laditka, S. B. (2001). Anticipatory caregiving anxiety among older women and men. *Women and Aging, 13*(1), 3–18.

7. van Hout, H. P., Beekman, A.T., de Beurs, E., Comijis, H., van Marwijk, H., de Hann, M, et al. (2004). Anxiety and the risk of death in older men and women. *British Journal of Psychiatry, 185,* 399–404.

8. Rudinger, G., & Thomae, H. (1993). The Bonn longitudinal study of aging: Coping, life adjustment, and life satisfaction. In P. B. Baltes & M. M. Baltes (Eds.), *Successful aging: Perspectives from the behavioral sciences* (pp. 265–295). Cambridge: Cambridge University Press.

9. U.S. Bureau of the Census. (1986). *Statistical abstract of the United States, 1987.* Washington, DC: U.S. Government Printing Office.

10. All About Vision. (2007). Macular degeneration. Retrieved from www.allaboutvision.com.

11. All About Vision (2007).

12. U.S. Bureau of the Census (1986).

13. National Institute on Deafness and Other Communication Disorders. (2002). Presbycusis. Retrieved from http://www.nidcd.nih.gov/health/hearing.

14. National Institute on Deafness and Other Communication Disorders (2002).

15. National Institute on Deafness and Other Communication Disorders (2002).

16. Tambs, K. (2004). Moderate effects of hearing loss on mental health and subjective well-being: Results from the Nord-Trondelag Hearing Loss Study. *Psychosomatic Medicine, 66,* 776–782.

17. Jakes, S. (1988). Ontological symptoms and emotion. *Advances in Behavioral Research and Therapy, 10,* 78.

18. Cacciatore, F., Naspoli, C., Abete, P., Marciano, E, Triassi, M., & Rengo, F. (1999). Quality of life determinants and hearing function in an elderly population. *Gerontology, 45,* 323–328; Maggi, S., Minicuci, N., Martini, A., Langlois, J., Siviero, P., Pavan, M., et al. (1998). Prevalence rates of hearing impairment and comorbid conditions in older people. *Journal of American Geriatric Society, 46,* 1069–1074; Strawbridge, W. J., Wallhagen, M. I., Shema, S. J., & Kaplan, G. A. (2000). Negative consequences of hearing impairment and comorbid conditions in older people. *Gerontologist, 40,* 320–326.

19. Kart, C. S. (1990). *The realities of aging: An introduction to gerontology* (3rd ed.). Boston: Allyn and Bacon.

20. Atchly, R. (1977). *Social forces in later life* (2nd ed.). Belmont, CA: Wadsworth Publishing Co., Inc.

21. Rudinger & Thomae (1993).

22. Coke, M. M., & Twaite, J. A. (1995). *The black elderly: Satisfaction and quality of later life.* New York: The Haworth Press; Hill, R. (1978). A demographic profile of the black elderly. *Aging, 7,* 287–288; Jackson, J. J. (1985). Race, national origin, ethnicity, and aging. In R. H. Binstock & E. Shanas (Eds.), *Handbook of aging and the social sciences* (2nd ed.). New York: Van Nostrand; Taylor, R. J., & Chatters, L. M. (1991). Correlates of education, income, and poverty among aged blacks. *The Gerontologist, 28*(4), 637–642.

23. Usui, W. M., Keil, T. J., & During, K. R. (1984). Homogeneity of friendship networks of elderly blacks and whites. *Journal of Gerontology, 40*(1), 110–114.

CHAPTER SIX

1. Crowley, C. & Lodge, H. S. (2004). *Younger next year.* New York: Workman Publishing.

2. Blazer, D. G. (1982). Social support and mortality in an elderly community population. *American Journal of Epidemiology, 115,* 684–694; Berkman, L. F., & Syme, S. L. (1979). Social networks, host resistance and mortality: A nine-year follow-up study of Alameda County residents. *American Journal of Epidemiology, 109,* 186–204; House, J. S., Robbins, C., & Metzner, H. L. (1982). The association of social relationships and mortality: Prospective evidence from the Tecumseh Community Health Study. *American Journal of Epidemiology, 116,* 123–140; Seeman, T. E., Kaplan, G. A., Knudsen, L., Cohen, R., & Guralnik, J. (1987). Social network ties and mortality among the elderly in the Alameda County Study. *American Journal of Epidemiology, 126,* 714–723.

3. Berkman & Syme (1979).

4. House, Robbins, & Metzner (1982).

5. Rowe, J. W., & Kahn, R. L. (1999). *Successful aging.* New York: Random House.

6. Haynes, S. G., Feinlib, M., Devine, S., Scotch, N., & Kannel, W. E. (1978). The relationship of psychological factors to coronary heart disease in the Framingham Study. *American Journal of Epidemiology, 107,* 384–402; Reed, D., McGee, D., & Yano, K. (1983). Social networks and coronary heart disease among Japanese men in Hawaii. *American Journal of Epidemiology, 117,* 384–386.

7. Coke, M. M., & Twaite, J. A. (1995). *The black elderly: Satisfaction and quality of later life.* New York: Haworth Press.

8. Coke & Twaite (1995).

9. Kooden, H., & Flowers, C. (2000). *Golden men: The power of gay midlife.* New York: Harper Collins, p. 28.

10. Wierzalis, E. A., Barret, B., Pope, M., & Rankins, M. (2006). Gay men and aging: Sex and intimacy. In D. Kimmel, T. Rose, & S. David (Eds.), *Lesbian, gay, bisexual, and transgender aging* (pp. 91–109). New York: Columbia University Press.

11. Wierzalis, E. A. (2001). *Gay men and experiences with aging.* Unpublished doctoral dissertation. University of Virginia, Charlottesville.

12. Wierzalis et al. (2006), pp. 101–102.

CHAPTER SEVEN

1. Kart, C. S. (1990). *The realities of aging: An introduction to gerontology* (3rd ed.). Boston: Allyn and Bacon.

2. Verwoerdt, A., Pfeiffer, E., & Wang, H. S. (1969a). Sexual behavior in senescence: I: Changes in sexual activity and interest in aging men and women. *Journal of Geriatric Psychiatry, 2,* 163–180; Verwoerdt, A., Pfeiffer, E., & Wang, H. S. (1969b). Sexual behavior in senescence: II: Patterns of change in sexual activity and interest. *Geriatrics, 24,* 163–180.

3. Masters, W., & Johnson, V. (1970). *Human sexual response.* Boston: Little, Brown, and Company.

4. Crowley, C., & Lodge, H. S. (2004). *Younger next year: A guide to living like 50 until you're 80 and beyond.* New York: Workman Publishing.

5. Crowley & Lodge (2004), p. 286.

6. Rowe, J. W., & Kahn, R. L. (1999). *Successful aging.* New York: Dell, p. 32.

7. Rowe & Kahn (1999).

8. Rowe & Kahn (1999).

9. Crowley & Lodge (2004), p. 287.

10. Crowley & Lodge (2004), p. 287.

11. Shippen, E., & Fryer, W. (1998). *The testosterone syndrome: The critical factor for energy, health, and sexuality—reversing the male menopause.* New York: M. Evans and Company.

12. Shippen & Fryer (1998), p. 4.

13. Shippen & Fryer (1998), p. 4.

14. Liverman, C. T., & Blazer, D. G. (Eds.). (2004). *Testosterone and aging: Clinical research directions.* Washington, DC: The National Academies Press, pp. 24–25.

15. Rose, K. (2003). Extent and nature of testosterone use. Presentation at the March 21, 2003, Workshop of the Institute of Medicine Committee on Assessing the Need for Clinical Trials of Testosterone Replacement Therapy, Phoenix, AZ.

16. Liverman & Blazer (2004), p. 25.

17. Liverman & Blazer (2004), pp. 87–88.

18. Shippen & Fryer (1998), p. 108.

19. Erectile Dysfunction or Impotence. (2007). Retrieved from www.urologychannel.com.

20. Erectile Dysfunction or Impotence (2007).

21. Erectile Dysfunction. (2007). Retrieved from www.mayoclinic.com/health/erectile-dysfunction.

22. Erectile Dysfunction (2007).

23. Erectile Dysfunction or Impotence (2007).

24. Erectile Dysfunction or Impotence (2007).

CHAPTER EIGHT

1. Seligman, M.E.P. (1990). *Learned optimism.* New York: Simon & Shuster.
2. Seligman (1990), p. 53.
3. Kart, G. S. (1990). *The realities of aging.* Boston: Allyn and Bacon.

CHAPTER NINE

1. Vaillant, G. E. (2002). *Aging well: Surprising guideposts to a happier life from the land-mark Harvard study of adult development.* New York: Little, Brown and Company, p. 278. Courtesy of Little, Brown and Company.
2. Erikson, E. H. (1950). *Childhood and society.* New York: Norton.
3. Perls, T. T., Silver, M. H., & Lauerman, J. F. (1999). *Living to 100: Lessons in living to your maximum potential at any age.* New York: Basic Books.
4. Trafford, A. (2004). *My time: Making the most of the bonus decades after 50.* New York: Basic Books, p. 240.
5. Trafford (2004), p. 241.
6. Neill, C. M., & Kahn, A. S. (1999). The role of personal spirituality and religious social activity on the life satisfaction of older retired women. *Sex Roles: A Journal of Research, 40*(3–4), 319–327.
7. Vaillant (2002), p. 260.
8. Vaillant (2002), p. 261.
9. Vaillant (2002), pp. 259, 260.
10. Trafford (2004), p. 239.
11. Koenig, H. G. (2000). Religion, spirituality, and medicine: An application to clinical practice. *Journal of the American Medical Association, 284,* 1708.
12. Matthews, D. A., & Clark, C. (1998). *The faith factor.* New York: Viking.
13. Koenig, H. G., & Lawson, D. M. (2004). *Faith in the future: Healthcare, aging, and the role of religion.* Radnor, PA: Templeton Foundation.
14. Risberg, T., Wist, E., Kaasa, S., Lund, E., & Norum, J. (1996). Spiritual healing among Norwegian hospitalized cancer patients and patients' religious needs and preferences of pastoral services. *European Journal of Cancer, 32a,* 274–281.
15. Shuler, P. A., Gelberg, L., & Brown, M. (1994). The effects of spiritual/religious practices on psychological well-being among inner city homeless women. *Nurse Practitioner Forum, 5*(2), 106–113; Gordon, P. A., Feldman, D., Crose, R., Schoen, E., Griffing, G., & Shankar, J. (2002). The role of religious beliefs in coping with chronic illness. *Counseling and Values, 46,* 162–168.
16. Durkheim, E. (1951 [1897]). *Suicide.* Translated by J. A. Spaulding & G. Simpson. New York: Free Press; Durkheim, E. (1965 [1915]). *Elementary forms of the religious life.* Translated by Joseph W. Swain. New York: Free Press.
17. Idler, E. L., & Kasl, S. V. (1991). Health perceptions ad survival: Do global evaluations of health status really predict mortality? *Journal of Gerontology: Social Sciences, 46,* S55–S65.
18. Levin, J. S., & Schiller, P. L. (1987). Is there a religious factor in health? *Journal of Religion and Health, 26,* 9–36.
19. Berger, P. L. (1967). *The sacred canopy: Elements of a sociological theory of religion.* New York: Doubleday.
20. Idler, E. L. (1987). Religious involvement and the health of the elderly: Some hypotheses and an initial test. *Social Forces, 66,* 226–238; Idler, E. L. (1993). *Cohesiveness and coherence: Religion and the health of the elderly.* New York: Garland.

21. Lewis, C. S. (1996 [1940]). *The problem of pain.* San Francisco: HarperCollins.

22. Idler (1987).

23. Berger (1967).

24. Koenig, H. G. (1993). Religion and hope for the disabled elder. In J. Levin (Ed.), *Religion in aging and health* (pp. 18–51). Thousand Oaks, CA: Sage.

25. Pollner, M. (1989). Divine relations, social relations, and well-being. *Journal of Health and Social Behavior, 30,* 92–102.

26. Schoenfeld, D. E., Malmrose, L. C., Blaser, D. G., Gold, D. T., & Seeman, T. E. (1994). Self-rated health and mortality in the high-functioning elderly: A closer look at healthy individuals: MacArthur Field Study of Successful Aging. *Journal of Gerontology: Medical Sciences, 49,* M109–M115.

27. Feinberg, S. E., Loftus, E. F., & Tanur, T. L. (1983) Cognitive aspects of health survey methodology: An overview. *Milbank Memorial Fund Quarterly, 63,* 547–564; Groves, R. M., Fultz, N. H., & Martin, E. (1992). Direct questioning about comprehension in a survey setting. In J. M. Tanur (Ed.), *Questions about questions: Inquires into the cognitive bases of surveys* (pp. 49–61). Russell Sage; Schecter, S. (Ed.). (1994). Proceedings of the 1993 NCHS Cognitive aspects of Self-Reported Health Status Hyattsville, MD.

28. Charmaz, K. (1991). *Good days, bad days: The self in chronic illness and time.* New Brunswick, NJ: Rutgers University Press.

29. Blazer, D., & Palmore, E. (1976). Religion and aging in a longitudinal panel. *The Gerontologist, 16,* 82–84; Hadaway, C. K. (1978). Life satisfaction and religion: A reanalysis. *Social Forces, 57,* 636–643; Steinitz, L. (1980). Religiosity, well-being, and weltanschauung among the elderly. *Journal for the Scientific Study of Religion, 19,* 60–67.

30. Hunsberger, B. E. (1985). Religion, age, life satisfaction, and perceived sources of religiousness: A study of older persons. *Journal of Gerontology, 40,* 615–620.

31. Coke, M. M., & Twaite, J. A. (1995). *The black elderly: Satisfaction and quality of later life.* New York: Haworth.

32. Diener, E., Emmons, R. A., Larsen, R. J., & Griffen, S. (1985). The Satisfaction with Life Scale: A measure of global life satisfaction. *Journal of Personality Assessment, 40,* 71–75.

33. Trafford (2004), p. 232.

34. Trafford (2004), p. 239.

35. Hollis, J. (2005). *Finding meaning in the second half of life.* New York: Gotham Books, p. 185.

36. Hollis (2005), p. 204.

CHAPTER TEN

1. Trafford, A. (2004). *My time: Making the most of the bonus decades after 50.* New York: Basic Books, p. xxii.

2. Rowe, J. W., & Kahn, R. L. (1999). *Successful aging.* New York: Random House, p. 165.

3. For example, Erikson stated that Freud defined mental health as the ability to love and to work (Erikson, E. [1950]. *Childhood and society.* New York: Norton). Hazan and Shaver stated that "Freud is purported to have said that the goal of psychotherapy is to allow the patient to love and to work" (Hazan, C., & Shaver, P. R. [1990]. Love and work: An attachment perspective. *Journal of Personality and Social Psychology, 59,* 270–280). Brodie stated that "Freud said that man has two basic needs: work and love" (Brodie, R. [1999]. *Love and work.* Retrieved from www.memecentral.com/L3LoveandWork.htm).

4. Freud, S. (1930). *Civilization and its discontents.* (Standard Edition, vol. XXI). London: Hogarth Press, p. 101.

5. Erikson (1950); Maslow, A. H. (1968). *Toward a psychology of being* (2nd ed.). Princeton: Van Nostrand.

6. Morrow-Howell, N., Hinterlung, J., & Sherraden, M. (2003). Development of institutional capacity for elder service. *Social Development Issues, 25*(1/2), 189–204.

7. Morrow-Howell, Hinterlung, & Sherraden (2003).

8. Harlow-Rosentraub, K., Wilson, L., & Steele, J. (2006). Expanding youth service concepts for older adults: Americorps results. In L. Wilson & S. Simpson (Eds.), *Civic engagement and the baby boomer generation: Research, policy, and practice perspectives.* New York: Haworth Press.

9. Creighton, S., & Hudson, L. (2002). *Participation trends and patterns in adult education: 1991 to 1999 (NCES 2002–119).* U.S. Department of Education. Washington, DC: National Center for Education Statistics; Kim, K., & Creighton, S. (2000). *Participation in adult education in the United States: 1998–99 (NCES 2000–027).* U.S. Department of Education. Washington, DC: National Center for Education Statistics.

10. Leider, R. J., & Shapiro, D. (2004). *Claiming your place at the fire: Living the second half of your life on purpose.* San Francisco: Berrett-Koehler, p. vii. Reprinted with permission of the publisher. From *Claiming Your Place at the Fire,* copyright © 2004 by Richard Leider and David Shapiro, Berrett-Koehler Publishers, Inc., San Francisco, CA. All rights reserved. www.bkconnection.com.

CHAPTER ELEVEN

1. AARP. (2007). Retirement planning: Deciding when to retire. Retrieved from www.aarp.org/money/financial_planning.

2. Brain, M. (2007). Understanding and controlling your finances: Retirement planning. Retrieved from www.bygpub.com/finance/finance7.htm.

3. Brain (2007).

4. University of Iowa Extension Service. (2007). Retirement: Secure your dreams: Begin planning today. Retrieved from www.extension.iastate.edu/finances.

5. University of Iowa Extension Service (2007).

6. Bedel, E. E. (2007). Retirement planning: When to start Social Security benefits. Retrieved from www.aarp.org/money/financial_planning.

7. Bedel (2007).

8. Bedel (2007).

CHAPTER TWELVE

1. Bucholz, K. K., Sheline, Y., & Helzer, J. E. (1995). The epidemiology of alcohol use, problems, and dependence in elders: A review. In T. Beresford & E. Gomberg (Eds.), *Alcohol and aging* (pp. 19–41). New York: Oxford University Press.

2. Quoted in Kaplan, A. (2005). Alcohol and drug dependence in older adults. *Geriatric Times, 1*(3) 1–4. Retrieved from www.cmellc.com/geriatrictimes/g0011023.html.

3. Schuckit, M. A. (1999). *Drug and alcohol abuse: A clinical guide to diagnosis and treatment* (5th ed.). New York: Kluwer Academic Press.

4. Rigler, S. K. (2000). Alcoholism in the family. *American Family Physician 61*(6), 1710–1716.

5. Substance Abuse and Mental Health Services Administration. (2003). *2003 Treatment Episode Data Set* (TEDS). Retrieved from https://ncadistore.samhsa.gov/catalog.

6. Quoted in 4Therapy.com Network. (2007). Older men more likely to seek treatment for alcohol. Retrieved from www.4Therapy.com/consumer/life_topics/article/84444.

7. National Institute on Alcohol Abuse and Alcoholism. (2007). Does alcohol affect older people differently? *FAQs for the General Public.* Retrieved from http://www.niaaa.nih.gov/FAQs.

8. American Psychiatric Association. (2000). *Diagnostic and statistical manual of mental disorders* (4th ed., text rev.). Washington, DC: Author.

9. Surgeon General. (2007). *Mental health: A report of the Surgeon General.* Retrieved from www.surgeongeneral.gov/library/mentalhelath/chapter5.

10. Special Committee on Aging. (1987). *Medicare prescription drug issues: Report to the chairman, Special Committee on Aging.* Washington, DC: General Accounting Office.

11. Kofoed, L. L. (1984). Abuse and misuse of over-the-counter drugs by the elderly. In R. M. Atkinson (Ed.), *Alcohol and drug abuse in old age* (pp. 49–59). Washington, DC: American Psychiatric Press.

12. Schuckit, M. A. (1999). New findings in the genetics of alcoholism. *Journal of the American Medical Association, 281*(20), 1875–1876.

13. Finlayson, R. E., & Davis, L. J. (1994). Prescription drug dependence in the elderly population: Demographic and clinical features of 100 inpatients. *Mayo Clinic Proceedings, 69,* 1137–1145.

14. Robins, C., & Clayton, R. R. (1989). Gender-related differences in psychoactive drug use among older adults. *Journal of Drug Issues, 19,* 207–219.

15. Elseviers, M. M., & DeBroe, M. E. (1998). Analgesic abuse in the elderly: Renal sequelae and management. *Drugs & Aging, 12,* 391–400.

16. Regier, D. A., Boyd, J. H., Burke, J. D., Rae, D. S., Myers, J. K., Kramer, M., et al. (1988). One-month prevalence of mental disorders in the United States based on five Epidemiologic Catchment Area sites. *Archives of General Psychiatry, 45,* 977–986.

CHAPTER THIRTEEN

1. Trafford, A. (2004). *My time: Making the most of the bonus decades after 50.* New York: Basic Books.

2. Williams, A., & Nussbaum, J. F. (2001). *Intergenerational communication across the life span.* Mahwah, NJ: Lawrence Erlbaum Associates, p. 151.

3. Nussbaum, J. E, Hummert, M. L., Williams, A., & Harwood, J. (1995). Communication and older adults. In B. Burleson (Ed.), *Communication yearbook 19* (pp. 1–47). Thousand Oaks, CA: Sage.

4. Williams & Nussbaum (2001), p. 162.

5. Lye, D. N. (1996). Adult-child relationships. *Annual Review of Sociology, 22,* 79–98.

6. Lye, D. N., Klepinger, D., Hyle, P. D., & Nelson, A. (1995). Childhood living arrangements and adult children's relations with their parents. *Demography, 32,* 261–280.

7. Coke, M. M., & Twaite, J. A. (1995). *The black elderly: Satisfaction and quality of later life.* Binghamton, NY: Haworth Press.

8. For example, Lye (1996) reported that researchers had employed all of the following techniques to assess the quality of adult child-elderly parent relationships: (1) single item relationship rating scales (e.g., Aquilino, W. S. [1994]. The impact of childhood family disruption on young adults' relationships with parents. *Journal of Marriage and the Family, 56,* 296–313); (2) multi-item scale measures of relationship quality (e.g., Booth, A., & Amato, P. R. [1994]. Parental marital quality, parental divorce and relations with parents. *Journal of Marriage and the Family, 56,* 21–34; and Cooney, T. M. [1994].

Young adults' relations with parents: The influence of recent parental divorce. *Journal of Marriage and the Family, 56*, 45–56); (3) measures of feelings of attachment and closeness (e.g., Lawton, L., Silverstein, M., & Bengston, V. L. [1994]. Solidarity between generations in families. In V. L. Bengston & R. A. Harootyan (Eds.), *Intergenerational linkages: Hidden connections in American society* [pp. 19–42]. New York: Springer); (4) measures of the exchange of emotional support and advice (e.g., Umberson, D. [1992]. Relationships between adult children and their parents: Psychological consequences for both generations. *Journal of Marriage and the Family, 45*, 841–849); (5) measures of strain and parental dissatisfaction with adult children (e.g., Umberson, [1992]); and (6) measures of disagreement (e.g., Aldous, J. [1995]. New views of grandparents in intergenerational context. *Journal of Family Issues, 16*, 104–122). Lye (1996) reviewed these diverse studies and concluded that regardless of the measure of relationship quality employed, adult children and their parents were close.

    9. Lawton, Silverstein, & Bengston (1994).

    10. Cooney, T. M., & Uhlenberg, P. (1992). Support from parents over the life course: The adult child's perspective. *Social Forces, 71*, 63–84.

    11. Antonucci, T. C., & Akiyama, H. (1987). Social networks in adult life and a preliminary examination of the convoy model. *Journal of Gerontology, 42*, 519–27; Becker, G. S. (1981). *A treatise on the family.* Cambridge, MA: Harvard University Press; Hogan, D. P., Eggebeen, D. J., & Clogg, C. C. (1993). The structure of intergenerational exchanges in American families. *American Journal of Sociology, 98*, 1428–1458.

    12. Aldous (1995).

    13. Clark, M., & Anderson, B. (1967). *Culture and aging.* Springfield, IL: Charles C. Thomas, Publisher.

    14. Williams & Nussbaum (2001), p. 184.

    15. Nussbaum et al. (1995), p. 153.

    16. Nydegger, C. N. (1986). Asymmetrical kin and the problematic son-in-law. In N. Datan, A. L. Greene, & H. W. Reese (Eds.), *Life-span developmental psychology: Intergenerational relations* (pp. 99–123). Hillsdale, NJ: Lawrence Erlbaum Associates.

    17. Hollis, J. (2005). *Finding meaning in the second half of life.* New York: Gotham Books, p. 138.

    18. Hollis (2005), p. 139.

CHAPTER FOURTEEN

    1. Kart, C. S. (1990). *The realities of aging: An introduction to gerontology* (3rd ed.). Boston: Allyn and Bacon.

    2. Neugarten, B., & Weinstein, K. (1964). The changing American grandparent. *Journal of Marriage and the Family, 26*(2), 199–204.

    3. Goodfellow, J. (2003). Grandparents as regular child care providers: Unrecognised, under-values and under-resourced. *Australian Journal of Early Childhood, 28*(3), 7–20.

    4. Trafford, A. (2004). *My time: Making the most of the bonus decades after fifty.* New York: Basic Books, p. 225.

    5. Kornhaber, A. (1996). *Contemporary grandparenting.* Thousand Oaks, CA: Sage.

    6. Goodfellow (2003).

    7. Davies, C. (2002). *The grandparent study 2002 report.* Washington, DC: AARP.

    8. Davies (2002), p. 34.

    9. Fuller-Thomson, E., Minkler, M., & Driver, D. (1997). A profile of grandparents raising grandchildren in the United States. *The Gerontologist, 37*(3), 406–411.

10. Pyle, R. (2002). Providing critical tools for grandparents raising grandchildren. Grandparent Resource Center, New York City Department for the aging. Retrieved from http://www.naswncy.org/g5.html.

11. Hagestad, G., & Neugarten, B. (1985). Age and the life course. In R. Binstock & R. Shanas (Eds.), *Handbook of aging and the social sciences.* New York: Van Nostrand Reinhold.

12. Burton, L. M., Dilworth-Anderson, P., & Merriwether-de-Vries, C. (1995). Context of surrogate parenting among contemporary grandparents. *Marriage and Family Review, 20,* 349–366; Pinson-Millburn, N. M., Fabian, E. S., Schlossberg, N. K., & Pyle, M. (1996). Grandparents raising grandchildren. *Journal of Counseling and Development, 74,* 548–554.

13. Morrow-Kondos, D., Weber, J.A.Q., Cooper, K., & Hesser, J. L. (1997). Becoming parents again: Grandparents raising grandchildren. *Journal of Gerontological Social Work, 28*(1/2), 35–46.

14. Minkler, M., Fuller-Thomson, E., Miller, D., & Driver, D. (2000). Grandparent caregiving and depression. In B. Hayslip & R. Goldberg-Glen (Eds.), *Grandparents raising grandchildren: Theoretical, empirical, and clinical perspectives* (pp. 207–220). New York: Springer; Solomon, J. C., & Marx, J. (2000). The physical, mental, and social health of custodial grandparents. In B. Hayslip & R. Goldberg-Glen (Eds.), *Grandparents raising grandchildren: Theoretical, empirical, and clinical perspectives* (pp. 183–206). New York: Springer.

15. Silverthorn, P., & Durant, S. L. (2000). Custodial grandparenting and the difficult child: Learning from the parenting literature. In B. Hayslip & R. Goldberg-Glen (Eds.), *Grandparents raising grandchildren: Theoretical, empirical, and clinical perspectives* (pp. 47–64). New York: Springer.

16. Gomez, K. A., Haiken, H. J., & Lewis, S. Y. (1995). Support group for children with HIV/AIDS. In N. Boyd-Franklin, G. L. Steiner, & M. G. Boland (Eds.), *Children, families, and HIV/AIDS: Psychosocial and therapeutic issues* (pp. 156–166). New York: Guilford Press; Herek, G. M. (1999). AIDS and stigma. *American Behavioral Scientist, 42*(7), 1106–1116; Landau, S., Pryor, J. P., & Haefli, K. (1995). Pediatric HIV: School-based sequelae and curricular interventions for infection prevention and social acceptance. *School Psychology Review, 24*(2), 213–229.

17. Hirshorn, B. A., Van Meter, M. J., & Brown, D. R. (2000). When grandparents raise grandchildren due to substance abuse: Responding to a uniquely destabilizing factor. In B. Hayslip & R. Goldberg-Glen (Eds.), *Grandparents raising grandchildren: Theoretical, empirical, and clinical perspectives* (pp. 269–288). New York: Springer.

18. Edwards, O. W. (1998). Helping grandkin—grandchildren raised by grandparents: Expanding psychology in the schools. *Psychology in the Schools, 35*(2), 173–180.

19. Herek (1999).

20. Chenoweth, L. (2000). Grandparent education. In B. Hayslip & R. Goldberg-Glen (Eds.), *Grandparents raising grandchildren: Theoretical, empirical, and clinical perspectives* (pp. 307–326). New York: Springer.

21. Albert, R. (2000). Legal issues for custodial grandparents. In B. Hayslip & R. Goldberg-Glen (Eds.), *Grandparents raising grandchildren: Theoretical, empirical, and clinical perspectives* (pp. 327–341). New York: Springer.

22. Grant, R., Gordon, S. G., & Cohen, S. T. (1997). An innovative school-based intergenerational model to serve grandparent caregivers. *Journal of Gerontological Social Work, 281*(1–2), 47–61.

23. Chenowith (2000).

24. Kelley, S. J. (1993). Caregiver stress in grandparents raising grandchildren. *Image: The Journal of Nursing Scholarship, 25*(4), 331–337.

25. Coke, M. M., & Twaite, J. A. (1995). *The black elderly: Satisfaction and quality of later life.* New York: Haworth.

26. Burton, L., & deVries, C. (1992). African American grandparents as surrogate parents. *Generations, 16,* 51–54; Burton, L. M., & Dilworth-Anderson, P. (1991). The intergenerational roles of aged black Americans. *Marriage and Family Review, 16,* 311–330.

27. Burnette, D. (1997). Grandparents raising grandchildren in the inner city. *Families in Society: The Journal of Contemporary Human Services, 72*(September–October), 489–499; Burnette, D. (1998). Grandparents rearing grandchildren: A school-based small group intervention. *Research on Social Work Practice, 8*(1), 10–27; Woodworth, R. S. (1996). You're not alone…You're one in a million. *Child Welfare, 75*(5), 619–635.

CHAPTER FIFTEEN

1. Beauchesne, E., & Morris, H. (2007, September 27). Older couples at odds over retirement. Saskatoon Star Phoenix. Retrieved from http://www.canada.com/saskatoonstarphoenix.

2. Bair, D. (2007). *Calling it quits: Late-life divorce and starting over.* New York: Random House, p. xiv.

3. Bair (2007), p. 4.

CHAPTER SIXTEEN

1. Farberman, H. A. (2003). A survey of family care giving to elders in Suffolk County, New York. (Unpublished survey.) Courtesy of VanderWyk and Burnham.

2. Hawthorne, L. S. (2006). *Husbands and wives all these years: From caring to caretaking.* Acton, MA: VanderWyk & Burnham.

3. Hawthorne (2006), p. 17.

4. Farberman (2003), p. 27.

5. Hawthorne (2006), p. 25.

6. Cahill, S. (2000). Elderly husbands caring at home for wives diagnosed with Alzheimer's disease: Are male caregivers really different? *Australian Journal of Social Issues, 35*(1), 53–59.

7. Twig, J., & Atkin, K. (1995). Carers and services: Factors mediating service provision. *Journal of Social Policy, 24*(1), 5–30.

8. Miller, B., & Guo, S. (2000). Social support for spouse caregivers of persons with dementia. *Journal of Gerontology, 558,* 5163–5172.

9. Coe, M., & Neufield, A. (1999). Male caregivers' use of formal support. *Western Journal of Nursing Research, 21,* 568–588.

10. Kramer, B. J. (2002). Husbands caring for wives with dementia: A longitudinal study of continuity and change. *Health and Social Work, 25*(2), 97–104.

11. Archer, C. K., & MacLean, M. J. (1993). Husbands and sons of caregivers of chronically-ill elderly women. *Journal of Gerontological Social Work, 21*(1/2), 5–23.

12. Parsons, K. (1997). The male experience of caregiving for a family member with Alzheimer's disease. *Qualitative Health Research, 7,* 391–407.

13. Russell, R. (2004). Social networks among elderly men caregivers. *The Journal of Men's Studies, 13*(1), 121.

14. Slotkin, J. (2001, April 9–12). Invisible labor in patriarchal capitalism: Demystifying women's unwaged domestic work. Paper presented at the Southern Sociological Society, Richmond, VA.

15. Bedini, L. A., & Guinan, D. M. (1996). The leisure of caregivers of older adults: Implications for CTRS's in non-traditional settings. *Therapeutic Recreation Journal, 30*(4), 274–288.

16. Dunn, N. J., & Strain, L. A. (2002). Caregivers at risk? Changes in leisure participation. *The Journal of Leisure Research, 33*(1), 32–43.

17. Aronson, J. (1992). Women's sense of responsibility for the care of old people: But who else is going to do it? *Gender and Society, 6*(1), 8–29.

18. Brattain Rogers, N. (1997). Centrality of caregiving role and integration of leisure in everyday life: A naturalistic study of older wife caregivers. *Therapeutic Recreation Journal, 31*(4), 230–243.

19. Rapp, S. R., Shumaker, S., Schmidt, S., & Anderson, R. (1998). Social resourcefulness: Its relationship to social support and well-being among caregivers to dementia victims. *Aging and Mental Health, 2*(1), 40–48.

20. Miller & Guo (2000).

21. Chappell, N. L., & Reid, R. C. (2002). Burden and well-being among caregivers: Examining the distinction. *The Gerontologist, 42,* 772–780.

22. Chang, B. H., Noonan, A. E., & Tennstedt, S. L. (1998). The role of religion/spirituality in coping with caregiving for disabled elders. *The Gerontologist, 38,* 463–470.

23. Farberman (2003), p. 33.

24. Cahill (2000), p. 53.

25. DeLongis, A., & O'Brien, T. (1990). An interpersonal framework for stress and coping: An application to the families of Alzheimer's patients. In M. A. Stevens, J. H. Crowther, S. E. Hobfoll, & D. L. Tennenbaum (Eds.), *Stress and coping in later-life families* (pp. 221–239). New York: Hemisphere Publishing Company.

26. Deimling, G. T., & Bass, D. M. (1986). Symptoms of mental impairment among elderly adults and their effects on family caregivers. *Journal of Gerontology, 41,* 778–784.

27. Chenowith, B., & Spencer, B. (1986). Dementia: The experience of family caregivers. *The Gerontologist, 26,* 267–272.

28. Brody, E. M. (1988). The long haul: A family odyssey. In L. F. Jarvik & C. H. Winograd (Eds.), *Treatments for the Alzheimer's patient: The long haul* (pp. 1–23). New York: Springer.

29. Cohen, D., & Eisdorfer, C. (1986). *The loss of self: A family resource for the care of Alzheimer's disease and related disorders.* New York: Norton.

30. DeLongis & O'Brien (1990), p. 223.

31. Mace, N., & Rabins, P. V. (1981). *The 36-hour day.* Baltimore, MD: The Johns Hopkins University Press.

32. Kaye, L. W., & Applegate, J. S. (1990). *Men as caregivers to the elderly: Understanding and aiding unrecognized family support.* Lexington, MA: Lexington Books.

33. Stephens, M.A.P., Kinney, J. M., & Ogrocki, P. K. (1991). Stressors and well-being among caregivers to older adults with dementia: The in-home versus nursing home experience. *The Gerontologist, 31,* 217–223.

34. Colerick, E. J., & George, L. K. (1986). A comprehensive approach to working with families of Alzheimer's patients. In R. Dobrof (Ed.), *Social work and Alzheimer's disease* (pp. 27–39). New York: Haworth Press; Cramer, B. J. (2000). Husbands caring for wives with dementia: A longitudinal study of continuity and change. *Health and Social Work, 25*(2), 97–104.

35. King, S., Collins, C., Given, B., & Vredevoogd, J. (1991). Institutionalization of an elderly family member: Reactions of spouse and nonspouse caregivers. *Archives of Psychiatric Nursing, 5*, 323–330.

36. Zarit, S. H., & Whitlach, C. J. (1993). The effects of placement in nursing homes on family caregivers: Short and long term consequences. *Irish Journal of Psychology, 14*, 25–37.

37. Rosenthal, C. J., & Dawson, P. (1991). Wives of institutionalized elderly men: The first stage of the transition to quasi-widowhood. *Journal of Aging and Health, 3*, 315–334.

38. Schultz, R., & Williamson, G. M. (1991). A 2-year longitudinal study of depression among Alzheimer's caregivers. *Journal of Psychology and Aging, 6*, 569–578; Wright, L. K. (1994). AD spousal caregivers: Longitudinal changes in health, depression, and coping. *Journal of Gerontological Nursing, 20*(10), 33–45.

CHAPTER SEVENTEEN

1. The leading causes of death today among those 65 years old or older are heart disease, cancer, cerebrovascular disease (stroke), chronic lower respiratory disease, influenza and pneumonia, and diabetes mellitus. Each of these diseases is typically accompanied by serious symptoms and disability. Approximately 20 percent of Americans over the age of 65 have some chronic disability, including arthritis, osteoporosis, and senile dementia. Olshansky, S. J., & Ault, A. B. (1986). The fourth stage of the epidemiologic transition: The age of delayed degenerative disease. *Milbank Memorial Fund Quarterly, 64*, 355–391.

2. Carr, D., Wortman, C. B., & Wolff, K. (2006). How older Americans die today: Implications for surviving spouses. In D. Carr, R. M. Nesse, & C. Wortment (Eds.), *Spousal bereavement in late life* (pp. 49–80). New York: Springer.

3. Brock, D., & Foley, D. (1998). Demography and epidemiology of dying in the U.S., with emphasis on the deaths of older persons. *The Hospice Journal, 13*, 49–60.

4. Lindeman, E. (1944). Symptomatology and management of acute grief. *American Journal of Psychiatry, 151*, 155–160.

5. Gerber, I., Rusalem, R., Hannon, N., Battin, D., & Arkin, A. (1975). Anticipatory grief and aged widows and widowers. *Journal of Gerontology, 30*, 225–229; Rando, T. A. (1986). A comprehensive analysis of anticipatory grief: Perspectives, processes, promises, and problems. In T. A. Rando (Ed.), *Loss and anticipatory grief* (pp. 3–38). Lexington, MA: Lexington Books; Vachon, M. L., Rogers, C., Lyall, J., Lancee, W., Sheldon, A., & Freeman, S. (1982). Stress reactions to bereavement. *Essence: Issues in the Study of Aging, Dying, and Death, 1*, 23–33.

6. Blauner, R. (1966). Death and social structure. *Psychiatry, 29*, 378–394.

7. Rando (1986).

8. Studies suggesting that forewarning is associated with better adjustment on the part of the surviving spouse include: Farberow, N. L., Gallagher-Thompson, D., Gilewski, M., & Thompson, L. (1992). Changes in the grief and mental health of bereaved spouses of older suicides. *Journal of Gerontology, 47*, 357–366; and Wells, Y. D., & Kendig, H. L. (1997). Health and well-being of spouse caregivers and the widowed. *The Gerontologist, 37*(5), 666–674. Studies suggesting that forewarning is associated with poor adjustment of the surviving spouse following the death include: Fengler, A. P., & Goodrich, R. (1979). Wives of elderly, disabled men: The hidden patients. *The Gerontologist, 19*(2), 175–183; and Sanders, C. M. (1982–1983). Effects of sudden vs. chronic illness on bereavement outcome. *Omega: The Journal of Death and Dying, 13*, 227–241.

9. Studies reporting no significant relationship between forewarning and the adjustment of the surviving spouse following a death include: Hill, C. D., Thompson, L. W., &

Gallagher, D. (1988). The role of anticipatory bereavement in older women's adjustment to widowhood. *The Gerontologist, 28*(6), 792–796; and Roach, M. J., & Kitson, C. (1989). Impact of forewarning on adjustment to widowhood and divorce. In D. A. Lund (Ed.), *Older bereaved spouses: Research with practical applications* (pp. 185–200). New York: Hemisphere Publishing.

10. Bennett, K. M. (1998). Longitudinal changes in mental and physical health among elderly, recently widowed men. *Mortality, 3,* 265–273.

11. Thompson, L. W., Breckenridge, J. N., Gallagher, D., & Peterson, J. (1984). Effects of bereavement on self-perceptions of physical health in elderly widows and widowers. *Journal of Gerontology, 39,* 309–314.

12. Bradbeer, M., Helme, R. D., & Young, H. (2003). Widowhood and other demographic associations of pain in independent older people. *Clinical Journal of Pain, 19,* 247–254.

13. Prigerson, H. G., Maciejewski, P. K., & Rosencheck, R. A. (2000). Preliminary explorations of the harmful interactive effects of widowhood and marital harmony on health, health service use, and health care costs. *The Gerontologist, 40,* 349–357.

14. Charlton, R., Sheahan, K., Smith, G., & Campbell, I. (2001). Spousal bereavement—Implications for health. *Family Practice, 18,* 614–618.

15. Clayton, P. J. (1998). The model of stress: The bereavement reaction. In B. P. Dohrenwend (Ed.), *Adversity, stress, and psychopathology* (pp. 96–110). London: Oxford University Press.

16. Hall, M., & Irwin, M. (2001). Physiological indices of functioning in bereavement. In M. S. Stroebe & R. O. Hansson (Eds.), *Handbook of bereavement research: Consequences, coping, and care* (pp. 473–492). Washington, DC: American Psychological Association.

17. Moss, M. S., Moss, S. Z., & Hansson, R. O. (2001). Bereavement in old age. In M. S. Stroebe & R. O. Hansson (Eds.), *Handbook of bereavement research: Consequences, coping and care* (pp. 241–260). Washington, DC: American Psychological Association.

18. Miller, E., & Wortman, C. B. (2002). Gender differences in mortality and morbidity following a major stressor: The case of conjugal bereavement. In G. Weidner, S. M. Kopp, & M. Kristenson (Eds.), *Heart disease: Environment, stress, and gender.* NATO Science Series, Series 1: Life and Behavioral Sciences. Volume 237. Amsterdam: IOS Press.

19. Wortman, C. B., & Silver, R. C. (2001). Successful mastery of bereavement and widowhood: A life course perspective. In P. B. Baltes & M. M. Baltes (Eds.), *Handbook of bereavement research: Consequences, coping and care* (pp. 405–430). Washington, DC: American Psychological Association Press.

20. Neugarten, B. L. (1968). *Middle age and aging: A reader in social psychology.* Chicago: University of Chicago Press.

21. Rosenzweig, A., Prigerson, H., Miller, H. D., & Reynolds, C. F. (1997). Bereavement and late life depression: Grief and its complications in the elderly. *Annual Review of Medicine, 48,* 421–428.

22. Baltes, M. M., & Skrotzki, E. (1995). Death in old age: Finality and the loss of spouse. In R. Oerter & L. Montada (Eds.), *Entwicklungpsychologie* (3rd ed., pp. 1137–1146). Munich, Germany: PVU.

23. Hayslip, B., & Panek, P. E. (2002). *Adult development and aging* (3rd ed.). Malabar, FL: Krieger Publishing, p. 197.

24. Moss et al. (2001).

25. Lund, D. A., Caserta, M. S., & Diamond, M. F. (1993). The course of spousal bereavement in later life. In M. S. Stroebe & W. Stroebe (Eds.), *Handbook of bereavement: Theory, research, and intervention* (pp. 240–254). New York: Cambridge University Press.

26. U.S. Bureau of the Census. (2002). *Current population survey (CPS) reports: Detailed tables for current population report, P20–547.* Washington, DC: U.S. Government Printing Office.

27. Schneider, D. S., Sledge, P. A., Shucter, S.R., & Zishook, S. (1996). Dating and remarriage over the first two years of widowhood. *Annals of Clinical Psychiatry, 8,* 51–57.

28. Goldman, N., Korenman, S., & Weinstein, R. (1995). Marital status and health among the elderly. *Social Science and Medicine, 40,* 1717–1730.

29. Fry, P. S. (2001). The unique contribution of key existential factors to the prediction of psychological well-being of older adults following spousal loss. *The Gerontologist, 41*(1), 69–81.

30. Lee, G. R., DeMaris, A., Bavin, S., & Sullivan, R. (2001). Gender differences in the depressive effect of widowhood in later life. *Journals of Gerontology: Series B: Psychological Sciences & Social Sciences, 56B*(1), 56–61.

31. Christakis, N., & Iwashyna, T. (2003). The health impact of health care on families: A matched cohort study of hospice use by decedents and mortality outcomes in surviving, widowed spouses. *Social Science and Medicine, 57*(3), 465–475.

32. Li, G. (1995). The interaction effect of bereavement and sex on the risk of suicide in the elderly: A historical cohort study. *Social Science and Medicine, 40,* 825–828.

33. Wolff, K., & Wortman, C. B. (2006). Psychological consequences of spousal loss among older adults: Understanding the diversity of responses. In D. Carr, R. M. Nesse, & C. B. Wortman (Eds.), *Spousal bereavement in late life* (pp. 81–115). New York: Springer.

34. Stroebe, M. S., & Stroebe, W. (1983). Who suffers more? Sex differences in health risks of the widowed. *Psychological Bulletin, 93,* 279–301.

35. Wolff & Wortman (2006), p. 98.

36. Umberson, D., Wortman, C. B., & Kessler, R. C. (1992). Widowhood and depression: Explaining long-term gender differences in vulnerability. *Journal of Health and Social Behavior, 33,* 10–24.

37. Miller & Wortman (2002).

38. Barnett, R. (2004). Women and multiple roles: Myths and reality. *Harvard Review of Psychiatry, 12*(3), 158–164.

39. The Shell Poll. (2000). *Women on the move.* Shell Oil Company. Retrieved from http://www.shellus.com.

40. Utz, R., Reidy, E., Carr, D., Nesse, R. M., & Wortman, C. B. (2004). The daily consequences of widowhood: The role of gender and intergenerational transfers on subsequent housework performance. *Journal of Family Issues, 25*(5), 683–712.

41. Umberson, D. (1992). Gender, marital status, and the social control of health behavior. *Social Science and Medicine, 34,* 907–917.

42. Umberson (1992).

43. Freud (1917/1957). Mourning and melancholia. In J. Strachey (Ed.), *The standard edition of the complete works of Sigmund Freud* (vol. 14, pp. 152–170). London: Hogarth Press; Bowlby, J. (1980). *Loss: Sadness and depression* (vol. 3). New York: Basic Books.

44. Bonanno, G. A., Notarious, C. I., Gunzerath, L., Keltner, D., & Horowitz, M. J. (2002). When avoiding unpleasant emotion might not be such a bad thing: Verbal-autonomic response dissociation and midlife conjugal bereavement. *Journal of Consulting and Clinical Psychology, 66*(6), 1012–1022; Carr, D., House, J. S., Kessler, R. C., Nesse, R. M., Sonnega, J., & Wortman, C. (2000). Marital quality and psychological adjustment to widowhood among older adults: A longitudinal analysis. *Journal of Gerontology: Series B: Psychological Sciences & Social Sciences, 55B*(4), S197–S207.

45. Pargament, K. I., & Park, C. L. (1995). Merely a defense? The variety of religious means and ends. *Journal of Social Issues, 51,* 13–32; Park, C. L., & Cohen, L. H. (1993).

Religious and nonreligious coping with the death of a friend. *Cognitive Therapy and Research, 17,* 561–577.

46. Kirkpatrick, L. A. (1997). A longitudinal study of changes in religious belief and behavior as a function of individual differences in adult attachment style. *Journal for the Scientific Study of Religion, 2,* 3–28.

47. Clayton, P. J. (1998). The model of stress: The bereavement reaction. In B. P. Dohrenwend (Ed.), *Adversity, stress, and psychopathology* (pp. 96–110). London: Oxford University Press; Stroebe, W., & Schut, H. (2001). Risk factors in bereavement outcome: A methodological and empirical review. In H. Schut (Ed.), *Handbook of bereavement research: Consequences, coping and care* (pp. 349–371). Washington, DC: American Psychological Association.

48. Stroebe, M., Stroebe, W., & Schut, H. (2001). Gender differences in adjustment to bereavement: An empirical and theoretical review. *Review of General Psychology, 5,* 62–83.

49. Nolen-Hoeksema, S., & Larson, J. (1999). *Coping with loss.* Mahwah, NJ: Lawrence Erlbaum Associates.

50. Taylor, J., & Turner, J. (2001). A longitudinal study of the role and significance of mattering to other for depressive symptoms. *Journal of Health and Social Behavior, 42,* 310–325.

51. Brown, S. L., Nesse, R., House, J. S., & Utz, R. L. (2004). Religion and emotional compensation: Results from a prospective study of widowhood. *Personality and Social Psychology Bulletin, 30,* 1165–1174.

52. Kart, C. S. (1981). *The realities of aging: An introduction to gerontology* (3rd ed.). Boston: Allyn and Bacon.

53. Lindeman (1944).

54. Neimeyer, R. A. (2006). Widowhood, grief, and the quest for meaning: A narrative perspective on resilience. In D. Carr, R. M. Nesse, & C. B. Wortman (Eds.), *Spousal bereavement in late life* (pp. 227–252). New York: Springer.

55. Neimeyer (2006), p. 240.

56. Neimeyer, R. A., Prigerson, H., & Davies, B. (2002). Mourning and meaning. *American Behavioral Scientist, 46,* 235–251.

57. Prigerson, H. G., & Jacobs, S. C. (2001). Diagnostic criteria for traumatic grief. In M. S. Stroebe, R. O. Hansson, W. Stroebe, & H. Schut (Eds.), *Handbook of bereavement research* (pp. 614–646). Washington, DC: American Psychological Association.

58. Bonanno, G. A., Wortman, C. B., & Nesse, R. M. (2004). Prospective patterns of resilience and maladjustment during widowhood. *Psychology and Aging, 19,* 260–271.

59. Neimeyer et al. (2002).

60. Bonanno et al. (2002).

61. Bonanno et al. (2002).

62. Neimeyer (2006), p. 235.

63. Bonanno et al. (2002).

CHAPTER EIGHTEEN

1. Bair, D. (2007). *Calling it quits: Late-life divorce and starting over.* New York: Random House; Wolf, K., & Wortman, C. B. (2006). Psychological consequences of spousal loss among older adults; Understanding the diversity of responses. In D. Carr, R. M. Nesse, & C. B. Wortman, (Eds.), *Spousal bereavement in late life* (pp. 81–115). New York: Springer.

2. Bair (2007), p. 243.

3. Davidson, K. (2001). Late life widowhood, selfishness and new partnership choices: A gendered perspective. *Aging and Society, 21*, 362–371.

4. Schneider, D. S., Sledge, P. A., Shuchter, S. R., & Zisook, S. (1996). Dating and re-marriage over the first two years of widowhood. *Annals of Clinical Psychiatry, 8*, 51–57.

5. Gentry, M., & Schulman, A. D. (1988). Remarriage as a coping response for widow-hood. *Psychology and Aging, 3*(2), 191–196.

6. Schneider et al. (1996).

7. Davidson (2001).

8. Carr, D. (2004). The desire to date and remarry among older widows and widowers. *Journal of Marriage and the Family, 66*, 220–235.

9. Carr (2004).

CHAPTER NINETEEN

1. U.S. Senate Special Committee on Aging. (1986). *Aging America: Trends and predictions.* Washington, DC: U.S. Government Printing Office.

2. Havighurst, R. (1969). Research and development goals in social gerontology. *Gerontologist, 9*, 1–90.

3. Chapman, N. J., & Beaudet, M. (1983). Environmental predictors of well-being for at-risk older adults in a mid-sized city. *Journal of Gerontology, 38*(2), 237–244.

4. Senioroutlook.com, An after 55 Housing and Resource Guide. (2007, October 10). Types of senior housing facilities and services. Retrieved from http://www.senioroutlook. com.

5. Senioroutlook.com (2007).

6. Eckert, J. K. (1980). *The unseen elderly: A study of marginally subsistent hotel dwellers.* San Diego, CA: Campanile Press.

CHAPTER TWENTY

1. AARP. (2007). Saving money: Inheritance tips. Retrieved from www.aarp.org/ money/financial_planning/sessionfour/inheritance_tips.html.

2. CNN. (2007). Estate planning: Top things to know. Retrieved from http: money.cnn. com/magazines/moneymag/money101/lesson21.

3. CNN (2007).

4. AARP. (2007). Private insurance: When you're losing your group health insurance. Retrieved from http://www.aarp.org/health/insurance/private.

5. AARP. (2007). Insurance: Long-term care insurance. Retrieved from http://www. aarp.org/money/financial_planning/sessionfive/longterm_care-insurances.

CHAPTER TWENTY-ONE

1. Butler, R. N. (1969). Age-ism: Another form of bigotry. *The Gerontologist, 9*, 243–246.

2. Butler, R. N. (1975). *Why survive? Being old in America.* New York: Harper and Row.

3. Palmore, E. (1990). *Ageism: Negative and positive.* New York: Springer, pp. 151–152.

4. Griffith, R. W. (2003). What is ageism, and how should we combat it? Retrieved from http://www.healthandage.com/public/health-center/40/article.

5. Dittman, M. (2003). Fighting ageism. APA Online: Monitor on Psychology. Retrieved from http://www.apa.org/monitor/may03/fighting.html.

6. Dittman (2003).

7. Robinson, B. (1994). *Ageism.* Berkeley, CA: The Academic Geriatric Resource Program, University of California, Berkeley.

8. AARP. (2007). Job loss help: Age discrimination at work. Retrieved from http://aarp.org/money/careers/jobloss/a2004–04–28-agediscrimination.html.

9. U.S. Equal Employment Opportunity Commission. (2007). Facts about age discrimination. Retrieved from http://www.eeoc.gov/facts/age.html.

10. Net Industries. (2007). Age discrimination: Older patients in the health care system. Retrieved from http://medicine.jrank.org/pages/48/Age-Discrimination-Older-patients-in-health-care-system.html.

11. Net Industries (2007).

12. Net Industries (2007).

13. Palmore (1990).

14. Solomon, K. (1981). The depressed patient: Social antecedents of psychopathologic changes in the elderly. *Journal of the American Geriatric Society, 29,* 14–17.

15. Dittman (2003).

16. Dittman (2003).

17. Butler (1975).

18. Palmore (1990).

19. Adapted from Kuypers, J. A., & Bengston, V. L. (1984). The cycle of structurally induced dependence. In W. H. Quinn & G. A. Hugston (Eds.), *Independent ageing.* Rockville, MD: Aspen Publications.

20. Palmore (1990), p. 152.

CHAPTER TWENTY-TWO

1. Hollis, J. (2005). *Finding meaning in the second half of life: How to finally, really grow up.* New York: Gotham Books, p. 209.

2. Erikson, E. (1950). *Childhood and society.* New York: Norton.

3. Knight, B. G. (1996). Overview of psychotherapy with the elderly: A contextual cohort based maturity specific-challenge model. In S. Zarit & B. Knight (Eds.), *A guide to psychotherapy and aging* (pp. 17–34). Washington, DC: American Psychological Association.

4. Hayslip, B., & Panek, P. E. (2002). *Adult development and aging* (3rd ed.). Malabar, FL: Krieger Publishing, p. 182.

5. Leider, R. J., & Shapiro, D. (2004). *Claiming your place at the fire: Living the second half of your life on purpose.* San Francisco: Berrett-Koehler, p. vii.

6. Hollis (2005), p. 204.

INDEX

Courtesy of Arnaldo Anaya.

About the Author

ROBERT SCHWALBE, PhD, is a psychoanalyst in private practice in New York City, specializing in therapy for men and issues brought on by aging. Also a Licensed Social Worker, Schwalbe is Chairman of the Board for the Wurzweiler School of Social Work, and is a recipient of the Distinguished Humanitarian of the Year Award from Yeshiva University.

About the Series Editor

JUDY KURIANSKY, PhD, is a licensed Clinical Psychologist, adjunct faculty in the Department of Clinical Psychology at Columbia University Teachers College, and also the Department of Psychiatry at Columbia University College of Physicians and Surgeons. Kuriansky is a United Nations representative for the International Association of Applied Psychology and for the World Council for Psychotherapy. She is also a Visiting Professor at the Peking University Health Sciences Center, a Fellow of the American Psychological Association, Founder of the APA Media Psychology Division, and a widely known journalist for CBS, CNBC, LIFETIME and A&E, as well as a regular weekly columnist for the *New York Daily News*. She has been a syndicated radio talk show host for more than 20 years.